Selections from Longman World History

Primary Sources and Case Studies

Volume 2

George F. Jewsbury

Centre d'Études du Monde Russe
École des Hautes Études en Sciences Sociales

New York San Francisco Boston
London Toronto Sydney Tokyo Singapore Madrid
Mexico City Munich Paris Cape Town Hong Kong Montreal

Vice President/Publisher: Priscilla McGeehon
Acquisitions Editor: Erika Gutierrez
Marketing Manager: Sue Westmoreland
Project Coordination, Text Design, and
    Electronic Page Makeup: Pre-Press Company, Inc.
Cover Design Manager: Wendy Fredericks
Cover Designer: David G. Bartow
Cover Photographs: *Background:* Thai relief sculpture of Bodhisattvas, © James
Chen/Corbis RF; *Counterclockwise from top left:* Face of Thai Golden Statue of the
Buddha, © Reed Kaestner/Corbis RF; © Steve Allen/Brand X Pictures/Picture-
Quest; Thai sculpture of a guardian figure, © Reed Kaestner/Corbis RF; detail of a
Ndebele painting showing a shield and spear, © Ralph A. Clevenger/Corbis RF;
Longman World History website logo, Janette Afsharian
Senior Print Buyer: Dennis Para
Printer and Binder: Hamiliton Printing Co.
Cover Printer: Lehigh Press, Inc.

Library of Congress Cataloging-in-Publication Data

Selections from Longman world history--primary sources and case studies
/ [edited by] George F. Jewsbury.
    v. cm.
Selected from the website "Longman world history--primary sources and
case studies" http://longmanworldhistory.com.
Includes bibliographical references.
  --ISBN 0-321-09848-X (v. 2)
  1. World history--Sources. I. Jewsbury, George F. II. Longman world
history--primary sources and case studies.
  D20.S4142002
  909--dc21

                                                        2002034008

Please visit our website at http://www.ablongman.com

ISBN 0-321-09848-X

10 9 8 7 6 5 4 3 2 1—HT—05 04 03 02

Contents

Topic and Theme Contents

LAWGIVERS AND LAW CODES

TECHNOLOGY, SCIENCE, MEDICINE, AND HEALTH

ART, ARCHITECTURE, AND LITERATURE

SOCIAL STRUCTURE

GENDER AND SEX

EVERYDAY LIFE, FAMILY, HOUSEHOLD AND LINEAGE

STATE AND POLITICS

CROSS-CULTURE PERCEPTIONS

REVOLUTIONS AND REVOLTS

Preface

"The historical sense involves a perception, not only of the pastness of the past, but of its presence."

T.S. Eliot

By not only studying the works of the historians but also the documents which make up their foundations, students gain a deeper understanding of the past and its meanings for the present. By reading primary documents, students gain direct access to the identities of the world's peoples expressed through their religious practices, oral traditions, literatures, and governmental archives. These documents are the touchstones of who our global neighbors are, where they come from, and where they—and we—are going.

This reader grew out of *Longman World History—Primary Sources and Case Studies*, *http://longmanworldhistory.com*, a Web site composed of primary sources, maps, images, and global comparative case studies. This book, as does the site, encourages students to analyze the themes, issues, and complexities of world history in a meaningful, exciting, and informative way. While the Web site contains an enormous database of material for professors and students, it is understood that in certain cases, a printed book is sometimes optimal where Internet access is limited. Thus the idea for this print reader was born. *Selections from Longman World History* is in essence the best of that wonderful site.

Selections from Longman World History helps readers handle the evidence of these documents "scientifically," as they advance their understanding as to why events have occurred. Unlike physical scientists, who can verify their hypotheses under controlled conditions in a laboratory, those who study history have to pay special attention to the uniqueness of documents because each event takes place at a particular time and at a particular place. Historians analyze documents with the same objective attitude employed by scientists examining natural phenomena. This scientific spirit requires historians to deal with the documents according to established rules of historical analysis, to recognize biases and to make conclusions as the evidence seems to warrant. The documents here have been subjected to the demands of *external criticism*—they are genuine as sources. It is up to the reader to take the next stage, *internal criticism*, to see what the documents' meanings and implications are.

SELECTIONS AND ORGANIZATION

The documents in this reader were carefully chosen to give a balance among the social, cultural, economic, political, and military aspects of each era. They also represent an attempt to provide global coverage—giving equal treatment to the Americas, Africa and the Middle East, Asia, and Europe.

To ensure a book of manageable length, difficult choices had to be made when selecting material to include from the Web site. The reader includes such selections as excerpts from The Holy Qur'an, Lady Murasaki Shikibu's Diary, and Martin Luther's *Sermon at the Castle Pleissenburg*. There were many wonderful selections and case studies that I simply could not include because of space limitations. In order to offer the best of both worlds, print and technology, each copy of *Selections from Longman World History* contains a free twelve-month subscription to the Web site. As we have become more comfortable and familiar with technology we realize that it is best to integrate the two forms of media to create a seamless flow that is accessible to all. Throughout the chapters, readers will find marginal icons that point students to key images and maps related to the sources at hand. The end of chapter material also includes an extensive list of pertinent Web links for students interested in further research. Because there were many selections that did not fit in this printed reader, the Web links section of each chapter begins with a link to the accompanying Web site with suggestions for other readings and case studies available online for that chapter.

There are many ways in which a reader can be organized and just as many ways that professors go about incorporating this type of material into their classes. In the case of this reader, the documents are arranged chronologically, for ease of use, and by region. There is also a table of contents included that references the documents according to topic and theme. Finally, should professors desire to organize the material around the chapters of their Longman World History survey textbook, the Web site provides a correlation for each book on the Longman list. This can be found on the Web site's home page.

FEATURES AND PEDAGOGICAL AIDS

Selections from Longman World History contains a number of pedagogical aids to promote student learning, provide a basis for unfamiliar information, and develop students' analytical skills.

- Marginal icons link students directly to photos and interactive and static maps found on the Longman World History Web site.
- Comparative Case Studies—At the end of each chronological part, there is an accompanying case study that introduces a topic and asks students to examine multiple primary sources related to it. These activities encourage students to act as historians and think analytically. Each case study is prefaced by its own introduction and is well suited to be the nucleus of class discussion or the basis for a project. The case study ends with a set of thought-provoking questions that encourage students' deeper analysis. An excellent example is the case study entitled "Battlefields to Courtrooms: Conflict and Agency in the Americas," which has students examine The Second Letter of Hernan Cortéz to King Charles V of Spain (1519) and *The New Laws of the Indies for the Good Treatment and Preservation of the Indians* (1542). This case study urges the student to consider the issues and debate surrounding the treatment of Indians in the New World.
- Each chapter and document is accompanied by introductory information giving students enough context and background to begin interpreting the written or visual source.
- Footnotes with definitions of potentially unfamiliar words can be found throughout the book.
- Each document is concluded by a set of Analysis and Review Questions prompting students to think closely about the readings.

- Each chapter ends with a number of Selected Weblinks, carefully chosen for their educational value, that offer students at least one direction for further research. A list of other documents and case studies found on the Web site can also be found in this section.

SUPPLEMENTS

The Instructor's Manual to accompany Longman World History is a comprehensive resource that guides instructors through the basics of logging on to the site and suggests how to relate the primary sources to the students. Introductions explain the basic navigation and pedagogical aspects of the site, and in-depth analysis of each chapter, topics for class discussion, and key questions for each source are also provided.

ACKNOWLEDGMENTS

As the general editor for this reader, I would like to thank the many historians, known for their fine classroom work and scholarship, who contributed to the product as a whole: Wayne Ackerson, Salisbury University; Eric Bobo, Hinds Community College; Wade G. Dudley, East Carolina University; James Halverson, Judson College; David L. Ruffley, United States Air Force Academy; Denise Le Blanc Scifres, Hinds Community College; Deborah Schmitt, United States Airforce Adacemy; John VanderLippe, State University of New York at New Paltz; Bryan E. Vizzini, West Texas A&M University; Pingchao Zhu, University of Idaho. This book is dedicated to their students and all who seek to know the past through the words of those who lived, worked, brought up families, and struggled to maintain their communities.

Much appreciation also goes to the fine people at Longman whose creativity and hard work brought this project to life: my acquisitions editor, Erika Gutierrez, Lisa Pinto, Nancy Crochiere, Beth Strauss, Patrick McCarthy, Doug Tebay, Marie Iacobellis, and Charles Annis.

Last of all, thank you to the reviewers who have been so enthusiastic about *Longman World History—Primary Sources and Case Studies* from the very beginning and who graciously offered their suggestions about selections, usability, features, and pedagogy: Richard H. Bradford, West Virginia University Institute of Technology; Pingchao Zhu, University of Idaho; Wade G. Dudley, East Carolina University; Aran S. MacKinnon, State University of West Georgia; Robert Chisholm, Columbia Basin College; Jon Lee, San Antonio College; Eric Bobo, Hinds Community College; Jessica Sheetz-Nguyen, Oklahoma City Community College; David Flaten, Plymouth State College; Richard Baldwin, Gulf Coast Community College; J. Lee Annis, Montgomery College; Richard S. Williams, Washington State University; Jim Halverson, Judson College; Kenneth A. Osgood, Florida Atlantic University; John A. Nichols, Slippery Rock University; Norman D. Love, El Paso Community College; Oscar Schmiege, Alliant International University; Clifford F. Wargelin, Georgetown College; Jennifer Hevelone-Harper, Gordon College; Deborah Gerish, Emporia State University.

George F. Jewsbury

CHAPTER 14

The West: The Reformation

The period in European history between 1450 and 1750 is usually referred to as the Early Modern Period. In many ways this period is more like the Middle Ages than the modern West. Even in 1750, most Europeans were illiterate, rural peasants living within traditional social and political structures. Economic productivity still depended heavily on human and animal energy. Yet the political, economic, and technological features that define western Europe today were built on the foundations laid during this period. The voyages of exploration and colonization created a new world economy with western countries at the center. The Scientific Revolution was causing many intellectuals to rethink the role and purpose of science in society. Although experimenting with different visions of royal power, both France and England developed from feudal monarchies into national monarchies, a critical step on the road to the modern nation state.

Yet it was the Protestant Reformation, with the cultural, political, and military upheaval that it spawned, that impacted the people of that time most directly. In 1517, an obscure monk and theology professor named Martin Luther proposed an academic debate on certain esoteric points of Christian doctrine. Within 40 years of this event, Europe had split into permanent and hostile religious camps. Indeed, by 1650, a significant percentage of Europeans had died in wars arising from this religious conflict.

Such a chain of events seems strange to us. That strangeness is a clue to us that something central to early modern European culture was at stake in the Reformation. Indeed, Europeans in the sixteenth century were religious to a degree that is not easily understood in our modern culture. Few Europeans of any class seriously questioned the basic teachings of the Church or the truth of the Bible. Moreover, religion permeated and gave structure to European society at that time. The social and economic centers of villages and cities were churches. Religious organizations were the primary places of socialization outside of the family. The Church administered all levels of formal education. The rulers of Europe enforced religious unity, and Church officials exercised tremendous political power. Thus, the Protestant challenge to the religious culture of the time affected every aspect of European society.

Map 14.1
Religious Diversity in
Western Europe

MARTIN LUTHER, *SERMON AT CASTLE PLEISSENBURG*

About the Document

*Image 14.1
Martin Luther*

In 1539 Martin Luther delivered a sermon at Castle Pleissenberg, in Leipzig. Twenty years before, Luther had debated Johann Eck, a papal representative, in Leipzig concerning the sale of indulgences. During this debate, Luther began to realize that his understanding of salvation was not in the mainstream of Medieval theology, which caused him to widen the focus of both his theological investigations and his criticism of the Church. Luther returned to Leipzig in 1539 to celebrate the implementation of Protestant reforms in the city. The Reformation was unsettling for many people. The conflicting claims to authority by Protestants and Roman Catholics caused many to wonder which was the true church. In an age in which almost all people believed in a god who would judge them after death, a conflict over how best to follow God cut to the heart of people's lives. Luther devoted this sermon to explaining the Protestant view of religious authority and the marks of the true church against the views of the papacy.

The Document

But when they are asked: What is the Christian church? What does it say and do? They reply: The church looks to the pope,° cardinals, and bishops. This is not true! Therefore we must look to Christ and listen to him as he describes the true Christian church in contrast to their phony shrieking. For one should and one must rather believe Christ and the apostles, that tone must speak God's Word and do as St. Peter and here the Lord Christ says: He who keeps my Word, there is my dwelling, there is the Builder, my Word must remain in it; otherwise it shall not be my house. Our papists° want to improve on this, and therefore they may be in peril. Christ says: "We will make our home with them"; there the Holy Spirit will be at work. There must be a people that loves me and keeps my commandments. Quite bluntly, this is what he wants.

Here Christ is not speaking of how the church is built, as he spoke above concerning the dwelling. But when it has been built, then the Word must certainly be there, and a Christian should listen to nothing but God's Word. Elsewhere, in worldly affairs, he hears other things, how the wicked should be punished and the good protected, and about the economy. But here in the Christian church it should be a house in which only the Word of God° resounds. Therefore let them shriek themselves crazy with their cry: church, church! Without the Word of God it is nothing. My dear Christians are steadfast confessors of the Word, in life and in death. They will not forsake this dwelling,

---

pope: The word "pope" comes from the Italian word for father. It refers to the Bishop of Rome. According to Roman Catholic teaching, the Bishop of Rome stands in the place of the Apostle Peter, who was the first leader of the Church at Rome. Using texts from the Gospels in which Jesus seems to give Peter special authority, Roman Catholics teach that the pope is the earthly leader of the Church.
papists: Derogatory name for Roman Catholics used by Protestants.
Word of God: According to Luther and other Protestants the term "Word of God," or simply "Word," could mean one of three things. First, it referred to Jesus as he is described in the Gospel of John. Second, it often referred to the Bible, since the Bible revealed the Word of God (Jesus) to humans. Finally, it could refer to the correct (to Protestants) preaching or teaching of the biblical message of salvation.

so dearly do they love this Prince. Whether in favor or not, for this they will leave country and people, boy and life. Thus we read of a Roman centurion, a martyr, who, when he was stripped of everything, said, "This I know; they cannot take away from me my Lord Christ." Therefore a Christian says: This Christ I must have, though it cost me everything else; what I cannot take with me can go; Christ alone is enough for me. Therefore all Christians should stand strong and steadfast upon the Word alone, as St. Peter says, "by the strength which God supplies" (1 Pet. 4:11).

Behold, how it all happens in weakness. Look at baptism,° it is water; where does the hallowing and the power come from? From the pope? No, it comes from God, who says, "He who believes and is baptized" (Mark 16:16). For the pope puts trust in the consecrated water. Why, pope? Who gave you the power? The ecclesia, the church? Yes, indeed, where is it written? Nowhere! Therefore the consecrated water is Satan's goblin bath (Kobelbad), which cripples, blinds, and consecrates the people without the Word. But in the church one should teach and preach nothing besides or apart from the Word of God. For the pastor who does the baptizing says: It is not I who baptize you; I am only the instrument of the Father, Son, and Holy Spirit; this is not my work.

Likewise, the blessed sacrament° is not administered by men, but rather by God's commands; we only lend our hands to it. Do you think this is an insignificant meal, which feeds not only the soul but also the mortal boy of a poor, condemned sinner for the forgiveness of sins in order that the body too may live? This is God's power, this Householder's power, not men's. So also in the absolution,° when a distressed sinner is pardoned. By what authority and command is he pardoned? Not by human command, but by God's command. Behold, here by God's power I deliver you from the kingdom of the devil and transfer you to the kingdom of God (Col. 1:13). So it is too with our prayer, which gains all things from God, not through its own power, or because it is able to do this, but because it rests in God's promise. In the world you see how hard it is to approach the Roman emperor and gain help; but a devout Christian can always come to God with a humble, believing prayer and be heard.

baptism: In the sacrament of baptism the individual is washed or sprinkled with water signifying death to sin and a new life as a Christian. In Medieval and later Roman Catholic theology, baptism is administered to infants and washes away the penalty of sin inherited from Adam and Eve, called original sin. Protestants disputed with Roman Catholics and among each other over the proper method and meaning of baptism. For all Christians, baptism is seen as a mark of membership in the universal church.
sacrament: According to Medieval theology, sacraments were the means by which God gave grace to human beings so that they might be saved. Roman Catholics recognize seven sacraments: baptism, the Lord's Supper (also called communion or the Eucharist), penance, confirmation, marriage, ordination, and last rites (extreme unction). At first, Luther retained only three (baptism, the Lord's Supper, penance), but later rejected penance. Protestants also differ from Roman Catholics over how sacraments work. Roman Catholics believe that sacraments convey divine grace whenever the ritual is performed. Protestants believe that the effectiveness of the sacrament depends on the faith of the recipient.
absolution: Absolution is part of the sacrament of penance by which sinners are forgiven for their sins. By the late Middle Ages, penance consisted of several parts. First a penitent must confess his or her sins to a priest in private. The priest had to determine whether the penitent was truly remorseful for the sins committed and resolved not to do them again. If the priest judged the penitent remorseful and committed to not sinning again, he would grant absolution. Absolution is the pronouncement of the forgiveness of sins in the name of Jesus Christ. Although forgiven, the penitent was still liable for the penalty for the sin. Thus, the priest assigned penitential acts such as charitable giving, restitution to a wronged party, or acts of self-denial like fasting. This part was called satisfaction. Much religious behavior in the late Middle Ages revolved around penitential acts of satisfaction.

. . . It is the Word which we believe—this is what makes our hearts so bold that we dare to call ourselves the children of the Father. Where does this come from? The answer is: From God, who teaches us to pray in the Lord's Prayer and puts into our hands the book of Psalms. For if we prayed without faith, this would be to curse twice over, as we learned in our nasty papistical holiness. But where there is a believing heart and that heart has before it the promise of God it quite simply and artlessly prays its "Our Father" and is heard. Outside of this church of God you may present your prayers and supplications to great lords and potentates to the best of your ability, but here you have no ability to pray except in Christ Jesus, in order that we may not boast that we are holy as they do in the papacy, who protest, of course, and say: Oh, it would be a presumption for anybody to call himself holy and fit; and yet they teach that man of himself has a "certain preparation" for prayer.

They also teach prayer according to this doctrine in their chants and say: I have prayed in despair as a poor sinner. Oh, stop that kind of praying! It would be better to drop such praying altogether if you despair. For despair ruins everything and if you go to baptism, prayer, and the sacrament without faith and in despair, you are actually mocking God. What you should quickly say, however, is this: I am certain that my dear God has so commanded and that he has assured me of the forgiveness of sins; therefore I will baptize, absolve, and pray. And immediately you will receive this treasure in your heart. It does not depend on our worthiness or unworthiness, for both of these can only make us despair. Therefore do not allow yourself by any means to be driven to despair. "Go and baptize" (Matt. 28:19), that is, baptize those who repent and are sorry for their sins. Here you hear that this is not human work; but the work of God and the Father; he is the Householder who wills to dwell here. But if we despair, then we should stay away from the sacrament and from prayer, and first learn to say: All right, it makes no difference that I am unworthy, God is truthful nevertheless, and he has most certainly promised and assured us; I'll stake my life on this.

And this we did not know under the papacy. Indeed, I, Martin Luther, for a long time could not find my way out of this papistical dream, because they were constantly blathering to me about my worthiness and unworthiness. Therefore, you young people, learn to know the church rightly.

Concerning penitence or penance we teach that it consists in the acknowledgment of sins and genuine trust in God, who forgives them all for Christ's sake. The pope, on the contrary, does nothing but scold and devise intolerable burdens; and besides he knows nothing of grace and faith, much less does he teach what the Christian church really is.

But don't you forget the main point here, namely, that God wants to make his dwelling here. Therefore, when the hand is laid upon your head and the forgiveness of sins is proclaimed to you in the words: "I absolve you from all your sins in the name of Christ," you should take hold of this Word with a sure faith and be strengthened out of the mouth of the preacher. And this is what Christ and St. Peter are saying: He, the Lord, wants to dwell in this church; the Word alone must resound in it.

In short, the church is a dwelling, in order that God may be loved and heard. Not wood or stones, not dumb animals, it should be people, who know, love, and praise God. And that you may be able to trust God with certainty in all things, including cross and suffering, you should know that it is the true church, even though it be made up of scarcely two believing persons. That's why Christ says: He who loves me keeps my Word; there I will dwell, there you have my church.

So now you must guard yourselves against the pope's church, bedaubed and bedizened with gold and pearls; for here Christ teaches us the opposite. To love God and keep his Word is not the pope's long robe and crown, nor even his decretals. There is a great difference between what God commands and what men command. Look how the pope brazenly announces—we should invoke the saints and conduct ourselves according to his human precepts. Does God's Word command this too? I still do not see it. But this I know very well, that God's Word says: I, Christ, go to the Father, and he who believes in me will be saved. For, I have suffered for him and I also give him the Holy Spirit from on high.

So the Lord Christ and the pope each have their own church, but with this mighty difference, which Christ himself, the best dialectitian (*der beste Dialecticus*), here describes, telling us what it is and where it is, namely, where his Word is purely preached. So where you hear this, there you may know that this is the true church. For where the Word of God is not present, there also are not true-believing confessors and martyrs. And if the World of God were lacking, then we would have been deceived by Christ; then he really would have betrayed us!

Oh, if we could only stake it all on Christ and mock and laugh at the pope, since Christ clearly says here, not "he who has my Word," but "he who keeps it loves me" and is also my disciple. There are many of you who have the Word, true enough, but do not keep it, and in time of trouble and trial fall away altogether and deny Christ.

It would, of course, be desirable if we could always have both: the Word and our temporal crumbs, but the good venison, peace, is very scarce in the kingdom of heaven. It's therefore something which must be recognized as a great blessing of God when there is peace among temporal lords and mutual understanding. But if not, then let them all go—goods, fame, wife, and child—if only this treasure remain with us.

I fear, however, that unfortunately there will be among us many weathercocks, false brethren, and such like weeds; and yet I am not going to be a prophet, because I must prophesy nothing but evil, and who would presume to be able to fathom it all? It will turn out all right; now we have it, let us see to it that we hold on to it. But let us be valiant against Satan, who intends to sift us like wheat (cf. Luke 22:31). For it may well be that you will have your bit of bread under a good government and then the devil will soon set a snare for you in your security and presumption, so that you will no longer trust and give place to the Word of God as much as you did before. That's why Christ says: My sheep not only hear me, they also obey and follow me (John 10:3–5); they increase in faith daily through hearing the Word of God and the right and perfect use of the blessed sacraments. There is strengthening and comfort in this church. And it is also the true church, not cowls, tonsures, and long robes, of which the Word of God knows nothing, but rather wherever two or three are gathered together (Matt. 18:20), not matter whether it be on the ocean or in the depths of the earth, if only they have before them the Word of God and believe and trust in the same, there is most certainly the real, ancient, true, apostolic church.

But we were so blinded in the papacy that, even though St. Peter tells us that "we have the prophetic word made more sure" and that we "do well to pay attention to this as to a lamp shining in a dark place" (11 Pet. 1:19), we still cannot see what a bright light we have in the gospel. Therefore we must note here once again the description of the Christian church which Christ gives us, namely, that it is a group of people who not only have his Word but also love and keep it and forsake everything for the sake of love.

. . . But Christ tells you and me something far different. He says: My church is where my Word is preached purely and is unadulterated and kept. Therefore St. Paul warns that we should flee and avoid those who would lead us away from God's Word, for if anyone defiles God's temple, which we are, God will destroy him (1 Cor. 3:17). And St. Peter also says: Take heed, if you are going to preach, then you should preach nothing but God's Word (1 Pet. 4:11), otherwise you will defile God's church.

. . . If anybody wants to teach human precepts, let him do so in secular and domestic affairs and leave the church alone. After all, the papists are really empty spewers and talkers, since Christ himself here says: He who hears my Word and keeps it, to him will I and my Father come and make our home with him. This is the end of Jerusalem and Moses; here there is to be a little band of Christ (*Heufflein Christi*), who hear God's Word and keep the same and rely upon it in every misfortune. This is my church. This Lord we shall believe, even though the pope blows his top over it.

But in these words Christ was also answering the apostle Judas, who also allowed himself to imagine that Christ would become a great secular emperor and that they, the apostles, would become great lords in the nations when he should manifest himself. But how wrong he was! Here Christ tells them straight out that his kingdom is not of this world, but that they and all believers should be that kingdom of heaven in which God the Father, Son, and Holy Spirit himself dwells. He does not install angels, emperors, kings, princes, and lords in that church. He himself wants to be the householder and be the only one to speak and act; there I will dwell, he says, and with me all believers from everlasting to everlasting.

But Judas, the good man, still cannot understand this and therefore the Holy Spirit must come and teach it to him. Of this future and this ministry, dear Christians, you will hear tomorrow, God willing. If I cannot do it, then it will be done by others who can do it better than I, though they will not admit it. Let this today serve as an introduction or the morning sermon. May the Lord help us, I cannot go on further now.

Analysis and Review Questions

1. What is the Church, according to Luther?
2. What role do activities like baptism, communion, and confession play in Luther's concept of the Church?
3. What are Luther's criticisms of the "papists" in this document?
4. If this document were the only evidence we had concerning Luther, what could we say about his religious views?
5. The contrast between faith and despair is a central theme in this document. What does Luther mean by faith? What does he mean by despair? What do his definitions have to do with the nature of the Church?

IGNATIUS LOYOLA, *RULES FOR THINKING WITH THE CHURCH*

Image 14.2
Ignatius of Loyola

About the Document

Ignatius Loyola (d. 1556) was born to a noble family in the Basque region of Spain and spent his early life as a soldier. In 1521, the same year that Luther was excommunicated, Loyola was severely injured and spent a year convalescing. Bedridden, he spent his time reading devotional literature and underwent a spiritual conversion. He renounced his inheritance and began to live as a monk.

Eventually he gathered a few followers, whom he led through his now-classic spiritual program, *The Spiritual Exercises*. In 1540 Loyola and his companions were recognized by the papacy as an official order, The Society of Jesus. Jesuits (as members of the Society came to be called) became the agents of the papacy in its efforts both to reconvert European Protestants and to convert pagans encountered by European explorers to Roman Catholicism. In this selection from *The Spiritual Exercises*, Loyola describes the proper attitude of the believer toward the teachings and practices of the Roman Catholic Church.

The Document *

1. Always to be ready to obey with mind and heart, setting aside all judgement of one's own, the true spouse of Jesus Christ, our holy mother, our infallible and orthodox mistress, the Catholic Church, whose authority is exercised over us by the hierarchy.
2. To commend the confession of sins to a priest as it is practised in the Church; the reception of the Holy Eucharist once a year, or better still every week, or at least every month, with the necessary preparation.
3. To commend to the faithful frequent and devout assistance at the holy sacrifice of the Mass, the ecclesiastical hymns, the divine office, and in general the prayers and devotions practised at stated times, whether in public in the churches or in private.
4. To have a great esteem for the religious orders, and to give the preference to celibacy or virginity over the married state.
5. To approve of the religious vows of chastity, poverty, perpetual obedience, as well as to the other works of perfection and supererogation. Let us remark in passing, that we must never engage by vow to take a state (such as marriage) that would be an impediment to one more perfect.
6. To praise relics,° the veneration and invocation of Saints: also the stations, and pious pilgrimages, indulgences, jubilees, the custom of lighting candles in the churches, and other such aids to piety and devotion.
7. To praise the use of abstinence and fasts as those of Lent, of Ember Days, of Vigils, of Friday, Saturday, and of others undertaken out of pure devotion: also voluntary mortifications, which we call penances, not merely interior, but exterior also.
8. To commend moreover the construction of churches, and ornaments; also images, to be venerated with the fullest right, for the sake of what they represent.
9. To uphold especially all the precepts of the Church, and not censure them in any manner; but, on the contrary, to defend them promptly, with reasons drawn from all sources, against those who criticize them.
10. To be eager to commend the decrees, mandates, traditions, rites and customs of the Fathers in the Faith or our superiors. As to their conduct; although there may not

---

relic: Material object held to have special powers because of its association with a saint or another holy person.

*Reprinted by permission of Oxford University Press, from *Documents of the Christian Church*, 3rd ed., Henry Bettenson, 364–67.

always be the uprightness of conduct that there ought to be, yet to attack or revile them in private or in public tends to scandal and disorder. Such attacks set the people against their princes and pastors; we must avoid such reproaches and never attack superiors before inferiors. The best course is to make private approach to those who have power to remedy the evil.

11. To value most highly the sacred teaching, both the Positive and the Scholastic, as they are commonly called.

12. It is a thing to be blamed and avoided to compare men who are living on the earth (however worthy of praise) with the Saints and Blessed, saying: This man is more learned than St. Augustine, etc.

13. That we may be altogether of the same mind and in conformity with the Church herself, if she shall have defined anything to be black which to our eyes appears to be white, we ought in like manner to pronounce it to be black. For we must undoubtedly believe, that the Spirit of our Lord Jesus Christ, and the Spirit of the Orthodox Church His Spouse, by which Spirit we are governed and directed to Salvation, is the same.

14. It must also be borne in mind, that although it be most true, that no one is saved but he that is predestinated, yet we must speak with circumspection concerning this matter, lest perchance, stressing too much the grace or predestination of God, we should seem to wish to shut out the force of free will and the merits of good works; or on the other hand, attributing to these latter more than belongs to them, we derogate meanwhile from the power of grace.

15. For the like reason we should not speak on the subject of predestination frequently; if by chance we do so speak, we ought so to temper what we say as to give the people who hear no occasion of erring and saying, 'If my salvation or damnation is already decreed, my good or evil actions are predetermined'; whence many are wont to neglect good works, and the means of salvation.

16. It also happens not unfrequently, that from immoderate, preaching and praise of faith, without distinction or explanation added, the people seize a pretext for being lazy with regard to any good works, which precede faith, or follow it when it has been formed by the bond of charity.

17. Not any more must we push to such a point when the preaching and inculcating of the grace of God, as that there may creep thence into the minds of the hearers the deadly error of denying our faculty of free will. We must speak of it as the glory of God requires that we may not raise doubts as to liberty and the efficacy of good works.

18. Although it is very praiseworthy and useful to serve God through the motive of pure charity, yet we must also recommend the fear of God; and not only filial fear, but servile fear, which is very useful and often even necessary to raise man from sin. Once risen from the state, and free from the affection of mortal sin, we may then speak of that filial fear which is truly worthy of God, and which gives and preserves the union of pure love.

*Reprinted by permission of Oxford University Press, from *Documents of the Christian Church,* 3rd ed., Henry Bettenson, 364–67.

Analysis and Review Questions

1. According to Loyola, what should a Christian's attitude be toward the Church? Toward the pope?
2. What should the Christian life look like, according to Loyola?
3. What does Loyola say about faith? In what should a Christian believe?
4. Why would Loyola advocate such radical, unquestioning obedience to the authority of the Roman Catholic Church?
5. Loyola founded the Society of Jesus (Jesuits). One mission of the Jesuits was to convert Protestants to Roman Catholicism. In many cases they were successful. Given what you know, why do you think some Protestants were attracted to Loyola's vision?

JAMES I ON THE DIVINE RIGHT OF KINGS

About the Document

Map 14.2 European Population Density c. 1600

James Stuart (James VI of Scotland, 1567–1625; James I of England, 1603–1625) was an intellectual who was rarely able to implement his ideas. He had hoped to unify England, Scotland, and Ireland, but was thwarted by both political realities and his own personal failings. He sought to ease international tensions, but his efforts to prevent the conflict that would become the Thirty Years' War were unsuccessful. The outbreak of the Thirty Years' War also destroyed his hope of brokering a European religious compromise. In addition to his duties as monarch, James I wrote on a variety of topics. His most famous work, the *True Law of a Free Monarchy*, is a classic argument for divine-right monarchy. Interestingly, although James penned this work in 1598 before he assumed the throne of England, he never tried to implement divine-right rule in England. He firmly believed that his power and authority derived solely from God but acknowledged that as king of England, he had sworn oaths to govern according to the "laws and customs of England."

The Document

THE TREW LAW OF FREE MONARCHIES: OR THE RECIPROCK AND MUTUALL DUETIE BETWIXT A FREE KING AND HIS NATURALL SUBJECTS

As there is not a thing so necessarie to be knowne by the people of any land, next the knowledge of their God, as the right knowledge of their alleageance, according to the forme of governement established among them, especially in a Monarchie (which forme of government, as resembling the Divinitie, approacheth nearest to perfection, as all the learned and wise men from the beginning have agreed upon; Unitie being the perfection of all things,) So hath the ignorance, and (which is worse) the seduced opinion of the multitude blinded by them, who thinke themselves able to teach and instruct the ignorants, procured the wracke and overthrow of sundry flourishing Commonwealths; and heaped heavy calamities, threatening utter destruction upon others. And the smiling successe, that unlaw rebellions have oftentimes had against Princes in ages past (such hath bene the misery, and the iniquitie of the time) hath by way of practise strengthened many of their errour: albeit there cannot be a more deceivable argument; then to judge by the justnesse of the cause by the event thereof; as hereafter shall be proved more at length. And among others, no Common-wealth, that ever hath bene since the beginning, hath had greater need of the trew knowledge of this ground, then this our so long disordered, and distracted Common-wealth hath: the misknowledge hereof being the onely spring, from whence have flowed so many endlesse calamities, miseries, and confusions, as is better felt by many, then the cause thereof well knowne, and deepely considered. The naturall zeale therefore, that I beare to this my native countrie, with the great pittie I have to see the so-long disturbance thereof for lack of the trew knowledge of this ground (as I have said before) hath compelled me at last to breake silence, to discharge my conscience to you my deare country men herein, that knowing the ground from whence these your many endlesse troubles have proceeded, as well as ye have already too-long tasted the bitter fruites thereof, ye may by knowledge, and eschewing of the cause escape, and divert the lamentable effects that ever necessarily follow thereupon. I have chosen the onely to set downe in this short Treatise, the trew grounds of the mutuall deutie, and alleageance betwixt a free and absolute Monarche, and his people.

First then, I will set downe the trew grounds, whereupon I am to build, out of the Scriptures, since Monarchie is the trew paterne of Divinitie, as I have already said: next, from the fundamental Lawes of our own Kingdome, which nearest must concerne us: thirdly, from the law of Nature, by divers similitudes drawne out of the same.

By the Law of Nature the King becomes a naturall Father to all his Lieges at his Coronation: And as the Father of his fatherly duty is bound to care for the nourishing, education, and vertuous government of his children; even so is the king bound to care for all his subjects. As all the toile and paine that the father can take for his children, will be thought light and well bestowed by him, so that the effect thereof redound to their profite and weale; so ought the Prince to doe towards his people. As the kindly father ought to foresee all inconvenients and dangers that may arise towards his children, and though with the hazard of his owne person presse to prevent the same; so ought the King towards his people. As the fathers wrath and correction upon any of his children that offendeth, ought to be by a fatherly chastisement seasoned with pitie, as long as there is any hope of amendment in them; so ought the King towards any of his Lieges that offend in that measure. And shortly, as the Fathers chiefe joy ought to be in procuring his childrens welfare, rejoycing at their weale, sorrowing and pitying at their evil, to hazard for their safetie, travell for their rest, wake for their sleepe; and in a word, to thinke that his earthly felicitie and life standeth and liveth more in them, nor in himself; so ought a good Prince thinke of his people.

As to the other branch of this mutuall and reciprock band, is the duety and alleageance that the Lieges owe to their King: the ground whereof, I take out of the words of Samuel, dited by Gods Spirit, when God had given him commandement to heare the peoples voice in choosing and annointing them a King. And because that place of Scripture being well understood, is so pertinent for our purpose, I have insert herein the very words of the Text.

10. So Samuel tolde all the wordes of the Lord unto the people that asked a King of him.

11. And he said, this shall be the maner of the King that shall raigne over you: hee will take your sonnes, and appoint them to his Charets, and to be his horsemen, and some shall runne before his Charet.

12. Also, hee will make them his captaines over thousands, and captaines over fifties, and to eare his ground, and to reape his harvest, and to make instruments of warre and the things that serve for his charets.

13. Hee will also take your daughters, and make them Apothicaries, and Cookes, and Bakers.

14. And hee will take your fields, and your vineyards, and your best Olive trees, and give them to his servants.

15. And hee will take the tenth of your seed, and of your Vineyards, and give it to his Eunuches, and to his servants.

16. And hee will take your men servants, and your maid-servants, and the chief of your young men, and your asses, and put them to his worke.

17. Hee will take the tenth of your sheepe: and ye shall be his servants.

18. And ye shall cry out at that day, because of your King, whom ye have chosen you: and the Lord God will not heare you at that day.

19. But the people would not heare the voice of Samuel, but did say: Nay, but there shall be a King over us.

20. And we also will be all like other Nations, and our King shall judge us, and goe out before us, and fight out battles.

As likewise, although I have said, a good king will frame all his actions to be according to the Law; yet is hee not bound thereto but of his good will, and for good example—giving to his subjects: For as in the law of abstaining from eating of flesh in Lenton, the king will, for examples sake, make his owne house to observe the Law; yet no man will thinke he needs to take a licence to eate flesh. And although by our Lawes, the bearing and wearing of hag-buts, and pistolets be forbidden, yet no man can find any fault in the King, for causing his traine use them in any raide upon the Borderers, or other malefactours or rebellious subjects. So as I have alreadie said, a good King, although hee be above the Law, will subject and frame his actions thereto, for examples sake to his subjects, and of his owne free-will, but not as subject or bound thereto.

And the agreement of the Law of nature in this our ground with the Lawes and constitutions of God, and man, already alleged, will by two similitudes easily appeare. The King towards his people is rightly compared to a father of children, and to a head of a body composed of divers members: For as fathers, the good Princes, and Magistrates of the people of God acknowledged themselves to their subjects. And for all other well ruled Common-wealths, the stile of Pater patriae was ever, and is commonly used to Kings. And the proper office of a King towards his Subjects, agrees very wel with the office of the head towards the body, and all members thereof: For from the head, being the seate of Judgement, proceedeth the care and foresight of guiding, and preventing all evill that may come to the body, so doeth the King for his people. As the discourse and direction flowes from the head, and the execution according thereunto belongs to the rest of the members, every one according to their office: so it is betwixt a wise Prince, and his people. As the judgement coming from the head may not onely imploy the members, every one in their owne office, as long as they are able for it; but likewise in case any of them be affected with any infirmitie must care and provide for their remedy, in-case it be curable, and if otherwise, gar cut them off for feare of infecting of the rest: even so is it betwixt the Prince, and his people. And as there is ever hope of curing any diseased member of the direction of the head, as long as it is whole; but by contrary, if it be troubled, all the members are partakers of that paine, so is it betwixt the Prince and his people.

And now first for the fathers part (whose naturally love to his children I described in the first part of this my discourse, speaking of the dutie that Kings owe to their Subjects) consider, I pray you what duetie his children owe to him, & whether upon any pretext whatsoever, it wil not be thought monstrous and unnaturall to his sons, to rise up against him, to control him at their appetite, and when they thinke good to sley him, or to cut him off, and adopt to themselves any other they please in his roome: Or can any pretence of wickedness or rigor on his part be a just excuse for his children to put hand into him? And although wee see by the course of nature, that love useth to descend more than to ascend, in case it were trew, that the father hated and wronged the children never so much, will any man, endued with the least sponke of reason, thinke it lawful for them to meet him with the line? Yea, suppose the father were furiously following his sonnes with a drawen sword, is it lawful for them to turne and strike againe, or make any resistance but by flight? I thinke surely, if there were no more but the example of bruit beasts & unreasonable creatures, it may serve well enough to qualifie and prove this my argument. We reade often the pietie that the Storkes have to their olde and decayed parents: And generally wee know, that there are many sorts of beasts and fowles, that with violence and many bloody strokes will beat and banish their yong ones from them, how soone they perceive them to be able to fend themselves; but wee never read or heard of any resistance on their part, except among the vipers; which prooves such persons, as ought to be reasonable creatures, and yet unnaturally follow this example, to be endued with their viperous nature.

And it is here likewise to be noted, that the duty and alleageance, which the people sweareth to their prince, is not bound to themselves, but likewise to their lawfull heires and posterity, the lineall to their lawfull heires and posterity, the lineall succession of crowns being begun among the people of God, and happily continued in divers Christian common-wealths: So as no objection either of heresie, or whatsoever private statute or law may free the people from their oathgiving to their king, and his succession, established by the old fundamentall lawes of the kingdom: For, as hee is their heritable over-lord, and so by birth, not by any right in the coronation, commeth to his crowne; it is a like unlawful (the crowne ever standing full) to displace him that succeedeth thereto, as to eject the former: For at the very moment of the expiring of the king reigning, the nearest and lawful heire entreth in his place: And so to refuse him, or intrude another, is not to holde out uncomming in, but to expell and put out their righteous King. And I trust at this time whole France acknowledgeth the superstitious rebellion of the liguers, who upon pretence of heresie, by force of armes held so long out, to the great desolation of their whole country, their native and righteous king from possessing of his owne crowne and naturall kingdome.

Not that by all this former discourse of mine, and Apologie for kings, I meane that whatsoever errors and intollerable abominations a sovereigne prince commit, hee ought to escape all punishment, as if thereby the world were only ordained for kings, & they without controlment to turne it upside down at their pleasure: but by the contrary, by remitting them to God (who is their onely ordinary Judge) I remit them to the sorest and sharpest school-master that can be devised for them: for the further a king is preferred by God above all other ranks & degrees of men, and the higher that his seat is above theirs, the greater is his obligation to his maker. And therfore in case he forget himselfe (his unthankfulness being in the same measure of height) the sadder and sharper will be correction be; and according to the greatnes of the height he is in, the weight of his fall wil recompense the same: for the further that any person is obliged to God, his offence becomes and growes so much the greater, then it would be in any other. Joves thunderclaps light oftner and sorer upon the high & stately oaks, then on the low and supple willow trees: and the highest bench is sliddriest to sit upon. Neither is it ever heard that any king forgets himself towards God, or in his vocation; but God with the greatnes of the plague revengeth the greatnes of his ingratitude: Neither thinke I by the force of argument of this my discourse so to perswade the people, that none will hereafter be raised up, and rebell against wicked Princes. But remitting to the justice and providence of God to stirre up such scourges as pleaseth him, for punishment of wicked kings (who made the very vermine and filthy dust of the earth to bridle the insolencie of proud Pharaoh) my onely purpose and intention in this treatise is to perswade, as farre as lieth in me, by these sure and infallible grounds, all such good Christian readers, as beare not onely the naked name of a Christian, but kith the fruites thereof in their daily forme of life, to keep their hearts and hands free from such monstrous and unnaturall rebellions, whensoever the wickednesse of a Prince shall procure the same at Gods hands: that, when it shall please God to cast such scourges of princes, and instruments of his fury in the fire, ye may stand up with cleane handes, and unspotted consciences, having prooved your selves in all your actions trew Christians toward God, and dutifull subjects towards your King, having remitted the judgement and punishment of all his wrongs to him, whom to onely of right it appertaineth.

But craving at God, and hoping that God shall continue his blessing with us, in not sending such fearefull desolation, I heartily wish our kings behaviour so to be, and continue among us, as our God in earth, and loving Father, endued with such properties as I described a King in the first part of this Treatise. And that ye (my deare countreymen, and charitable readers) may presse by all means to procure the prosperitie and welfare of your King; that as hee must on the one part thinke all his earthly felicitie and happiness grounded upon your weale, caring more for himselfe for your sake then for his owne, thinking himselfe onely ordained for your weale; such holy and happy emulation may arise betwixt him and you, as his care for your quietnes, and your care for his honor and preservation, may in all your actions daily strive together, that the Land may thinke themselves blessed with such a King, and the king may thinke himself most happy in ruling over so loving and obedient subjects.

Analysis and Review Questions

1. What are the responsibilities of a monarch to his subjects? What are the responsibilities of subjects to the monarch?
2. Are there any limits on the power of a king? What are they?
3. How does James defend divine-right monarchy?
4. What are his motives in this essay?
5. As king of England, James never tried to rule as a divine-right monarch. Does this make him a hypocrite or a realist?

Louis XIV Writes to His Son

About the Document

During the sixteenth and seventeenth centuries, England, for various reasons, was moving toward what we might call a "constitutional monarchy." In such a system, the power of a king or a queen is limited by a written constitution (or, in England's case, where there is no written constitution, a series of documents that serve the same general purpose as a constitution). In general, such a system tends to be more decentralized than centralized, as power is delegated to bodies such as a parliament. In contrast, France during the same period was developing, to the envy of the rest of Western Europe, a strong, centralized absolute monarchy, where the king's position was not limited in any way. Louis XIV, who ruled from 1643 to 1715, became the prototypical absolute monarch, even developing a sort of "cult of personality" around him.

Because ruling over and maintaining such a centralized system required care and attention, Louis XIV in 1661 wrote a series of memoirs to his son, the dauphin. These memoirs not only provided practical advice for the king's heir, they also provide us with insight into royal attitudes and priorities. Sadly for Louis XIV, the dauphin died before his father, and it was Louis's great-grandson who became Louis XV in 1715.

The Document

MANY REASONS, all very important, my son, have decided me, at some labour to myself, but one which I regard as forming one of my greatest concerns, to leave you these Memoirs of my reign and of my principal actions. I have never considered that kings, feeling in themselves, as they do, all paternal affection, are dispensed from the obligation common to fathers of instructing their children by example and by precept.

I have even hoped that in this purpose I might be able to be more helpful to you, and consequently to my subjects, than any one else in the world; for there cannot be men who have reigned of more talents and greater experience than I, nor who have reigned in France; and I do not fear to tell you that the higher the position the greater are the number of things which cannot be viewed or understood save by one who is occupying that position.

I have considered, too, what I have so often experienced myself—the throng who will press round you, each for his own ends, the trouble you will have in finding disinterested advice, and the entire confidence you will be able to feel in that of a father who has no other interest but your own, no ardent wish but for your greatness.

I have given, therefore, some consideration to the condition of Kings—hard and rigorous in this respect—who owe, as it were, a public account of their actions to the whole world and to all succeeding centuries, and who, nevertheless, are unable to do so to all and sundry at the time without injury to their greatest interests, and without divulging the secret reasons of their conduct.

[Louis talks briefly about his own reign.]

Two things without doubt were absolutely necessary; very hard work on my part, and a wise choice of persons capable of seconding it.

As for work, it may be, my son, that you will begin to read these Memoirs at an age when one is far more in the habit of dreading than loving it, only too happy to have escaped subjection to tutors and to have your hours regulated no longer, nor lengthy and prescribed study laid down for you.

There is something more, my son, and I hope that your own experience will never teach it to you: nothing could be more laborious to you than a great amount of idleness if you were to have the misfortune to fall into it through beginning by being disgusted with public affairs, then with pleasure, then with idleness itself, seeking everywhere fruitlessly for what can never be found, that is to say, the sweetness of repose and leisure without having the preceding fatigue and occupation.

I laid a rule on myself to work regularly twice every day, and for two or three hours each time with different persons, without counting the hours which I passed privately and alone, nor the time which I was able to give on particular occasions to any special affairs that might arise. There was no moment when I did not permit people to talk to me about them, provided that they were urgent; with the exception of foreign ministers who sometimes find too favourable moments in the familiarity allowed to them, either to obtain or to discover something, and whom one should not hear without being previously prepared.

I cannot tell you what fruit I gathered immediately I had taken this resolution. I felt myself, as it were, uplifted in thought and courage; I found myself quite another man, and with joy reproached myself for having been too long unaware of it. This first timidity, which a little self-judgment always produces and which at the beginning gave me pain, especially on occasions when I had to speak in public, disappeared in less than no time. The only thing I felt was that I was King, and born to be one. I experienced next a delicious feeling, hard to express, and which you will not know yourself except by tasting it as I have done. For you must not imagine, my son, that the affairs of State are like some obscure and thorny path of learning which may possibly have already wearied you, wherein the mind strives to raise itself with effort above its purview, more often to arrive at no conclusion, and whose utility or apparent utility is repugnant to us as much as its difficulty. The function of Kings consists principally in allowing good sense to act, which always acts naturally and without effort. What we apply ourselves to is sometimes less difficult than what we do only for our amusement. Its usefulness always follows. A King, however skilful and enlightened be his ministers, cannot put his own hand to work without its effect being seen. Success, which is agreeable in everything, even in the smallest matters, gratifies us in these as well as in the greatest, and there is no satisfaction to equal that of noting every day some progress in glorious and lofty enterprises, and in the happiness of the people which has been planned and thought out by oneself. All that is most necessary to this work is at the same time agreeable; for, in a word, my son, it is to have one's eyes open to the whole earth; to learn each hour the news concerning every province and every nation, the secrets of every court, the mood and the weaknesses of each Prince and of every foreign minister; to be well-informed on an infinite number of matters about which we are supposed to know nothing; to elicit from our subjects what they hide from us with the greatest care; to discover the most remote opinions of our own courtiers and the most hidden interests of those who come to us with quite contrary professions. I do not know of any other pleasure we would not renounce for that, even if curiosity alone gave us the opportunity.

I have dwelt on this important subject longer than I had intended, and far more for your sake than for my own; for while I am disclosing to you these methods and these alleviations attending the greatest cares of royalty I am not aware that I am likewise depreciating almost the sole merit which I can hope for in the eyes of the world. But in this matter, my son, your honour is dearer to me than my own; and if it should happen that God call you to govern before you have yet taken to this spirit of application and to public affairs of which I am speaking, the least deference you can pay to the advice of a father, to whom I make bold to say you owe much in every kind of way, is to begin to do and to continue to do for some time, even under constraint and dislike, for love of me who beg it of you, what you will do all your life from love of yourself, if once you have made a beginning.

Analysis and Review Questions

1. What do you think Louis XIV means when he writes "the function of kings consists principally in allowing good sense to act"?
2. Does Louis XIV seem arrogant, or is he simply offering experienced advice?
3. List three things Louis believes a successful ruler must do.
4. Is there anything Louis suggests *not* to do?
5. Overall, do you feel Louis gives his son good or bad advice? Why?

WEB LINKS

Selections from Longman World History—Primary Sources and Case Studies

http://longmanworldhistory.com
The following additional readings and case studies can be found on the Web site.
Document 14.3, Galileo Galilei, *Letter to the Grand Duchess Christina*
Document 14.5, English Bill of Rights
Document 14.6, Pope Boniface VIII, *Unam sanctam*
Document 14.9, Juan Luis Vives, the Office and Dutie of a Husband
Case Study 14.1, Role and Authority of the Papacy
Case Study 14.2, A Question of Trust
Case Study 14.3, God and Nature

Martin Luther

http://www.iclnet.org/pub/resources/text/wittenberg/wittenberg-home.html
Project Wittenberg is an extensive site devoted to works by and about Martin Luther. It is a good place to start.

http://www.mun.ca/rels/reform/index.html
Hans Rollman's Reformation Home Page focuses on Luther but includes resources on other Reformers and Protestant groups. It has an excellent index of links to Reformation documents on the Web and other interesting Reformation Web sites.

http://gbgm-umc.org/umw/bible/ref.html
Produced by the United Methodist Women, this site has excellent summaries of Reformation events, helpful reference materials, and good external links about the Reformation.

http://www.fordham.edu/halsall/mod/modsbook02.html
Part of Paul Halsall's *Internet Modern History Sourcebook*. It is very thorough. Other pages in the *Internet Modern History Sourcebook* have excellent resources for other aspects of the period covered in this chapter.

Ignatius Loyola and the Catholic Reformation

http://www.jesuit.org/
The official Web site of the order of Jesus.

http://campus.northpark.edu/history/WebChron/WestEurope/CatholicRef.html
Good summary of the Catholic Reformation, along with excellent links to information about Loyola and the Council of Trent.

Medieval Background

http://cedar.evansville.edu/~ecoleweb/
The Ecole Initiative is a site devoted to the History of Christianity up to 1500. It contains many documents and images produced in that period, as well as essays on various topics.

http://www.fordham.edu/halsall/sbook.html
Paul Halsall's Internet Medieval Sourcebook.

CHAPTER 15

Eastern Europe and Russia, 1450–1750

Between 1450 and 1750, Eastern Europe and Russia lagged behind Western Europe culturally, socially, and politically. These areas had been controlled by more powerful neighbors, and their pace of development and cultural outlook were affected by years of constant domination. The diverse ideas of their conquerors, both in terms of ruling methods and religion, made the cultures of Russia and Eastern Europe even more distinct from that of their Western European counterparts.

From 1450 to 1750, Europe went from the high Middle Ages through the Renaissance. The Scientific Revolution emerged to give western Europe its "rational" mind and set it on a course of secular thought. Kings and queens consolidated their power by wresting control from feudal lords and introducing the concept of absolutism. Explorers ventured off into the unknown and brought back knowledge of newly discovered lands. The countries of Europe established colonies in these faraway places to claim the riches they found there and bring them back to Europe.

NICOLAUS COPERNICUS:
ON THE REVOLUTION OF THE HEAVENLY SPHERES

About the Document

It was almost inevitable that the beginnings of modern science (the Scientific Revolution) in the sixteenth and seventeenth centuries would upset the scientific and religious status quo in Europe. The acceptance of radically new ideas about the universe was difficult for both Protestants and Catholics alike because these ideas refuted the old Ptolemaic view of an earth-centered universe, a view that fit neatly with the Bible.

A Polish canon° with a doctorate in theology, Nicolaus Copernicus was also one of the great scientific minds of the late fifteenth and early sixteenth centuries. In the preface to his work excerpted below, Copernicus tries to explain to Pope Paul III why he believes what he believes about the movement of the earth around the sun.

Image 15.1
Copernicus's Drawing of the Heliocentric Theory

The Document

I can readily imagine, Holy Father, that as soon as some people hear that in this volume, which I have written about the revolutions of the spheres of the universe, I ascribe certain motions to the terrestrial globe, they will shout that I must be immediately repudiated together with this belief. For I am not so enamored of my own opinions that I disregard what others may think of them. I am aware that a philosopher's ideas are not subject to the judgement of ordinary persons, because it is his endeavor to seek the truth in all things, to the extent permitted to human reason by God. Yet I hold that completely erroneous views should be shunned. Those who know that the consensus of many centuries has sanctioned the conception that the earth remains at rest in the middle of the heaven as its center would, I reflected, regard it as an insane pronouncement if I made the opposite assertion that the earth moves. Therefore I debated with myself for a long time whether to publish the volume which I wrote to prove the earth's motion or rather to follow the example of the Pythagoreans° and certain others, who used to transmit philosophy's secrets only to kinsmen and friends, not in writing but by word of mouth. . . . And they did so, it seems to me, not, as some suppose, because they were in some way jealous about their teachings, which would be spread around; on the contrary, they wanted the very beautiful thoughts attained by great men of deep devotion not to be ridiculed by those who are reluctant to exert themselves vigorously in any literary pursuit unless it is lucrative; or if they are stimulated to the nonacquisitive study of philosophy by the exhortation and example of others, yet because of their dullness of mind they play the same part among philosophers as drones among bees. When I weighed these considerations, the scorn which I had reason to fear on account of the novelty and unconventionality of my opinion almost induced me to abandon completely the work which I had undertaken.

But while I hesitated for a long time and even resisted, my friends [encouraged me]. . . . Foremost among them was the cardinal of Capua [a city in southern Italy], Nicholas Schönberg, renowned in every field of learning. Next to him was a man who loves me dearly, Tiedemann Giese, bishop of Chelmno [a city in northern Poland], a close student of sacred letters as well as of all good literature. For he repeatedly encouraged me and, sometimes adding reproaches, urgently requested me to publish this volume and finally permit it to appear after being buried among my papers and lying concealed not merely until the ninth year but by now the fourth period of nine years. The same conduct was recommended to me by not a few other very eminent scholars. They exhorted me no longer to refuse, on account of the fear which I felt, to make my work available for the general use of students of astronomy. The crazier my doctrine of the earth's motion now appeared to most people, the argument ran, so much the more admiration and thanks would it gain after they saw the publication of my writings

---

canon: A member of the clery belonging to the staff of a cathedral or of a collegiate church.
Pythagoreans: Followers of the Greek mathematician and philosopher Pythagoras.

dispel the fog of absurdity by most luminous proofs. Influenced therefore by these per-suasive men and by this hope, in the end I allowed my friends to bring out an edition of the volume, as they had long besought me to do....

But you [your Holiness] are rather waiting to hear from me how it occurred to me to venture to conceive any motion of the earth, against the traditional opinion of as-tronomers and almost against common sense.... [Copernicus then describes some of the problems connected with the Ptolemaic° system.]

For a long time, then, I reflected on this confusion in the astronomical traditions concerning the derivation of the motions of the universe's spheres. I began to be an-noyed that the movements of the world machine, created for our sake by the best and most systematic Artisan of all [God], were not understood with greater certainty by the philosophers, who otherwise examined so precisely the most insignificant trifles of this world. For this reason I undertook the task of rereading the works of all the philoso-phers which I could obtain to learn whether anyone had ever proposed other motions of the universe's spheres than those expounded by the teachers of astronomy in the schools. And in fact first I found in Cicero that Hicetas supposed the earth to move. Later I also discovered in Plutarch that certain others were of this opinion....

Therefore, having obtained the opportunity from these sources, I too began to con-sider the mobility of the earth.... I thought that I too would be readily permitted to ascertain whether explanations sounder than those of my predecessors could be found for the revolution of the celestial spheres on the assumption of some motion of the earth.

Having thus assumed the motions which ascribe to the earth later on in the volume, by long and intense study I finally found that if the motions of the other planets are correlated with the orbiting of the earth, and are computed for the revolution of each planet, not only do their phenomena follow therefrom but also the order and size of all the planets and spheres, and heaven itself is so linked together that in no portion of it can anything be shifted without disrupting the remaining parts and the universe as a whole. Accordingly in the arrangement of the volume too I have adopted the following order. In the first book I set forth the entire distribution of the spheres together with the motions which I attribute to the earth, so that this book contains, as it were, the general structure of the universe. Then in the remaining books I correlate the motions of the other planets and of all the spheres with the movement of the earth so that I may thereby determine to what extent the motions and appearances of the other planets and spheres can be saved if they are correlated with the earth's motions. I have no doubt that acute and learned astronomers will agree with me if, as this discipline especially requires, they are willing to examine and consider, not superficially but thoroughly, what I adduce in this volume in proof of these matters. However, in order that the educated and uned-ucated alike may see that I do not run away from the judgement of anybody at all, I have preferred dedicating my studies to Your Holiness rather than to anyone else. For even in this very remote corner of the earth where I live you are considered the highest author-ity by virtue of the loftiness of your office and your love for all literature and astronomy too. Hence by your prestige and judgement you can easily suppress calumnious attacks although, as the proverb has it, there is no remedy for a backbite.

Perhaps there will be babblers who claim to be judges of astronomy although com-pletely ignorant of the subject and, badly distorting some passage of Scripture to their purpose, will dare to find fault with my undertaking and censure it. I disregard them

---

Ptolemaic: Referring to the ancient geographer Ptolemy, whose conception of the universe placed the earth at its center with the heavenly bodies moving around it.

even to the extent of despising their criticism as unfounded. For it is not unknown that Lactantius, otherwise an illustrious writer but hardly an astronomer, speaks quite childishly about the earth's shape, when he mocks those who declared that the earth has the form of a globe. Hence scholars need not be surprised if any such persons will likewise ridicule me. Astronomy is written for astronomers. To them my work too will seem, unless I am mistaken, to make some contribution.

Analysis and Review Questions

1. Why has Copernicus hesitated for so long before publishing his ideas on the movement of the earth? Why was he tempted to follow the example of the Pythagoreans?
2. Who encouraged Copernicus to publish his work? Why was he careful to include their names and reasons?
3. What forms the basis of Copernicus's reasoning on the movement of the earth?
4. What were the steps—the sequence of events—he formulated to bring him to his theory?
5. Why has Copernicus dedicated his work to the pope? What was his rationale?

OGIER GHISELIN DE BUSBECQ: AN AMBASSADOR'S REPORT ON THE OTTOMAN EMPIRE, 1555

About the Document

Ogier Ghiselin de Busbecq was the ambassador from the Holy Roman Empire to the court of the Ottoman Empire from 1555 to 1562. The Ottoman Turks controlled much of Eastern Europe and periodically pushed westward toward central Europe. This made them enemies of the European states. De Busbecq was given the task of using diplomatic means to put an end to the Turk raids into Europe. The years he spent in Constantinople gave de Busbecq close contact with Suleiman the Great and life at the Ottoman Court. Through his letters to a friend and his official reports, de Busbecq gives us a fascinating look into the world of the Ottoman Turks. Here was an empire the Europeans had to deal with, but whose lifestyle and customs were very different from what Europeans were accustomed to.

The Document

The Sultan's hall was crowded with people, . . . but there was not in all that great assembly a single man who owed his position to aught save valour and his merit. . . . Those who receive the highest offices from the Sultan are for the most part the sons of shepherds or herdsmen, and so far from being ashamed of their parentage, they actually glory in it, and consider it a matter of boasting that they owe nothing to the accident of birth. . . . Among the Turks, therefore, honours, high posts, and judgeships are the rewards of great ability and good service. . . . These are not our ideas, with us there is no opening left for merit; birth is the standard for everything; the prestige of birth is the sole key to advancement in the public service. . . .

When they [the Turkish army] are hard pressed . . . they take out a few spoonfuls of flour and put them into water, adding some butter, and seasoning the mess with salt and spices; these ingredients are boiled, and a large bowl of gruel is thus obtained. Of this they eat once or twice a day, according to the quantity they have, without any bread, unless they have brought some biscuit with them. In this way they are able to support themselves from their own supplies for a month, or if necessary longer. . . .

From this you will see that it is the patience, self-denial, and thrift of the Turkish soldier that enable him to face the most trying circumstances, and come safely out of the dangers that surround him. What a contrast to our men! Christian soldiers on a campaign refuse to put up with their ordinary food and call for thrushes, becaficos, and such like dainty dishes! If these are not supplied they grow mutinous and work their own ruin; and, if they are supplied, they are ruined all the same. For each man is his own worst enemy, and has no foe more deadly than his own intemperance, which is sure to kill him, if the enemy be not quick. It makes me shudder to think of what the result of a struggle between such different systems must be; one of us must prevail and the other be destroyed, at any rate we cannot both exist in safety. On their side is the vast wealth of their empire, unimpaired resources, experience and practice in arms, a veteran soldiery, an uninterrupted series of victories, readiness to endure hardships, union, order, discipline, thrift, and watchfulness. On ours are found an empty exchequer,° luxurious habits, exhausted resources, broken spirits, a raw and insubordinate soldiery, and greedy generals; there is no regard for discipline, license runs riot, the men indulge in drunkenness and debauchery, and, worst of all, the enemy are accustomed to victory, we, to defeat. Can we doubt what the result must be? . . .

Against us stands Solyman, that foe whom his own and his ancestors' exploits have made so terrible; he tramples the soil of Hungary with 200,000 horses, he is at the very gates of Austria, threatens the rest of Germany, and brings in his train all the nations that extend from our borders to those of Persia. The army he leads is equipped with the wealth of many kingdoms. Of the three regions, into which the world is divided, there is not one that does not contribute its share towards our destruction. Like a thunderbolt he strikes, shivers, and destroys everything in his way. The troops he leads are trained veterans, accustomed to his command; he fills the world with the terror of his name. Like a raging lion he is always roaring around our borders, trying to break in, now in this place, now in that.

Analysis and Review Questions

1. For those in the Sultan's service, to what do they owe their positions?
2. How does de Busbecq compare this system of service with the way the Europeans operate?
3. Compare Turkish and Christian soldiers.
4. What are the differences between the two systems in terms of wartime operations.
5. How does de Busbecq describe "Solyman"? How does he describe Solyman's strategy in war?

---

exchequer: Treasury.

ADAN OLEARIUS: A FOREIGN TRAVELER IN RUSSIA

About the Document

To Europeans, seventeenth-century Russia seemed both strange and exciting. Russia's distance from Europe and her distinct culture made it difficult for Europeans of that era to understand the Russian view of things. Few Europeans traveled to Russia, and those who did observed things that could not be interpreted accurately without an understanding of the Russian people and their culture. The result was that Europeans held very stereotypical and sometimes incorrect ideas about Russians. Because of Russia's isolation from European culture and ideas and its Mongol background, the Russians were seen as barbarians.

The most famous of the travel accounts of this era was written by a German, Adan Olearius. Olearius was sent to Russia on three diplomatic missions in the 1630s. Although his report indicates that he was well informed about Russian culture, it nevertheless gives a very unflattering view of the Russian people.

*Map 15.1
(Interactive) Russia*

The Document

The government of the Russians is what political theorists call a "dominating and despotic monarchy," where the sovereign, that is, the tsar or the grand prince who has obtained the crown by right of succession, rules the entire land alone, and all the people are his subjects, and where the nobles and princes no less than the common folk—towns-people and peasants—are his serfs and slaves, whom he rules and treats as a master treats his servants. . . .

If the Russians be considered in respect to their character, customs, and way of life, they are justly to be counted among the barbarians. . . . The vice of drunkenness is so common in this nation, among people of every station, clergy and laity, high and low, men and women, old and young, that when they are seen now and then lying about in the streets, wallowing in the mud, no attention is paid to it, as something habitual. If a cart driver comes upon such a drunken pig whom he happens to know, he shoves him onto his cart and drives him home, where he is paid his fare. No one ever refuses an opportunity to drink and to get drunk, at any time and in any place, and usually it is done with vodka. . . .

The Russians being naturally tough and born, as it were, for slavery, they must be kept under a harsh and strict yoke and must be driven to do their work with clubs and whips, which they suffer without impatience, because such is their station, and they are accustomed to it. Young and half-grown fellows sometimes come together on certain days and train themselves in fisticuffs, to accustom themselves to receiving blows, and, since habit is second nature, this makes blows given as punishment easier to bear. Each and all, they are slaves and serfs. . . .

Because of slavery and their rough and hard life, the Russians accept war readily and are well suited to it. On certain occasions, if need be, they reveal themselves as courageous and daring soldiers. . . .

Although the Russians, especially the common populace, living as slaves under a harsh yoke, can bear and endure a great deal out of love for their masters, yet if the pressure is beyond measure, then it can be said of them: "Patience, often wounded, finally turned into fury." A dangerous indignation results, turned not so much against their sovereign as against the lower authorities, especially if the people have been much oppressed by them and by their supporters and have not been protected by the higher authorities.

And once they are aroused and enraged, it is not easy to appease them. Then, disregarding all dangers that may ensue, they resort to every kind of violence and behave like mad-men. . . . They own little; most of them have no feather beds; they lie on cushions, straw, mats, or their clothes; they sleep on benches and, in winter, like the non-Germans [i.e., natives] in Livonia, upon the oven, which serves them for cooking and is flat on the top; here husband, wife, children, servants, and maids huddle together. In some houses in the countryside we saw chickens and pigs under the benches and the ovens. . . .

Russians are not used to delicate food and dainties; their daily food consists of porridge, turnips, cabbage, and cucumbers, fresh and pickled, and in Moscow mostly of big salt fish which stink badly, because of the thrifty use of salt, yet are eaten with relish. . . .

The Russians can endure extreme heat. In the bathhouse they stretch out on benches and let themselves be beaten and rubbed with bunches of birch twigs and wisps of bast° (which I could not stand); and when they are hot and red all over and so exhausted that they can bear it no longer in the bathhouse, men and women rush outdoors naked and pour cold water over their bodies; in winter they even wallow in the snow and rub their skin with it as if it were soap; then they go back into the hot bathhouse. And since bathhouses are usually near rivers and brooks, they can throw themselves straight from the hot into the cold bath. . . .

Generally noble families, even the small nobility, rear their daughters in secluded chambers, keeping them hidden from outsiders; and a bridegroom is not allowed to have a look at his bride until he receives her in the bridal chamber. Therefore some happen to be deceived, being given a misshapen and sickly one instead of a fair one, and sometimes a kinswoman or even a maidservant instead of a daughter; of which there have been examples even among the highborn. No wonder therefore that often they live together like cats and dogs and that wife-beating is so common among Russians. . . .

In the Kremlin and in the city there are a great many churches, chapels, and monasteries, both within and without the city walls, over two thousand in all. This is so because every nobleman who has some fortune has a chapel built for himself, and most of them are of stone. The stone churches are round and vaulted inside. . . . They allow neither organs nor any other musical instruments in their churches, saying: Instruments that have neither souls nor life cannot praise God. . . .

In their churches there hang many bells, sometimes five or six, the largest not over two hundred-weights. They ring these bells to summon people to church, and also when the priest during mass raises the chalice. In Moscow, because of the multitude of churches and chapels, there are several thousand bells, which during the divine service create such a clang and din that one unaccustomed to it listens in amazement.

Analysis and Review Questions

1. How does Adan Olearius describe the Russian government?
2. What prejudices does Olearius bring to his narrative?
3. Describe the Russian marriage customs. What does the author see as the consequences of these customs?
4. What assumptions does Olearius make about the Russians based purely on his observations? Speculate on what effects these observations had once they were published in Western Europe.

---

bast: A strong woody fiber used in making ropes.

PRINCE MIKHAIL MIKHAILOVICH SHCHERBATOV, ON THE CORRUPTION OF MORALS IN RUSSIA

Map 15.2
*Eastern Europe
c. 1550*

About the Document

Russia was in many ways a closed society, shut off from Europe by geography, culture, and religion. While some Russians welcomed the Westernization begun by Peter the Great, others saw the influx of Western ideas as dangerous to Russian culture. The Russian Orthodox Church was concerned about the introduction of "false" religious thought.

Prince Shcherbatov admired Peter, but was concerned by Peter's reforms and by the result of this contact with the West. The old aristocracy felt that their place in Russian society was being undermined. The introduction of Western ideas seemed to be changing the very nature of Russian culture and undermining Russian moral values.

Shcherbatov, a scholar and historian, was given the task of editing Peter's private and public papers. This gave him direct access to Peter's "thoughts," and thus great insight into Peter himself. Shcherbatov wrote this essay late in life, and can give us a view as to the long-term effects of Peter's reforms.

The Document

Peter the Great, in imitating foreign nations, not only strove to introduce to his realm a knowledge of sciences, arts and crafts, a proper military system, trade, and the most suitable forms of legislation; he also tried to introduce the kind of sociability, social intercourse and magnificence, which he first learnt from Lefort, and which he later saw for himself. Amid essential legislative measures, the organization of troops and artillery, he paid no less attention to modifying the old customs which seemed crude to him. He ordered beards to be shaved off, he abolished the old Russian garments, and instead of long robes he compelled the men to wear German coats, and the women, instead of the "telogreya" to wear bodices, skirts, gowns and "samaras," and instead of skull-caps, to adorn their heads with fontanges and cornettes. He established various assemblies where the women, hitherto segregated from the company of men, were present with them at entertainments. . . .

The monarch himself kept to the old simplicity of morals in his dress, so that apart from plain coats and uniforms, he never wore anything costly; and it was only for the coronation of the Empress Catherine Alexeevna, his wife, that he had made a coat of blue gros-de-tours with silver-braid; they say he also had another coat, grey with gold braid, but I do not know for what great occasion this was made.

Image 15.2
Peter the Great

The rest was all so plain that even the poorest person would not wear it today, as can be seen from such of his clothes as have remained, and are kept in the Kunst-Kamera at the Imperial Academy of Sciences.

He disliked cuffs and did not wear them, as his portraits attest. He had no costly carriages, but usually travelled in a gig in towns, and in a chaise on a long journey.

He did not have a large number of retainers and attendants, but had orderlies, and did not even have a bodyguard, apart from a Colonel of the Guard.

However, for all his personal simplicity, he wanted his subjects to have a certain magnificence. I think that this great monarch, who did nothing without farsightedness, had it as his object to stimulate trade, industries and crafts through the magnificence and luxury of his subjects, being certain that in his lifetime excessive magnificence and voluptuousness would not enthrone themselves at the royal court. . . .

As far as his domestic life was concerned, although the monarch himself was content with the plainest food, he now introduced drinks previously unknown in Russia, which he drank in preference to other drinks; namely, instead of domestic brandy, brewed from ordinary wine—Dutch aniseed brandy which was called "state" brandy, and Hermitage and Hungarian wine, previously unknown in Russia.

His example was followed by the grandees and those who were close to the court; and indeed it was proper for them to provide these wines; for the monarch was fond of visiting his subjects, and what should a subject not do for the monarch? . . .

Closely copying him, as they were bound to do by their very rank, other leading officials of the Empire also kept open table, such as Admiral-of-the-Fleet, Count Fyodor Matveevich Apraxin, Field-Marshal-in-Chief, Count Boris Petrovich Sheremetev, the Chancellor, Count Gavrilo Ivanovich Golovkin, and the boyar, Tikhon Nikitich Streshnev, who as first ruler of the Empire during Peter the Great's absence abroad, was given estates in order to provide for such meals.

As these eminent men were copied by their inferiors, so the custom of keeping an open table was now introduced in many homes. The meals were not of the traditional kind, that is, when only household products were used; now they tried to improve the flavor of the meat and fish with foreign seasonings. And of course, in a nation in which hospitality has always been a characteristic virtue, it was not hard for the custom of these open tables to become a habit; uniting as it did the special pleasure of society and the improved flavour of the food as compared with the traditional kind, it established itself as a pleasure in its own right. . . .

With this change in the way of life, first of the leading officials of state, and then, by imitation, of the other nobles, and as expenditure reached such a point that it began to exceed income, people began to attach themselves more and more to the monarch and to the grandees, as sources of riches and rewards.

I fear someone may say that this, at any rate, was a good thing, that people began to attach themselves more and more to the monarch. No, this attachment was no blessing, for it was not so much directed to the person of the monarch as to personal ends; this attachment became not the attachment of true subjects who love their sovereign and his honour and consider everything from the point of view of the national interest, but the attachment of slaves and hirelings, who sacrifice everything for their own profit and deceive their sovereign with obsequious zeal.

Coarseness of morals decreased, but the place left by it was filled by flattery and selfishness. Hence came sycophancy, contempt for truth, beguiling of the monarch, and the other evils which reign at court to this day and which have ensconced themselves in the houses of the grandees. . . .

But despite [his] love of truth and his aversion to flattery, the monarch could not eradicate this encroaching venom. Most of those around him did not dare to contradict him in anything, but rather flattered him, praising everything he did, and never resisting his whims, while some even indulged his passions. . . .

I said that it was voluptuousness and luxury that were able to produce such an effect in men's hearts; but there were also other causes, stemming from actual institutions, which eradicated resoluteness and good behaviour.

The abolition of rights of precedence (a custom admittedly harmful to the service and the state), and the failure to replace it by any granting of rights to the noble families, extinguished thoughts of noble pride in the nobility. For it was no longer birth that was respected, but ranks and promotions and length of service. And so everyone started to strive after ranks; but since not everyone is able to perform straightforward deeds of merit, so for lack of meritorious service men began to try and worm their way up, by flattering and humouring the monarch and the grandees in every way. Then there was the introduction of regular military service under Peter the Great, whereby masters were conscripted into the ranks on the same level as their serfs. The serfs, being the first to reach officer's rank through deeds suited to men of their kind, became commanders over their masters and used to beat them with rods. The noble families were split up in the service, so that a man might never see his own kinsman.

Could virtue, then, and resolution, remain in those who from their youth had gone in fear and trembling of their commanders' rods, who could only acquire respect by acts of servility, and being each without any support from his kinsmen, remained alone, without unity or defence, liable to be subjected to violent treatment?

It is admirable that Peter the Great wished to rid religion of superstition, for indeed, superstition does not signify respect for God and his Law, but rather an affront. For to ascribe to God acts unbecoming to him is blasphemy.

In Russia, the beard was regarded as being in the image of God, and it was considered a sin to shave it off, and through this, men fell into the heresy of the Anthropomorphites.° Miracles, needlessly performed, manifestations of ikons, rarely proven, were everywhere acclaimed, attracted superstitious idolatry, and provided incomes for dissolute priests.

Peter the Great strove to do away with all this. He issued decrees, ordering beards to be shaved off, and by the Spiritual Regulation, he placed a check on false miracles and manifestations and also on unseemly gatherings at shrines set up at crossways. Knowing that God's Law exists for the preservation of the human race, and not for its needless destruction, with the blessing of the Synod and the Ecumenical patriarchs, he made it permissible to eat meat on fast-days in cases of need, and especially in the Navy where, by abstaining even from fish, the men were somewhat prone to scurvy; ordering that those who voluntarily sacrificed their lives by such abstinence, should, when they duly fell ill, be thrown into the water. All this is very good, although the latter is somewhat severe.

But when did he do this? At a time when the nation was still unenlightened, and so, by taking superstition away from an unenlightened people, he removed its very faith in God's Law. This action of Peter the Great may be compared to that of an unskilled gardener who, from a weak tree, cuts off the water-shoots which absorb its sap. If it had strong roots, then this pruning would cause it to bring forth fine, fruitful branches; but since it is weak and ailing, the cutting-off of these shoots (which, through the leaves which received the external moisture, nourished the weak tree) means that it fails to produce new fruitful branches; its wounds fail to heal over with sap, and hollows are formed which threaten to destroy the tree. Thus, the cutting-off of superstitions did harm to the most basic articles of the faith; superstition decreased, but so did faith. The servile fear of Hell disappeared, but so did love of God and his Holy Law; and morals, which for lack of other enlightenment used to be improved by faith, having lost this support began to fall into dissolution. . . .

Anthropomorphites: Those who ascribe human qualities to god(s).

And so, through the labours and solicitude of this monarch, Russia acquired fame in Europe and influence in affairs. Her troops were organized in a proper fashion, and her fleets covered the White Sea and the Baltic; with these forces she overcame her old enemies and former conquerors, the Poles and the Swedes, and acquired important provinces and sea-ports. Sciences, arts and crafts began to flourish there, trade began to enrich her, and the Russians were transformed—from bearded men to clean-shaven men, from long-robed men to short-coated men; they became more sociable, and polite spectacles became known to them.

But at the same time, true attachment to the faith began to disappear, sacraments began to fall into disrepute, resoluteness diminished, yielding place to brazen, aspiring flattery; luxury and voluptuousness laid the foundation of their power, and hence avarice was also aroused, and, to the ruin of the laws and the detriment of the citizens, began to penetrate the law-courts.

Such was the condition with regard to morals, in which Russia was left at the death of this great monarch (despite all the barriers which Peter the Great in his own person and by his example had laid down to discourage vice).

Analysis and Review Questions

1. What were the areas in which the author says Peter makes changes or "Westernizes"?
2. What societal changes does the author see?
3. How do the "magnificence and luxury" spread downward through the various ranks of people?
4. What were the problems that resulted from Peter's "Westernization"?
5. Why do Peter's ideas and reforms lead to a decline in faith?

WEB LINKS

Selections from Longman World History—Primary Sources and Case Studies

http://longmanworldhistory.com
The following additional readings and case studies can be found on the Web site.
Case Study 15.1, Two Western Views of Russia and Eastern Europe
Case Study 15.2, Reflections on the Accomplishments of Peter the Great
Case Study 15.3, The Conflict Between Science and Religion
Case Study 15.4, Lomonosov: Panegyric to the Sovereign Emperor Peter the Great.
Comparative Document 14.3, Galileo Galilei, Letter to the Grand Duchess Christina.

General History Sites

http://www.fordham.edu/halsall/mod/modsbookfull.html
Modern History Sourcebook is a collection of full-text documents that correspond with more popular reading assignments given in college classes in many areas of history.

http://www.fordham.edu/halsall/islam/islamsbook.html
Islamic History Sourcebook is a collection of full-text documents that correspond with more popular reading assignments given in college classes on Islamic history.

The Scientific Revolution

http://mars.acnet.wnec.edu/~grempel/courses/wc2/lectures/scientificrev.html
This site is a lecture on Copernicus and the Scientific Revolution.

http://www.fordham.edu/halsall/mod/modsbook09.html
This is from the *Modern History Sourcebook* and contains links on the Scientific Revolution.

Peter the Great

http://mars.acnet.wnec.edu/~grempel/courses/russia/lectures/12peter1.html
Gives a description of the personality of Peter the Great.

CHAPTER 16

Latin America, 1450–1750:
Conflicts in the Contact Zone

In the late 1400s, the Latin American contact zone became a crucible in which people from different cultures struggled for power, advantage, and control. Conflicts between Europeans and America's indigenous peoples lay at the heart of such struggles. If the conquest of the Americas had been just a war between two cultures, though, the vastly outnumbered Europeans should have suffered swift defeat. Likewise, had Europeans fully conquered, converted, and assimilated their indigenous opponents, much of the subsequent contestation by which the period is characterized would not have taken place.

The history of Latin America was as much the history of conflicts within cultures as between cultures. Conflicts between and among various Indian groups enabled small numbers of Europeans to form alliances critical to their ascent to power. For their parts, contested aims and agendas divided Europeans and provided America's indigenous peoples with substantial maneuvering room long after the conquest ended. The lines of divisiveness were many and the future anything but certain.

EXCERPTS FROM THE *ACCOUNT OF ALVA IXTLILXOCHILTL*

About the Document

Following the treaty with the Tlaxcalans, the Spaniards marched to the Aztec capital of Tenochtitlan (present site of Mexico City) where they captured the Aztec emperor, Montezuma. Subsequently, a battle took place between Cortéz's men and the Aztecs, forcing the conquistador and his men to flee the city. During the flight and ensuing battle, Montezuma was killed. His death marked a point of no return for Spaniards and Aztecs alike, though there is considerable debate over who exactly killed Montezuma. That the Aztecs and Spaniards each tried to vilify and hold the other accountable is not surprising. Excerpts from two versions—one Aztec and one Spanish—of what happened, though, demonstrate more than just finger-pointing and the inability to determine exactly what happened. They demonstrate the divisions and tensions that the Aztecs experienced even at the heart of their own empire. Moreover, they suggest that the Spaniards, in assuming Montezuma had no cause to be accountable to his people, might have allowed their own assumptions about kingship in Europe to mislead them.

Image 16.1
The Arrival of
Cortéz in Mexico

The Document

EXCERPTS FROM THE *ACCOUNT OF ALVA IXTLILXOCHITL*

Cortés turned in the direction of Tenochtitlan and entered the city of Tezcoco. He was received only by a group of knights, because the legitimate sons of King Nezahualpilli had been hidden by their servants, and the other lords were being held by the Aztecs as hostages. He entered Tenochtitlan with his army of Spaniards and allies on the day of St. John the Baptist, without being molested in any way.

The Mexicans gave them everything they needed, but when they saw that Cortés had no intention of leaving the city or of freeing their leaders, they rallied their warriors and attacked the Spaniards. This attack began on the day after Cortés entered the city and lasted for seven days.

On the third day, Motecuhzoma climbed onto the rooftop and tried to admonish his people, but they cursed him and shouted that he was a coward and a traitor to his country. They even threatened him with their weapons. It is said that an Indian killed him with a stone from his sling, but the palace servants declared that the Spaniards put him to death by stabbing him in the abdomen with their swords.

On the seventh day, the Spaniards abandoned the city along with the Tlaxcaltecas, the Huexotzincas and their other allies. They fled down the causeway that leads out to Tlacopan. But before they left, they murdered King Cacama of Tezcoco, his three sisters and two of his brothers.

There are several accounts by Indians who took part in the fighting that ensued. They tell how their warriors killed a great many of the Spaniards and their allies, and how the army took refuge on a mountain near Tlacopan and then marched to Tlaxcala.

ACCOUNT OF MONTEZUMA'S DEATH IN BERNAL DÍAZ'S *TRUE STORY OF THE CONQUEST OF MEXICO*

Here Cortés showed himself to be every inch a man, as he always was. Oh, what a fight! What a battle we had! It was something to see us dripping blood and covered with wounds, and others killed, but it pleased Our Lord that we should make our way to the place where we had kept the image of Our Lady. We did not find it, and it seems, as we learned later, Montezuma had become devoted to her and had ordered her to be cared for. We set fire to their idols and burned a good part of the room, with great help from the Tlaxcalans.

After this was done, while we were making our way back down, the priests that were in the temple and the three or four thousand Indians made us tumble six or even ten steps. There were other squadrons in the breastworks and recesses of the great *cu,* discharging so many javelins and arrows that we could not face one group or another, so we decided to return to our quarters, our towers destroyed and everybody wounded, with sixteen dead and the Indians continually pressing us. However clearly I try to tell about this battle, I can never explain it to anyone who wasn't there. We captured two of their principal priests and Cortés ordered us to take good care of them.

Many times I have seen paintings of this battle among the Mexicans and Tlaxcalans, showing how we went up the great temple, for they look upon it as a very heroic feat.

The night was spent in treating wounds and burying the dead, preparing to fight the next day, strengthening the walls they had torn down, and consulting as to how we could fight without sustaining so many casualties, but we found no solution at all. I want to tell about the curses that the followers of Narváez threw at Cortés, and how they damned him and the country and even Diego Velázquez for sending them there, when they had been peacefully settled in their homes in Cuba.

To return to our story. We decided to ask for peace so that we could leave Mexico. With dawn came many more squadrons of warriors, and when Cortés saw them, he decided to have Montezuma speak to them from a rooftop and tell them to stop the fighting and that we wished to leave his city. They say that he answered, very upset, "What more does Malinche want from me? I do not want to live, or listen to him, because of the fate he has forced on me." He would not come, and it was said too that he said that he did not want to see or hear Cortés, or listen to any more of his promises and lies.

The Mercedarian father and Cristóbal de Olid went to him, and showed him great reverence and spoke most affectionately, but Montezuma said, "I do not believe that I can do anything to end this war, for they have already elevated another lord and have decided not to let you leave here alive."

Nevertheless Montezuma stationed himself behind a battlement on a roof top with many of our soldiers to guard him and began to speak to the Mexicans in very affectionate terms, asking them to stop the war and telling them that we would leave Mexico. Many Mexican chiefs and captains, recognizing him, ordered their men to be quiet, and not to shoot stones or arrows. Four of them reached a place where they were able to talk to Montezuma, and they said, crying as they talked, "Oh, Lord, our great lord, how greatly we are afflicted by your misfortune, and that of your sons and relations! We have to let you know that we have already raised one of your kinsmen to be our lord."

They said that he was named Coadlavaca, lord of Iztapalapa. They also said that the war would have to go on to the end, for they had promised their idols not to stop until all of us were killed, and they prayed every day that he would be kept free and safe from our power. As everything would come out as they desired, they would not fail to hold him in higher regard as their lord than before, and they asked him to pardon them.

They had hardly finished this speech when there was such a shower of stones and javelins that Montezuma was hit by three stones, one on the head, another on the arm, and the third on the leg, for our men who were shielding him neglected to do so for a moment, because they saw that the attack had stopped while he was speaking with his chiefs.

They begged him to be doctored and to eat something, speaking very kindly to him, but he wouldn't, and when we least expected it they came to say that he was dead.

Cortés wept for him, and all of our captains and soldiers. There were men among us who cried as though he had been our father, and it is not surprising, considering how good he was. It was said that he had ruled for seventeen years and that he was the best king Mexico had ever had.

I have already told about the sorrow we felt when we saw that Montezuma was dead. We even thought badly about the Mercedarian father, who was always with him, for not having persuaded him to turn Christian. He gave as an excuse that he didn't think Montezuma would die from those wounds, but he did say that he should have ordered something given to stupefy him.

Finally Cortés directed that a priest and a chief among those we had imprisoned should be freed so that they could go and tell Coadlavaca and his captains that the great Montezuma was dead and that they had seen him die from the wounds his own people had caused him.

Map 16.1
European Empires
in Latin America,
1660

Analysis and Review Questions

1. How do the Aztec and Spanish versions of Montezuma's death differ?
2. To what extent do the two accounts share an assessment of Aztec divisiveness concerning their emperor?
3. What can we infer from these documents about how Aztec society was structured, and what kinds of obligations were required to maintain one's rule?
4. What are the various groups or levels that wield power in Aztec society?
5. To what extent did Aztec divisiveness aid the Spaniards in their conquest of Mexico? In what respects might such divisions have made the Spaniards' goals more difficult to attain?
6. In what ways were the Aztec society and society in Europe mirror images of one another? How were they different?

EXCERPT FROM BARTOLOMÉ DE LAS CASAS' *IN DEFENSE OF THE INDIANS*

About the Document

As Spain struggled in the mid 1500s to consolidate control over its New World possessions, a great debate erupted over the status and treatment of the Indians. At the heart of the debate lay the issue of whether Indians were civilized. An Aristotle treatise enshrined in Spanish law gave civilized peoples the right to wage war on uncivilized peoples and take them as slaves. Consequently, assessments of Indians as barbarians benefited many Spanish settlers who sought both to impose jurisdiction on the Indians and to take advantage of their labor. The Iberian scholar and theologian Juan Ines de Sepúlveda became a spokesperson for such interests.

Sepúlveda faced stiff opposition. Bartolomé de las Casas, who had served several years as a bishop in Mexico, represented the other side of the debate. Arguing that Indians were civilized, the theologian sought, on behalf of both Indians and priests outraged at the settlers' excesses, to persuade the Spanish Crown to impose stricter controls on its colonists. The debate's outcome would determine and shape Spain's policy toward *all* of its New World inhabitants.

The Document

Now if we shall have shown that among our Indians of the western and southern shores (granting that we call them barbarians and that they are barbarians) there are important kingdoms, large numbers of people who live settled lives in a society, great cities, kings, judges and laws, persons who engage in commerce, buying, selling, lending, and the other contracts of the law of nations, will it now stand proved that the Reverend Doctor Sepúlveda has spoken wrongly and viciously against peoples like these, either out of malice or ignorance of Aristotle's teaching, and, therefore, has falsely and perhaps irreparably slandered them before the entire world? From the fact that the Indians are barbarians it does not necessarily follow that they are incapable of government and have to be ruled by others, except to be taught about the Catholic faith and to be admitted to the holy sacraments. They are not ignorant, inhuman, or bestial. Rather, long before they had heard the word Spaniard they had properly organized states, wisely ordered by excellent laws, religion, and custom. They cultivated friendship and, bound together in common fellowship, lived in populous cities in which they wisely administered the affairs of both peace and war justly and equitably, truly governed by laws that at very many points surpass ours, and could have won the admiration of the sages of Athens, as I will show in the second part of this *Defense*.

Now if they are to be subjugated by war because they are ignorant of polished literature, let Sepúlveda hear Trogus Pompey:

Nor could the Spaniards submit to the yoke of a conquered province until Caesar Augustus, after he had conquered the world, turned his victorious armies against them and organized that barbaric and wild people as a province, once he had led them by law to a more civilized way of life.

Now see how he called the Spanish people barbaric and wild. I would like to hear Sepúlveda, in his cleverness, answer this question: Does he think that the war of the Romans against the Spanish was justified in order to free them from barbarism? And this question also: Did the Spanish wage an unjust war when they vigorously defended themselves against them?

Next, I call the Spaniards who plunder that unhappy people torturers. Do you think that the Romans, once they had subjugated the wild and barbaric peoples of Spain, could with secure right divide all of you among themselves, handing over so many head of both males and females as allotments to individuals? And do you then conclude that the Romans could have stripped your rulers of their authority and consigned all of you, after you had been deprived of your liberty, to wretched labors, especially in searching for gold and silver lodes and mining and refining the metals? And if the Romans finally did that, as is evident from Diodorus, [would you not judge] that you also have the right to defend your freedom, indeed your very life, by war? Sepúlveda, would you have permitted Saint James to evangelize your own people of Córdoba in that way? For God's sake and man's faith in him, is this the way to impose the yoke of Christ on Christian men? Is this the way to remove wild barbarism from the minds of barbarians? Is it not, rather, to act like thieves, cut-throats, and cruel plunderers and to drive the gentlest of people headlong into despair? The Indian race is not that barbaric, nor are they dull witted or stupid, but they are easy to teach and very talented in learning all the liberal arts, and very ready to accept, honor, and observe the Christian religion and correct their sins (as experience has taught) once priests have introduced them to the sacred mysteries and taught them the word of God. They have been endowed with excellent conduct, and before the coming of the Spaniards, as we have said, they had political states that were well founded on beneficial laws.

From this it is clear that the basis for Sepúlveda's teaching that these people are uncivilized and ignorant is worse than false. Yet even if we were to grant that this race has no keenness of mind or artistic ability, certainly they are not, in consequence, obliged to submit themselves to those who are more intelligent and to adopt their ways, so that, if they refuse, they may be subdued by having war waged against them and be enslaved, as happens today. For men are obliged by the natural law to do many things they cannot be forced to do against their will. We are bound by the natural law to embrace virtue and imitate the uprightness of good men. No one, however, is punished for being bad unless he is guilty of rebellion. Where the Catholic faith has been preached in a Christian manner and as it ought to be, all men are bound by the natural law to accept it, yet no one is forced to accept the faith of Christ. No one is punished because he is sunk in vice, unless he is rebellious or harms the property and persons of others. No one is forced to embrace virtue and show himself as a good man. One who receives a favor is bound by the natural law to return the favor by what we call antidotal obligation. Yet no one is forced to this, nor is he punished if he omits it, according to the common interpretation of the jurists.

Analysis and Review Questions

1. On what grounds does las Casas argue that the Indians are civilized?
2. Las Casas was a master of rhetoric. How does his language in describing the Spanish settlers and their actions incline his audience to accept his bias or position? Do you think he was successful?
3. Referring to the reading, tell how important you think legal and philosophical precedents were in making a successful case before the Spanish Crown? Do you think this form of logic and argument was based on Roman precedent? Why or why not?
4. In comparing the Spaniards with the Romans, what do you think las Casas was trying to achieve?
5. How does the position of las Casas on the role of Christianity in the New World differ from that which he ascribes to Sepúlveda? What are some of the implications of this division within the Church?

*Image 16.2
Spanish Mistreatment
of the Indians*

SOR JUANA INÉZ DE LA CRUZ, FROM *LA RESPUESTA**

About the Document

Arguably one of the greatest divides in the contact zone was that between the sexes. The patriarchal nature of Spanish rule and of the Catholic Church ensured that legally, at least, women were restricted to inferior positions and to lives with few rights. This was as true of Spanish women as it was of indigenous women. Perhaps the most impressive example of gender conflict involved Sor Juana Inéz de la Cruz, a Mexican nun in the late 1600s.

A brilliant and talented scholar, Sor Juana in 1690 wrote a daring critique of an earlier Jesuit sermon. Her critique prompted the Bishop of Puebla to admonish her for overstepping herself as a woman. Sor Juana subsequently defended herself in a lengthy reply *(respuesta)* that challenged the foundations of the society in which she lived. Her 1695 response to the bishop set off a struggle that highlighted not only divisions between the sexes, but also those within the Church, and between the Church and the Spanish government, in which Sor Juana found many powerful and influential supporters.

The Document

I see many and illustrious women; some blessed with the gift of prophecy, like Abigail, others of persuasion, like Esther; others with pity, like Rehab; others with perseverance, like Anna, the mother of Samuel; and an infinite number of others, with diverse gifts and virtues.

... for all were nothing more than learned women, held, and celebrated—and venerated as well as such by antiquity. Without mentioning an infinity of other women whose names fill books. For example, I find the Egyptian Catherine, studying and influencing the wisdom of all the wise men of Egypt. I see a Gertrudis studying, writing, and teaching. And not to overlook examples close to home, I see my most holy mother Paula, learned in Hebrew, Greek, and Latin, and most able in interpreting the Scriptures. And what greater praise than, having as her chronicler a Jeronimus Maximus, that Saint scarcely found himself competent for his task, and says, with that weighty deliberation and energetic precision with which he so well expressed himself: "If all the members of my body were tongues, they still would not be sufficient to proclaim the wisdom and virtue of Paula."

The venerable Doctor Arce (by his virtue and learning a worthy teacher of the Scriptures) in his scholarly *Bibliorum* raises this question: *Is it permissible for women to dedicate themselves to the study of the Holy Scriptures, and to their interpretation?* and he offers as negative arguments the opinions of many saints, especially that of the Apostle: *Let women keep silence in*

*The Spanish text for this 17th century declaration of women's intellectual freedom was discovered by Gabriel North Seymour during her Fulbright Scholarship in Mexico in 1980, following graduation from Princeton University. The English language translation by Margaret Sayers Peden was commissioned by Lime Rock Press, a small independent press in Connecticut, and was originally published in 1982 in a limited edition that included Seymour's black-and-white photographs of Sor Juana sites, under the title, "A Woman of Genius: The Intellectual Autobiography of Sor Juana Inès de la Cruz." The publication was honored at a special convocation of Mexican and American scholars at the Library of Congress. Copyright 1982 by Lime Rock Press, Inc. Reprinted by permission.

the churches; for it is not permitted them to speak, etc. He later cites other opinions and, from the same Apostle, verses from his letter to Titus: *The aged women in like manner, in holy attire teaching well*, with interpretations by the Holy Fathers. Finally he resolves, with all prudence, that teaching publicly from a University chair, or preaching from the pulpit, is not permissible for women; but that to study, write, and teach privately not only is permissible, but most advantageous and useful. It is evident that this is not to be the case with all women, but with those to whom God may have granted special virtue and prudence, and who may be well advanced in learning, and having the essential talent and requisites for such a sacred calling. This view is indeed just, so much so that not only women, who are held to be so inept, but also men, who merely for being men believe they are wise, should be prohibited from interpreting the Sacred Word if they are not learned and virtuous and of gentle and well-inclined natures; that this is not so has been, I believe, at the root of so much sectarianism and so many heresies. For there are many who study but are ignorant, especially those who are in spirit arrogant, troubled, and proud, so eager for new interpretations of the Word (which itself rejects new interpretations) that merely for the sake of saying what no one else has said they speak a heresy, and even then are not content. Of these the Holy Spirit says: *For wisdom will not enter into a malicious soul*. To such as these more harm results from knowing than from ignorance. A wise man has said: he who does not know Latin is not a complete fool; but he who knows it is well qualified to be. And I would add that a fool may reach perfection (if ignorance may tolerate perfection) by having studied his title of philosophy and theology and by having some learning of tongues, by which he may be a fool in many sciences and languages: a great fool cannot be contained solely in his mother tongue.

For such as these, I reiterate, study is harmful, because it is as if to place a sword in the hands of a madman; which, though a most noble instrument for defense, is in his hands his own death and that of many others. So were the Divine Scriptures in the possession of the evil Pelagius and the intractable Arius, of the evil Luther, and the other heresiarchs like our own Doctor (who was neither ours nor a doctor) Cazalla. To these men, wisdom was harmful; although it is the greatest nourishment and the life of the soul; in the same way that in a stomach of sickly constitution and adulterated complexion, the finer the nourishment it receives, the more arid, fermented, and perverse are the humors it produces; thus these evil men: the more they study, the worse opinions they engender, their reason being obstructed with the very substance meant to nourish it, and they study much and digest little, exceeding the limits of the vessel of their reason. Of which the Apostle says: *For I say, by the grace that is given me, to all that are among you, not to be more wise than it behoveth to be wise, but to be wise unto sobriety, and according as God hath divided to every one the measure of faith*. And in truth, the Apostle did not direct these words to women, but to men; and that *keep silence* is intended not only for women, but for *all* incompetents. If I desire to know as much, or more, than Aristotle or Saint Augustine, and if I have not the aptitude of Saint Augustine or Aristotle, though I study more than either, not only will I not achieve learning, but I will weaken and dull the workings of my feeble reason with the disproportionateness of the goal.

Analysis and Review Questions

1. On what grounds does Sor Juana defend her right to exercise her intellect?
2. What examples does Sor Juana offer of noted and influential women? What does the variety of sources from which she draws her examples tell us of Sor Juana's education?

3. What reasons does Sor Juana give for agreeing with Doctor Arce's argument for barring women from the pulpit?

4. How does Sor Juana turn her agreement with Arce into an attack on the male-dominated society in which she lived? Do you think the Church in particular would have found Sor Juana's argument more threatening than, say, the average male Spaniard? Why or why not?

5. In her "Respuesta," Sor Juana treats intellect as a veritable weapon. To what extent do you agree with her? What examples might you provide that would support or contradict her?

Map 16.2
Spanish and Portuguese
Explorations: 1400–1600

Web Links

Selections from Longman World History—Primary Sources and Case Studies

Comparative Document

Document 22.1, Catherine the Great's Constitution

http://longmanworldhistory.com
The following additional readings and case studies can be found on the Web site.
Document 16.1, *The Second Letter of Hernan Cortéz to King Charles V of Spain (1519)*
Document 16.5, *The New Laws of the Indies for the Good Treatment and Preservation of the Indians (1542)*
Case Study 16.1, Battlefields to Courtrooms: Conflict and Agency in the Americas
Case Study 16.2, Policy-making in the Americas: Subjects or Slaves?
Case Study 16.3, Challenges of Empire: The "Song" Remains the Same

Spanish Colonial Policy and the New Laws

http://www.fordham.edu/halsall/mod/1542newlawsindies.html
Brief introduction to and context for the 1542 New Laws. Includes more expansive excerpts from the New Laws.

http://www.mexconnect.com/mex_/history/jtuck/jtviceroymendoza.html
Site devoted to the colonial career of Viceroy Mendoza, the Crown bureaucrat charged with implementing and enforcing the New Laws in Mexico. Describes in detail the political backlash that forced many of the New Laws to be suspended in the New World.

The Encomienda and Its Relation to Spanish Abuses

http://muweb.millersv.edu/~columbus/papers/scott-m.html
Article-length history of the encomienda in the Americas.

The New Laws and Their Relation to the Spanish "Black Legend"

http://www.freerepublic.com/forum/a39d38e0d14db.htm
Comprehensive assessment of las Casas, the encomienda, the New Laws, and their relation to the Spanish "Black Legend" so often invoked as propaganda by Spain's enemies at home and abroad.

http://www.unl.edu/LatAmHis/RoleofChurch.html
This site deals more directly with the Church's role in unwittingly creating and sustaining the Spanish "Black Legend."

http://www.xxicentury.org/HCA/reform.html
Historical assessment of the Church's role in helping to establish and reform Spanish colonial policy; not limited to the New Laws and the abuses which prompted them.

The Age of Discovery and European Reactions to the New World

http://muweb.millersv.edu/~columbus
Extensive collection of indexed articles and issues pertaining to Columbus, the Age of Discovery, and both the short- and long-term impacts of Columbus's epic voyages on both Spain and the New World.

East Asia in Transition, 1450–1700

The intellectual and religious developments beginning in the fourteenth century brought changes not only in the West but also in the East. Early European outreach to East Asia had a significant impact on the region and precipitated the beginning of the Enlightenment in East Asia. Although China, Japan, and Korea managed to keep their political unity while remaining isolated to the outside world, Western influence became almost irresistible. The guns, the cross, and the trade would eventually reshape the minds of East Asia and bring in a new era of change.

The fall of the Mongol Empire left a political vacuum that led to the restoration of Chinese imperial glory. China under the Ming Dynasty (1368–1644) regained its political centralization and resumed its commercial expansion. The traditional tribute system, designed to maintain China's political and economic superiority to its neighboring small states, was reorganized in the face of increasing Western commercial activities. In 1405, nearly 90 years before Christopher Columbus set off on his westward expedition to the "new world," China's Zheng He led the imperial treasure fleet of 62 ships through the southwestern Pacific and Indian Oceans to reach the east coast of Africa. However, such courageous voyages lasted for only 28 years, until 1433, when the Ming emperor called the missions off.

Japan, on the other hand, withdrew from its limited contact with the Europeans into isolation and remained that way until mid-nineteenth century. Both Japanese government and society became increasingly rigid under the rule of the shogun, especially during the Tokugawa period (1604–1868). On the Korean Peninsula, the Yi Dynasty (1392–1910) gave the Koreans over five centuries of peace and unity. Chinese patterns continued to affect Korea in a significant way.

The period between the fifteenth and eighteenth centuries was a time of recovery and consolidation for East Asia. Soon, the region would have to face the challenge from the West. Collision with European powers and different solutions to deal with them would lead to different paths toward modernization for the major countries in the region.

MATTEO RICCI'S JOURNALS

About the Document

Matteo Ricci was an Italian Jesuit missionary who went to China in 1583. He first learned to adapt to the Chinese way of life before attempting to convert the Chinese to Christianity. His modest manner amazed many Chinese, including the emperor. In 1601 Ricci was offered a position in the imperial court in charge of studies in mathematics and astronomy, as well as teaching Christianity to the Chinese elite class. Fluent in Chinese and well-versed in Confucian teaching, Ricci also composed a number of books in Chinese on various subjects. One of the most important was his *History of the Introduction of Christianity into China*. The imperial court was so impressed by his achievements that Ricci was awarded an honorable title as the Doctor from the Great West Ocean.

While in China, Ricci kept a journal reflecting on his experience and impression of the Chinese government and society.

*Image 17.1
Matteo Ricci and a
Chinese Convert to
Christianity*

The Document

We shall touch upon this subject only insofar as it has to do with the purpose of our narrative. It would require a number of chapters, if not of whole books, to treat this matter in full detail. . . . Chinese imperial power passes on from father to son, or to other royal kin, as does our own. Two or three of the more ancient kings are known to have bequeathed the throne to successors without royal relationship rather than to their sons, whom they judged to be unfitted to rule. More than once, however, it has happened that the people, growing weary of an inept ruler, have stripped him of his authority and replaced him with someone pre-eminent for character and courage whom they henceforth recognized as their legitimate King. It may be said in praise of the Chinese that ordinarily they would prefer to die an honorable death rather than swear allegiance to a usurping monarch. In fact, there is a proverb extant among their philosophers, which reads: "No woman is moral who has two husbands, nor any vassal faithful to two lords."

There are no ancient laws in China under which the republic is governed in perpetuum, such as our laws of the twelve tables and the Code of Caesar. Whoever succeeds in getting possession of the throne, regardless of his ancestry, makes new laws according to his own way of thinking. His successors on the throne are obliged to enforce the laws which he promulgated as founder of the dynasty, and these laws cannot be changed without good reason. . . .

The extent of their kingdom° is so vast, its borders so distant, and their utter lack of knowledge of a transmaritime world is so complete that the Chinese imagine the whole world as included in their kingdom. Even now, as from time beyond recording, they call their Emperor, Thiencu, the Son of Heaven, and because they worship Heaven as the Supreme Being, the Son of Heaven and the Son of God are one and the same. In ordinary speech, he is referred to as Hoamsi, meaning supreme ruler or monarch, while other and subordinate rulers are called by the much inferior title of Guam.

kingdom: Ricci often used the term kingdom instead of dynasty or empire to refer to China.

Only such as have earned a doctor's degree or that of licentiate are admitted to take part in the government of the kingdom, and due to the interest of the magistrates and of the King himself there is no lack of such candidates. Every public office is therefore fortified with and dependent upon the attested science, prudence, and diplomacy of the person assigned to it, whether he be taking office for the first time or is already experienced in the conduct of civil life. This integrity of life is prescribed by . . . law . . . , and for the most part it is lived up to, save in the case of such as are prone to violate the dictates of justice from human weakness and from lack of religious training among the gentiles. All magistrates, whether they belong to the military or to the civil congress, are called Quon-fu, meaning commander or president, though their honorary or unofficial title is Lau-ye or Lau-sie, signifying lord or father. The Portuguese call the Chinese magistrates, mandarins, probably from mandando, mando mandare, to order or command, and they are now generally known by this title in Europe.

Though we have already stated that the Chinese form of government is monarchical, it must be evident from what has been said, and it will be made clearer by what is to come, that it is to some extent an aristocracy. Although all legal statutes inaugurated by magistrates must be confirmed by the King in writing on the written petition presented to him, the King himself makes no final decision in important matters of state without consulting the magistrates or considering their advice. . . .

Tax returns, impost, and other tribute, which undoubtedly exceed a hundred and fifty million a year, as is commonly said, do not go into the Imperial Exchequer, nor can the King dispose of this income as he pleases. The silver, which is the common currency, is placed in the public treasury, and the returns paid in rice are placed in the warehouses belonging to the government. The generous allowance made for the support of the royal family and their relatives, for the palace eunuchs and the royal household, is drawn from this national treasury. In keeping with the regal splendor and dignity of the crown, these annuities are large, but each individual account is determined and regulated by law. Civil and military accounts and the expenses of all government departments are paid out of this national treasury, and the size of the national budget is far in excess of what Europeans might imagine. Public buildings, the palaces of the King and of his relations, the upkeep of city prisons and fortresses, and the renewal of all kinds of war supplies must be met by the national treasury, and in a kingdom of such vast dimensions the program of building and of restoration is continuous. One would scarcely believe that at times even these enormous revenues are not sufficient to meet the expenses. When this happens, new taxes are imposed to balance the national budget.

Relative to the magistrates in general, there are two distinct orders or grades. The first and superior order is made up of the magistrates who govern the various courts of the royal palace, which is considered to be a model for the rule of the entire realm. The second order includes all provincial magistrates or governors who rule a province or a city. For each of these orders of magistrates, there are five or six large books containing the governmental roster of the entire country. These books are for sale throughout the kingdom. They are being continually revised, and the revision, which is dated twice a month in the royal city of Pekin, is not very difficult because of the singular typographical arrangement in which they are printed. The entire contents of these books consist of nothing other than the current lists of the names, addresses, and grades of the court officers of the entire government, and the frequent revision is necessary if the roster is to be kept up to date. In addition to the daily changes, occasioned by deaths, demotions, and dismissals in such an incredibly long list of names, there are the frequent departures of some to visit their homes at stated periods. We shall say more later on of this last instance, which is occasioned by the custom requiring every magistrate to lay aside his official duties and return to his home for three full years, on the death of his father or his mother. One result of these numerous changes is that there are always a great many in the city of Pekin awaiting the good fortune of being appointed to fill the vacancies thus created.

Besides the regular magistrates there are in the royal palace various other organizations, instituted for particular purposes. The most exalted of these is what is known as the Han-Iin-yuen, made up of selected doctors of philosophy and chosen by examination. Members of this cabinet have nothing to do with public administration but outrank all public officials in dignity of office. Ambition for a place in this select body means no end of labor and of sacrifice. These are the King's secretaries, who do both his writing and his composing. They edit and compile the royal annals and publish the laws and statutes of the land. The tutors of kings and princes are chosen from their number. They are entirely devoted to study and there are grades within the cabinet which are determined by the publications of its members. Hence, they are honored with the highest dignity within the regal court, but not beyond it. . . .

The Chinese can distinguish between their magistrates by the parasols they use as protection against the sun when they go out in public. Some of these are blue and others yellow. Sometimes for effect they will have two or three of these sunshades, but only one if their rank does not permit of more. They may also be recognized by their mode of transportation in public. The lower ranks ride on horseback, the higher are carried about on the shoulders of their servants in gestatorial chairs. The number of carriers also has a significance of rank; some are allowed only four, others may have eight. There are other ways also of distinguishing the magistracy and the rank of dignity therein; by banners and pennants, chains and censer cups, and by the number of the guards who give orders to make way for the passage of the dignitary. The escort itself is held in such high esteem by the public that no one would question their orders. Even in a crowded city everyone gives way at the sound of their voices with a spontaneity that corresponds to the rank of the approaching celebrity.

Before closing this chapter on Chinese public administration, it would seem to be quite worthwhile recording a few more things in which this people differ from Europeans. To begin with, it seems to be quite remarkable when we stop to consider it, that in a kingdom of almost limitless expanse and innumerable population, and abounding in copious supplies of every description, though they have a well-equipped army and navy that could easily conquer the neighboring nations, neither the King nor his people ever think of waging a war of aggression. They are quite content with what they have and are not ambitious of conquest. In this respect they are much different from the people of Europe, who are frequently discontent with their own governments and covetous of what others enjoy. While the nations of the West seem to be entirely consumed with the idea of supreme domination, they cannot even preserve what their ancestors have bequeathed them, as the Chinese have done through a period of some thousand of years. . . .

Another remarkable fact and quite worthy of note as marking a difference from the West, is that the entire kingdom is administered by the Order of the Learned, commonly known as The Philosophers. The responsibility for orderly management of the entire realm is wholly and completely committed to their charge and care. The army, both officers and soldiers, hold them in high respect and show them the promptest obedience and deference, and not infrequently the military are disciplined by them as a schoolboy might be punished by his master. Policies of war are formulated and military questions are decided by the Philosophers only, and their advice and counsel has more weight with the King than that of the military leaders. In fact very few of these, and only on rare occasions, are admitted to war consultations. Hence it follows that those who aspire to be cultured frown upon war and would prefer the lowest rank in the philosophical order to the highest in the military, realizing that the Philosophers far excel military leaders in the good will and the respect of the people and in opportunities of acquiring wealth.

Analysis and Review Questions

Map 17.1
Trade Routes
to Asia

1. In your view, how well did Ricci understand Chinese traditions and society?
2. How does Ricci compare Chinese law with that from European tradition?
3. According to Ricci's account, what was the attitude of the Chinese magistrates to the Jesuits?
4. What was Ricci's description of the Chinese government?
5. Who might be Ricci's intended readers?

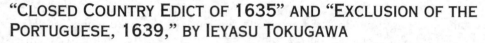

"CLOSED COUNTRY EDICT OF 1635" AND "EXCLUSION OF THE PORTUGUESE, 1639," BY IEYASU TOKUGAWA

About the Document

Ieyasu Tokugawa was granted the title of shogun in 1603 after defeating his rivals by using guns brought into Japan by the Europeans. His successors, however, began to fear that the growing trade with the West and influence of Christianity would directly challenge the Japanese value system. Below are two major shogun edicts intended to force foreign trade and missionaries out of Japan. Japan remained an isolated country for the next 200 years, until the Americans tried to open relations with Japan in 1853.

The Document

Closed Country Edict of 1635

1. Japanese ships are strictly forbidden to leave for foreign countries.
2. No Japanese is permitted to go abroad. If there is anyone who attempts to do so secretly, he must be executed. The ship so involved must be impounded and its owner arrested, and the matter must be reported to the higher authority.
3. If any Japanese returns from overseas after residing there, he must be put to death.
4. If there is any place where the teachings of padres° is practiced, the two of you must order a thorough investigation.
5. Any informer revealing the whereabouts of the followers of padres must be rewarded accordingly. If anyone reveals the whereabouts of a high ranking padre, he must be given one hundred pieces of silver. For those of lower ranks, depending on the deed, the reward must be set accordingly.

padres: Fathers (priests) of the Roman Catholic Church.

6. If a foreign ship has an objection [to the measures adopted] and it becomes necessary to report the matter to Edo,° you may ask the Omura° domain to provide ships to guard the foreign ship. . . .

7. If there are any Southern Barbarians° who propagate the teachings of padres, or otherwise commit crimes, they may be incarcerated in the prison. . . .

8. All incoming ships must be carefully searched for the followers of padres.

9. No single trading city shall be permitted to purchase all the merchandise brought by foreign ships.

10. Samurai are not permitted to purchase any goods originating from foreign ships directly from Chinese merchants in Nagasaki.

11. After a list of merchandise brought by foreign ships is sent to Edo, as before you may order that commercial dealings may take place without waiting for a reply from Edo.

12. After settling the price, all white yarns brought by foreign ships shall be allocated to the five trading cities° and other quarters as stipulated.

13. After settling the price of white yarns, other merchandise [brought by foreign ships] may be traded freely between the [licensed] dealers. However, in view of the fact that Chinese ships are small and cannot bring large consignments, you may issue orders of sale at your discretion. Additionally, payment for goods purchased must be made within twenty days after the price is set.

14. The date of departure homeward of foreign ships shall not be later than the twentieth day of the ninth month. Any ships arriving in Japan later than usual shall depart within fifty days of their arrival. As to the departure of Chinese ships, you may use your discretion to order their departure after the departure of the Portuguese galeota.°

15. The goods brought by foreign ships which remained unsold may not be deposited or accepted for deposit.

16. The arrival in Nagasaki of representatives of the five trading cities shall not be later than the fifth day of the seventh month. Anyone arriving later than that date shall lose the quota assigned to his city.

17. Ships arriving in Hirado° must sell their raw silk at the price set in Nagasaki, and are not permitted to engage in business transactions until after the price is established in Nagasaki.

You are hereby required to act in accordance with the provisions set above. It is so ordered.

Image 17.2
A Japanese view
of European
Missionaries

Exclusion of the Portuguese, 1639

1. The matter relating to the proscription of Christianity is known [to the Portuguese]. However, heretofore they have secretly transported those who are going to propagate that religion.

2. If those who believe in that religion band together in an attempt to do evil things, they must be subjected to punishment.

Edo: Old name of what today is Tokyo, before Meiji Reforms of 1868.
Omura: Area around Nagasaki.
Southern Barbarians: Westerners.
five trading cities: Foreigners could do business in Kyoto, Edo/Tokyo, Osaka, Sakai, and Nagasaki.
galeota: Portuguese ship.
Hirado: Island southwest of Nagasaki.

3. While those who believe in the preaching of padres are in hiding, there are incidents in which that country [Portugal] has sent gifts to them for their sustenance.

In view of the above, hereafter entry by the Portuguese galeota is forbidden. If they insist on coming [to Japan], the ships must be destroyed and anyone aboard those ships must be beheaded. We have received the above order and are thus transmitting it to you accordingly.

The above concerns our disposition with regard to the galeota.

Memorandum

With regard to those who believe in Christianity, you are aware that there is a proscription, and thus knowing, you are not permitted to let padres and those who believe in their preaching to come aboard your ships. If there is any violation, all of you who are aboard will be considered culpable. If there is anyone who hides the fact that he is a Christian and boards your ship, you may report it to us. A substantial reward will be given to you for this information.

This memorandum is to be given to those who come on Chinese ships. [A similar note to the Dutch ships.]

Analysis and Review Questions

1. What were the major restrictions imposed on the Japanese?
2. What were the major restrictions on foreign traders?
3. What was the primary purpose of the 1635 Edict?
4. What was the argument behind the shogun's decision of 1639 to expel the Christians?
5. How would these two edicts affect Japan's relations with the outside world?

Map 17.2 Voyages of Zheng He

A MING NAVAL EXPEDITION

About the Document

Zheng He's daring adventures to explore the outside world came nearly 90 years earlier than Christopher Columbus's journey westward. Although the voyages did not last long, they proved to the Chinese, as well as the world, that China was able to carry out long-distance travel on the high seas.

Reading this stone tablet text commemorating the expeditions, it is not difficult to understand the pride of the Chinese in demonstrating their maritime power. One wonders what kind of naval power China would have become if the Ming emperor had not called off such voyages in 1433 and China had not lost its technological edge to the Europeans.

The Document

The Imperial Ming dynasty in unifying seas and continents . . . even goes beyond the Han and the Hang . . . the countries beyond the horizon and from the ends of the earth have all become subjects . . . Thus the barbarians from beyond the seas have come to audience bearing precious objects. . . . The Emperor has ordered us, Zheng He . . . to make manifest the transforming power of the Imperial virtue and to treat distant people with kindness. . . . We have seven times received the commission and ambassadors [and have visited] altogether more than thirty countries, large and small. We have traversed immense water spaces and have beheld huge waves like mountains rising sky high, and we have set eyes on barbarian regions far away hidden in a blue transparency of light vapors, while our sails loftily unfolded like clouds day and night controlled their course, traversing those savage waves as if we were treading a public thoroughfare. . . We have received the high favor of a gracious commission of our Sacred Lord, to carry to the distant barbarians the benefits of his auspicious example. . . . Therefore we have recorded the years and months of the voyages. [Here follows a detailed record of places visited and things done on each of the seven voyages.] We have anchored in this port awaiting a north wind to take the sea, and have thus recorded an inscription in stone . . . erected by the principal envoys, the Grand Eunuchs Cheng Ho and Wang Ching-hung and the assistant envoys.

Analysis and Review Questions

1. How did the Chinese view their overseas expeditions?
2. What was China's view of itself and the world?
3. What is the point of the description of the weather and waves on the high sea?
4. What role was played by the imperial power in China's overseas expeditions?
5. What might be the major contributions of these Chinese voyages to the world?

WEB LINKS

Selections from Longman World History—Primary Sources and Case Studies

http://longmanworldhistory.com
The following additional readings and case studies can be found on the Web Site.
Document 17.3A, European View of Asia
Case Study 17.1, A Chinese and a Japanese View of Europeans
Jesuits in China

*http://www.ibiblio.org/expo/vatican.exhibit/exhibit/
i-rome_to_china/Jesuits_in_China.html*

*http://www.ibiblio.org/expo/vatican.exhibit/exhibit/
i-rome_to_china/Rome_to_china.html*

http://mb-soft.com/believe/text/jesuit.htm

http://www.christianitytoday.com/ch/52h/52h024.html

Christians in Japan

http://www.baobab.or.jp/~stranger/mypage/chrinjap.htm
http://www.pnsnet.co.jp/users/cltembpt/cronology.html
http://satucket.com/lectionary/Japan_martyrs.htm
http://members.aol.com/DoJourney/Keikyo/

Zheng He's Voyage

http://www.chinapage.com/chengho.html
http://campus.northpark.edu/history/WebChron/World/Voyages.html
http://www.askasia.org/frclasrm/lessplan/l000069.htm
http://www.cronab.demon.co.uk/china.htm

CHAPTER 18

Foreign Rulers in South Asia, 1450–1750

Between 1450 and 1750 C.E., southern India was invaded and controlled by numerous foreign rulers. Many of these rulers, such as the Delhi Sultans and Babur, came from powerful entities within South Asia, but as these empires began to crumble, the English saw their opportunity to pick up the broken pieces for their own economic gain. With England's rise to power in South Asia came the influence of the Western world. As the fifteenth century dawned in South Asia, the Delhi Sultanate, a Muslim empire, had ruled northern India since 1192 C.E. Southern India was ruled mostly by local rulers and princes. On the horizon, though, were powerful foreign entities with an interest in India. The Delhi Sultans had come to India from Afghanistan, and the next invader came from there as well. In 1523 Babur invaded India, conquering Delhi and destroying the remnants of the Delhi Sultanate. Babur was the founder of the Mughal Empire, which ruled much of India until the early 1700s.

Around this time, after a century of increasing influence, the English became a dominant force in India. England's East India Company established commercial and financial monopolies, especially in the area of Bengal in eastern India. As it did so, it weakened the Mughal Empire. After the death of the Mughal emperor Aurangzeb in 1707, the empire was on the verge of collapse, and the English and the East India Company were there to pick up the pieces.

THE ENGLISH IN SOUTH ASIA AND THE INDIAN OCEAN

About the Document

Many European nations (especially Spain and Portugal) began overseas exploration and serious overseas trade during the sixteenth century. Preoccupied mainly by religious issues during the Reformation and Counter-Reformation, other nations, such as France, England, and later the Netherlands, followed suit only in the seventeenth century. Relatively poor trade connections in British and French America led these countries increasingly to seek commercial contacts in Asia.

European trade with Asia was nothing new, but it soon took on an unparalleled intensity. Nearly all of the aforementioned nations, except Spain, tried to increase their presence in India as well as in outer areas of the Indian Ocean such as Indonesia.

In 1614 King James I of England sent a diplomat, Sir Thomas Roe, to visit the Mughal emperor, Jahangir, and negotiate a trade treaty. The trade mission was successful, and the emperor wrote a letter, the first document here, to James afterward. A few years later, however, the English found things more difficult as they tried to encroach on Indonesia, already being plied by the Dutch. A French traveler recounts in the second document what happened between the Dutch and the English in 1617.

Map 18.1
The Delhi Sultanate
and Mughal India

The Document

Part One: Letter from Jahangir to James I of England

When your majesty shall open this letter let your royal heart be as fresh as a sweet garden. Let all people make reverence at your gate; let your throne be advanced higher; amongst the greatness of the kings of the prophet Jesus, let your Majesty be the greatest, and all monarchies derive their counsel and wisdom from your breast as from a fountain, that the law of the majesty of Jesus may revive and flourish under your protection.

The letter of love and friendship which you sent and the presents, tokens of your good affection toward me, I have received by the hands of your ambassador, Sir Thomas Roe (who well deserveth to be your trusted servant), delivered to me in an acceptable and happy hour; upon which mine eyes were so fixed that I could not easily remove them to any other object, and have accepted them with great joy and delight.

Upon which assurance of your royal love I have given my general command to all the kingdoms and ports of my dominions to receive all the merchants of the English nation as the subjects of my friend; that in what place soever they choose to live, they may have reception and residence to their own content and safety; and what goods soever they desire to sell or buy, they may have free liberty without any restraint; and at what port soever they shall arrive, that neither Portugal nor any other shall dare to molest their quiet; and in what city soever they shall have residence, I have commanded all my governors and captains to give them freedom answerable to their own desires; to sell, buy, and to transport into their country at their pleasure.

For confirmation of our love and friendship, I desire your Majesty to command your merchants to bring in their ships of all sorts of rarities and rich goods fit for my palace; and that you be pleased to send me your royal letters by every opportunity, that I may rejoice in your health and prosperous affairs; that our friendships may be interchanged and eternal.

Your Majesty is learned and quick-sighted as a prophet, and can conceive so much by few words that I need write no more.

The God of heaven give you and us increase of honor.

Part Two: Dutch Hostility toward English Merchants

[The original source refers to the Dutch as "Hollanders," but the more modern "Dutch" has been inserted in its place. A few other words have also been modernized.]

A relation of the Frenchmen which lately arrived into France in a ship of Dieppe out of the East Indies concerning the wrongs and abuses which the Dutch had lately done to the English there (1617):

Two English ships coming to Banda, in course of trade and traffic, the Dutch assaulted with certain of their ships, which English ships in their resistance and defense the said Dutch took, slew seven or eight of their men (whereof one was a chief factor), chained the captain, merchants, and mariners, and put the mariners in their galleys. All the munitions and victuals in the said English ships did the Dutch take out and carried the same ashore, challenged all to be theirs as their proper inheritance, and therefore will be lords of the same.

The Dutch likewise took an English ship going from Bantam (in Dutch Java°) to Jakarta, slew some of her men, wounded many more, chained the captain and mariners, and carried away the said ship at the stern of one of their ships into Bantam Road, and there anchored close by the admiral of the English in most despiteful and daring manner, making their vaunts that they were the chief people of all Europe; and to make a show of the same they advanced their own arms and colors, and under them placed the colors of England and France, and then shot at the said English and French colors in most contemptuous and disdainful manner.

At Bantam the English and Dutch had great disputes, insomuch as it was verily thought they would have fought together in the road, for the general of the Dutch had brought thither fourteen great ships, ready to fight, where the English had nine, which they fitted for defense; but they fought not, for the governor of Bantam forbad them to fight in his road, and threatened them that if they did fight contrary to his command he could cut the throats of all their men that he should find upon the land.

The 27th of November the Dutch declared war against all the English at the Mulluccoes, Banda, and Amboyna, threatening to make one and all prize and to put them to the edge of the sword; which proclamation of theirs they fixed upon the doors of their lodgings at Bantam, challenging all to be theirs as their proper inheritance.

Analysis and Review Questions

1. Are English merchants to be protected in any way in Jahangir's territory?
2. What restrictions are being placed on English merchants?
3. What prevented fighting between the English and Dutch at Bantam?
4. How did the Dutch offend the French?
5. From reading these two selections, why do you think the English gained a firm foothold in India, but failed to do so in Indonesia?

ABU TALEB ON THE WEST AND WESTERN INFLUENCE

About the Document

Muslims filled the top positions in much of India during the Mughal Dynasty. As European influence and trade increased, however, the Muslim empires and kingdoms weakened substantially. Upper-caste Hindus began to have their children

Java: Former Dutch colony, essentially today's Indonesia.

educated in Western schools, and, while relatively few Hindus had the chance to travel to Europe, many started to affect English ways and attitudes. The same cannot be said for Indian Muslims, who generally resisted Western influence on their lives and customs, but who were often more able to travel (unlike Hindus, they had no religious prohibitions against foreign travel).

One of the first educated Indians to travel to Europe was Abū Tāleb. Born in 1752, Abū Tāleb served the Mughal government for much of his early life, and, after retiring, spent three years in Europe. When he returned to Calcutta, he wrote *The Travels of Mirza Abū Tāleb Khan.* Written in Persian for his Muslim audience, the book illustrates Abū Tāleb's interest in English ways and life, but also displays the attitudes between the English and Indian Muslims.

The Document

Glory be to God, the Lord of all worlds, who has conferred innumerable blessings on mankind, and accomplished all the laudable desires of his creatures. Praise be also to the Chosen of Mankind [Muhammad], the traveler over the whole expanse of the heavens, and benedictions without end on his descendants and companions.

The wanderer over the face of the earth, Abū Tāleb, the son of Mohammed of Ispahan, begs leave to inform the curious in biography, that, owing to several adverse circumstances, finding it inconvenient to remain at home, he was compelled to undertake many tedious journeys, during which he associated with men of all nations and beheld various wonders, both by sea and by land.

It therefore occurred to him, that if he were to write all the circumstances of his journey through Europe, to describe the curiosities and wonders which he saw, and to give some account for the manner and customs of the various nations he visited, all of which are little known to Asiatics, it would afford a gratifying banquet to his countrymen.

He was also of opinion, that many of the customs, inventions, sciences, and ordinances of Europe, the good effects of which are apparent in those countries, might with great advantage be imitated by Mohammedans.

Impressed with these ideas, he, on his first setting out on his travels, commenced a journal, in which he daily inserted every event, and committed to writing such reflections as occurred to him at the moment: and on his return to Calcutta, in the year of the Hejira 1218 (A.D. 1803), having revised and abridged his notes, he arranged them in the present form.

[Here Abū Tāleb changes from the third to the first person, and laments:] I have named this work ... "The Travels of Tāleb in the Regions of Europe"; but when I reflect on the want of energy and the indolent dispositions of my countrymen, and the many erroneous customs which exist in all Mohammedan countries and among all ranks of Mussulmans, I am fearful that my exertions will be thrown away. The great and the rich, intoxicated with pride and luxury, and puffed up with the vanity of their possessions, consider universal science as comprehended in the circle of their own scanty acquirements and limited knowledge; while the poor and common people, from the want of leisure, and overpowered by the difficulty of procuring a livelihood, have not time to attend to their personal concerns, much less to form desires for the acquirement of information on new discoveries and inventions; although such a passion has been implanted by nature in every human breast, as an honor and an ornament to the species. I therefore despair of their reaping any fruit from my labors, being convinced that they will consider this book of no greater value than the volumes of tales and romances which they peruse merely to pass away their

time, or are attracted thereto by the easiness of the style. It may consequently be concluded, that as they will find no pleasure in reading a work which contains a number of foreign names, treats on uncommon subjects, and alludes to other matters which cannot be understood at the first glance, but require a little time for consideration, they will, under pretense of zeal for their religion, entirely abstain and refrain from perusing it.

. . .

ODE TO LONDON

Henceforward we will devote our lives to London, and its heart-alluring Damsels:
Our hearts are satiated with viewing fields, gardens, rivers, and palaces.

We have no longing for the Toba, Sudreh, or other trees of Paradise:
We are content to rest under the shade of these terrestrial Cypresses.

If the Shaikh of Mecca is displeased at our conversion, who cares?
May the Temple which has conferred such blessings on us, and its Priests, flourish!

Fill the goblet with wine! If by this I am prevented from returning
To my old religion, I care not; nay, I am the better pleased.

If the prime of my life has been spent in the service of an Indian Cupid,
It matters not: I am now rewarded by the smiles of the British Fair.

Adorable creatures! Whose flowing tresses, whether of flaxen or of jetty hue,
Or auburn gay, delight my soul, and ravish all my senses!

Whose ruby lips would animate the torpid clay, or marble statue!
Had I a renewal of life, I would, with rapture, devote it to your service!

These wounds of Cupid, on your heart, Tāleba, are not accidental:
They were engendered by Nature, like the streaks on the leaf of a tulip.

. . .

The first and greatest defect I observed in the English is their want of faith in religion, and their great inclination to philosophy [atheism]. The effects of these principles, or rather want of principle, is very conspicuous in the lower orders of people, who are totally devoid of honesty. They are, indeed, cautious how they transgress against the laws, from fear of punishment; but whenever an opportunity offers of purloining any thing without the risk of detection, they never pass it by. They are also ever on the watch to appropriate to themselves the property of the rich, who, on this account, are obliged constantly to keep their doors shut, and never to permit an unknown person to enter them. At present, owing to the vigilance of the magistrates, the severity of the laws, and the honor of the superior classes of people, no very bad consequences are to be apprehended; but if ever such nefarious practices should become prevalent and should creep in among the higher classes, inevitable ruin must ensue.

The second defect most conspicuous in the English character is pride, or insolence. Puffed up with their power and good fortune for the last fifty years, they are not apprehensive of adversity, and take no pains to avert it. Thus, when the people of London, some time ago, assembled in mobs on account of the great increase of taxes and high price of provisions, and were nearly in a state of insurrection—although the magistrates, by their vigilance in watching them, and by causing parties of soldiers to patrole the streets day and night, to disperse all persons whom they saw assembling together, succeeded in quieting the disturbance—yet no pains were afterwards taken to eradicate the evil. Some of the men in power said it had been merely a plan of the artificers to obtain higher wages (an attempt frequently made by the English tradesmen); others were of opinion that no remedy could be applied; therefore no further notice was taken of the affair. All this, I say, betrays a blind confidence, which, instead of meeting the danger and endeavoring to prevent it, waits till the misfortune arrives, and then attempts to remedy it. Such was the case with the late king of France, who took no step to oppose the Revolution till it was too late. This self-confidence is to be found, more or less, in every Englishman; it however differs much from the pride of the Indians and Persians.

Their third defect is a passion for acquiring money and their attachment to worldly affairs. Although these bad qualities are not so reprehensible in them as in countries more subject to the vicissitudes of fortune, (because, in England, property is so well protected by the laws that every person reaps the fruits of his industry, and, in his old age, enjoys the earnings or economy of his youth,) yet sordid and illiberal habits are generally found to accompany avarice and parsimony, and, consequently, render the possessor of them contemptible; on the contrary, generosity, if it does not launch into prodigality, but is guided by the hand of prudence, will render a man respected and esteemed.

Analysis and Review Questions

1. In the first section of the excerpt, does Abū Tāleb think Muslims are going to take to Western learning? Explain.
2. Is the poem about London positive or negative? What makes you think so?
3. List two of the defects of the English pointed out by Abū Tāleb.
4. What is the overall consequence of the English arrogance toward social problems, according to the author?
5. What appears to you to be the biggest problem pointed out? Why?

*Image 18.1
Akbar, Emperor
of India*

AKBAR AND THE JESUITS

About the Document

During the sixteenth through eighteenth centuries, many European countries were vying for trade and commercial arrangements in India and other parts of Asia. Some nations, primarily the dominant Catholic nations such as Spain, Portugal, and France, also brought a religious element to their contacts, sending missionaries and religious scholars to meet with their counterparts or rulers in Asia.

A group well-suited for missionary activity was one created specifically for that purpose: the Jesuit order. Founded in 1524 by St. Ignatius Loyola, the Jesuits were used during Europe's Counter-Reformation to "take back" areas that had become Protestant—for example, reclaiming Poland and parts of Germany for the Catholic Church. The Jesuits also spent considerable time in India, China, and Japan; they were welcomed there more for their secular learning than for their religious doctrines. French Jesuits spent years in India between the mid-1500s and 1600s, including time at the court of Akbar the Great, one of India's most noted rulers. One of the French Jesuits, Father Pierre du Jarric, around 1610 compiled an account of the fathers' exploits at the court of Akbar. Known as a tolerant ruler, Akbar presided over the Mughal Empire at its height. By his death in 1605, the Mughal Empire was well prepared for the future.

The Document

That we may the better understand the motives which led the Great Mogor to summon the Fathers of the Company from Goa,° we must bear in mind that the Viceroy in India of the Portuguese king, had, in the year 1578, sent as ambassador to his court a Portuguese gentleman named Antoine Cabral, who was accompanied by several others of the same nation. Whilst they were at his court, Akbar closely watched their behavior and manner of life, gaining thereby some idea of other adherents of the Christian religion, of which he had heard so much. He was very favourably impressed by what he saw of these persons; and showed himself so anxious to know something of the law they followed, that the ambassador did his best to explain to him its main principles, telling him also of the Fathers of the Company who were preaching it in India.

About the month of March in the year 1578, the good priest, whose name I have not discovered, reached Pateful, where the King then held his court, and was received with much kindness. It was not long before his Majesty told him the reason why he had sent for him, which was, he said, that he might clear his mind of certain doubts which prevented him from deciding whether it was better to follow the law of the Christians or the law of Mahomet.° The priest, accordingly, expounded to him the main principles of our faith, at the same time opening his eyes to the worthlessness of the law of Mahomet.

Akbar heard these things with evident gladness; and so strongly was he moved to abandon his faith that, one evening while conversing with his Caziques, or Mullas, as the priests of the Mahometan religion are called, he told them frankly that he had decided to follow the counsel of the good priest, and pray to God for light to see the truth, and the path to salvation.

A few days later, he asked the same priest to teach him to speak Portuguese; for he had a great desire (or so he said) to know that tongue, that he might the better understand his exposition of the Christian law. This the priest commenced to do with much care and zeal; and the first word that he taught the King was the sweet name of Jesus.

One evening the same priest was disputing with the Mullas in the royal ante-chamber, while the King sat listening in his private apartment. In the course of the dispute, the priest said that the law of Mahomet was a tissue of errors and lies. This so enraged the Mullas that they were on the point of laying violent hands on him when the King entered and restrained them, appeasing their anger by telling them that it was no unusual thing for one engaged in a disputation to hold his own views to be true, and those of his adversaries to be false.

While conversing with the King, the priest told him one day that there were in the town of Goa some very learned and holy Fathers, who had spread a knowledge of Jesus-Christ in many parts of India; and that if he would communicate his doubts to

---

Goa: The Portuguese-held port city in India.
Mahomet: Old European spelling of Mohammed, the founder of Islam.

them, he would learn from them, much better than from himself, all that he desired to know touching the Christian faith, in as much as they were much more learned in the holy scriptures.

[Another group of priests were sent to see Akbar.]

So great was the King's anxiety to see them that, during this period (as they subsequently learnt), he constantly calculated the number of days necessary for the completion of their journey, and repeatedly asked those about him when they would arrive. The moment he heard that they had come, he summoned them to his palace, where he received them with many marks of friendship, and entertained them in various ways until far into the night. Before they took their leave, a large quantity of gold and silver was brought to be presented to them. The Fathers thanked him very respectfully, but would not take any of the money, courteously excusing themselves on the ground of their calling. As for their livelihood, for which the King urged them to accept what he offered them, they said that it was sufficient happiness for them to enjoy his favour, and that they trusted to God to supply their daily needs. The King was much impressed by their refusal of the money, and for a long time could talk to his courtiers of nothing else.

Three or four days later, the Fathers again visited the King, who received them as cordially as on the first occasion. As he had asked to be shown the books of the law of the Creator (meaning thereby the holy Scriptures), the Fathers took with them and presented to him all the volumes of the Royal Bible, in four languages, sumptuously bound, and clasped with gold. The King received these holy books with great reverence; taking each into his hand one after the other and kissing it, after which he placed it on his head, which, amongst these people, signifies honour and respect. He acted thus in the presence of all his courtiers and captains, the greater part of whom were Mahometans.

Some time afterwards, he again sent for the Fathers, summoning at the same time his Mullas and Caziques, in order that they might dispute together in his presence, so that he might discover which were in truth the holy scriptures on which to place his faith. The Fathers clearly established the authenticity and truth of the scriptures contained in the Old and New Testaments, laying bare at the same time the falsehoods and fallacies with which the Koran is filled. This first dispute ended in the complete discomfiture of the Mullas and Caziques, who, unable to find any answer to the arguments of the Fathers, took refuge in silence.

Three days after the first dispute, another took place concerning the paradise which the Mahometan law promises to its followers. The Fathers assailed the infamous and carnal paradise of Mahomet with arguments so clear and convincing that the Mullas blushed for shame, not knowing what to say in reply. The King, seeing their perplexity, essayed to take up their cause; but he was as little able as they to disprove the incongruities that had been pointed out.

The Fathers now became anxious to ascertain what effect these disputes had had on the King, and whether the adoption of the Christian faith was a step that he was seriously deliberating. They accordingly made their way to the palace, the fact that they had not seen the King for some days affording a sufficient excuse for their visit. He received them with his accustomed courtesy and good-will. After some conversation on general subjects, the Fathers begged him to give them private audience; and when this was granted, Father Rodolfe Aquauiua, who was the superior of the others, thus addressed him—"Your Majesty wrote a letter to our R.P. Provincial demanding that some Fathers of the Company should be sent to you to expound the law of God.

We three have, accordingly, been sent; and we count it a peculiar happiness that God has led us to a Prince who is so powerful, and who desires so earnestly to know the divine law. This happiness was intensified when you made known to us that you had no other desire in the world but to discover and to embrace the true law. Our thoughts have been given day and night to this matter, and the means of attaining the end for which we have been sent here; and after earnest consideration, and continual prayers to God for guidance, it seems to us fitting that your Majesty should now, for the sake of your temporal and spiritual welfare, the preservation of your life, the increase of your dominions, the comfort of your conscience, and the salvation of your soul, set apart a time for hearing the interpretation of the divine law, and that, recognizing it to be true, and that there is no other which leads to salvation, your Majesty should adopt it as your own, and renounce that which is preached in all your kingdoms and provinces." In reply to these words, the King said that the matter was in the hands of God, who possessed the power to accomplish what they desired; and that, for his part, there was nothing in the world he desired more. By what he said, he gave them to understand that there were weighty reasons why he should not, at that juncture, declare himself a Christian.

Image 18.2
Portuguese Church
in Southern India

Analysis and Review Questions

1. Does Akbar appear to favor the priests or his own religious advisors? Explain.
2. Is the author favorably inclined towards Islam? Give evidence for your answer.
3. What is a Mulla?
4. Why didn't the priests accept gold or silver from Akbar?
5. Why do you think Akbar was not willing to convert to Christianity?

Map 18.2
The Maratha
Kingdom

AURANGZEB, MUGHAL RULER

About the Document

India's Mughal Empire was constantly trying to address the practical problems facing a minority Muslim population ruling over a much larger Hindu population. Some rulers, such as Akbar the Great (1556–1605), proved tolerant and accommodating to Hindus and other local religious groups. Akbar even attempted, unsuccessfully, to create a new religion that brought together elements from Islam, Hinduism, and Zoroastrianism, among others. Akbar's successors generally continued his tolerant policies.

There was, of course, another approach to the Mughal issue. Rather than accommodating Hindus, a ruler might oppress them to solve some of the problems of governance. A ruler who is remembered for doing so is Aurangzeb, who ruled from 1658–1707 and even executed his brother for being too tolerant of other faiths. In the early 1680s, an advisor of Aurangzeb, Baktha'war Khan, wrote a history of the world up through the time of Aurangzeb's reign. The following excerpt not only discusses the ruler's religious attitudes, it also addresses his personality and overall attitudes.

The Document

Be it known to the readers of this work that this humble slave of the Almighty is going to describe in a correct manner the excellent character, the worthy habits and the refined morals of this most virtuous monarch, Aurangzeb, according as he has witnessed them with his own eyes. The Emperor, a great worshiper of God by natural propensity, is remarkable for his rigid attachment to religion. . . . Having made his ablutions [ritual washings], he always occupies a great part of his time in adoration of the Deity, and says the usual prayers, first in the mosque and then at home, both in congregation and in private, with the most heartfelt devotion. He keeps the appointed fasts on Fridays and other sacred days, and he reads the Friday prayers in the mosque with the common people of the Muslim faith. He keeps vigils during the whole of the sacred nights, and with the light of the favor of God illumines the lamps of religion and prosperity. From his great piety, he passes whole nights in the mosque which is in his palace, and keeps company with men of devotion. In privacy he never sits on a throne. He gave away in alms before his accession a portion of his allowance of lawful food and clothing, and now devotes to the same purpose the income of a few villages in the district of Delhi, and the proceeds of two or three salt-producing tracts, which are appropriated to his private purse. . . . During the whole month of Ramadan he keeps fast, says the prayers appointed for that month, and reads the holy Qur'an in the assembly of religious and learned men, with whom he sits for that purpose during six, and sometimes nine hours of the night. During the last ten days of the month, he performs worship in the mosque, and although, on account of several obstacles, he is unable to proceed on a pilgrimage to Mecca, yet the care which he takes to promote facilities for pilgrims to that holy place may be considered equivalent to the pilgrimage.

Though he has collected at the foot of his throne those who inspire ravishment in joyous assemblies of pleasure, in the shape of singers who possess lovely voices and clever instrumental performers, and in the commencement of his reign sometimes used to hear them sing and play, and though he himself understands music well, yet now for several years past, on account of his great restraint and self-denial . . . he entirely abstains from this amusement. If any of the singers and musicians becomes ashamed of his calling, he makes an allowance for him or grants him land for his maintenance. . . .

In consideration of their rank and merit, he shows much honor and respect to the saints and learned men, and through his cordial and liberal exertions, the sublime doctrines of our pure religion have obtained such prevalence throughout the wide territories of Hindustan° as they never had in the reign of any former king.

Hindu writers have been entirely excluded from holding public offices, and all the worshiping places of the infidels [Hindus] and the great temples of these infamous people have been thrown down and destroyed in a manner which excites astonishment at the successful completion of so difficult a task. . . .

As it is a great object with this Emperor that all Muslims should follow the principles of the religion . . . and as there was no book which embodied them all, and as until many books had been collected and a man had obtained sufficient leisure, means and knowledge of theological subjects, he could not satisfy his inquiries on any disputed point, therefore His Majesty, the protector of the faith, determined that a body of eminently learned and able men of Hindustan should take up the volumi-

Hindustan: Old European name for India

nous and most trustworthy works which were collected in the royal library, and having made a digest of them, compose a book which might form a standard canon of the law, and afford to all an easy and available means of ascertaining the proper and authoritative interpretation. The chief conductor of this difficult undertaking was the most learned man of the time, Shaikh Nizam, and all the members of the society were very handsomely and liberally paid, so that up to the present time a sum of about two hundred thousand rupees has been expended in this valuable compilation, which contains more than one hundred thousand lines. When the work, with God's pleasure, is completed, it will be for all the world the standard exposition of the law. . . .

The Emperor is perfectly acquainted with the commentaries, traditions, and law. . . . One of the greatest excellences of this virtuous monarch is, that he has learned the Qur'an by heart. Though in his early youth he had committed to memory some chapters of that sacred book, yet he learned the whole by heart after ascending the throne. He took great pains and showed much perseverance in impressing it upon his mind. He writes in a very elegant hand, and has acquired perfection in this art. He has written two copies of the holy book with his own hand, and having finished and adorned them with ornaments and marginal lines, at the expense of seven thousand rupees, he sent them to the holy cities of Mecca and Medina . . . . He is a very elegant writer in prose, and has acquired proficiency in versification, but agreeably to the words of God, "Poets deal in falsehoods," he abstains from practicing it. He does not like to hear verses except those which contain a moral. "To please Almighty God he never turned his eye towards a flatterer, nor gave his ear to a poet."

The Emperor has given a very liberal education to his fortunate and noble children, who, by virtue of his attention and care, have reached to the summit of perfection, and made great advances in rectitude, devotion, and piety, and in learning the manners and customs of princes and great men. Through his instruction they have learned the Book of God by heart, obtained proficiency in the sciences and polite literature, writing the various hands, and in learning the Turkish and the Persian languages.

In like manner, the ladies of the household also, according to his orders, have learned the fundamental and necessary tenets of religion, and all devote their time to the adoration and worship of the Deity, to reading the sacred Qur'an, and performing virtuous and pious acts. The excellence of character and the purity of morals of this holy monarch are beyond all expression. As long as nature nourishes the tree of existence, and keeps the garden of the world fresh, may the plant of the prosperity of this preserver of the garden of dignity and honor continue fruitful!

Analysis and Review Questions

1. Why didn't Aurangzeb generally listen to poetry?
2. What was Aurangzeb's attitude toward Hinduism?
3. Does the author claim the king was dedicated to his religion? Explain.
4. What qualities does the author seem to respect in his ruler?
5. What do you think Aurangzeb's attitudes were toward what we might call "social welfare"?

WEB LINKS

http://longmanworldhistory.com
Document 18.5, St Francis Xavier, Jesuit in India
Case Study 18.1, Islamic Commentators in India
Case Study 18.2, Jesuits in India
Case Study 18.3, Two Very Different Mughal Emperors

http://www.freeindia.org
A massive site with large sections devoted to biographies of notable Indian gods, goddesses, and leaders. Search engine focusing on Indian Web sites is included as well.

http://www.123india.com
The site portrays itself as "India's Premier Portal" with good reason. Everything from current Indian news, online India chat, to Indian search engines can be found here.

http://www.museum.rbi.org.in/general.html
An online "monetary museum," this site shows currency from all periods of Indian history.

http://www.indianmuseum-calcutta.org
Exhibits, images, and other useful information from one of the world's oldest museums.

CHAPTER **19**

African Kingdoms and Early European Contacts, 1450–1750

This chapter will examine primary documents that reflect the first extensive cultural interactions between African kingdoms and Europeans. As the Portuguese expanded their influence along the West African coastline, they engaged heavily in trade and sugar growing. They learned to interact with powerful African rulers who often dictated the terms of trade and, of course, controlled access to land.

For the most part, a special landlord-stranger relationship existed, marked by the need for reciprocity and accommodation to political, religious, ideological, economic, and social differences. The king of the Kongo hoped to consolidate his political control by promoting contacts with the Portuguese, who had weapons and mercenaries who could strengthen his army. Endemic warfare became a way of life in central Africa, as wars were encouraged to gain slaves. From the 1530s, São Thomé developed as a major transit point for captives being transported across the Atlantic to the new plantations in Brazil. With the increased demand for slaves, the São Thomé slavers evaded Portuguese royal control by establishing a slaving station at Luanda.

The Portuguese always took along missionaries who had a "civilizing" mission that was important in the minds of European monarchs. That mission was to convert Africans to Christianity in the hopes of building stronger ties with Europe. The king of the Kongo, Afonso I (1506–1543), became a Christian convert in 1506. Christianity was seen by some African kings as a tool to undermine the authority of local religious leaders. In the case of Ethiopian kings, Christianity was well established, and they resisted Portuguese efforts at reforming their traditional beliefs along Roman Catholic lines.

*Image 19.1
Loango, the capital
of the kingdom of
the Kongo*

"VOYAGE FROM LISBON TO THE ISLAND OF SÃO THOMÉ," BY AN ANONYMOUS PORTUGUESE PILOT, C. 1540

About the Document

Early descriptions of Portuguese travelers to West Africa are vital to our understanding of African life before the advent of colonial rule. These descriptions portray the nature of kingship, religion, social life, economic activity, and slavery in

Africa in the sixteenth century. This early account is particularly interesting because it describes the trade in gold and slaves in West Africa from someone other than an Arab traveler. It is well known that gold from West Africa was heavily traded in the trans-Saharan trade by Berber° merchants making their way to the major trading centers in North Africa and Egypt. This is perhaps one of the earliest accounts of gold being traded directly with Europeans along the Atlantic coast. Eventually this shift in trade routes would undermine the caravan traders in the north, as Europeans made direct contact with African merchants nearer the gold fields.

The Portuguese pilot is fascinated by the extent of the slave trade and the items that are given up in the trade, including cowrie shells, glass beads, coral, copper, brass items, and cotton cloth. Portuguese merchants and traders are also involved in the buying and selling of sugar grown on the islands off the west coast of Africa. Sugar was a lucrative trade item that was in high demand in Europe. It wasn't long after this time that Europeans began to set up sugar plantations in the New World.

The Document

The Ships which leave Lisbona to go to the island of São Thomé to load sugar, the wind they sail by to the Canarie islands, called by the ancients the Fortunate islands, the island of Palme, and the promontory called Capo di Boiador.

As your excellency knows, before I left Venetia, signor Hieronimo Gracastor ordered me, in his letters from Verona, to transcribe for him, as soon as I reached the Villa di Conde, from some notes which I had told your excellency I had with me, the whole of the voyage which we pilots made to the island of S. Thomé, when we went there to transport a cargo of sugar; together with all that happened during our voyage to this island, that seemed to him so wonderful and worthy of the study of a scholar. Your excellency also, on my departure, made the same request to me; and so, having arrived here, I began at once to write an account of the voyage in question, communicating also with some of my friends who took part in it. . . .

The various provinces of the West Coast of Africa, Guinea, the coast of Melegete [Malagueta], Benin, Manicongo; and the lords and kings of these lands; how the people worship their kings believing that they have descended from heaven; and of some of the ceremonies and customs of the kingdom of Benin on the death of the king.

To understand the negro traffic, one must know that over all the African coast facing west there are various countries and provinces, such as Guinea, the coast of Melegete, the kingdom of Benin, the kingdom of Manicõgo, six degrees from the equator and towards the south pole. There are many tribes and negro kings here, and also communities which are partly mohammedan and partly heathen. These are constantly making war among themselves. The kings are worshipped by their subjects, who believe that they come from heaven, and speak of them always with great reverence, at a distance and on bended knees. Great ceremony surrounds them, and many of these kings never allow themselves to be seen eating, so as not to destroy the belief

Berber: The people of northwest Africa.

of their subjects that they can live without food. They worship the sun, and believe that spirits are immortal, and that after death they go to the sun. Among others, there is in the kingdom of Benin an ancient custom, observed to the present day, that when the king dies, the people all assemble in a large field, in the centre of which is a very deep well, wider at the bottom than at the mouth. They cast the body of the dead king into this well, and all his friends and servants gather round, and those who are judged to have been most dear to and favoured by the king (this includes not a few, as all are anxious for the honour) voluntarily go down to keep him company. When they have done so, the people place a great stone over the mouth of the well, and remain by it day and night. . . .

The Negroes of Guinea are unmethodical even in their way of eating; they live long; certain superstitions among some of the negroes in this country; melegete spices; the tailed pepper; certain bushes with stems that have the flavour of ginger; soap made with oil of palms and with ashes.

The negroes of Guinea and Benin are very haphazard in their habits of eating. They have no set times for meals, and eat and drink four or five times a day, drinking water, or a wine which they distil from palms. They have no hair except for a few bristly strands on top of the head, and none grows; and the rest of the bodies are completely hairless. They live for the best part of 100 years, and are always vigorous, except at certain times of the year when they become very weak, as if they had fever. They are then bled, and recover, having a great deal of blood in their system. Some of the negroes in this country are so superstitious that they worship the first object they see on the day of recovery. . . .

Why the fathers and mothers of these negroes send their own children to be sold, and what they take in exchange; and how these slaves are taken to the island of San Jacobo, where they are sold in couples, that is, the same number of males and females; the coast of Mina, and why the catholic king has built a castle there.

All the coast, as far as the kingdom of Manicongo, is divided into two parts, which are leased every four or five years to whoever makes the best offer, that is, to be able to go to contract in those lands and ports, and those in this business are called contractors, though among us they would be known as *appaltadori*, and their deputies, and no others may approach and land on this shore, or even buy or sell. Great caravans of negroes come here, bringing gold and slaves for sale. Some of the slaves have been captured in battle, others are sent by their parents, who think they are doing their children the best service in the world by sending them to be sold in this way to other lands where there is an abundance of provisions. They are brought as naked as they are born, both males and females, except for a sheepskin cloth; and they have glass rosaries of various colours, and articles made of glass, copper, brass, and cotton cloths of different colours, and other similar things used throughout Ethiopia. These contractors take the slaves to the island of San Jacobo, where they are bought by merchant captains from various countries and provinces, chiefly from the Spanish Indies. These give their merchandise in exchange and always wish to have the same number of male and female slaves, because otherwise they do not get good service from them. During the voyage, they separate the men from the women, putting the men below the deck and the women above, where they cannot see when the men are given food; because otherwise the women would do nothing but look at them. Regarding these negroes, our king has had a castle built on the said coast, at

Mina, 6 degrees north of the equator, where none but his servants are allowed to live; and large numbers of negroes come to this place with grains of gold, which they have found in the river beds and sand, and bargain with these servants, taking various objects from them in exchange; principally glass necklaces or rosaries, and another kind made of a blue stone, not lapis lazuli, but another stone which our king causes to be brought from Manicõgo, where it is found. These rosaries are in the form of necklaces, and are called coral; and a quantity of gold is given in exchange for them, as they are greatly valued by all the negroes. They wear them round their necks as a charm against spirits, but some wear necklaces of glass, which are very similar, but which will not bear the heat of fire.

Description of the island of São Thomé, nowadays inhabited by many traders; the island called il Principe, the island of Anobon, and the city called Pouoasan.

The island of São Thomé, which was discovered 80 or 90 years ago by the sea-captains of our king, and which was unknown to the ancients, is round. It is 60 Italian miles in diameter, that is, one degree; and is situated under the line of the equator and half way between the north and south poles. The days and nights are of equal length, and one never sees the least difference, whether the sun is in cancer or capricorn. The Pole Star cannot be seen, but by turning a little one can see it; and the constellation called *il crusero* appears very far away. To the east of this island, 120 miles distant, there is a small island called Il Principe [O Principe]. This island is inhabited and cultivated at the present time, and the profits made from its sugar trade go to the king's eldest son; this is why it is called Il Principe. . . .

There is a bishop here, and the present one comes from Villa di Conde by order of the archbishop at the desire of the king. A corregedor° dispenses justice. There must be 600 to 700 families living here as well as many Portuguese, Castilian, French and Genoese merchants; and people of any nationality, who wish to settle here are welcome. They all have wives and children, and some of the children who are born there are as white as ours. It sometimes happens that, when the wife of a merchant dies, he takes a negress, and this is an accepted practice, as the negro population is both intelligent and rich; the children of such unions are brought up to our customs and way of dressing. Children born of these negresses are mischievous and difficult to manage, and are called *Mulati* [mulattoes].

Description of how the inhabitants of this island treat sugar; of the goods which the ships bring in exchange for sugar; of the fertility of the land and the way they cultivate sugar cane and trade it; of why the flesh of pigs in this land is so healthy and easy to digest.

The chief industry of the people is to make sugar, which they sell to the ships which come each year, bringing flour, Spanish wines, oil, cheese, and all kinds of leather for shoes, swords, glass vessels, rosaries, and shells, which in Italia are called *porcellette* [porcelains]—little white ones—which we call *buzios*, and which are used for money in Ethiopia. If the ships which bring these goods did not come, the white merchants would die, because they are not accustomed to negro food. All the population, therefore, buys negro slaves and their women from Guinea, Benin and Manicongo, and sets them to work on the land to grow and make sugar. There are rich men here, who have 150, 200 and even 300 negroes and negresses, who are obliged to work for their masters all the week, except on Saturdays, when they work on their own account. . . .

corregedor: Representative of the king.

Analysis and Review Questions

1. What can we deduce from this document about the relationship of African kings to their native subjects? What importance does this relationship have to early Portuguese travelers to West Africa?

2. How is the business of trade conducted within the Manicongo (Kongo) kingdom? What elements of capitalism are present in the indigenous system of land allocation?

3. Why do some African fathers and mothers send their own children into slavery? What items are taken in exchange for African slaves? Why do you suppose these items are acceptable as equal to a human life?

4. What is the value of gold in West African societies? What is the value of coral in the Manicongo (Kongo) kingdom? How do the Portuguese begin to tap into the thriving local economy of African kingdoms?

5. It is evident from this primary account that Europeans had a precarious existence in the early days of trade and exploration along the west coast of Africa. Since only men went to Africa to trade and grow sugar, what accommodations to African life did these Portuguese men have to deal with? What aspects of daily life were most life-threatening to Europeans? What might have been the importance of mulattoes to the Portuguese as they established long-term connections to African kingdoms and the trade that made their existence so viable?

Map19.1
(Interactive)
*African Empires in
the Western Sudan*

"A DEFENSE OF THE SLAVE TRADE," JULY 1740

About the Document

Justifying European involvement in the trans-Atlantic slave trade often involved the use of ideas that made the endeavor seem moral; it was considered part of the "white man's burden" to release Africans from a worse bondage at home. Merchants, in particular, felt the need for some justification for transporting and selling human cargo. In this document, an anonymous person writes about conditions along the Guinea Coast of West Africa and the cruel power of the local kings to control African slaves. The anonymous writer is responding to a letter published in the *Gentleman's Magazine* under the pseudonym Mercator Honestus, which argued against slavery and the slave trader.

It is well known that many of the great kingdoms of West Africa had dealt in a local slave trade for centuries. Slaves were used in agricultural production, in households, and as part of court life. These slaves were under varying degrees of bondage outside the realm of what we call "chattel slavery";° that is, under African customs, the condition of slavery was not hereditary and even

chattel slavery: Slavery based on the principle that men and women who are slaves enjoy no rights and can hold no property. In most cases, this type of slavery is hereditary, and humans are bought and sold as property by the owners. It was the prevalent form of slavery used by Europeans during the age of the Atlantic slave trade from the sixteenth to the eighteenth century.

slaves had some rights. What is interesting about this account is the heavy emphasis on Enlightenment° ideas such as the right of every human being to liberty and happiness. European merchants believed they were freeing Africans from an even worse fate, slavery without Western laws and Christianity.

The Document

Sir, The Guinea Trade, by the Mistake of some, or Misrepresentation of others, hath been charged with Inhumanity, and a Contradiction to good Morals. Such a Charge at a Time when private and publick Morals are laugh'd at, as the highest Folly, by a powerful Faction; and Self-interest set up as the only Criterion of true Wisdom, is certainly very uncourtly: But yet as I have a profound Regard for those superannuated Virtures; you will give me Leave to justify the African Trade, upon those Stale Principles, from the Imputations of "Mercator Honestus"; and shew him that there are People in some boasted Regions of Liberty, under a more wretched Slavery, than the Africans transplanted to our American Colonies.

The Inhabitants of Guinea are indeed in a most deplorable State of Slavery, under the arbitrary Powers of their Princes both as to Life and Property. In the several Subordinations to them, every great Man is absolute lord of his immediate Dependents. And lower still; every Master of a Family is Proprietor of his Wives, Children, and Servants; and may at his Pleasure consign them to Death, or a better Market. No doubt such a State is contrary to Nature and Reason, since every human Creature hath an absolute Right to Liberty. But are not all arbitrary Governments, as well in Europe, as Africa, equally repugnant to that great Law of Nature? And yet it is not in our Power to cure the universal Evil, and set all the Kingdoms of the Earth free from the Domination of Tyrants, whose long Possession, supported by standing Armies, and flagitious Ministers, renders the Thraldom without Remedy, while the People under it are by Custom satisfied with, or at least quiet under Bondage.

All that can be done in such a Case is, to communicate as much Liberty, and Happiness, as such circumstances will admit, and the People will consent to: And this is certainly by the Guinea Trade. For, by purchasing, or rather ransoming the Negroes from their national Tyrants, and transplanting them under the benign Influences of the Law, and Gospel, they are advanced to much greater Degrees of Felicity, tho' not to absolute Liberty.

That this is truly the Case cannot be doubted by any one acquainted with the Constitution of our Colonies, where the Negroes are governed by Laws, and suffer much less Punishment in Proportion to their Crimes, than the People in other Countries more refined in the Arts of Wickedness; and where Capital Punishment is inflicted only by the Civil Magistrates. . . .

Perhaps my Antagonist calls the Negroes Allowance of a Pint of Corn and an Herring, penurious, in Comparison of the full Meals of Gluttony: But if not let him compare that Allowance, to what the poor Labourer can purchase for Tenpence per Day to subsist himself and Family, and he will easily determine the American's Advantage. . . .

Nevertheless, Mercator will say, the Negroes are Slaves to their Proprietors: How Slaves? Nominally: Not really so much Slaves, as the Peasantry of all Nations is to Neces-

---

Enlightenment: The period in Europe when thinkers supported scientific advances and social scientific knowledge based on rational laws. Most important, the Enlightenment produced a set of basic principles about human affairs: human beings were good, could be educated, and were entitled to basic rights of life, liberty, and the pursuit of wealth. In sixteenth-century Europe, the enslavement of "barbarians" or nonbelievers was seen as positive—as a way to civilize others; however, during the Enlightenment, slavery came to be seen as backward and immoral. The slave trade in particular was criticized. It was the symbol of slavery's inhumanity and cruelty.

sity; not so much as those of Corruption, or Party Zeal; not in any Sense, such abject Slaves, as every vicious Man is to his own Appetites. Indeed there is this Difference between Britons, and the Slaves of all other Nations; that the latter are so by Birth, or tyrannical Necessity; the former can never be so, but by a wicked Choice, or execrable Venality. . . .

Analysis and Review Questions

1. What role do Enlightenment ideas play in justifying the trans-Atlantic slave trade? To what degree do you think English ideas on law, government, and justice contributed to merchant activity in the slave trade?
2. What was the author's attitude toward African indigenous slavery? Are there religious overtones to the passage? If so, describe and explain them.
3. What can we deduce from this document about the relationship between merchants and other elements of European society about the slave trade? Who might be particularly interested in the content and flavor of this publication?
4. What do the descriptions of African life along the west coast of Africa tell us about European perceptions of African slavery?
5. In addition to arguments based on moral principles, what other justifications *against* the slave trade might Mercator Honestus have used to criticize merchants involved in the traffic of human lives? Do you think these are valid claims? Why or why not?

Map 19.2
Africa 1500–1800

FRANCISCO ALVAREZ, "THE LAND OF PRESTER JOHN," C. 1540

About the Document

Ethiopia had long been the heart of Coptic° Christianity and was regarded as part of the ancient archdiocese of Alexandria. The Ethiopian Church developed its own individual characteristics. Ethiopians saw themselves as an outpost of Christianity—a sort of chosen people of God surrounded by pagans and Muslims. The Ethiopian kings built churches out of solid rock cut into mountains and caves. There is a total of 11 churches carved out near the capital, which was named Lalibela after the reign of Lalibela, who ruled between 1200 and 1250 C.E.

Conflict with the Muslim sultanates dominated life in the region. In 1526 a Muslim general named Ahmad ibn Ibrahim decided to wage a *jihad*, or holy war, against the Christian aristocracy. The Ethiopians kings sought Portuguese help in defeating Ahmad's army. The Portuguese responded by landing a small but well-equipped force in the north of the country. The combination of Portuguese and Ethiopians managed to save the Christian kingdom by inflicting a sharp defeat on the Muslim army in 1543. In the attached document, Father

Coptic: In Egypt, the bulk of Christians adopted a doctrine of Monophysitism which was unacceptable to the Roman Church. The Monophysites emphasized the divinity of Christ and denied that He could have been also human. In 451 C.E. the Roman Church declared this doctrine a "heresy," and many believers were expelled from the official Christian Church. Monophysite Christian missionaries pushed southward, carrying their distinctive doctrine and a strong monastic tradition into Nubia, Aksum, and Ethiopia.

Francisco Alvarez, chaplain to the first Portuguese embassy to Ethiopia, commented on life in sixteenth-century Ethiopia. Alvarez refers to the Ethiopian ruler as "Prester John," after a legendary priest-king of Ethiopia.

The Document

At a day's journey from this church of Imbra Christo are edifices, the like of which and so many, cannot, as it appears to me, be found in the world, and they are churches entirely excavated in the rock, very well hewn. The names of these churches are these: Emanuel, St. Saviour, St. Mary, Holy Cross, St. George, Golgotha, Bethlehem, Marcoreos, the Martyrs. The principal one is Lalibela. This Lalibela, they say, was a King in this same country for eighty years, and he was King before the one before mentioned who was named Abraham. This King ordered these edifices to be made. He does not lie in the church which bears his name, he lies in the church of Golgotha, which is the church of the fewest buildings here. It is in this manner: all excavated in the stone itself, a hundred and twenty spans in length, and seventy-two spans in width. The ceiling of this church rests on five supports, two on each side, and one in the centre, like fives of dice, and the ceiling or roof is all flat like the floor of the church, the sides also are worked in a fine fashion, also the windows, and the doors with all the tracery, which could be told, so that neither a jeweller in silver, nor a worker of wax in wax, could do more work. The tomb of this King is in the same manner as that of Santiago of Galicia, at Compostella, and it is in this manner: the gallery which goes round the church is like a cloister, and lower than the body of the church, and one goes down from the church to this gallery; there are three windows on each side, that is to say, at that height which the church is higher than the gallery, and as much as the body of the church extends, so much is excavated below, and to as much depth as there is height above the floor of the church. And if one looks through each of these windows which is opposite the sun, one sees the tomb at the right of the high altar. In the centre of the body of the church is the sign of a door like a trap door, it is covered up with a large stone, like an altar stone, fitting very exactly in that door. They say that this is the entrance to the lower chamber, and that no one enters there, nor does it appear that that stone or door can be raised. This stone has a hole in the centre which pierces it through, its size is three palms. All the pilgrims put their hands into this stone (which hardly find room), and say that many miracles are done here. On the left hand side, when one goes from the principal door before the principal chapel, there is a tomb cut in the same rock as the church, which they say is made after the manner of the sepulchre of Christ in Jerusalem. . . . This church and its chapels have their altars and canopies, with their supports, made of the rock itself, it also has a very great circuit cut out of the rock. The circuit is on the same level as the church itself, and is all square: all its walls are pierced with holes the size of the mouth of a barrel. All these holes are stopped up with small stones, and they say that they are tombs, and such they appear to be, because some have been stopped up since a long time, others recently. The entrance of this circuit is below the rock, at a great depth and measure of thirteen spans, all artificially excavated, or worked with the pick-axe, for here there is no digging, because the stone is hard, and for great walls like the Porto in Portugal.

The church of St. Saviour stands alone, cut out of a rock; it is very large. Its interior is two hundred spans in length, and a hundred and twenty in width. It has five naves, in each one seven square columns; the large one has four, and the walls of the church have as much. The columns are very well worked, with arches which hang down a span below the vaulted roof. The vaulted roofs are very well worked, and of great height, principally the centre one, which is very high. It is of a handsome height; most of the ends

Image 19.2
Solid Rock
Churches of
Lalibela, Ethiopia

are lower, all in proportion. . . . Above this church, where it should be roofed, there are on each side nine large arches, like cloisters, which descend from the top to the bottom, to the tombs along the sides, as in the other church. The entrance to this church is by a descent through the rock itself, eighty steps cut artificially in the stone, of a width that ten men can go side by side, and of the height of a lance or more. This entrance has four holes above, which give light to the passage above the edges. From this rock to the enclosure of the church is like a field; there are many houses, and they sow barley in it.

. . .

On the 4th day of the month of January Prester John° sent to tell us to order our tents, both that of the church and our own, to be taken from this place to a distance of about half a league, where they had made a large tank of water, in which they were to be baptized on the day of the Kings, because on that day it is their custom to be baptized every year, as that was the day on which Christ was baptized. We took thither a small tent for resting in and the church tent. The next day, which was the vigil of the day of the Kings, the Prester sent to call us, and we saw the enclosure where the tank was. The enclosure was a fence, and very large, in a plain. He sent to ask us if we intended to be baptized. I replied that it was not our custom to be baptized more than once, when we were little. Some said, principally the ambassador, that we would do what His Highness commanded. When they perceived that, they came back again with another message to me, asking what I said as to being baptized. I answered that I had been already baptized, and should not be so again. They still sent word that if we did not wish to be baptized in their tank, they would send us water to our tent. To this the ambassador replied that it should be as His Highness ordered. The Franks and our people had arranged to give a representation of the Kings, and they sent to tell him of it. A message came that it pleased him, and so they got ready for it, and they made it in the inclosure and plain close to the King's tent, which was pitched close to the tank. They gave the representation, and it was not esteemed, nor hardly looked at, and so it was a cold affair. Now that it was night they told us to go to our tent, which was not far off. In all this night till dawn a great number of priests never ceased chaunting over the said tank, saying that they were blessing the water, and about midnight, a little earlier or later, they began the baptism. They say, and I believe that such is the truth, that the first person baptized is the Prester, and after him the Abima, and after him the Queen, the wife of the Prester. They say that these three persons wear cloths over their nakedness, and that all the others were as their mothers bore them. When it was almost the hour of sunrise, and the baptism in fullest force, the Prester sent to call me to see the said baptism. I went and remained there till the hour of tierce, seeing how they were baptized; they placed me at one end of the tank, with my face towards Prester John, and they baptize in this manner.

. . .

In the tank stood the old priest, the master of the Prester, who was with me Christmas night, and he was naked as when his mother bore him (and quite dead of cold, because it was a very sharp frost), standing in the water up to his shoulders or

Prester John: A legendary East African priest-king who held many cities along the coast. The inhabitants of these cities were great merchants and owned big ships. The king was supposedly Christian, and many Portuguese accounts report looking for Prester John in order to forge an alliance against the Muslims along the Swahili coast. Father Francisco Alvarez called the ruler of Ethiopia in c. 1540 "Prester John," although that was not an accurate name. The title was obviously used to signify the special religious and political power of the kings in Ethiopia.

thereabouts, for so deep was the tank that those who were to be baptized entered by the steps, naked, with their backs to the Prester, and when they came out again they showed him their fronts, the women as well as the men. When they came to the said priest, he put his hands on their head, and put it three times under the water, saying in his language: "In name of the Father, of the Son, and of the Holy Spirit," he made the sign of the cross as a blessing, and they went away in peace. (The "I baptize thee," I heard him say it.) . . . After a great number of baptized persons had passed, he sent to call me to be near him; and so near that the Cabeata did not stir to hear what the Prester said, and to speak to the interpreter who was close to me: and he asked me what I thought of that office. I answered him that the things of God's service which were done in good faith and without evil deceit, and in His praise, were good, but such an office as this, there was none in our Church, rather it forbade us baptizing without necessity on that day, because on that day Christ was baptized, so that we should not think of saying of ourselves that we were baptized on the same day as Christ; also the Church does not order this sacrament to be given more than once. Afterwards he asked whether we had it written in books not to be baptized more than once. I replied, Yes, that we had. . . . Then they said to me that such was the truth, and so it was written in their books; but what were they to do with many who turned Moors and Jews after being Christians and then repented, and with others who did not believe well in baptism, what remedy would they have? I answered: For those who do not rightly believe, teaching and preaching would suffice for them, and if that did not profit, burn them as heretics. . . . And as to those who turned Moors or Jews, and afterwards of their own free will recognised their error, and asked for mercy, the *Abima* would absolve them, with penances salutary for their souls, if he had powers for this, if not, let them go to the Pope of Rome, in whom are all the powers. And those who did not repent, they might take them and burn them, for such is the use in Frankland and the Church of Rome. To this there came the reply, that all this seemed to him good, but that his grandfather had ordained this baptism by the counsel of great priests, in order that so many souls should not be lost, and that it had been the custom until now. . . . To this there came no answer except that I might go in peace to say mass. I said it was no longer time for saying mass, that midday was long passed. So I went to dine with our Portuguese and the Franks.

. . . This day, later in the afternoon, Prester John sent to call the ambassador and all his company. The baptism was already ended, and His Highness was still within his curtain where I left him. We entered there, and he at once asked the ambassador what he thought of it. He replied that it was very good, although we had not got such a custom. The water was then running into the tank, and he asked if there were here Portuguese who could swim. At once two jumped into the tank, and swam and dived as much as the tank allowed of. He enjoyed greatly, as he showed by his looks, seeing them swim and dive. After this he desired us to go outside and go to one end of the enclosure or circuit; and here he ordered a banquet to be made for us of bread and wine (according to their custom and the use of the country), and he desired us to raise our church tent and the tent we were lodging in, because he wished to return to his quarters, and that we should go in front of him because he was ordering his horsemen to skirmish in the manner in which they fight with the Moors in the field. So we went in front of him, looking at the said skirmish. They began, but soon there came such heavy rain that it did not allow them to carry out the skirmish which they had begun well.

Analysis and Review Questions

1. Father Francisco Alvarez wrote this vivid account of Abyssinia, or the "land of Prester John," so-called because of the legendary priest-king whose dominions were thought to be in Ethiopia. What indications are there that this kingdom in the Ethiopian highlands was extensive, wealthy, and powerful? Why the very detailed descriptions of the Lalibela churches?

2. Despite the fact that Arab conquests across northern Africa were very successful, there were islands of Christianity. The Egyptian Christian community, the Copts, maintained contact with Byzantium but later split away because of doctrinal and political reasons. The Ethiopian Church, too, developed along unique lines. What evidence does Father Alvarez provide that the Christian kings took their religious traditions very seriously?

3. What can we deduce from this document about the relationship between the Ethiopian Church and Rome? What are the Portuguese motives for accommodating the many differences in religious beliefs and customs?

4. Ideological, religious, political, and economic rivalries play themselves out along the coasts of the Red Sea and East Africa in the sixteenth century. Why do you suppose that the Portuguese were able to defeat the Muslims in nearly every instance?

5. According to the Ethiopian ruler, what is the purpose of annual baptisms? What is the role of the king in the religious ceremonies of his people? What seems to shock Father Alvarez most about the baptisms?

WEB LINKS

http://longmanworldhistory.com
The following additional readings and case studies can be found on the Web site.
Case Study 19.1, Portuguese Travelers in Africa
Case Study 19.2, "The White Man's Burden" across Two Centuries
Comparative Document 21.5, Imperialism and the White Man's Burden

http://vi.uh.edu/pages/mintz/primary.htm
A collection of excerpts from slave narratives.

http://www.law.umkc.edu/faculty/projects/ftrials/amistad/AMI_ACT.HTM
The career of the *Amistad*, a slave schooner that became the subject of a major motion picture on the trade.

http://docsouth.unc.edu/fpn/fpn.html
Narratives of slaves who lived in the American south.

http://www.bethel.edu/~letnie/AfricanChristianity/WesternNorthAfricaHomepage.html
A discussion on the history of Christianity in West Africa.

CHAPTER 20

The Middle East, 1450–1750

This era was a vibrant and creative period for the still-expanding Islamic world. It was also a time of great urbanization. The city of Baghdad remained a major intellectual and religious center, and cities such as Cairo, Egypt, and Cordova, Spain, played important roles as well. Islam retained a firm footing in northern India and South Asia, as Muslim rulers there steadily expanded their control over parts of India.

However, the political unity of the Islamic empire had begun to decrease after the thirteenth century. The ruling Abbasid Dynasty was in decline, and separate Muslim states began to emerge. While religion was an important common denominator for these states, local differences became more pronounced. Indeed, even religion was not immune to local adaptation—variability in how Islam was practiced was noticeable in this period, especially in the Muslim areas of sub-Saharan Africa. By the eighteenth century, much of the Islamic world was in decline and about to confront a new period of European expansion.

Map 20.1 (Interactive) The Middle East

MEHMED II

About the Document

As the ruling Abbasid Dynasty was declining in the late thirteenth century C.E., powerful local states emerged to take its place. One of these, the Ottoman Empire, was arguably the dominant Muslim state for the next 500 years. Centered in modern-day Turkey, the Ottoman Empire experienced its own period of vibrant cultural growth, but it is best remembered for its political and military complexity.

Writing in the fifteenth century, the Greek author Kritovoulos focused on one of the most important Ottoman emperors, Mehmed II, known as the "Conqueror." Mehmed II ruled from 1451–1481 and was responsible for conquering the last remnant of the old Byzantine Empire, the fortress city of Constantinople, in 1453. The following excerpt discusses the events before the takeover of the city and the actual attack, as well as what the emperor himself was like. Following this victory, the Muslim Ottomans would slowly push into southeastern Europe, forever changing the cultural and religious culture there.

The Document

16. It was the year [A.D. 1451] when the Sultan° Murad came to the end of his life, having lived a total of fifty-two years and having reigned thirty-one, a very good man in every way, high-minded, and also a very great general who had exhibited throughout his life many brave and wonderful deeds, as indeed these exploits show.

19. So when this Murad, of whom I spoke, died, his son Mehmed succeeded to the sultanate, he being the seventh Sultan and now in the twentieth year of his life. He was sent for from Asia, for it was there that he had his province which had been assigned him by his father.

20. Just at that period the Divine power sent many unusual, unexpected, and prodigious signs. These occurred both at the birth of this man and also at his entering on his rule as Sultan. For strange and exceptional earthquakes took place, and subterranean rumblings, also severe thunder and lightning from heaven, and whirlwinds and terrible storms, and an unusual light appeared in the sky, and many similar signs which the Divine power is accustomed to exhibit at the time of the greatest events and changes in the customary order.

21. The soothsayers,° sages and prophets and inspired persons foretold and foresaw many things that were to happen, and announced that the new Sultan would have every sort of good fortune and virtue, that his dominion would be very large in every way, and that he would surpass all the sultans before him in the very great abundance of his glory and wealth and power and accomplishments.

23. His physical powers helped him well. His energies were keen for everything, and the power of his spirit gave him ability to rule and to be kingly. To this end also his wisdom aided, as well as his fine knowledge of all the doings of the ancients. For he studied all the writings of the Arabs and Persians [Ottomans], and whatever works of the Greeks had been translated into the language of the Arabs and Persians—I refer particularly to the works of the Peripatetics and Stoics. So he used the most important philosophies of the teachers of the Arabs and Persians.

24. He did not postpone anything or put off any action, but immediately carried everything through. First he made a treaty with the Romans and the Emperor Constantine and after that, with Karaman, the ruler of Upper Phrygia and Cilicia, believing that for the present this move was beneficial to his affairs.

25. Then he gave himself to an examination of his whole realm. Using his judgment about the governorships of the nations under him, he deposed some of the governors and substituted others who he deemed to be superior to the former in strategy and knowledge and justice.

26. He also went over the registers and battle order of the troops, cavalry and infantry, which are paid from the royal treasuries.

27. In addition to this, he collected a supply of arms and arrows and other things needful and useful in preparation for war. Then he examined his family treasury, looking especially closely into its overseers. He carefully questioned the officials in charge of the annual taxes and obliged them to render accounts.

Sultan: Common Islamic title for "emperor" or "king."
soothsayer: Predictor.

28. And he discovered that much of the public and royal revenue was being badly spent and wasted to no good purpose, about one-third of the yearly revenues which were recovered for the royal treasury. So he set the keeping of this in good order. He greatly increased the annual revenue.

29. . . . Thus he prepared for greater things; and so everything contributed to the plan he had before him.

30. And this plan was: he meant to build a strong fortress on the Bosporus° on the European side, opposite to the Asiatic fortress on the other side; at the point where it is narrowest and swiftest, and so to control the straits by uniting both continents, Asia and Europe; and to cross there whenever he should choose, quite independently of any other individuals and with no least question that it was the Sultan himself who controlled the passage.

31. . . . Meanwhile the Emperor of the Romans [Byzantines] reigned securely in the City, always watching the times and the events, for the most part controlling the sea, making use of it sometimes to the advantage of his own nation, and injuring whom he pleased. In addition, the Italians, and especially the Venetians, in their quarrels with these others, often cruised in long triremes through the Bosporus and the Hellespont, preventing the crossing of these straits.

33. With this plan in mind, that winter he ordered all the materials to be prepared for building, namely, stone and timbers and iron and whatever else would be of use for this purpose.

34. The Emperor Constantine, on the other hand, and the men of the City, when they learned this, regarded it as terrible and as the beginning of great evils. Considering it a certain danger of enslavement—as indeed it was—they decided to fortify their town and to prepare the whole City. They were sorely troubled.

35. Hence he [Constantine] decided to send an embassy composed of his associates to try by any possible means to forestall this threat.

36. And they, when they arrived, used all sorts of arguments, citing the treaties and agreements. They told how, in all the previous treaties which had been drawn up and ratified, both with his forefathers and with his father, and indeed with him also, it was in every case promised that no one should build a fortress or anything else in this place. Furthermore it was specified that, if any such undertaking was begun, both sides would oppose this by every possible means. So the country had been saved from danger of this until now and was free. They said they would agree simply to the passing across of the Sultan's armies and other equipment from continent to continent, but they demanded that he should not in any way break the treaties, concluded but yesterday and the day before, for any trivial reason. For surely he did not wish to commit any injustice, as they certainly were not doing any injustice on their part.

37. The Sultan replied to them: "I have no intention to do you any injustice, O Romans, nor to do anything contrary to the agreements and treaties in this undertaking of mine, but only to protect my possessions while doing no injury to you. It is, however, just and right for each of us to guard and make sure of his own, not in the least injuring those with whom he has a treaty, and this is the desire of all. But, as you see, I rule over both Asia and Europe, continents separated from each other, and in each of these I have many opponents and enemies of my rule. . . . Besides, this place where I am now going to build a fortress is our own, being the place for crossing into our own territory,

Bosporus: The strait between the Byzantine Empire and the Ottoman Empire; today it separates European and Asian Turkey.

whether from Asia into Europe or from Europe into Asia. So you must not interfere too much. If you wish to enjoy peace, and if you have no intention on your part of preventing us from having this crossing-place, I on my part will neither break my pledges nor desire to do so, provided you will stay in your own place and not meddle at all in our affairs nor wish to be too prying."

38. With this reply, he dismissed the ambassadors. They on their return told everything to the Emperor Constantine and all the Romans [Byzantines]—the whole story and especially that it was not possible to prevent this undertaking entirely, either by argument or by persuasion, but only by resort to force, if indeed that were possible. And they, since they fully realized the exceeding gravity of the situation and that there was nothing they could do, kept an unwilling silence.

54. He also resolved to carry into execution immediately the plan which he had long since studied out and elaborated in his mind and toward which he had bent every purpose from the start, and to wait no longer nor delay. This plan was to make war against the Romans [Byzantines] and their Emperor Constantine and to besiege the city. For he thought . . . that if he could succeed in capturing it and becoming master of it, there was nothing to hinder him from sallying forth from it in a short time . . . and overrunning all and subduing them to himself. For this reason he could no longer be restrained at all.

234. So saying, he led them himself. And they, with a shout on the run and with a fearsome yell, went on ahead of the Sultan, pressing on up to the palisade. After a long and bitter struggle they hurled back the Romans from there and climbed by force up the palisade.° The dashed some of their foe down into the ditch between the great wall and the palisade, which was deep and hard to get out of, and they killed them there. The rest they drove back to the gate.

235. He had opened this gate in the great wall, so as to go easily over to the palisade. Now there was a great struggle there and great slaughter among those stationed there, for they were attacked by the heavy infantry and not a few others in irregular formation, who had been attracted from many points by the shouting. There the Emperor Constantine, with all who were with him, fell in gallant combat.

236. The heavy infantry were already streaming through the little gate into the City, and others had rushed in through the breach in the great wall. Then all the rest of the army, with a rush and a roar, poured in brilliantly and scattered; all over the City. And the Sultan stood before the great wall, where the standard also was and the ensigns, and watched the proceedings. The day was already breaking.

Analysis and Review Questions

1. Would you say that the author's account of Mehmed is generally positive or negative? Why?
2. Who were the soothsayers and sages?
3. Does Mehmed honor his treaties or not, according to the author?
4. How does the Byzantine emperor Constantine die?
5. Where was Mehmed when his father died?

palisade: A fence of stakes used for defense.

VENETIAN OBSERVATIONS ON THE OTTOMAN EMPIRE

About the Document

After Constantinople was conquered, the city was renamed Istanbul and was soon on its way back to the greatness it had enjoyed during the height of the Byzantine Empire. Indeed, just as the city had been the cultural, intellectual, and political heart for the Byzantines, so, too, would it be for the Ottoman Empire.

But, in many ways, the history of the Ottoman Empire was of a quick, decisive rise to power followed by a long, steady decline. Even by the seventeenth century, European observers, who admittedly tended to be biased against Muslim institutions anyway, were noticing signs of decay and weakness. One such individual was a Venetian ambassador to Istanbul, Gianfrancesco Morosini, who was in Turkey during the 1580s. His reports not only discuss the organization of the military and the government, but also provide a European view of the perceived strengths and weaknesses of the Turkish people. These and other dispatches also describe the Turkish capital.

Image 20.1
Mehmet II

The Document

They succeed to the throne without any kind of ceremony of election or coronation. According to Turkish law of succession, which resembles most countries' laws in this respect, the oldest son should succeed to the throne as soon as the father dies. But in fact, whichever of the sons can first enter the royal compound in Constantinople is called the sultan and is obeyed by the people and by the army. Since he has control of his father's treasure he can easily gain the favor of the janissaries and with their help control the rest of the army and the civilians.

Because this government is based on force, the brother who overcomes the others is considered the lord of all. The same obedience goes to a son who can succeed in overthrowing his father, a thing which bothers the Turks not at all. As a result, when his sons are old enough to bear arms, the sultan generally does not allow them near him, but sends them off to some administrative district where they must live under continual suspicion until their father's death. And just as the fathers do not trust their own sons, the sons do not trust their fathers and are always afraid of being put to death. This is the sad consequence of unbridled ambition and hunger for power—a miserable state of affairs where there is no love between father and sons, and much less between sons and father.

This lord has thirty-seven kingdoms covering enormous territory. His dominion extends to the three principal parts of the world, Africa, Asia, and Europe; and since these lands are joined and contiguous with each other, he can travel for a distance of eight thousand miles on a circuit through his empire and hardly need to set foot in another prince's territories.

The principal cities of the Turks are Constantinople, Adrianople,° and Bursa, the three royal residence places of the sultans. Buda is also impressive, as are the Asian cities—Cairo, Damascus, Aleppo, Bagdad and others—but none of these have the things which usually lend beauty to cities. Even Constantinople, the most important of them all, which is posted in the most beautiful and enchanting situation that can be imagined, still lacks those amenities that a great city should have, such as beautiful streets, great squares, and handsome palaces. Although Constantinople has many mosques, royal

---

Adrianople: Turkish city on the European side of the Bosporus.

palaces, inns, and public baths, the rest of the city is mazy and filthy; even these [public buildings], with their leaded domes studded with gilded bronze ornaments, only beautify the long-distance panorama of the city.

The security of the empire depends more than anything else on the large numbers of land and sea forces which the Turks keep continually under arms. These are what make them feared throughout the world.

The sultan always has about 280,000 well-paid men in his service. Of them about 80,000 are paid every three months out of his personal treasury. These include roughly 16,000 janissaries, who form the Grand Signor's advance guard; six legions, or about 12,000 cavalry called "spahi," who serve as his rear guard; and about 1,500 other defenders. . . . The other 200,000 cavalry . . . are not paid with money like the others, but are assigned landholdings [called timars].

The timariots are in no way inferior as fighting men to the soldiers paid every three months with cash, because the timars are inherited like the fiefs distributed by Christian rulers.

What about the fighting qualities of these widely feared Turkish soldiers? I can tell you the opinion I formed at Scutari, where I observed the armies of Ferrad Pasha and Osman Pasha (Ferrad's army was there for more than a month, and Osman's for a matter of weeks). I went over to Scutari several times to confer with the two pashas and also, unofficially, to look at the encampment, and I walked through the whole army and carefully observed every detail about the caliber of their men, their weapons, and the way they organize a bivouac site and fortify it. I think I can confidently offer this conclusion: they rely more on large numbers and obedience than they do on organization and courage.

Although witnesses who saw them in earlier times claim they are not as good as they used to be, it appears that the janissaries are still the best of the Turkish soldiers. They are well-made men, and they can handle their weapons—the arquebus, club, and scimitar—quite well. These men are accustomed to hardships, but they are only used in battle in times of dire necessity.

As for the cavalry, some are lightly armed with fairly weak lances, huge shields, and scimitars.

If I compare these men with Christian soldiers, such as those I saw in the wars in France or in the Christian King's conquest of Portugal, I would say they are much better than Christian soldiers in respect to obedience and discipline. However, in courage and enthusiasm, and in physical appearance and weapons, they are distinctly inferior.

The naval forces which the Great Turk uses to defend his empire are vast and second to none in the world. True, at present they do not have at hand all the armaments they would need to outfit the as yet uncompleted galleys, . . . But his resources are so great that if he wanted to he could quickly assemble what he needs; he has already begun to attend to this.

Analysis and Review Questions

1. From the document, how does it appear that a new king is selected in the Ottoman Empire?
2. Does the author consider Constantinople to be an attractive city?
3. What are the three principal Turkish cities?
4. How does the author evaluate the Ottoman army?
5. Would you consider this a positive or a negative account? Why?

THE DECLINE OF THE OTTOMANS

About the Document

*Image 20.2
The Suleymaniye
Mosque*

Istanbul, the former Constantinople, became a great cultural center under the Ottoman Turks. In the 200 years after its conquest in 1453, Istanbul took on an increasingly Islamic character, as society was irrevocably altered, buildings were modified, and architectural styles changed. Islam replaced Orthodox Christianity as the dominant faith.

However, despite the fact that the Ottoman Empire became powerful quickly, it had already started to decay by the seventeenth century. This fact was quickly noticed by European observers such as Gianfrancesco Morosini (see document 20.2) and Lorenzo Bernardo, both ambassadors from Venice to the Ottoman sultans in the late 1500s. While accounts of the decline may have been somewhat exaggerated by these European observers, Bernardo was also quick to praise the Turks for various accomplishments. In spite of any predictions about its collapse, the Ottoman Empire would exist until after 1918.

The Document

Three basic qualities have enabled the Turks to make such remarkable conquests, and rise to such importance in a brief period: religion, frugality, and obedience.

From the beginning it was religion that made them zealous, frugality that made them satisfied with little, and obedience that produced men ready for any dangerous campaign.

In former times, Serene Prince, all Turks held to a single religion, whose major belief is that it is "written" when and how a man will die, and that if he dies for his God and his faith he will go directly to Paradise. It is not surprising, then, that one reads in histories about Turks who vied for the chance to fill a ditch with their bodies, or made a human bridge for others to use crossing a river, going to their deaths without the slightest hesitation. But now the Turks have not a single religion, but three of them. The Persians are among the Turks like the [Protestant] heretics among us [Christians], because some of them hold the beliefs of Ali, and others those of Omar, both of whom were followers of Mohammed, but held different doctrines. Then there are the Arabs and Moors, who claim they alone preserve the true, uncorrupted religion and that the "Greek Turks" (as they call these in Constantinople) are bastard Turks with a corrupted religion, which they blame on their being mostly descended from Christian renegades who did not understand the Muslim religion.

As for frugality, which I said was the second of the three sources of the Turks' great power, this used to be one of their marked characteristics. At one time the Turks had no interest in fine foods or, if they were rich, in splendid decorations in their houses. Each was happy with bread and rice, and a carpet and a cushion; he showed his importance only by having many slaves and horses with which he could better serve his ruler. No wonder then that they could put up with the terrible effort and physical discomfort involved in conquering and ruling. What a shameful lesson to our own state, where we equate military glory with sumptuous banquets and our men want to live in their camps and ships as if they were back home at weddings and feasts!

But now that the Turks have conquered vast, rich lands they too have fallen victims to the corruption of wealth. They are beginning to appreciate fine foods and game, and most of them drink wine. They furnish their houses beautifully and wear clothes of gold and silver with costly linings. Briefly, then, they become fonder every day of luxury, comfort, and display.

Obedience was the third source of the great power of the Turkish empire. In the old days obedience made them united, union made them strong, and strength rendered their armies invincible. They are all slaves by nature, and the slaves of one single master; only from him can they hope to win power, honors, and wealth and only from him do they have to fear punishment and death. Why should it be surprising, then, that they used to compete with each other to perform stupendous feats in his presence? This is why it is said that the Turks' strict obedience to their master is the foundation of the empire's security and grandeur. But when the foundation weakens, when the brake is released, ruin could easily follow. The point is that with those other state-preserving qualities changing into state-corroding qualities, disobedience and disunion could be the agents which finally topple it.

This is all the more likely now that the chief officials have no other goal but to oppose each other bitterly. They have all the normal rivalries and ambitions of ministers of state, but they also have unusual opportunities for undercover competition with each other, because many of them have married daughters, sisters, and nieces of the Grand Signor. These women can speak with His Majesty whenever they want and they often sway him in favor of their husbands. This practice throws government affairs into confusion and is a real source of worry to the first vizier, who fears to take the smallest step without notifying the sultan.

Just as obedience to a prince creates a spirit of unity, so disobedience causes discord and strife. I have already said how much the pashas who are in office hate each other. In the same way, the *massuli* or dismissed pashas think of nothing but ruining the ones in office so they can return to their former posts.

The Grand Signor himself stirs up hatred and indignation among his subjects by making himself the heir of those who die rich, and grabbing their goods from their children. His avarice and penny-pinching are subjects for loud grumbling in every tavern and gathering place in the empire.

It seems reasonable to say that if the Ottoman Empire rose so remarkably fast in a short time because the Grand Sultan went on the major campaigns and because his men hoped and struggled for rewards, then its decline may now be under way. Sultan Selim, the father of the present Grand Signor, was the first to hold that a king or emperor's real satisfaction is not to be found in brave deeds on the field of glory but in peace and quiet, in gratifying all his physical senses, in enjoying the pleasures and comforts of the seraglios in the company of women and jesters, and treating himself to jewels, palaces, loggias, and every other human creation his heart desires. Sultan Murad has followed his father's example—in fact, he has gone further, because at least Sultan Selim occasionally left the seraglio and hunted as far away as Adrianople, but the present Grand Signor, as I said, hardly ever goes out.

My conclusion, distinguished gentlemen, is that the three basic qualities which made the Turks a great power—religion, frugality, and obedience—are vanishing. If this trend continues, and if the sultan's successors follow his example of remaining in the seraglios and letting others lead campaigns, then we can hope for the decline of the empire. Just as it rose to great strength very rapidly, it seems logical to expect it to decline very rapidly, in the same way that those plants which quickly mature and produce fruit are also quick to wither.

Even if the Turks have enormous armed forces, this does not mean their state will not decline. If armed might guaranteed that an empire would last forever, think how many examples one can find of powerful Greek and Roman empires, especially the Roman one (the world has never seen a mightier power), and yet it was totally ruined in little more than two hundred years. If having more money, more land, and more inhabitants always made one country more powerful than the others, the world would not have seen so many of those reversals in which countries with smaller but better armies wiped out larger ones. It is good government, not armies, that conserve an empire; fine laws and institutions have maintained our republic, with God's help, in a world where many states are more powerful.

This is a law of nature, that the same forces which caused a thing to grow must also keep it alive when mature. If the Turkish empire rose so high with the aid of the three qualities I have discussed, then when it lacks its wings it will surely fall.

Analysis and Review Questions

1. How well do Ottoman officials get along, according to the author?
2. What are the three "basic qualities [that] have enabled the Turks" to build their empire?
3. How did the Ottoman Empire rise so quickly to prominence, according to this excerpt?
4. Does the author make any evaluation of Ottoman military strength?
5. Is there anything positive pointed out in this excerpt?

WEB LINKS

http://longmanworldhistory.com
The following additional case study can be found on the Web site.
Case Study 20.1, The Ottoman Empire in the Late Sixteenth Century

http://ccat.sas.upenn.edu/~rs143/map.html
A Web page dedicated to maps relating to the history of Islam and the Ottoman Empire.

http://www.islamic.org
An all-inclusive Muslim-oriented site that includes the text of the Quran as well as excellent discussions on the history of Islam.

http://www.greece.org/projects/Romiosini/fall.html
A detailed account of the fall of Constantinople in 1453.

http://www.cyberiran.com
A complete site dealing with all manner of things Iranian, past and present.

PART III Comparative Case Study

BATTLEFIELDS TO COURTROOMS: CONFLICT AND AGENCY IN THE AMERICAS

Spaniards on both sides of the Atlantic contested issues of how to define, and subsequently treat, the Indians. To be sure, agendas varied considerably given the different circumstances and positions of the people acting within them. Even particular individuals might find their goals changing in a relatively short time. With the exception of the Indians' obvious religious differences, for example, Cortéz initially described the Tlaxcalans in terms that las Casas himself might have found agreeable. Yet the conquistadors, despite their earlier appraisals of the New World inhabitants, quickly reversed themselves and argued as to the Indians' barbarism, savagery, and need for instruction. Consider the circumstances Cortéz faced when writing his letter to Charles V, and consider as well the advantages he sought to gain through his carefully wrought depictions of the Tlaxcalans. The Spaniards' changing motivations and circumstances, however, were only part of the contested milieu. The Indians did not remain silent or passive. They also entered the debates, often through the less obvious means of the Spanish courts, acts that spoke highly of the Indians' level of civilization and political acumen. Over time, their "voice" helped to influence the king of Spain in his decision to implement the New Laws.

THE SECOND LETTER OF HERNAN CORTÉZ TO KING CHARLES V OF SPAIN (1519)

About the Document

In 1519 the Spanish attempted to expand their sphere of control in the New World. After several abortive and costly efforts to explore Mexico's Yucatán peninsula, the Spaniards embarked on an exploration of what is now central Mexico. Hernan Cortéz, who led the mission, kept King Charles V informed of events in the Americas through a series of five extensively detailed letters. Under constant pressure to justify both his own leadership and the expenses of conquest, Cortéz missed no opportunity to expound on either the riches of the New World or the willingness of many indigenous peoples to accept Spanish tutelage and rule. In the following excerpt, Cortéz relates his meeting with the Tlaxcalans, an indigenous civilization not fully under Aztec control. Despite Cortéz's ability to embellish and put a positive spin on the events taking place, on closer reading, his letter reveals many of the ambiguities he experienced in attempting to understand the Tlaxcalans and their motives.

The Document

When we had rested somewhat, I went out one night, after inspecting the first watch, with a hundred foot soldiers, our Indian allies and the horsemen; and one league from the camp five of the horses fell and would go no further, so I sent them back. And although all those who were with me in my company urged me to return, for it was an evil omen, I continued on my way secure in the belief that God is more powerful than Nature. Before it was dawn I attacked two towns, where I killed many people, but I did not burn the houses lest the fires should alert the other towns nearby. At dawn I came upon another large town containing, according to an inspection I had made, more than twenty thousand houses. As I took them by surprise, they rushed out unarmed, and the women and children ran naked through the streets, and I began to do them some harm. When they saw that they could not resist, several men of rank of the town came to me and begged me to do them no more harm, for they wished to be Your Highness's vassals and my allies. They now saw that they were wrong in not having been willing to assist me; from thenceforth I would see how they would do all that I, in Your Majesty's name, commanded them to do, and they would be Your faithful vassals. Then, later, more than four thousand came to me in peace and led me outside to a spring and fed me very well.

And so I left them pacified and returned to our camp where I found that those who had remained behind were very afraid that some danger had befallen me because of the omen they had seen in the return of the horses the night before. But after they heard of the victory which God had been pleased to give us, and how we had pacified those villages, there was great rejoicing, for I assure Your Majesty that there was amongst us not one who was not very much afraid, seeing how deep into this country we were and among so many hostile people and so entirely without hope of help from anywhere. Indeed, I heard it whispered, and almost spoken out loud, that I was a Pedro Carbonero to have led them into this place from which they could never escape. And, moreover, standing where I could not be seen, I heard certain companions in a hut say that if I was crazy enough to go where I could not return, they were not, and that they were going to return to the sea, and if I wished to come with them, all well and good, but if not, they would abandon me. Many times I was asked to turn back, and I encouraged them by reminding them that they were Your Highness's vassals and that never at any time had Spaniards been found wanting, and that we were in a position to win for Your Majesty the greatest dominions and kingdoms in the world. Moreover, as Christians we were obliged to wage war against the enemies of our Faith; and thereby we would win glory in the next world, and, in this, greater honor and renown than any generation before our time. They should observe that God was on our side, and to Him nothing is impossible, for, as they saw, we had won so many victories in which so many of the enemy had died, and none of us. I told them other things which occurred to me of this nature, with which, and Your Highness's Royal favor, they were much encouraged and determined to follow my intentions and to do what I wished, which was to complete the enterprise I had begun.

On the following day at ten o'clock, Sintengal, the captain general of this province, came to see me, together with some fifty men of rank, and he begged me on his own behalf, and on behalf of Magiscasin, who is the most important person in the entire province, and on behalf of many other lords, to admit them to Your Highness's Royal service and to my friendship, and to forgive them their past errors, for they did not know who we were. They had tried with all their forces both by day and by night to avoid being subject to anyone, for this province never had been, nor had they ever had an over-all ruler. For they had lived in freedom and independence from time immemorial and had always defended themselves against the great power of Mutezuma and against his ancestors, who had subjugated all those lands but had never been able to reduce them to servitude, although they were surrounded on all sides and had not place by which to leave their land. They ate no salt because there was none in their land; neither could they go and buy it elsewhere, nor did they wear cotton because it did not grow there on account of the cold; and they were lacking in many other things through being so enclosed.

All of which they suffered willingly in return for being free and subject to no one, and with me they had wished to do the same; to which end, as they said, they had used all their strength but saw clearly that neither it nor their cunning had been of any use. They would rather be Your Highness's vassals than see their houses destroyed and their women and children killed. I replied that they should recognize they were to blame for the harm they had received, for I had come to their land thinking that I came to a land of friends because the men of Cempoal had assured me that it was so. I had sent my messengers on ahead to tell them that I was coming and that I wished to be their friend. But without reply they had attacked me on the road while I was unprepared and had killed two horses and wounded others. And after they had fought me, they sent messengers to tell me that it had been done without their consent by certain communities who were responsible; but they were not involved and had now rebuked those others for it and desired my friendship. I had believed them and had told them that I was pleased and would come on the following day and go among them as I would among friends. And again they had attacked me on the road and had fought all day until nightfall. And I reminded them of everything else that they had done against me and many other things which in order not to tire Your Highness I will omit. Finally, they offered themselves as vassals in the Royal service of Your Majesty and offered their persons and fortunes and so they have remained until today and will, I think, always remain so for what reason Your Majesty will see hereafter.

Analysis and Review Questions

1. What problems does Cortéz experience with his own men?
2. What greater reasons or purposes does Cortéz offer as justification for his actions and those of his fellow conquistadors?
3. What reasons do the Tlaxcalans (through their representatives Sintengal and Magiscasin) give for wishing to support the Spaniards?
4. Were the Tlaxcalans sincere in their arguments, or were they simply trying to minimize the consequences of the earlier conflicts they lost? Is there evidence of other motives or perhaps of conflicting agendas within the Tlaxcalan ranks?
5. How would you characterize Cortéz's assessment of the Tlaxcalans' hospitality and sincerity of motive? What reasons might he have for providing an assessment perhaps more positive than events suggested?

THE NEW LAWS OF THE INDIES FOR THE GOOD TREATMENT AND PRESERVATION OF THE INDIANS (1542)

About the Document

In 1542 Spain's King Charles V instituted a sweeping administrative reform of his New World colonies. Designed to ensure fairer treatment for the Indians while weakening his more ambitious Spanish subjects, the New Laws sparked serious resentment and led to several rebellions against Crown rule. The oft-cited phrase "I obey but I cannot comply" is said to have originated when Spanish bureaucrats were unable to enforce the king's new legislation. Charles V subsequently suspended several of the New Laws—most notably those concerning the enslavement of Indians—until he could consolidate his power enough to guarantee their enforcement.

Despite the level of attention that the treatment of Indians received in the reforms, the New Laws dealt as much with issues of how the Spanish monarchy might extend and consolidate its power over its own peoples as they did with issues of how to treat new subjects. Like the Romans before them, and the globe-spanning empires to follow, the Spanish monarchs found that the challenges of empire often diminished the rewards of empire.

The Spanish arrival in the Americas arguably posed as many challenges for the Iberian monarchy and its peoples as it did for their New World counterparts. In a very short time span, Spain grew from a loose confederation of kingdoms into a global empire. Even as Christopher Columbus was embarking on his epic voyage to the West, King Ferdinand and Queen Isabella were struggling to consolidate their power over the Iberian peninsula. The more than 700-year effort to repel the Moorish invasion from North Africa had just ended in 1492, and the monarchs faced considerable obstacles. On the one hand, they had to contend with the question of how to assimilate peoples that geography, culture, and religion (the Moors, for instance, were Muslims) long had distanced from one another. On the other hand, and in the absence of a clearly defined common enemy, they had to find a means of maintaining and strengthening their hold over the sizeable population of nobles (*hidalgos*) who earlier had offered them their loyalty in exchange for the possibilities of material gain. With the fighting over, the monarchs could no longer offer the longstanding incentives of land, honor, and treasure as a means of reigning in the nobility. Ferdinand and Isabella sat atop a veritable powder keg.

Columbus's arrival in the New World drew Spain's internal conflicts and challenges into the global arena where distance made them even more problematic. Spanish encounters with indigenous civilizations, for example, exacerbated the issue of how successfully to assimilate different peoples and cultures under the rubric of a single empire or identity. While the discovery of new lands provided much needed incentives for hidalgos and, at least temporarily, a means by which the monarchy could continue to direct and control their impulses, the two often were at odds. Ferdinand and Isabella sought to find in the Indians loyal and obedient subjects. The hidalgos, by contrast, sought to find uncivilized barbarians whom they could then rob, plunder, and enslave. By the time that Cortéz and Pizarro began their conquests of Mexico and Peru, Spanish priests and missionaries already were complaining to the Crown of the conquistadors' abuses of the native populations.

Realizing that their control over affairs in the New World and over their Spanish subjects depended on their ability to both administer the Indian populations and continue to provide material incentives to the hidalgos, Ferdinand and Isabella instituted the practice of the encomienda.° Not to be confused with a land grant—since, after all, there was still considerable debate over whether the Indians were civilized enough to possess their own lands—the encomienda entrusted the indigenous inhabitants of a particular area or region to a hidalgo for the duration of his life. In exchange for administering, protecting, and Christianizing the inhabitants entrusted to him, the *encomendero* was entitled to some of their labor. The institution was, in sum, a short-term means of establishing control over the Americas and pacifying the Spaniards until an effective bureaucracy could be established in the New World.

Affairs went from bad to worse almost immediately. The encomienda often proved little more than a pretext for enslaving, robbing, and otherwise abusing the Indians. In their search for wealth, the encomenderos frequently placed their own material interests above the spiritual interests of the people they were entrusted with Christianizing. Consequently, rifts in the Spanish community occurred as settlers squared off against missionaries and priests. In the Yucatán region of Mexico the struggles grew especially bitter. Franciscan missionaries contended, for example, that Spanish abuses had led entire villages of Mayan Indians to revert to idolatry and human sacrifice. Worse, in the eyes of many members of the Spanish religious community, was the fact that encomiendas were becoming hereditary in practice.

By the 1530s, Spain's King Charles V recognized the severity of the crisis he faced. While engaged with conflicts in Europe, he had lost control of his new colonies. Nowhere was this more evident than in relation to the treatment of the Indians. Despite a 1537 papal bull declaring the Indians to be human beings, complete with souls and reason, and despite the protestations of Bishop Bartolomé de las Casas, Spanish settlers continued to enslave and wage war on the indigenous peoples in their care. The hidalgos demonstrated repeatedly their reluctance to obey any orders, whether from Church or King, that might conflict with their aims. Corruption and conflicts of interest virtually ensured that a fair administration of the new lands and their peoples would not be possible so long as the hidalgos were entrusted with such responsibilities. King Charles V subsequently focused his attentions on the enforcement of his rule. The 1542 New Laws of the Indies were the king's response to affairs in the Americas.

encomienda: This was the practice of entrusting the care of a specific indigenous population to a hidalgo. In exchange for Christianizing and protecting them, the hidalgo had the right to some of their labor.

The Document

Whereas one of the most important things in which the Audiencias° are to serve us is in taking very especial care of the good treatment of the Indians and preservation of them, We command that the said Audiencias enquire continually into the excesses and ill treatment which are or shall be done to them by governors or private persons; and how the ordinances and instructions which have been given to them, and are made for the good treatment of the said Indians have been observed. And if there had been any excesses, on the part of the said Governors, or should any be committed hereafter, to take care that such excesses are properly corrected, chastizing the guilty parties with all rigour conformably to justice. The Audiencias must not allow that in the suits between Indians, or with them, there be ordinary proceedings at law, nor dilatory expedients, as is wont to happen through the malice of some advocates and solicitors, but that they be determined summarily, observing their usages and customs, unless they be manifestly unjust; and that the said Audiencias take care that this be so observed by the other, inferior judges.

Item, We ordain and command that from hence forward for no cause of war nor any other whatsoever, though it be under title of rebellion, nor by ransom nor in other manner can an Indian be made a slave, and we will that they be treated as our vassals of the Crown of Castile° since such they are.

No person can make use of the Indians by way of Naboria or Tapia or in any other manner against their will.

As we have ordered provision to be made that from henceforward the Indians in no way be made slaves, including those who until now have been enslaved against all reason and right and contrary to the provisions and instructions thereupon, We ordain and command that the Audiencias having first summoned the parties to their presence, without any further judicial form, but in a summary way, so that the truth may be ascertained, speedily set the said Indians at liberty unless the persons who hold them for slaves show title why they should hold and possess them legitimately. And in order that in default of persons to solicit the aforesaid, the Indians may not remain in slavery unjustly, We command that the Audiencias appoint persons who may pursue this cause for the Indians and be paid out of the Exchequer fines, provided they be men of trust and diligence.

Also, we command that with regard to the lading of the said Indians the Audiencias take especial care that they be not laden, or in case that in some parts this cannot be avoided that it be in such a manner that no risk of life, health and preservation of the said Indians may ensue from an immoderate burthen; and that against their own will and without their being paid, in no case be it permitted that they be laden, punishing very severely him who shall act contrary to this. In this there is to be no remission out of respect to any person.

Because report has been made to us that owing to the pearl fisheries not having been conducted in a proper manner deaths of many Indians and Negroes have ensued, We command that no free Indian be taken to the said fishery under pain of death, and that the bishop and the judge who shall be at Veneçuela direct what shall seem to them most fit for the preservation of the slaves working in the said fishery, both Indians and Negroes, and that the deaths may cease. If, however, it should appear to them that the

Audiencias: Spanish courts of justice established in the colonies to which, theoretically, both Spaniards and Indians had recourse.
Castile: Castile was the name of the Iberian kingdom in which the Spanish monarchy was housed. It was also the birthplace of Queen Isabella and a powerful kingdom at the time of her marriage to Ferdinand of Aragon.

risk of death cannot be avoided by the said Indians and Negroes, let the fishery of the said pearls cease, since we value much more highly (as is right) the preservation of their lives than the gain which may come to us from the pearls.

Whereas in consequence of the allotments of Indians made to the Viceroys,° Governors, and their lieutenants, to our officials, and prelates, monasteries, hospitals, houses of religion and mints, offices of our Hazienda° and treasury thereof, and other persons favoured by reason of their offices, disorders have occurred in the treatment of the said Indians, it is our will, and we command that forthwith there be placed under our Royal Crown all the Indians whom they hold and possess by any title and cause whatever, whoever the said parties are, or may be, whether Viceroys, Governors, or their lieutenants, or any of our officers, as well of Justice as of our Hazienda, prelates, houses of religion, or of our Hazienda, hospitals, confraternities, or other similar institutions, although the Indians may not have been allotted to them by reason of the said offices; and although such functionaries or governors may say that they wish to resign the offices or governments and keep the Indians, let this not avail them nor be an excuse for them not to fulfill what we command.

Moreover, We command that from all those persons who hold Indians without proper title, having entered into possession of them by their own authority, such Indians be taken away and be placed under our Royal Crown.

And because we are informed that other persons, although possessing a sufficient title, have had an excessive number of Indians allotted to them, We order that the Audiencias, each in its jurisdiction diligently inform themselves of this, and with all speed, and reduce the allotments made to the said persons to a fair and moderate quantity, and then place the rest under our Royal Crown notwithstanding any appeal or application which may be interposed by such persons: and send us a report with all speed of what the said Audiencias have thus done, that we may know how our command is fulfilled. And in New Spain let it be especially provided as to the Indians held by Joan Infante, Diego de Ordas, the Maestro Roa, Francisco Vasquez de Coronado, Francisco Maldondo, Bernardino Vazquez de Tapia, Joan Xaramillo, Martin Vazquez, Gil Goncales de Venavides, and many other persons who are said to hold Indians in very excessive quantity, according to the report made to us. And, whereas we are informed that there are some persons in the said New Spain who are of the original Conquistadores and have no repartimiento° of Indians, We ordain that the President and Auditors of the said New Spain do inform themselves if there be any persons of this kind, and if any, to give them out of the tribute which the Indians thus taken away have to pay, what to them may seem fit for the moderate support and honourable maintenance of the said original Conquistadores who had no Indians allotted to them.

So also, the said Audiencias are to inform themselves how the Indians have been treated by the persons who have held them in encomienda, and if it be clear that in justice they ought to be deprived of the said Indians for their excesses and the ill-usage to which they have subjected them, We ordain that they take away and place such Indians under our Royal Crown. And in Peru, besides the aforesaid, let the Viceroy and Audiencia inform themselves of the excesses committed during the occurrences between

Viceroys: Situated atop the colonial bureaucracy, viceroys were royal bureaucrats who served as the king's New World proxies. Though subordinate to the king himself, the great distances between Spain and the colonies often necessitated that the viceroys act independently and without outside council.
Hazienda: The Hacienda was the Spanish equivalent of a Department of the Interior.
repartimiento: Forced labor draft in which up to one-seventh of a given indigenous population could be drafted to labor for a set amount of time on a plantation, in the mines, etc.

Governors Pizarro and Almagro in order to report to us thereon, and from the principal persons whom they find notoriously blameable in those feuds they then take away the Indians they have, and place them under our Royal Crown.

Moreover, we ordain and command that from hence forward no Viceroy, Governor, Audiencia, discoverer, or any other person have power to allot Indians in encomienda by new provision, or by means of resignation, donation, sale, or any other form or manner, neither by vacancy nor inheritance, but that the person dying who held the said Indians, they revert to our Royal Crown. And let the Audiencias take care to inform themselves then particularly of the person who died, of his quality, his merits and services, of how he treated the said Indians whom he held, if he left wife and children or what other heirs, and send us a report thereof together with the condition of the Indians and of the land, in order that we may give directions to provide what may be best for our service, and may do such favour as may seem suitable to the wife and children of the defunct. If in the meantime it should appear to the Audiencia that there is a necessity to provide some support for such wife and children, they can do it out of the tribute which the said Indians will have to pay, or allowing them a moderate pension, if the said Indians are under our Crown, as aforesaid.

Analysis and Review Questions

1. To what extent do you think Cortéz's descriptions of the Tlaxcalans make a strong case for the Indians' level of civilization and autonomy being sufficiently high so as to dictate against enslaving them?

2. In less than 25 years, Spaniards and Indians transferred their conflicts from the battlefield to the courtrooms *(audiencias)*. To what extent did this mark a transformation from Indian to Spanish rule? What might be the long-term significance of the Indians' utilization of the Spanish courts?

3. Cortéz cited the Spaniards' religious imperative in conquering the Aztecs. From your reading of the New Laws and the abuses they sought to end, do you think the Indians' Christianization remained a priority for Spanish settlers?

4. In comparing the two documents, to what extent do you believe that the Spanish abuses were part of a longer tradition of struggle and contest that preceded the Spaniards' arrival?

CHAPTER 21

The Nineteenth-Century West

The nineteenth century was a period of social, political, and economic upheaval. Throughout this period, Western nations struggled to create true nationalism—a political unity based on an expression of common culture—despite the difficulties involved. Major political revolutions had swept through the West in the late 1700s, inspired by the ideas of the Enlightenment and the political theories of John Locke. In the 1700s, English colonists revolted against their mother country; absolute monarchy in France was replaced first by a republic, then by a dictator in Napoleon; and Spain witnessed colonial revolts in Central and South America based on nationalism. Revolution gave way to conservatism for only a brief period. In 1848 revolutions occurred in Germany, Austria, Hungary, France, and Belgium. These upheavals changed the political landscape in the West and provided an impetus for the unification of other states, including Germany and Italy.

Map 21.1
(Interactive)
The Unification of
Germany 1815–1871

Economically, the Industrial Revolution destroyed mercantilism and rural craft-based economies, ushering in the age of capitalism. This shift wrought drastic social change for those caught up in the creation of what Marx called the proletariat—the working classes that were at the mercy of the industrial system. The creation of the Socialist Party and Marx's ideas concerning Communism can be traced to the social impacts of industrialization. Despite their political struggles, many Western nations turned their attention to the creation of empires abroad instead of improving conditions at home. This age of imperialism witnessed Western domination of many nations, often at tremendous social and political costs to the conquered nations. However, the political domination of an area also had economic implications that helped fuel the spread of capitalism.

CAPITALISM CHALLENGED: THE COMMUNIST MANIFESTO

About the Document

Karl Marx (1818–1883) was born and educated in Germany. He earned his doctorate degree from the University of Jena in 1841, and was soon caught up in the atmosphere of social revolution in his homeland. Prussian authorities closed the newspaper Marx edited for its radical beliefs, and he was soon forced into exile in France. While there, Marx began to collaborate with Friedrich Engels, an upper-middle-class German who was a partner in his father's textile mill in Manchester,

England. Engels was unlike most factory owners in that he had a genuine concern for the working classes. Together, Marx and Engels wrote the *Manifesto of the Communist Party* and had it published in 1848, the same year that political revolution was sweeping Europe.

Designed primarily as a propaganda piece, the Manifesto outlined modern socialism. Marx believed that laws governed both scientific and historical events. In order to understand history and possibly predict the future, Marx relied on an economic interpretation and predicted that the unequal distribution of wealth between different social classes would finally lead to open class conflict—revolution—in which eventually the working classes would seize power and create a classless society.

The Document

In what relation do the Communists stand to the proletarians as a whole?

The Communists do not form a separate party opposed to other working-class parties.

They have no interests separate and apart from those of the proletariat as a whole.

They do not set up any sectarian principles of their own, by which to shape and mould the proletarian movement.

The Communists are distinguished from the other working-class parties by this only: 1. In the national struggles of the proletarians of the different countries, they point out and bring to the front the common interests of the entire proletariat, independently of all nationality. 2. In the various stages of development which the struggle of the working class against the bourgeoisie has to pass through, they always and everywhere represent the interests of the movement as a whole.

The Communists, therefore, are on the one hand, practically, the most advanced and resolute section of the working-class parties of every country, that section which pushes forward all others; on the other hand, theoretically, they have over the great mass of the proletariat the advantage of clearly understanding the line of march, the conditions, and the ultimate general results of the proletarian movement.

The immediate aim of the Communists is the same as that of all the other proletarian parties: formation of the proletariat into a class, overthrow of the bourgeois supremacy, conquest of political power by the proletariat.

The theoretical conclusions of the Communists are in no way based on ideas or principles that have been invented, or discovered, by this or that would-be universal reformer.

They merely express, in general terms, actual relations springing from an existing class struggle, from a historical movement going on under our very eyes. The abolition of existing property relations is not at all a distinctive feature of Communism.

All property relations in the past have continually been subject to historical change consequent upon the change in historical conditions.

The French Revolution, for example, abolished feudal property in favour of bourgeois property.

The distinguishing feature of Communism is not the abolition of property generally, but the abolition of bourgeois property. But modern bourgeois private property is the final and most complete expression of the system of producing and appropriating products, that is based on class antagonisms, on the exploitation of the many by the few.

In the sense, the theory of the Communists may be summed up in the single sentence: Abolition of private property.

. . .

We have seen above, that the first step in the revolution by the working class, is to raise the proletariat to the position of the ruling class, to win the battle of democracy.

The proletariat will use its political supremacy to wrest, by degrees, all capital from the bourgeoisie, to centralize all instruments of production in the hands of the State, i.e., of the proletariat organized as the ruling class; and to increase the total of productive forces as rapidly as possible.

Of course, in the beginning, this cannot be effected except by means of despotic inroads on the rights of property, and on the conditions of bourgeois production; by means of measures, therefore, which appear economically insufficient and untenable, but which, in the course of the movement, outstrip themselves, necessitate further inroads upon the old social order, and are unavoidable as a means of entirely revolutionizing the mode of production.

These measures will of course be different in different countries.

Nevertheless, in the most advanced countries, the following will be pretty generally applicable:

1.   Abolition of private [ownership] in land and application of all rents of land to public purposes.

2.   A heavy progressive or graduated income tax.

3.   Abolition of all right of inheritance.

4.   Confiscation of the property of all emigrants and rebels.

5.   Centralization of credit in the hands of the State, by means of a national bank with State capital and an exclusive monopoly.

6.   Centralization of the means of communication and transport in the hands of the State.

7.   Extension of factories and instruments of production owned by the State; the bringing into cultivation of wastelands, and the improvement of the soil generally in accordance with a common plan.

8.   Equal liability of all to labour. Establishment of industrial armies, especially for agriculture.

9.   Combination of agriculture with manufacturing industries; gradual abolition of the distinction between town and country, by a more equable distribution of the population over the country.

10.   Free education for all children in public schools. Abolition of children's factory labour in its present form. Combination of education with industrial production, &c., &c.

When, in the course of development, class distinctions have disappeared, and all production has been concentrated in the whole nation, the public power will lose its political character. Political power, property so called, is merely the organized power of one class for oppressing another. If the proletariat during its contest with the bourgeoisie is compelled, by the force of circumstances, to organize itself as a class, if, by means of a revolution, it makes itself the ruling class, and, as such, sweeps away by force the old conditions of production, then it will, along with these conditions, have swept away the conditions for the existence of class antagonisms and of classes generally, and will thereby have abolished its own supremacy as a class.

Image 21.2:
Karl Marx
and His Daughter

In place of the old bourgeois society, with its classes and class antagonisms, we shall have an association, in which the free development of each is the condition for the free development of all.

. . .

In short, the Communists everywhere support every revolutionary movement against the existing social and political order of things.

In all these movements they bring to the front, as the leading question in each, the property question, no matter what its degree of development at the time.

Finally, they labour everywhere for the union and agreement of the democratic parties of all countries.

The Communists disdain to conceal their views and aims. They openly declare that their ends can be attained only by the forcible overthrow of all existing social conditions. Let the ruling classes tremble at a Communistic revolution. The proletarians have nothing to lose but their chains. They have world to win.

Working Men of all Countries Unite!

Analysis and Review Questions

1. Marx and Engels write that the beliefs of the Communists can be summed up in a single thought. What is it?
2. Using the selection, outline the progression of the revolution Marx and Engels describe. What are the steps involved? What will finally be achieved?
3. What is meant by class conflict? What examples are provided? What classes are involved in the conflict Marx and Engels outline?
4. What is the condition of the working class under capitalism, and how will it change under a Communist system? Who will have political power?
5. Can Marx's and Engels's system work? Have any of his ideas been put into practice, and have they been successful? Observe closely the list Marx provided of measures applied to successful countries; do you see these in everyday society today?

DECLARATION OF THE RIGHTS OF MAN AND THE CITIZEN

About the Document

The year 1789 was pivotal for France. Faced with a deteriorating economy, poor harvests, and pressure from the nobility, King Louis XVI agreed to call into session the Estates General for May of 1789. The Medieval representative body of France had not met since 1614 because of France's absolute monarchy. It was hoped that the meeting would produce a solution for France's economic difficulties, but, instead, it released frustration with the ancient regime and led to the first stage of the revolution. Once convened, the Third Estate demanded individual voting on the issues instead of the traditional vote by estate, and the wrangling continued into June 1789. Joined by some members of the clergy, the Third Estate walked out of the Estates General and proclaimed itself to be the National Assembly on June 17, 1789.

Image 21.1:
Oath of the
Tennis Court

The French National Assembly issued the Declaration of the Rights of Man and the Citizen on August 27, 1789. Designed as a preamble for a new constitution that the body had promised to write during the Oath of the Tennis Court, the document drafted was heavily influenced by the political philosophy of the Enlightenment. The ideas of John Locke, Rousseau, Voltaire, and the American Declaration of Independence are melded together to form the foundations of French liberal government.

The Document

The representatives of the French people, organized as a National Assembly,° believing that the ignorance, neglect, or contempt of the rights of man are the sole cause of public calamities and of the corruption of governments, have determined to set forth in a solemn declaration the natural, unalienable, and sacred rights of man, in order that this declaration, being constantly before all the members of the Social body, shall remind them continually of their rights and duties; in order that the acts of the legislative power, as well as those of the executive power, may be compared at any moment with the objects and purposes of all political institutions and may thus be more respected, and, lastly, in order that the grievances of the citizens, based hereafter upon simple and incontestable principles, shall tend to the maintenance of the constitution and redound to the happiness of all. Therefore the National Assembly recognizes and proclaims, in the presence and under the auspices of the Supreme Being, the following rights of man and of the citizen:

Articles:

1. Men are born and remain free and equal in rights. Social distinctions may be founded only upon the general good.

2. The aim of all political association is the preservation of the natural and imprescriptible rights of man. These rights are liberty, property, security, and resistance to oppression.

3. The principle of all sovereignty resides essentially in the nation. No body nor individual may exercise any authority which does not proceed directly from the nation.

4. Liberty consists in the freedom to do everything which injures no one else; hence the exercise of the natural rights of each man has no limits except those which assure to the other members of the society the enjoyment of the same rights. These limits can only be determined by law.

5. Law can only prohibit such actions as are hurtful to society. Nothing may be prevented which is not forbidden by law, and no one may be forced to do anything not provided for by law.

6. Law is the expression of the general will. Every citizen has a right to participate personally, or through his representative, in its foundation. It must be the same for all, whether it protects or punishes. All citizens, being equal in the eyes of the law, are equally eligible to all dignities and to all public positions and occupations, according to their abilities, and without distinction except that of their virtues and talents.

National Assembly: When members of the Third Estate walked out of the meeting of the Estates General, taking with them some of the members from the first and second estates, they met nearby and declared themselves to be the National Assembly. In other words, this body claimed that it, not the Estates General, was the representative body of France and her people.

7. No person shall be accused, arrested, or imprisoned except in the cases and according to the forms prescribed by law. Any one soliciting, transmitting, executing, or causing to be executed, any arbitrary order, shall be punished. But any citizen summoned or arrested in virtue of the law shall submit without delay, as resistance constitutes an offense.

8. The law shall provide for such punishments only as are strictly and obviously necessary, and no one shall suffer punishment except it be legally inflicted in virtue of a law passed and promulgated before the commission of the offense.

9. As all persons are held innocent until they shall have been declared guilty, if arrest shall be deemed indispensable, all harshness not essential to the securing of the prisoner's person shall be severely repressed by law.

10. No one shall be disquieted on account of his opinions, including his religious views, provided their manifestation does not disturb the public order established by law.

11. The free communication of ideas and opinions is one of the most precious of the rights of man. Every citizen may, accordingly, speak, write, and print with freedom, but shall be responsible for such abuses of this freedom as shall be defined by law.

12. The security of the rights of man and of the citizen requires public military forces. These forces are, therefore, established for the good of all and not for the personal advantage of those to whom they shall be intrusted.

13. A common contribution is essential for the maintenance of the public forces and for the cost of administration. This should be equitably distributed among all the citizens in proportion to their means.

14. All the citizens have a right to decide, either personally or by their representatives, as to the necessity of the public contribution; to grant this freely; to know to what uses it is put; and to fix the proportion, the mode of assessment and of collection and the duration of the taxes.

15. Society has the right to require of every public agent an account of his administration.

16. A society in which the observance of the law is not assured, nor the separation of powers defined, has no constitution at all.

17. Since property is an inviolable and sacred right, no one shall be deprived thereof except where public necessity, legally determined, shall clearly demand it, and then only on condition that the owner shall have been previously and equitably indemnified.

Analysis and Review Questions

1. A great portion of the document addresses questions of law. What are some of the rights of the citizen in the legal system, according to the document?
2. What does the declaration say about property?
3. What are every citizen's four natural rights?
4. Individual freedoms are also addressed in the Declaration. What are they?
5. What is decided about taxation in the document?

IMPERIALISM AND THE WHITE MAN'S BURDEN

About the Document

The quest for empire dominated latter nineteenth-century Western affairs. Virtually every major European nation and the United States engaged in some type of territorial acquisition. The reasons behind the imperialistic movement are numerous and include quests for raw materials and markets to fuel the growing industrialization of Western nations, nationalism, and militarism. Even racism played a role in the movement as many nations, including Great Britain, argued that their civilization was the fittest and should be spread to "backward" peoples. These motivations led to European entry into the African interior after 1885 and the carving up of China into spheres of influence by 1900. By this time, the United States had emerged as an industrial power and needed markets; safe harbors for its military and coaling stations for its navy; and protection for American investments in foreign nations. The Spanish-American War demonstrated America's commitment as Puerto Rico, Guam, and the Philippines were added as U.S. possessions.

Rudyard Kipling's poem "The White Man's Burden" was published in *McClure's Magazine* in February 1899, at a pivotal point in the American debate over imperialism. Debate raged in American political circles over imperialism, highlighted by the terms of the Treaty of Paris that would give the U.S. control of Puerto Rico and the Philippines. Kipling's poem urged the United States to take up the burden of "civilizing" the former Spanish colonies; a thankless task but a noble undertaking. Kipling's poem also contains several warnings, and these seemed to come true. Beginning in 1899 and lasting into 1902, native Filipinos revolted against American dominance of their homeland just as they had against the Spanish in 1896. A bitter three-year war followed as America fought to maintain control of its new possession.

The Document

THE WHITE MAN'S BURDEN

Take up the White Man's burden—
    Send forth the best ye breed—
Go, bind your sons to exile
    To serve your captives' need;
To wait, in heavy harness,
    On fluttered folk and wild—
Your new-caught sullen peoples,
    Half devil and half child.

Take up the White Man's burden—
    In patience to abide,
To veil the threat of terror
    And check the show of pride;
By open speech and simple,

An hundred times made plain,
To seek another's profit
    And work another's gain.

Take up the White Man's burden—
    The savage wars of peace—
Fill full the mouth of Famine,
    And bid the sickness cease;
And when your goal is nearest
    (The end for others sought)
Watch sloth and heathen folly
    Bring all your hope to nought.

Take up the White Man's burden—
    No iron rule of kings,
But toil of serf and sweeper—
    The tale of common things.
The ports ye shall not enter,
    The roads ye shall not tread,
Go, make them with your living
    And mark them with your dead.

Take up the White Man's burden,
    And reap his old reward—
The blame of those ye better
    The hate of those ye guard—
The cry of hosys ye humour
    (Ah, slowly!) toward the light:—
"Why brought ye us from bondage,
    Our loved Egyptian night?"

Take up the White Man's burden—
    Ye dare not stoop to less—
Nor call too loud on Freedom
    To cloak your weariness.
By all ye will or whisper,
    By all ye leave or do,
The silent sullen peoples
    Shall weigh your God and you.

Take up the White Man's burden!
    Have done with childish days—
The lightly-proffered laurel,
    The easy ungrudged praise:
Comes now, to search your manhood
    Through all the thankless years,
Cold, edged with dear-bought wisdom,
    The judgment of your peers.

    RUDYARD KIPLING

Analysis and Review Questions

1. What is the "White Man's Burden"?
2. Kipling's poem and imperialism in general have racist undertones. What are some found in the poem?
3. Do any of the articles sound familiar? Are they similar to the ideas expressed in the Constitution of the United States?
4. A tremendous amount of time and effort went into the preparation of the document. Do you think it was worth it?
5. What do you think was the historical motivation for issuing the document? What contemporary events may have forced the document to the forefront?

*Map 21.2
(Interactive)
Industrialization
in Europe*

CHADWICK'S REPORT ON SANITARY CONDITIONS

About the Document

Edwin Chadwick (1800–1890) took an active role in trying to reform the conditions of the working poor in England. He served on many commissions and enquiries until a typhoid and influenza outbreak forced Parliament to seek answers. Chadwick was appointed head of a commission that investigated the relationship between disease and the filthy sanitary conditions found in most cities. The report, published in 1842, is a blueprint for public health, and it included recommendations for fresh water, better sanitation, and cleanliness.

The Document

After as careful an examination of the evidence collected as I have been enabled to make, I beg leave to recapitulate the chief conclusions which that evidence appears to me to establish.

First, as to the extent and operation of the evils which are the subject of this inquiry:—

That the various forms of epidemic, endemic, and other disease caused, or aggravated, or propagated chiefly amongst the labouring classes by atmospheric impurities produced by decomposing animal and vegetable substances, by damp and filth, and close and overcrowded dwellings prevail amongst the population in every part of the kingdom, whether dwelling in separate houses, in rural villages, in small towns, in the larger towns—as they have been found to prevail in the lowest districts of the metropolis.

That such disease, wherever its attacks are frequent, is always found in connexion with the physical circumstances above specified, and that where those circumstances are removed by drainage, proper cleansing, better ventilation, and other means of diminishing atmospheric impurity, the frequency and intensity of such disease is abated; and where the removal of the noxious agencies appears to be complete, such disease almost entirely disappears.

That high prosperity in respect to employment and wages, and various and abundant food, have afforded to the labouring classes no exemptions from attacks of epidemic disease, which have been as frequent and as fatal in periods of commercial and manufacturing prosperity as in any others.

That the formation of all habits of cleanliness is obstructed by defective supplies of water.

That the annual loss of life from filth and bad ventilation are greater than the loss from death or wounds in any wars in which the country has been engaged in modern times.

That of the 43,000 cases of widowhood, and 112,000 cases of destitute orphanage relieved from the poor's rates in England and Wales alone, it appears that the greatest proportion of deaths of the heads of families occurred from the above specified and other removable causes; that their ages were under 45 years; that is to say, 13 years below the natural probabilities of life as shown by the experience of the whole population of Sweden.

That the public loss from the premature deaths of the heads of families is greater than can be represented by any enumeration of the pecuniary burdens consequent upon their sickness and death.

That, measuring the loss of working ability amongst large classes by the instances of gain, even from incomplete arrangements for the removal of noxious influences from places of work or from abodes, that this loss cannot be less than eight or ten years.

That the ravages of epidemics and other diseases do not diminish but tend to increase the pressure of population.

That in the districts where the mortality is greatest the births are not only sufficient to replace the numbers removed by death, but to add to the population.

That the younger population, bred up under noxious physical agencies, is inferior in physical organization and general health to a population preserved from the presence of such agencies.

That the population so exposed is less susceptible of moral influences, and the effects of education are more transient than with a healthy population.

That these adverse circumstances tend to produce an adult population short-lived, improvident, reckless, and intemperate, and with habitual avidity for sensual gratifications.

That these habits lead to the abandonment of all the conveniences and decencies of life, and especially lead to the overcrowding of their homes, which is destructive to the morality as well as the health of large classes of both sexes.

That defective town cleansing fosters habits of the most abject degradation and tends to the demoralization of large numbers of human beings, who subsist by means of what they find amidst the noxious filth accumulated in neglected streets and bye-places.

That the expenses of local public works are in general unequally and unfairly assessed, oppressively and uneconomically collected, by separate collections, wastefully expended in separate and inefficient operations by unskilled and practically irresponsible officers.

That the existing law for the protection of the public health and the constitutional machinery for reclaiming its execution, such as the Courts Leet, have fallen into desuetude, and are in the state indicated by the prevalence of the evils they were intended to prevent.

Secondly. As to the means by which the present sanitary condition of the labouring classes may be improved:—

The primary and most important measures, and at the same time the most practicable, and within the recognized province of public administration, are drainage, the removal of all refuse of habitations, streets, and roads, and the improvement of the supplies of water.

That the chief obstacles to the immediate removal of decomposing refuse of towns and habitations have been the expense and annoyance of the hand labour and cartage requisite for the purpose.

That this expense may be reduced to one-twentieth or to one-thirtieth, or rendered inconsiderable, by the use of water and self-acting means of removal by improved and cheaper sewers and drains.

That refuse when thus held in suspension in water may be most cheaply and innoxiously conveyed to any distance out of towns, and also in the best form for productive use, and that the loss and injury by the pollution of natural streams may be avoided.

That for all these purposes, as well as for domestic use, better supplies of water are absolutely necessary.

That for successful and economical drainage the adoption of geological areas as the basis of operations is requisite.

That appropriate scientific arrangements for public drainage would afford important facilities for private land-drainage, which is important for the health as well as sustenance of the labouring classes.

That the expense of public drainage, of supplies of water laid on in houses, and of means of improved cleansing would be a pecuniary gain, by diminishing the existing charges attendant on sickness and premature mortality.

That for the protection of the labouring classes and of the ratepayers against inefficiency and waste in all new structural arrangements for the protection of the public health, and to ensure public confidence that the expenditure will be beneficial, securities should be taken that all new local public works are devised and conducted by responsible officers qualified by the possession of the science and skill of civil engineers.

That the oppressiveness and injustice of levies for the whole immediate outlay on such works upon persons who have only short interests in the benefits may be avoided by care in spreading the expense over periods coincident with the benefits.

That by appropriate arrangements, 10 or 15 per cent. on the ordinary outlay for drainage might be saved, which on an estimate of the expense of the necessary structural alterations of one-third only of the existing tenements would be a saving of one million and a half sterling, besides the reduction of the future expenses of management.

That for the prevention of the disease occasioned by defective ventilation and other causes of impurity in places of work and other places where large numbers are assembled, and for the general promotion of the means necessary to prevent disease, that it would be good economy to appoint a district medical officer independent of private practice, and with the securities of special qualifications and responsibilities to initiate sanitary measures and reclaim the execution of the law.

That by the combinations of all these arrangements, it is probable that the full ensurable period of life indicated by the Swedish tables; that is, an increase of 13 years at least, may be extended to the whole of the labouring classes.

That the attainment of these and the other collateral advantages of reducing existing charges and expenditure are within the power of the legislature, and are dependent mainly on the securities taken for the application of practical science, skill, and economy in the direction of local public works.

And that the removal of noxious physical circumstances, and the promotion of civic, household, and personal cleanliness, are necessary to the improvement of the moral condition of the population; for that sound morality and refinement in manners and health are not long found co-existent with filthy habits amongst any class of the community.

Analysis and Review Questions

1. What are some of the sanitary problems noted by the commission?
2. What are the recommendations of the commission?
3. Why do you think conditions were so poor? Do you think the conditions were factors in the high mortality rates? Why?

WEB LINKS

Selections from Longman World History—Primary Sources and Case Studies

http://longmanworldhistory.com
The following additional readings and case studies can be found on the Web site.
Document 21.2, The Declaration of Independence
Document 21.3, Industrial Society and Factory Conditions
Document 21.6, The Seneca Falls Convention
Document 21.8, Platform of the American Anti-Imperialist League
Document 21.9, Recommendations of the Salem Convention
Case Study 21.1, All *Men* Are Created Equal?
Case Study 21.2, Industrial Side Effects
Case Study 21.3, Conflicting Views on Imperialism

Declaration of Independence

http://memory.LOC.gov/const/declar.html

National Archives and Record Administration. This site provides a detailed history of the Declaration of Independence, including sections on the history of the document, the parchment used, and even the ink used to write the document. The site also discusses the problems associated with the preservation of the document. From this site, readers can link to the exhibit site, find pictures of the document in its current state, and link to further reading on the document. An excellent starting point for further research.

Industrial Revolution

http://dewey.chs.chico.k12.ca.us/irev.html
Chico High School organized a series of sites dedicated to the history of the Industrial Revolution. Links to different Industrial Revolution sites present a wide-ranging view of the accomplishments, inventors, and effects of industrialization.

Marxism

http://www.marxists.org
Comprehensive site dedicated to the founding and evolution of Marxism. The site includes biographies of Karl Marx and Friedrich Engels and other writers of Communist literature. It maintains an archive of documents concerning Communist theory, an encyclopedia of Marxism, and an image gallery.

Imperialism

http://www.boondocksnet.com/kipling
Site dedicated to the anti-imperialist cause. Thorough compilation of sources connected to opposition to imperialism in the United States. Cartoons, poems, and essays are linked for exploration.

http://www.smplanet.com/imperialism/toc.html
This site provides a simple outline of American imperialist efforts. Numerous pictures, links to speeches, and various maps provided. Focus is on the United States; there is no mention of European imperialism.

CHAPTER 22

Eastern Europe and Russia, 1750–1914

The development from 1750 to 1914 takes us from absolutism through the Enlightenment, the Industrial Revolution, and then to the French Revolution and Napoleon. The conservative culture of the nineteenth century was not strong enough to stem the tide of nationalism released by Napoleon and his wars of empire. Romanticism and socialism would have their effects on the thinking and politics of the nineteenth century. The period ended with European imperialism, the second Industrial Revolution, and the coming of World War I. In Eastern Europe, Russia, the Austrian Empire, and the Ottoman Empire dominated.

In Russia, Catherine the Great came to the throne with many ideas inspired by the French philosophers whom she adored. After benefiting from a coup d'etat that placed her on the throne, Catherine set out to rule as an enlightened monarch. She wanted to bring three things to Russia: sophisticated culture, domestic reform (via a new law code), and territorial expansion to keep the nobles rewarded with new lands. This same period witnessed the movement of Austria toward enlightenment under Maria Theresa and Joseph II. Despite being involved in the diplomatic turmoil of the time, both moved toward reform.

By the mid-nineteenth century, Russia was in crisis. Despite all the efforts at Westernization over the preceding 100 years, Russia remained a backward, agrarian society. The Crimean War, fought from 1853 to 1856, showed just how far behind Russia had fallen. Russia needed to reorganize her infrastructure and military, industrialize, and reform serfdom. In 1861 Alexander II freed the serfs. They were allowed to buy land, but only collectively, as a village, and at very high prices. There were reforms in the government and in education, as well. In 1881 Alexander II was assassinated. His successor, Alexander III, was a reactionary ruler, but even then, economic modernization moved forward. Foreigners were encouraged to visit. Steel and oil production boomed.

Then, the 1905 Russo-Japanese War began. Defeat in the Russo-Japanese War brought unrest at home. Business leaders, professionals, factory workers, and peasants all had grievances. A peaceful march on the Winter Palace in January

1905 turned into a slaughter, as imperial troops opened fire on the crowd. This infamous "Bloody Sunday" was the beginning of serious problems for the tsar. The uprising forced the tsar to sign the October Manifesto, which guaranteed fundamental civil liberties, promised to extend the right to vote, and proclaimed that no law would be passed without the approval of the Duma, or state parliament. By the time the first Duma met in May 1906, there was a new constitution. The tsar, however, would have absolute veto power. By World War I, while still an agrarian-based country, Russia had a conservative constitutional monarchy and was slowly modernizing.

The nineteenth century saw growing nationalism everywhere in Europe, but it was never more evident than in the unification efforts of Germany and Italy and the minority movements in the Austrian Empire. As a result of the Austro-Prussian War, Austria had to give virtual independence to the Magyars in Hungary, creating the Austro-Hungarian Empire. Each side in this dual monarchy ruled its own half. Within the Hungarian area, the Magyars moved to solidify their control. They dealt with minorities in much the same way that Austria had tried to deal with them. The forces of nationalism began to weaken and would ultimately destroy the Austro-Hungarian Empire and bring Europe to World War I.

Image 22.1
Catherine
the Great

Map 22.1
(Interactive)
The Growth of
Russia to 1914

CATHERINE THE GREAT'S CONSTITUTION

About the Document

Catherine II ruled Russia during a period of epic expansion in which Russia added nearly 20,000 square miles of territory to its domain. In order to administer the new lands and ensure the fair treatment of their inhabitants, Catherine ordered a royal commission in 1767 to compose a series of new laws that would fully reflect her vision for the Russian Empire. She provided the commission with lengthy instructions concerning the issues and principles to be woven into the new law code.

Catherine's constitution, or "Great Instructions," reflected her admiration of the French Enlightenment and Enlightenment thought. She wrote important Enlightenment figures regularly and even paid for Diderot's library. She subsidized his "Encyclopedia" when the French would not.

Catherine's "Instructions" were based on the premise that Russia was a European state and should be governed by European principles. This premise assumed Russia would be governed by an absolute monarch whose authority rested in the rule of law.

Catherine leaned on Montesquieu's *L'Esprit des lois* and Beccaria's ideas on crime and punishment. The "Instructions" were very general in scope and provided no real legislative structure. The royal commission convened in Moscow in July 1767, but when the Turkish War broke out in December, the commission adjourned, and no section of code was ever completed. Catherine's grand plan never came to fruition.

The Document

O Lord my God, hearken unto me, and instruct me; that I may administer Judgment unto thy People; as thy sacred Laws direct to judge with Righteousness!

The Instructions to the Commissioners for Composing a New Code of Laws

1. The Christian Law teaches us to do mutual Good to one another, as much as possibly we can.

2. Laying this down as a fundamental Rule prescribed by that Religion, which has taken, or ought to take Root in the Hearts of the whole People; we cannot but suppose, that every honest Man in the Community is, or will be, desirous of seeing his native Country at the very Summit of Happiness, Glory, Safety, and Tranquillity.

3. And that every Individual Citizen in particular must wish to see himself protected by Laws, which should not distress him in his Circumstances, but, on the Contrary, should defend him from all Attempts of others, that are repugnant to this fundamental Rule.

4. In order therefore to proceed to a speedy Execution of what *We* expect from such a general Wish, *We*, fixing the Foundation upon the above first-mentioned Rule, ought to begin with an Inquiry into the natural Situation of this Empire.

5. For those Laws have the greatest Conformity with Nature, whose particular Regulations are best adapted to the Situation and Circumstances of the People, for whom they are instituted.

This natural Situation is described in the three following Chapters.

Chapter I

6. Russia is an European State.

7. This is clearly demonstrated by the following Observations: The Alterations which *Peter the Great* undertook in Russia succeeded with the greater Ease, because the Manners, which prevailed at that Time, and had been introduced amongst us by a Mixture of different Nations, and the Conquest of foreign Territories, were quite unsuitable to the Climate. *Peter the First*, by introducing the Manners and Customs of Europe among the European People in his Dominions, found at that Time such Means as even he himself was not sanguine enough to expect.

Chapter II

8. The Possessions of the Russian Empire extend upon the terrestrial Globe to 32 Degrees of Latitude, and to 165 of Longitude.

9. The Sovereign is absolute; for there is no other Authority but that which centers in his single Person, that can act with a Vigour proportionate to the Extent of such a vast Dominion.

10. The Extent of the Dominion requires an absolute Power to be vested in that Person who rules over it. It is expedient so to be, that the quick Dispatch of Affairs, sent from distant Parts, might make ample Amends for the Delay occasioned by the great Distance of the Places.

11. Every other Form of Government whatsoever would not only have been prejudicial to Russia, but would even have proved its entire Ruin.

12. Another Reason is; That it is better to be subject to the Laws under one Master, than to be subservient to many.

13. What is the true End of Monarchy? Not to deprive People of their natural Liberty; but to correct their Actions, in order to attain the *Supreme Good.*

14. The Form of Government, therefore, which best attains this End, and at the same Time sets less Bounds than others to natural Liberty, is that which coincides with the Views and Purposes of rational Creatures, and answers the End, upon which we ought to fix a steadfast Eye in the Regulations of civil Polity.

15. The Intention and the End of Monarchy, is the Glory of the Citizens, of the State, and of the Sovereign.

16. But, from this Glory, a Sense of Liberty arises in a People governed by a Monarch; which may produce in these States as much Energy in transacting the most important Affairs, and may contribute as much to the Happiness of the Subjects, as even Liberty itself.

Chapter III

17. *Of the Safety of the Institutions of Monarchy.*

18. The intermediate Powers, subordinate to, and depending upon the supreme Power, form the essential Part of monarchical Government.

19. *I* have said, that the intermediate Powers, subordinate and depending, proceed from the supreme Power; as in the very Nature of the Thing the Sovereign is the Source of all imperial and civil Power.

20. The Laws, which form the Foundation of the State, send out certain Courts of Judicature, through which, as through smaller Streams, the Power of the Government is poured out, and diffused.

21. The Laws allow these Courts of Judicature to remonstrate, that such or such an Injunction is unconstitutional, and prejudicial, obscure, and impossible to be carried into Execution; and direct, beforehand, to which Injunction one ought to pay Obedience, and in what Manner one ought to conform to it. These Laws undoubtedly constitute the firm and immoveable Basis of every State.

Chapter IV

22. There must be a political Body, to whom the Care and strict Execution of these Laws ought to be confided.

23. This Care, and strict Execution of the Laws, can be no where so properly fixed as in certain Courts of Judicature, which announce to the People the newly-made Laws, and revive those, which are forgotten, or obsolete.

24. And it is the Duty of these Courts of Judicature to examine carefully those Laws which they receive from the Sovereign, and to remonstrate, if they find any Thing in them repugnant to the fundamental Constitution of the State, &c. which has been already remarked above in the third Chapter, and twenty-first Article.

25. But if they find nothing in them of that Nature, they enter them in the Code of Laws already established in the State, and publish them to the whole Body of the People.

26. In Russia the Senate is the political Body, to which the Care and due Execution of the Laws is confided.

27. All other Courts of Judicature may, and ought to remonstrate with the same Propriety, to the Senate, and even to the Sovereign himself, as was already mentioned above.

28. Should any One inquire, wherein the Care and due Execution of the Laws consists? I answer, That the Care, and due Execution of the Laws, produces particu-

lar Instructions; in consequence of which, the before-mentioned Courts of Judicature, instituted to the End that, by their Care, the Will of the Sovereign might be obeyed in a Manner comformable to the fundamental Laws and Constitution of the State, are obliged to act, in the Discharge of their Duty, according to the Rules prescribed.

29. These Instructions will prevent the People from transgressing the Injunctions of the Sovereign with impunity; but, at the same Time, will protect them from the Insults, and ungovernable Passions of others.

30. For, on the one Hand, they justify the Penalties prepared for those who transgress the Laws; and, on the other, they confirm the Justice of that Refusal to enter Laws repugnant to the good Order of the State, amongst those which are already approved of, or to act by those Laws in the Administration of Justice, and the general Business of the whole Body of the People.

Chapter V

31. *Of the Situation of the People in general.*

32. It is the greatest Happiness for a Man to be so circumstanced, that, if his Passions should prompt him to be mischievous, he should still think it more for his Interest not to give Way to them.

33. The Laws ought to be so framed, as to secure the Safety of every Citizen as much as possible.

34. The Equality of the Citizens consists in this; that they should all be subject to the same Laws.

35. This Equality requires Institutions so well adapted, as to prevent the Rich from oppressing those who are not so wealthy as themselves, and converting all the Charges and Employments intrusted to them as Magistrates only, to their own private Emolument.

36. General or political Liberty does not consist in that licentious Notion, *That a Man may do whatever he pleases.*

37. In a State or Assemblage of People that live together in a Community, where there are Laws, Liberty can only consist *in doing that which every One ought to do, and not to be constrained to do that which One ought not to do.*

38. A Man ought to form in his own Mind an exact and clear Idea of what Liberty is. *Liberty is the Right of doing whatsoever the Laws allow:* And if any one Citizen could do what the Laws forbid, there would be no more Liberty; because others would have an equal Power of doing the same.

39. The political Liberty of a Citizen is the Peace of Mind arising from the Consciousness, that every Individual enjoys his peculiar Safety; and in order that the People might attain this Liberty, the Laws ought to be so framed, that no one Citizen should stand in Fear of another; but that all of them should stand in Fear of the same Laws.

Chapter VI

40. *Of Laws in general.*

41. Nothing ought to be forbidden by the Laws, but what may be prejudicial, either to every Individual in particular, or to the whole Community in general.

42. All Actions, which comprehend nothing of this Nature, are in nowise cognizable by the Laws; which are made only with the View of procuring the greatest possible Advantage and Tranquillity to the People, who live under their Protection.

43. To preserve Laws from being violated, they ought to be so good, and so well furnished with all Expedients, tending to procure the greatest possible Good to the People; that every Individual might be fully convinced, that it was his Interest, as well as Duty, to preserve those Laws inviolable.

44. And this is the most exalted Pitch of Perfection which we ought to labour to attain to.

. . .

57. The Legislation ought to adapt its Laws to the general Sense of a Nation. We do nothing so well as what we do freely and uncontrouled, and following the natural Bent of our own Inclinations.

58. In order to introduce better Laws, it is essentially necessary to prepare the Minds of the People for their Reception. But that it may never be pleaded in Excuse, that it is impossible to carry even the most useful Affairs into Execution, because the Minds of the People are not yet prepared for it; you must, in that Case, take the Trouble upon yourselves to prepare them; and, by these Means, you will already have done a great Part of the Work.

59. Laws are the peculiar and distinct Institutions of the Legislator; but Manners and Customs are the Institutions of the whole Body of the People.

60. Consequently, if there should be a Necessity of making great Alterations amongst the People for their greater Benefit, that must be corrected by Laws, which has been instituted by Laws, and that must be amended by Custom, which has been introduced by Custom; and it is extreme bad Policy to alter that by Law, which ought to be altered by Custom.

61. There are Means of preventing the Growth of Crimes, and these are the Punishments inflicted by the Laws. At the same Time there are Means for introducing an Alteration in Customs, and these are Examples.

62. Besides, the more a People have an Intercourse with one another, the more easy it is for them to introduce a Change in their Customs.

63. In a Word, every Punishment, which is not inflicted through Necessity, is tyrannical. The Law has not its Source merely from Power. Things indifferent in their Nature, do not come under the Cognizance of the Laws.

Chapter VII

64. *Of the Laws in particular.*

65. Laws carried to the Extremity of Right, are productive of the Extremity of Evil.

. . .

123. The Usage of Torture is contrary to all the Dictates of Nature and Reason; even Mankind itself cries out against it, and demands loudly the total Abolition of it.

. . .

180. That Law, therefore, is highly beneficial to the Community where it is established, which ordains that every Man shall be judged by his Peers and Equals. For when the Fate of a Citizen is in Question, all Prejudices arising from the Difference of Rank

or Fortune should be stifled; because they ought to have no Influence between the Judges and the Parties accused.

. . .

194. No Man ought to be looked upon as guilty, before he has received his judicial Sentence; nor can the Laws deprive him of their Protection, before it is proved that he has forfeited all Right to it. What Right therefore can Power give to any to inflict Punishment upon a Citizen at a Time, when it is yet dubious, whether he is Innocent or guilty?

. . .

269. It seems too, that the Method of exacting their Revenues, newly invented by the Lords, diminishes both the Inhabitants, and the Spirit of Agriculture in Russia. Almost all the villages are heavily taxed. The Lords, who seldom or never reside in their Villages, lay an Impost on every Head of one, two, and even five Rubles, without the least Regard to the Means by which their Peasants may be able to raise this Money.

Map 22.2
Russian Serfs

270. It is highly necessary that the Law should prescribe a Rule to the Lords, for a more judicious Method of raising their Revenues; and oblige them to levy such a Tax, as tends least to separate the Peasant from his House and Family; this would be the Means by which Agriculture would become more extensive, and Population be more increased in the Empire.

Analysis and Review Questions

1. What were the reasons for declaring the power of the Sovereign of Russia absolute?
2. What was the foundation of the "political body," or Courts of Jurisdiction?
3. How does Catherine define liberty?
4. What are examples of Enlightenment ideas found in these instructions?
5. How did Catherine regard the lords' methods of taxing the peasants?

ADAM MICKIEWICZ: EXCERPTS FROM "THE BOOKS OF THE POLISH NATION"

About the Document

By 1830 Poland was under Russian rule. Nicholas I (1825–1855) visited Poland in 1828, took the oath of the Polish constitution, and was crowned King of Poland. Nicholas's relationship with Poland was uneasy because prominent Poles had been unjustly arrested and tried for taking part in the Decembrist uprising in Russia.

Nicholas's reaction to the 1830 uprisings in France and Belgium inflamed the Poles. They were upset that he was planning to intervene on the side of the "legitimate" rules in those countries and use Polish units in the army. Because of this, and the arrest of the Polish revolutionary leaders, it seemed like the time to act.

An uprising began in November 1830 when the residence of the Grand Duke Constantine was invaded, and the Russian troops attacked. Constantine withdrew to Russia. While at first the uprising was controlled by the aristocratic and conservative elements, it was quickly taken over by radicals. The Polish Diet deposed Nicholas.

Fighting followed until October 1831. The Poles were woefully outnumbered, but inflicted heavy losses on the Russians. The Poles appealed to Austria, Prussia, England, and France to come to their aid, but no aid was forthcoming. Finally, the uprising collapsed. From then on, Poland would be declared an "invisible part" of Russia. While Polish customs and rights were theoretically protected, even the Catholic Church was subjected to extreme restrictons by the Russian Orthodox Church. Polish authors were not mentioned in the press, and Russian was taught in the schools. While the other countries of Europe did nothing during this time, the treatment of the Poles would be one factor in the coming Crimean War.

In the following document, Adam Mickiewicz writes of the heroic efforts of his Polish countrymen. The use of Romantic verse gives his poem an epic feel and wraps the uprising in spiritual terms.

The Document

In the beginning there was belief in one God, and there was freedom in the world. And there were no laws, only the will of God, and there were no lords and slaves, only patriarchs and their children.

But later the people denied the one God, and made for themselves idols, and bowed themselves down to them, and slew in their honor bloody offerings, and waged war for the honor of their idols.

Therefore God sent upon the idolaters the greatest punishment, which is slavery.

. . .

Finally in idolatrous Europe there rose three rulers; the name of the first was Frederick the Second of Prussia°, the name of the second was Catherine the Second of Russia, the name of the third was Maria Theresa of Austria.

And this was a Satanic trinity, contrary to the Divine Trinity, and was in the manner of a mock and a derision of all that is holy.

Frederick, whose name signifieth friend of peace, contrived wars and pillage throughout his whole life, and was like Satan eternally panting for war, who in derision should be called Christ, the God of peace.

. . .

Now Catherine signifieth in Greek pure, but she was the lewdest of women, and it was as though the shameless Venus had called herself a pure virgin.

And this Catherine assembled a council for the establishing of laws, that she might turn lawmaking into a mockery, for the rights of her neighbors she overthrew and destroyed.

And this Catherine proclaimed that she protected freedom of conscience or tolerance, that she might make a mock of freedom of conscience, for she forced millions of

Prussia: One of the most powerful German states. Part of Prussia was just west of Poland.

her neighbors to change their faith. And Maria Theresa bore the name of the most meek and immaculate Mother of the Savior, that she might make a mock of humility and holiness.

For she was a proud she-devil, and carried on war to make subject the lands of others.

. . .

Then this trinity, seeing that not yet were the people sufficiently foolish and corrupt, fashioned a new idol, the most abominable of all, and they called this idol Interest, and this idol was not known among the pagans of old.

. . .

But the Polish nation alone did not bow down to the new idol, and did not have in its language the expression for christening it in Polish, neither for christening its worshipers, whom it calls by the French word *egoists*.

The Polish nation worshiped God, knowing that he who honoreth God giveth honor to everything that is good.

The Polish nation then from the beginning to the end was true to the God of its ancestors.

Its kings and men of knightly rank never assaulted any believing nation, but defended Christendom from the pagans and barbarians who brought slavery.

And the Polish kings went to the defense of Christians in distant lands, King Wladislaw to Varna, and King Jan to Vienna, to the defense of the east and the west.

And never did their kings and men of knightly rank seize neighboring lands by force, but they received the nations into brotherhood, uniting them with themselves by the gracious gift of faith and freedom.

And God rewarded them, for a great nation. Lithuania, united itself with Poland, as husband with wife, two souls in one body. And there was never before this such a union of nations. But hereafter there shall be.

For that union and marriage of Lithuania and Poland is the symbol of the future union of all Christian peoples in the name of faith and freedom.

And God gave unto the Polish kings and knights freedom, that all might be called brothers, both the richest and the poorest. And such freedom never was before. But hereafter there shall be.

The king and the men of knightly rank received into their brotherhood still more people; they received whole armies and whole tribes. And the number of brothers became as great as a nation, and in no nation were there so many people free and calling each other brothers as in Poland.

And finally, on the Third of May, the king and the knightly body determined to make all Poles brothers, at first the burghers and later the peasants.

And they called the brothers the nobility, because they had become noble, that is had become brothers with the Lachs, who were men free and equal.

And they wished to bring it about that every Christian in Poland should be ennobled and called a Nobleman, for a token that he should have a noble soul and always be ready to die for freedom.

Just as of old they called each man accepting the gospel a Christian, for a token that he was ready to shed his blood for Christ.

Nobility then was to be the baptism of freedom, and every one who was ready to die for freedom was to be baptized of the law and of the sword.

And finally Poland said: "Whosoever will come to me shall be free and equal, for I am Freedom."

But the kings when they heard of this were terrified in their hearts and said: "We banished freedom from the earth; but lo, it returneth in the person of a just nation, that doth not bow down to our idols! Come, let us slay this nation." And they plotted treachery among themselves.

And the King of Prussia came and kissed the Polish Nation and greeted it, saying: "My ally," but already he had sold it for thirty cities of Great Poland, even as Judas for thirty pieces of silver.

And the two other rulers fell upon and bound the Polish Nation. And Gaul° was judge and said: "Verily I find no fault in this nation, and France my wife, a timid woman, is tormented with evil dreams; nevertheless, take for yourselves and martyr this nation." And he washed his hands.

And the ruler of France said: "We cannot ransom this innocent nation by our blood or by our money, for my blood and my money belong to me, but the blood and money of my nation belong to my nation."

And this ruler uttered the last blasphemy against Christ, for Christ taught that the blood of the Son of Man belongeth to all our brother men.

And when the ruler had uttered these words, then the crosses fell from the towers of the godless capital, for the sign of Christ could no longer shine upon a people worshiping the idol Interest.

And this ruler was called Casimir-Périer, a Slavic first name and a Roman last name. His first name signifieth corrupter or annihilator of peace, and his last name signifieth, from the word perire or périr, destroyer or son of destruction. And these two names are anti-Christian. And they shall be alike accursed among the Slavic race and among the Roman race.

And this man rent the league of peoples as that Jewish priest rent his clothes upon hearing the voice of Christ.

And they martyred the Polish Nation and laid it in the grave, and the kings cried out: "We have slain and we have buried Freedom."

But they cried out foolishly, for in committing the last sin they filled up the measure of their iniquities, and their power was coming to an end at the time when they exulted most.

For the Polish Nation did not die: its body lieth in the grave, but its spirit hath descended from the earth, that is from public life, to the abyss, that is to the private life of people who suffer slavery in their country and outside of their country, that it may see their sufferings.

But on the third day the soul shall return to the body, and the Nation shall arise and free all the peoples of Europe from slavery.

And already two days have gone by. One day passed with the first capture of Warsaw, and the second day passed with the second capture of Warsaw, and the third day shall begin, but shall not pass.

And as after the resurrection of Christ bloody offerings ceased in all the world, so after the resurrection of the Polish Nation wars shall cease in all Christendom.

Gaul: The Roman name for the region that is now France.

Analysis and Review Questions

1. What does the author say is the "satanic trinity"? Why does he say this?
2. How does the author describe the history of Poland's relations with its neighbors?
3. How does the author describe the actions taken by Polish kings and noblemen on behalf of the Polish people? What evidence do you see that makes this description seem like an over-glorification of the relationship?
4. Compare the author's description of Poland with that of Prussia.
5. How does the author compare the suppression of Poland's uprising to the Crucifixion?

*Image 22.2
Early Russian
Factory*

J. A. MACGAHAN: THE TURKISH ATROCITIES IN BULGARIA

About the Document

Although a Middle Eastern empire in location, the Ottoman Empire dominated Eastern Europe for centuries. The conquered peoples were ruled ruthlessly by the Turks, who mercilessly put down uprising after uprising. The growing sense of nationalism in the nineteenth century would surface over and over In a multitude of uprisings. Slowly, the countries of Western Europe would begin to support autonomy for Eastern European and Balkan countries. This support was not always for altruistic reasons. Britain and France had political reasons as well.

In 1876 the Bulgarians revolted against Turkish rule. The actions of the Turkish troops in suppressing the revolt were savage in the eyes of Western Europeans. J. A. MacGahan, an American correspondent, filed the following report about his experiences in Bulgaria. The account so moved the British Prime Minister, William Gladstone, that he felt the West must do something about the situation of Bulgaria. Partly because of this report, the Congress of Berlin in 1878 granted the Bulgarians autonomous status. MacGahan became known as the "Liberator of Bulgaria."

The Document

Down in the bottom of one of these hollows we could make out a village, which our guide informed us it would still take us an hour and a half to reach, although it really seemed to be very near. This was the village of Batak, which we were in search of. The hillsides were covered with little fields of wheat and rye, that were golden with ripeness. But although the harvest was ripe, and over ripe, although in many places the well-filled ears had broken down the fast-decaying straw that could no longer hold them aloft, and were now lying flat, there was no sign of reapers trying to save them. The fields were as deserted as the little valley, and the harvest was rotting in the soil. In an hour we had neared the village.

As we approached our attention was directed to some dogs on a slope overlooking the town. We turned aside from the road, and, passing over the debris of two or three walls, and through several gardens, urged our horses up the ascent towards the dogs. They barked at us in an angry manner, and then ran off into the adjoining fields. I observed nothing peculiar as we mounted, until my horse stumbled. When looking down I perceived he had stepped on a human skull partly hid among the grass. It was quite dry and hard, and might, to all appearances, have been there for two or three years, so well had the dogs done their work. A few steps further there was another, and beside it part of a skeleton, likewise white and dry. As we ascended, bones, skeletons, and skulls became more frequent, but here they had not been picked so clean, for there were fragments of half-dry, half-putrid flesh still clinging to them. At last we came to a kind of little plateau or shelf on the hillside, where the ground was nearly level, with the exception of a little indentation where the head of a hollow broke through. We rode towards this, with the intention of crossing it, but all suddenly drew rein with an exclamation of horror, for right before us, almost beneath our horses' feet, was a sight that made us shudder. It was a heap of skulls, intermingled with bones from all parts of the human body, skeletons, nearly entire, rotting clothing, human hair, and putrid flesh lying there in one foul heap, around which the grass was growing luxuriantly. It emitted a sickening odour, like that of a dead horse, and it was here the dogs had been seeking a hasty repast when our untimely approach interrupted them.

In the midst of this heap I could distinguish one slight skeleton form still enclosed in a chemise, the skull wrapped about with a coloured handkerchief, and the bony ankles encased in the embroidered footless stockings worn by the Bulgarian girls. We looked about us. The ground was strewed with bones in every direction, where the dogs had carried them off to gnaw them at their leisure. At the distance of a hundred yards beneath us lay the town. As seen from our standpoint, it reminded one somewhat of the ruins of Herculaneum or Pompeii.

There was not a roof left, not a whole wall standing; all was a mass of ruins, from which arose, as we listened, a low plaintive wail, like the 'keening'° of the Irish over their dead, that filled the little valley and gave it voice . . .

On the other side of the way were the skeletons of two children lying side by side, partly covered with stones, and with frightful sabre cuts in their little skulls. The number of children killed in these massacres is something enormous. They were often spitted on bayonets, and we have several stories from eye witnesses who saw little babies carried about the streets, both here and at Otluk-kui, on the point of bayonets. The reason is simple. When a Mahometan has killed a certain number of infidels, he is sure of Paradise, no matter what his sins may be. Mahomet probably intended that only armed men should count, but the ordinary Mussulman takes the precept in broader acceptation, and counts women and children as well. Here in Batak the Bashi-Bazouks, in order to swell the count, ripped open pregnant women, and killed the unborn infants. As we approached the middle of the town, bones, skeletons, and skulls became more numerous. There was not a house beneath the ruins of which we did not perceive human remains, and the street besides was strewn with them. Before many of the doorways women were walking up and down wailing their funeral chant. One of them caught me by the arm and led me inside of the walls, and there in one corner, half covered with stones and mortar, were the remains of another young girl, with her long hair flowing wildly about among the stones and dust. And the mother fairly shrieked with agony, and beat her head madly against the wall. I could only turn round and walk out sick at heart, leaving her alone with her skeleton. A few steps further on sat a woman on a doorstep, rocking herself to and fro, and uttering moans heartrending beyond anything I could have imagined. Her head was buried in her hands, while her fingers were unconsciously twisting and tearing her hair as she gazed into her

keening: A lamentation for the dead uttered in a loud wailing voice or in a wordless cry.

lap, where lay three little skulls with the hair still clinging to them. How did the mother come to be saved, while the children were slaughtered? Who knows? Perhaps she was away from the village when the massacre occurred. Perhaps she had escaped with a babe in her arms, leaving these to be saved by the father; or perhaps, most fearful, most pitiful of all, she had been so terror-stricken that she had abandoned the three poor little ones to their fate and saved her own life by flight. If this be so, no wonder she is tearing her hair in that terribly unconscious way as she gazes at the three little heads lying in her lap . . .

The church was not a very large one, and it was surrounded by a low stone wall, enclosing a small churchyard about fifty yards wide by seventy-five long. At first we perceive nothing in particular, and the stench is so great that we scarcely care to look about us, but we see that the place is heaped up with stones and rubbish to the height of five or six feet above the level of the street, and upon inspection we discover that what appeared to be a mass of stones and rubbish is in reality an immense heap of human bodies covered over with a thin layer of stones. The whole of the little churchyard is heaped up with them to the depth of three or four feet, and it is from here that the fearful odour comes. Some weeks after the massacre, orders were sent to bury the dead. But the stench at that time had become so deadly that it was impossible to execute the order, or even to remain in the neighbourhood of the village. The men sent to perform the work contented themselves with burying a few bodies, throwing a little earth over others as they lay, and here in the churchyard they had tried to cover this immense heap of festering humanity by throwing in stones and rubbish over the walls, without daring to enter. They had only partially succeeded. The dogs had been at work there since, and now could be seen projecting from this monster grave, heads, arms, legs, feet, and hands, in horrid confusion. We were told there were three thousand people lying here in this little churchyard alone, and we could well believe it. It was a fearful sight—a sight to haunt one through life. There were little curly heads there in that festering mass, crushed down by heavy stones; little feet not as long as your finger on which the flesh was dried hard, by the ardent heat before it had time to decompose; little baby hands stretched out as if for help; babes that had died wondering at the bright gleam of sabres and the red hands of the fierce-eyed men who wielded them; children who had died shrinking with fright and terror; young girls who had died weeping and sobbing and begging for mercy; mothers who died trying to shield their little ones with their own weak bodies, all lying there together, festering in one horrid mass. They were silent enough now. There are no tears nor cries, no weeping, no shrieks of terror, nor prayers for mercy. The harvests are rotting in the fields, and the reapers are rotting here in the churchyard.

Analysis and Review Questions

1. How does the reporter describe the scene, as he approaches the village of Batak?
2. Describe what has happened in the village itself.
3. What picture does the writer give of the "Mussulman" and the reasons for the slaughter?
4. What might be some other reasons, besides the humanitarian reason, that the Western European nations would use this document in giving Bulgaria autonomy?
5. What elements of nationalism do you see in the account?

BORIJOVE JEVTIC: THE MURDER OF ARCHDUKE FRANZ FERDINAND AT SARAJEVO, 28 JUNE 1914

About the Document

Throughout the nineteenth century, the forces of conservatism, liberalism, social-ism, and nationalism had been working against each other—sometimes with cat-astrophic effects. Uprisings, rebellions, and all-out war occurred throughout the century. Nowhere was nationalism so evident as in the Austro-Hungarian Empire. As ethnic groups across Europe began to see themselves as distinct from other groups, there was great pressure for them to obtain their own countries. The Hungarians had already been successful in gaining autonomy under the Empire, making the Austro-Hungarian Empire a dual monarchy.

Nationalism was more of a problem in an era when the major countries of Europe were convinced that peace could be secured by bringing smaller and weaker countries under their control. Nationalistic feelings reached their height just before and after the beginning of the twentieth century.

The document below describes how, in the spring of 1914, the Archduke Franz Ferdinand had come on a state visit to Sarajevo in the recently annexed re-gion of Bosnia. As heir to the Austrian throne, Ferdinand was to view troop ma-neuvers, despite concerns about terrorist activity from Bosnians who wanted an independent country. A terrorist who was part of the Serbian Black Hand plot to assassinate Ferdinand writes his description of what happened on the fateful day of 28 June 1914.

The Document

A tiny clipping from a newspaper mailed without comment from a secret band of terrorists in Zagreb, a capital of Croatia, to their comrades in Belgrade, was the torch which set the world afire with war in 1914. That bit of paper wrecked old proud em-pires. It gave birth to new, free nations.

I was one of the members of the terrorist band in Belgrade which received it and, in those days, I and my companions were regarded as desperate criminals. A price was on our heads. Today my little band is seen in a different light, as pioneer patriots. It is recognized that our secret plans hatched in an obscure café in the capital of old Serbia, have led to the independence of the new Yugoslavia, the united nation set free from Austrian domination.

The little clipping was from the *Srobobran*, a Croatian journal of limited circulation, and consisted of a short telegram from Vienna. This telegram declared that the Austrian Archduke Franz Ferdinand would visit Sarajevo, the capital of Bosnia, 28 June, to direct army manoeuvres in the neighbouring mountains.

It reached our meeting place, the café called Zeatna Moruana, one night the latter part of April, 1914 . . . At a small table in a very humble café, beneath a flickering gas jet we sat and read it. There was no advice nor admonition sent with it. Only four letters and two numerals were sufficient to make us unanimous, without discussion, as to what we should do about it. They were contained in the fateful date, 28 June.

How dared Franz Ferdinand, not only the representative of the oppressor but in his own person an arrogant tyrant, enter Sarajevo on that day? Such an entry was a studied insult.

28 June is a date engraved deeply in the heart of every Serb, so that the day has a name of its own. It is called the vidovnan. It is the day on which the old Serbian kingdom was conquered by the Turks at the battle of Amselfelde in 1389. It is also the day on which in the second Balkan War the Serbian arms took glorious revenge on the Turk for his old victory and for the years of enslavement.

That was no day for Franz Ferdinand, the new oppressor, to venture to the very doors of Serbia for a display of the force of arms which kept us beneath his heel.

Our decision was taken almost immediately. Death to the tyrant!

Then came the matter of arranging it. To make his death certain twenty-two members of the organization were selected to carry out the sentence. At first we thought we would choose the men by lot. But here Gavrilo Princip intervened. Princip is destined to go down in Serbian history as one of her greatest heroes. From the moment Ferdinand's death was decided upon he took an active leadership in its planning. Upon his advice we left the deed to members of our band who were in and around Sarajevo under his direction and that of Gabrinovic, a linotype operator on a Serbian newspaper. Both were regarded as capable of anything in the cause.

The fateful morning dawned. Two hours before Franz Ferdinand arrived in Sarajevo all the twenty-two conspirators were in their allotted positions, armed and ready. They were distributed 500 yards apart over the whole route along which the Archduke must travel from the railroad station to the town hall.

When Franz Ferdinand and his retinue drove from the station they were allowed to pass the first two conspirators. The motor cars were driving too fast to make an attempt feasible and in the crowd were Serbians: throwing a grenade would have killed many innocent people.

When the car passed Gabrinovic, the compositor, he threw his grenade. It hit the side of the car, but Franz Ferdinand with presence of mind threw himself back and was uninjured. Several officers riding in his attendance were injured.

The cars sped to the Town Hall and the rest of the conspirators did not interfere with them. After the reception in the Town Hall General Potiorek, the Austrian Commander, pleaded with Franz Ferdinand to leave the city, as it was seething with rebellion. The Archduke was persuaded to drive the shortest way out of the city and to go quickly.

The road to the manoeuvres was shaped like the letter V, making a sharp turn at the bridge over the River Nilgacka. Franz Ferdinand's car could go fast enough until it reached this spot but here it was forced to slow down for the turn. Here Princip had taken his stand.

As the car came abreast he stepped forward from the curb, drew his automatic pistol from his coat and fired two shots. The first struck the wife of the Archduke, the Archduchess Sofia, in the abdomen. She was an expectant mother. She died instantly.

The second bullet struck the Archduke close to the heart.

He uttered only one word; 'Sofia'—a call to his stricken wife. Then his head fell back and he collapsed. He died almost instantly.

The officers seized Princip. They beat him over the head with the flat of their swords. They knocked him down, they kicked him, scraped the skin from his neck with the edges of their swords, tortured him, all but killed him.

Then he was taken to the Sarajevo gaol.° The next day he was transferred to the military prison and the round-up of his fellow conspirators proceeded, although he denied that he had worked with anyone.

gaol: jail.

He was confronted with Gabrinovic, who had thrown the bomb. Princip denied he knew him. Others were brought in, but Princip denied the most obvious things.

The next day they put chains on Princip's feet, which he wore till his death.

His only sign of regret was the statement that he was sorry he had killed the wife of the Archduke. He had aimed only at her husband and would have preferred that any other bullet should have struck General Potiorek.

The Austrians arrested every known revolutionary in Sarajevo and among them, naturally, I was one. But they had no proof of my connection with the crime. I was placed in the cell next to Princip's, and when Princip was taken out to walk in the prison yard I was taken along as his companion.

Analysis and Review Questions

1. Who is the "oppressor" that Franz Ferdinand represents? Why is Franz Ferdinand called the "new oppressor"?
2. Why is the date 28 June an unfortunate date for Franz Ferdinand to visit Sarajevo?
3. Describe the plans to kill Franz Ferdinand.
4. Describe the scene at the time of the murder.
5. How does the author justify the events?

WEB LINKS

http://longmanworldhistory.com
The following additional readings can be found on the Web site.
Document 21.3, Industrial Society and Factory Conditions
Document 22.4, M. I. Pokzovskaya, Working Conditions of Women in the Factories
http://www.fordham.edu/halsall/mod/modsbookfull.html
Modern History Sourcebook is a collection of full-text books and documents that correspond with more popular reading assignments given in college classes in many areas of history.

http://www.fordham.edu/halsall/islam/islamsbook.html
Islamic History Sourcebook is a collection of full-text books and documents that correspond with more popular reading assignments given in college classes on Islamic history.

http://www.dis.org/daver/anarchism/kropotkin/index.html
A collection of writings of Prince Peter Kropotkin.

http://www.poloniatoday.com/history9.htm
This site is from a brief history of Poland on the Polish uprisings of the nineteenth century.

http://www.alexanderpalace.org/tsarskoe/historyfive.html
A brief history of Catherine the Great.

http://www.alexanderpalace.org/catherinepalace/
Virtual tour of Catherine's palace of Tsarskoye Selo.

http://www.cats.ohiou.edu/~Chastain/ip/poleag.htm

Presents an account of this nationalist group's attempt to defend the Polish state against the Prussians using legal means.

http://www.dur.ac.uk/~dml0www/octmanif.html
A copy of the 1905 October Manifesto.

http://www.dur.ac.uk/~dml0www/Russhist.HTML
Russian history texts from 1800 to 1930.

http://www.shsu.edu/~his_ncp/365Read.html
Links on Russian history by major time periods. This has both primary and secondary sources.

http://www.law.emory.edu/EILR/volumes/win98/kaze.html
Reflections on Church and State in Russian History, by Firuz Kazemzadeh.

http://www.departments.bucknell.edu/russian/chrono.html
This site has links to different time periods in Russian history.

http://www.bulgaria.com/history/bulgaria/index.html
Bulgarian history links.

http://www.bulgaria.com/history/bulgaria/liber.html
The liberation of Bulgaria.

CHAPTER 23

Revolution! Contested Identities in Latin America, 1750–1914

Revolutionary winds swept across Latin America in the late eighteenth century, fanning to life sparks and embers that lay embedded in the very foundations of Spain and Portugal's New World colonies. By the turn of the century, long smoldering issues of race, class, and contested identity erupted in a full-blown conflagration that engulfed the former Iberian colonies and continued to flare up for the better part of 150 years.

Initially a response to revolutionary impulses in North America and Europe, the Latin American revolutions quickly showed just how fragmented and contested the colonial societies had become. The war to end colonial control became a series of wars and conflicts to determine both the nature of the societies that would replace the colonies and the collective identity of the people who would rule and live in these societies. Race, class, geography, and ideology divided Latin Americans. Only short-term political and military alliances united them. A single, collective identity remained elusive, if not improbable. Earlier, extensive militarization, factionalism, and decentralization impeded peaceful transitions to nationhood. Later, scientific racism kept Latin Americans divided and in conflict with one another. Today, nearly 200 years after their first tentative steps toward independence, Latin Americans still struggle with the issue of their identities.

THE PLAN OF IGUALA

About the Document

Map 23.1
(Interactive)
Latin Americans
Obtain Independence

The Mexican independence wars highlighted social divisions in colonial Latin America. On the one side, white, upper-class Latin Americans sought to replace foreign rule with governments that would act at their behest. On the other side, emboldened by the possibility of creating an entirely new order, *castas*, people of indigenous, African, or mixed ancestry, desired an end to the status quo that kept them subservient and disenfranchised. Two parish priests, Miguel Hidalgo and José María Morelos, led the first revolutionary movements in Mexico, fighting alongside their casta allies to end the marginalizing social stratification that had structured their society from the time of the Conquest. Such movements threatened the predominantly white upper classes, which quickly set aside their differences and joined forces. The ensuing counterrevolutions succeeded in suppressing, but not vanquishing, the castas' movement. Mexico remained a divided society. On the eve of declaring independence from Spain, Mexican elites intended the Plan of Iguala to act as a compromise between Mexico's divided classes.

The Document

ART. 1. The Mexican nation is independent of the Spanish nation, and of every other, even on its own Continent.

ART. 2. Its religion shall be the Catholic, which all its inhabitants profess.

ART. 3. They shall be all united, without any distinction between Americans and Europeans.

ART. 4. The government shall be a constitutional monarchy.

ART. 5. A junta shall be named, consisting of individuals who enjoy the highest reputation in the different parties which have shewn themselves.

ART. 6. This junta shall be under the presidency of his Excellency the Count del Venadito, the present Viceroy° of Mexico.

ART. 7. It shall govern in the name of the nation, according to the laws now in force, and its principal business will be to convoke, according to such rules as it shall deem expedient, a congress for the formation of a constitution more suitable to the country.

ART 8. His Majesty Ferdinand VII. shall be invited to the throne of the empire, and in case of his refusal, the Infantes Don Carlos and Don Francisco de Paula.

ART. 9. Should his Majesty Ferdinand VII. and his august brothers decline the invitation, the nation is at liberty to invite to the imperial throne any member of reigning families whom it may select.

ART. 10. The formation of the constitution by the congress, and the oath of the emperor to observe it, must precede his entry into the country.

ART. 11. The distinction of castes is abolished, which was made by the Spanish law, excluding them from the rights of citizenship. All the inhabitants of the country are citizens, and equal, and the door of advancement is open to virtue and merit.

ART. 12. An army shall be formed for the support of religion, independence, and union, guaranteeing these three principles, and therefore it shall be called the army of the three guarantees.

---

viceroy: The viceroy was the king's proxy in a given administrative subdivision of the colonies (a viceroyalty). While subordinate to the king of Spain, the viceroy's distance from the king meant that the viceroy acted or responded without instructions as often as he was charged with implementing orders from Madrid.

ART. 13. It shall solemnly swear to defend the fundamental bases of this plan.

ART. 14. It shall strictly observe the military ordinances now in force.

ART. 15. There shall be no other promotions than those which are due to seniority, or which shall be necessary for the good of the service.

ART. 16. This army shall be considered as of the line.

ART. 17. The old partisans of independence who shall immediately adhere to this plan, shall be considered as individuals of this army.

ART. 18. The patriots and peasants who shall adhere to it hereafter, shall be considered as provincial militiamen.

ART. 19. The secular and regular priests shall be continued in the state in which they now are.

ART. 20. All the public functionaries, civil, ecclesiastical, political, and military, who adhere to the cause of independence, shall be continued in their offices, without any distinction between Americans and Europeans.

ART. 21. Those functionaries, of whatever degree and condition, who dissent from the cause of independence, shall be divested of their offices, and shall quit the territory of the empire, taking with them their families and their effects.

ART. 22. The military commandants shall regulate themselves according to the general instructions in conformity with this plan, which shall be transmitted to them.

ART. 23. No accused person shall be condemned capitally by the military commandants. Those accused of treason against the nation, which is the next greatest crime after that of treason to the Divine Ruler, shall be conveyed to the fortress of Barrabas, where they shall remain until the congress shall resolve on the punishment which ought to be inflicted on them.

ART. 24. It being indispensable to the country that this plan should be carried into effect, in as much as the welfare of that country is its object, every individual of the army shall maintain it, to the shedding (if it be necessary) of the last drop of his blood.

Analysis and Review Questions

1. What form of government do the articles propose for independent Mexico?
2. What part, if any, is religion to play in the former colony?
3. Using your reading of this document, tell what kinds of racial divisions existed at the time of independence. To what extent does the Plan address such divisions? What evidence do you find that the Plan's authors sought to establish a compromise with members of the initial independence movements (lead by Hidalgo and Morelos)?
4. Post-independence Latin America is often perceived as militaristic. What degree of militarization, if any, did Mexicans experience in the early 1820s?

Image 23.1
The Great Liberator—
Independence Leader,
Caudillo, and Future
President, Simón Bolivar

THE JOURNAL OF EDWARD THORNTON TAYLOE

About the Document

Mexican elites earlier had set aside their differences to counter what they perceived as the threat from below, but the late 1820s found them more divided than ever. With Spain defeated and independence achieved, they were unable to agree on the structure, nature, or identity of their new society. Geographic, economic, and ideological differences kept elites divided. At the time of Tayloe's visit, Mexico's short-lived monarchy already had fallen victim to a republican coup, and bitter factionalism now threatened to destroy the struggling republic. Though the factions gravitated toward various York and Scottish-rite Masonic lodges, often even these were little more than coalitions of similar interests. Perhaps the most divisive issue was that of popular class (the former castas) inclusion. In their struggle to achieve supremacy over their political opponents, York-rite masons sought allies among the people, while Scottish-rite masons struggled to maintain the exclusiveness of the colonial status quo. The result was heightened politicization and conflict, as Mexicans struggled to define themselves as a people and a nation.

The Document

These charges have now been repeated in a Solemn Manifest presented to the world by the Legislature of the State of Vera Cruz, instigated, it seems, by that party which is avowedly hostile to the United States & without doubt hostile to every American interest. I speak of the party denominated Escoceses—a name adopted from the Scotch rite of masonry, under which they first organised themselves. It is composed, first of Borbonists, who insist upon the Treaty of Iguala being carried into effect so far as provided that a prince of the House of Borbon should be invited to a throne in Mexico, independent of Spain—the higher orders of the clergy, the shattered nobility, the wealthy aristocrats, and nearly all the Old Spaniards constitute this monarchical class; secondly, of the Centralists, or monarchists of another order, who are advocates either of a central form of government, like that of Colombia; or of a yet more aristocratic character, resembling as nearly as possible that of Great Britain, with a native Prince under the name of Liberator, Dictator or some such Bolivarian invention, with their House of Peers & other tinsel of royalty—those who would most probably acquire promotion & greater power under this system than they can hope to gain under the federal, some of a speculative disposition, such of the aristocracy as do not incline to Borbonism—in a word—all opposed to the existing Federal form, constitute this class.

This party, tho' defeated by the states in the establishment of the federal form of government, was at the head of affairs at the period of our arrival in this country in the spring of 1825. Both of the candidates for the presidency, Victoria & Bravo, were Centralists; and the first, on his election, formed his cabinet of the same materials. Possessing great advantages in the position it had acquired, this party was well organized, & was looking triumphantly forward to their accomplishment of its views. Its opponents, the Federalists, were not in the minority, but too badly provided with leaders to enable them to make much resistance to the almost overwhelming phalanxes of centralism, reinforced by the Borbonists, who sagely foresaw their own victory in the rear of their allies. But fortunately for the cause of liberty, the division that was created by espousing the election of Victoria & Bravo, both of their party, was too serious to heal. The Federalists wisely availed themselves of this moment to invite the union with them of the Iturbidists, who were until then indifferent spectators of what was passing—they also gained additional force by the junction with them of many of the friends & supporters of Victoria, whose administration was imprudently assailed by the advocates of the rival candidate. The Federalists, with their numbers suddenly increased by these several junctions, now availed themselves of the rite of the Ancient York Masons, & so became organised. Hence arises the name of Yorkinos, by which this party is now denominated—presenting, in a Catholic & fanatical country, the curious spectacle of two great parties, which derive their names from orders of Masonry, which the Mexicans have been taught by the priests to believe to be inimical to their religion.

The Yorkinos, soon after their organization, were successful in nearly all the elections of last year, and are now decidedly victorious—& their numbers daily increasing. The Escoceses have made great efforts to sustain their sinking cause—their union with the Borbonists they have attempted to draw still closer; and in the trials of the conspirators detected in January last, they have maintained their innocence. During the time that elapsed between the condemnation and execution—a period of more than four months—of Arenas,° their leading paper, the *Sol*, was constantly throwing out insinuations that a great personage, alluding to Mr. Poinsett, was implicated in this conspiracy. The revolutionary movement in Texas furnished occasion for them to persuade the Mexicans that the United States were fomenting these dissensions—that our two countries were natural enemies—and that the Minister of the United States should be furnished with his passports & sent out of the Mexican territory. And when Negrete & Echavarri, European Spaniards, & Borbonists, & Generals in the Mexican Army—when these were arrested, it was industriously reported by the Escoceses, forgetting their inconsistency, that Mr. Poinsett had a party of Yorkinos to celebrate that event in his house—a story, which they were successful in palming upon the credulity of Mr. Ward, the British Chargé d'affaires. These and other absurd attempts have been made to create a feeling against the U.S. and against their Minister, to whom they ascribed great agency in bringing about the happy change in favor of the Federal party, & consequently their own decline.

The rallying point of the Escoceses was now in Vera Cruz—where European Spaniards possess wealth and influence. Gen. Barragán, uniting the offices of Governor & Commanding General of that state, is an Escoces, & entertaining no other hopes of promotion than thro' that party, who flatter him with the title of 'Conqueror of Ulúa,' and with the prospect of his election, thro' them, to the presidency. Discovering the increase of Yorkinos in the very stronghold of the Escoceses, & entertaining a bitter enmity against Esteva, who deprived him of a share of the laurels he acquired in the siege of the Castle of Ulúa, Esteva being very active & possessed with full powers at the time of its reduction—these motives seem to have induced Gen. Barragán to prevent the advance of Yorkinos by a legislative barrier, which his obedient Congress raised by means of a decree prohibiting every secret association of any kind whatsoever in the State of Vera Cruz, adjudging heavy penalties & banishment against all offenders. Esteva, too, was known to be a Mason & Yorkino, & having been appointed by the President Com-

---

Arenas: Arenas was the name of a priest implicated in an 1827 conspiracy alleged to have as its goal the return of Mexico to Spanish control. Contemporaries, and especially the Yorkinos, charged that the Borbonists and Escoceses were in league with Arenas.

missary General of the Customs at Vera Cruz, was soon expected to enter upon the duties of his office. This was another inducement for the passage of that decree—which would rid him of Esteva, of whose influence he was fearful.

. . . I now come to the curious document that has given rise to the preceding observations, without which it would scarce be understood. The Legislature of Vera Cruz, sensible of the impropriety of its acts, aware of the unconstitutionality of its proceedings & conscious of the gross violation, in the person of Esteva, of the rights that belong to every citizen, has published a 'Manifest to the Mexican Nation' in defence of its conduct. In its outset it attacks the Minister of the United States, to whom while it pays him unintentional compliments, it attributes the evils under which Mexico is believed to groan. It charges him with zealously prosecuting the interests of his own country, & with enmity to the prosperity of Mexican States, the aggrandizement & glory of the one being inconsistent with the glory & aggrandizement of the other. It falsely attributed to the United States a policy which is decidedly opposite to what they have pursued—& consistently with the views of the Escoceses against liberty, it makes earnest exertions to throw into disrepute among the Mexicans the nation which shows too clearly the practical benefits resulting from Federal Institutions, & whose influence in the cause of freedom must prove inimical to their aristocratic purposes.

Under these circumstances it became the imperative duty of Mr. Poinsett to counteract the mischief that would otherwise result from this unjust and injurious attack upon the United States. In discharge of that duty, he has published "An Exposition of the Policy of the United States Towards the New Republics of America," in which he has unanswerably refuted by a mere statement of facts all the charges of the Congress of Vera Cruz. This document has already created a feeling that never before existed in favor of our country, whose enemies, in this manner, have themselves been the means of producing effects which they have strived to defeat. It has historically stated acts of friendship on the part of the United States towards these countries of which the most enlightened among their citizens have been hitherto ignorant, and has made our most decided friends many who only needed some such measure to fix their opinions— opinions that are irrevocably fixed by this outrageous attack upon liberty on the part of the Escoceses.

Since writing the above I have thought fit to send the same observations, with some modification, to Gales, that he may make use of them at his discretion. You will not be surprised, therefore, to see them in print, but in another shape. The shocking state of society which tolerates the scandal which the public presses are daily serving out to the morbid appetite of such a people has made me quite disgusted with Mexico.

Analysis and Review Questions

1. In Tayloe's assessment, what are the two major political factions in post-independence Mexico?
2. According to Tayloe, what persons or groups belong to the individual factions?
3. In what way are U.S. interests tied to Mexico's political factions and their ongoing struggle for supremacy?
4. To what extent is the political struggle that Tayloe describes a public one? To what extent does it take place through more secretive channels?
5. What do you believe are Tayloe's reasons for supporting one faction over the other?

REFLECTIONS ON REVOLUTIONS

About the Document

The proliferation of *caudillos* (military leaders) in the post-independence era added to the fledgling republics' fragility. Extensive militarization in the course of the revolutionary wars left the Latin American landscape littered with out-of-work generals at a time when national governments were unable to field and sustain large armies. Capable of overwhelming the national government, caudillos' ambitions tended to be more pragmatic than ideological in their motivations. Indeed, caudillos succeeded where politicians failed in terms of gauging or representing the identity of the people they led. Coming from diverse socioeconomic backgrounds, caudillos provided a voice for those at the bottom. The most successful caudillos, like Peru's José Rufino Echenique, moved skillfully through multiple layers of society and built their alliances on personal, as opposed to strictly political, loyalties. The excerpt from Echenique's memoirs provides a window into Peru in the 1840s, when efforts to create a national identity out of political alliances and divisions in Lima were outmatched by the more personal movements of caudillos in the countryside.

The Document

I had left my hacienda and come to Lima to buy some mules that I had heard were on sale near the port. Passing the street which runs in front of the Palace of Government, I met my friend Colonel Ros, who told me of Hercelles's defeat. He also said that Hercelles himself had been captured and was presently being brought as a prisoner to Lima, but that an order had been issued to execute him before arriving. Ros added that I could probably save Hercelles if I tried, because of the great influence that I had with [Acting President] Vidal. It was true that I did have influence with Vidal, and since I was Hercelles's friend I went straight to the Palace. Vidal was not there, but they told me that I might speak with La Fuente, a government minister with particular sway over Vidal, so I went to speak with him about the matter. I found him surrounded by many important figures, among them the minister Lazo, all talking about Hercelles. With his characteristic emphasis, La Fuente spoke of the order which had been given, saying that Hercelles should be shot the moment it was received, and declared that the government would do the same five hundred times to stop revolutions. Several of his interlocutors voiced their agreement. You may be sure that this resolution wounded my patriotism because I considered it tyranny. Overcome by my feelings, I said nothing, but withdrew, determined to reach Vidal. They had told me he was at his house, and I headed that way.

As it happened, I met Vidal on his way to the Palace, and we returned there together. As soon as we were alone, I told him why I was looking for him, and I was astonished to hear him simply repeat the same words I had heard from La Fuente. Sensitive by nature, I also have an unfortunately violent temper, and I took offense that he should speak to me in that way. His arbitrary threats constituted a horrible tyranny for the nation, and furthermore, the man he intended to destroy was my good friend. I made up my mind first to save my friend, and then to help overthrow a government of methods so antithetical to laws and rights. This decision, unhappily, became the cause of all that befell me later: the loss of my privileged situation and of the bright future that corresponded to it.

As soon as I got home, steadfast in my purpose, I sent for a well-known war captain named Contreras who was extremely loyal to me. I told him to gather twenty-five men of absolute trustworthiness, to arm them, to lead them out the road to Chancay, to ambush the party that was bringing Hercelles prisoner, and to rescue him. He agreed but, as he gathered the men and arms, the news arrived that Hercelles had been executed immediately upon receipt of the order to that effect. Not only that, his head had been cut off and sent to the place where he began the revolution, to be displayed as an example and a warning. Lazo, the Minister of Government, gave that order, and it was the last straw for me. I determined to move against the government at the first opportunity.

Shortly thereafter we learned of a revolution in favor of General Vivanco, which had taken place in Arequipa. The well-known patriotism, ability, honesty, and honorable sentiments of General Vivanco gave everyone high hopes for the future progress and stability of the country. By this time the government had fallen into complete disrepute. Besides not doing anything to benefit the nation, the government had lost even institutional legitimacy because, at the death of Gamarra, the presidency should have gone to Menéndez, who was chairman of the Executive Council, or to Vice President Figuerola, and not to Vidal, who had been merely assistant to the Vice President. Consequently, the revolution spread quickly to Cuzco, and then to Ayacucho, where General Pezet joined with his division. In Lima, there were four corps which I decided to bring into the revolution without having communicated with Vivanco. I began by establishing contact with some of the officers, and I found them favorably disposed. When Figuerola assumed the presidency and made Castilla Minister of War, these corps were now under his command. But I could not turn back because I had already made commitments to some supporters of Vivanco. In addition, I had the highest opinion of Vivanco and felt it my patriotic duty to help put him in power. Foolishly, I thought that my responsibilities would end with the triumph of the revolution and that I would then be able to return to the peace and quiet of my hacienda. Most important, two high officers had solemnly committed themselves to move the moment that I gave the command.

I do not know whether or not Castilla found out about the revolutionary plans, but for some reason he sent the four corps under his command to spend the night in the main plaza of Lima. I received word of this maneuver, which was taken for a sign that the revolution had been discovered, and without hesitation I went to talk with the officers loyal to me, judging that the time was ripe. We encountered little resistance from the officers in command of the other two corps. They, too, put themselves at my orders when I proclaimed Vivanco to be Supreme Chief of the Republic. The next day, most of the leading citizens of the city met to proclaim the same thing. They also named me mayor and military commander of Lima. I could find no way to decline these honors and so accepted them, trusting that it would be only until the arrival of Vivanco, at which time I could get rid of these responsibilities and go back to my private occupations. In the meantime, I persecuted no one and allowed Castilla himself to remain free in his own house.

A few days later I heard that Castilla was conspiring with another officer to bring down the revolution on a certain night. That night I went to the barracks where the reaction was supposed to begin, and I stayed there until dawn. Nothing happened, and people's apprehension began to dissipate. Then I learned that Colonel Alvarado Ortiz was on his way to Lima from Jauja with two battalions. Some said that he supported Vivanco; and others, that he meant to restore the constitutional government. When he arrived, I had him bivouac his troops in Lurín as a precaution, but without letting him know that I did not trust him. Next, General Pezet arrived with the force which had announced for Vivanco in Ayacucho. Because of his rank I put my soldiers at his disposition, but I continued in the office of mayor.

Everyone knows how well I executed my duties as mayor. It is enough to say that I neglected nothing and enjoyed wide popularity. Pezet and I got along excellently. He continued the policy of not bothering anyone for political reasons. Still, we could not rest easy because we had no news of Vivanco, not a word, and all the time we heard rumors of thriving conspiracies to bring back the constitutional government.

Finally, we learned that Vivanco had arrived in Jauja and was continuing to Lima, so we prepared him a splendid reception with the enthusiastic participation of the people, who seemed well pleased with the new order of things. Immediately after reporting on everything concerning the current situation of Lima, I asked Vivanco to appoint a new mayor, explaining my determination to return to my personal affairs, which were suffering from my neglect. But he asked me—one could even say he begged me—not to desert him at a time when my services were urgently needed for the regeneration of our country. I have always been too soft to deny a favor to a friend, and, believing that it would be unpatriotic to abandon Vivanco at this moment, I agreed to continue.

Analysis and Review Questions

1. Why does Echenique decide to lead a revolution?
2. What evidence do you find to suggest that personal ties or loyalties in mid-nineteenth-century Peru may have superseded more formal obligations and legalities when it came to accounting for people's actions?
3. What sense, if any, do you gain of the various actors' identities or agendas?
4. Given the document's insights into the inner-workings of mid-nineteenth-century Peruvian politics, what do you believe were the country's prospects for political or social stability?
5. Do Echenique's stated reasons for remaining involved in politics, despite pressing "personal affairs," ring true with you? Why or why not?

SYMBOLISM AND CONTESTED IDENTITIES IN ARGENTINA

About the Document

While Argentina had no large indigenous population to factor into its quest for national identity, racial considerations, nevertheless, played a critical part in how Argentines viewed themselves, especially in an era shaped by ideas of scientific racism. Indeed, Domingo Sarmiento's famous essay on civilization and barbarism in Latin American—a sustained critique of how Argentine caudillo Facundo Quiroga had prevented Argentina from taking its place on the world stage of civilized countries—used a racial duality as a means of understanding Argentina's post-independence successes and failures. The white upper-class population of Buenos Aires—of whom Sarmiento was an example—sought to mimic European culture, fashion, and political traditions. The caudillos who represented their rural counterparts, by contrast, were less impressed by all things European. In the following section, Sarmiento discusses how political symbolism embodied and reflected the essential dualities—civilization versus barbarism, and pure versus mixed blood—of Argentine society.

The Document

. . . Like all civil wars in which deep differences of education, belief, and motives divide the parties engaged in them, the internal warfare of the Argentine Republic was long and obstinate, until one of the elements of the strife was victorious. The Argentine Revolutionary War was twofold: 1st, a civilized warfare of the cities against Spain; 2d, a war against the cities on the part of the country chieftains with the view of shaking off all political subjection and satisfying their hatred of civilization. The cities overcame the Spaniards, and were in their turn overcome by the country districts. This is the explanation of the Argentine Revolution, the first shot of which was fired in 1810, and the last is still to be heard.

. . . To make the ruin and decadence of civilization and the rapid progress of barbarism perceptible to the reader, I must select two cities—one already annihilated, the other insensibly proceeding towards barbarism—La Rioja and San Juan. La Rioja was formerly a city of some account, but its own sons would fail to recognize it in its present condition.

. . . Let us now look at the condition of La Rioja, as exhibited by the answers given to one of the many inquiries I have instituted for the purpose of gaining a thorough knowledge of the facts on which I base my theories. These are the statements of a reliable person, who was unacquainted with my object in investigating his memory of matters that must have been fresh in his mind, for it was only four months before that he left Rioja.

1. What is about the actual amount of the population of Rioja city?

Ans. About fifteen hundred souls. It is said that only fifteen adult males reside in the city.

2. How many persons of note live in it?

Ans. Six or eight in the city.

3. How many lawyers' offices are open there?

Ans. None.

4. How many men wear dress-coats?

Ans. None.

5. How many young men from La Rioja are studying at Cordova or Buenos Ayres?

Ans. I know of only one.

. . . This was the famous fight at Tala, the first exploit of Quiroga beyond the limits of his province. He had conquered "the bravest of the brave," and kept his sword as a trophy of the victory. Will he stop there? But let us see the force which sustained itself against the colonel of the 13th regiment, who overthrew a government to equip his company. Facundo raised at Tala a flag which was not Argentine, but of his own invention; namely, a black ground with a skull and cross-bones in the center. This was the flag which he had lost early in the engagement, and which he intended to recover, as he said to his routed soldiers, even at the mouth of hell. Terror, death, hell, were represented on the banner and in the proclamations of this general of the Llanos.

And there was still another revelation of the Arab-Tartar spirit of that power which was to destroy the cities. The Argentine colors are blue and white; the clear sky of a fair day, and the bright light of the disk of the sun: "peace and justice for all." In our hatred of tyranny and violence, we reject on our national flag warlike devices. Two hands, as a sign of union, support the Phrygian cap of Liberty. "The United Cities" says this symbol, "will sustain their acquired liberty." The sun begins to illumine the background of this device, while the darkness of night is disappearing. The armies of the Republic, which were to spread over the whole country to enforce the coming of that promised light, wear a uniform of dark blue. But now, in the very heart of the Republic, the color red appears on the national banners, in the dress of the soldiers, and in the cockade which every native Argentine must wear under pain of death. Let us look up the significance of the color red. I have before me a picture of all the national flags of the world. In civilized Europe there is but one in which this color prevails, notwithstanding the barbaric origin of its banners. The *red* ones are: Algiers, a *red* flag with skull and crossbones; Tunis, a *red* flag; Mongolia, the same; Turkey, a *red* flag with a crescent; Morocco; Japan, *red* with the exterminating knife; Siam has the same.

I remember that travelers in the interior of Africa provide themselves with *red* cloth for the Negro princes. "The king of Elve," say the brothers Lander, "wore a Spanish coat of *red* cloth and pantaloons of the same color."

I remember that the presents sent by the government of Chili to the caciques° of Aranco, were *red* cloaks and coats, because savages liked this color especially.

Siam, the Africans, the savages, the Roman Neros, the barbarian kings, the hangmen, the Rosas, should be clothed in a color now proscribed by Christian and civilized communities? No, it is because red is the symbol of violence, blood, and barbarism. If not, why this antagonism?

The Argentine revolution of independence was symbolized by two blue stripes and one white one; signifying, *justice, peace, justice.*

The amendment made by Facundo and approved by Rosas, was a red band, signifying *terror, blood, barbarism.*

In all ages this significance has been given to the color purple or red; study the history of those nations who have hoisted this color, and you will always find a Rosas and a Facundo—terror, barbarism, and blood always prevailing. In Morocco, the emperor has the singular prerogative of killing criminals with his own hand. Each phase of civilization is expressed in its garments, and every style of apparel is indicative of an entire system of ideas. Why do we wear beards at the present day? Because of the researches recently made in mediæval history; the direction given to romantic literature is reflected in the fashions of the day. And why are these constantly changing? Because of the freedom of thought in Europe; let thought be stationary, enslaved, and the costume will remain unchanged. Thus in Asia, where men live under such governments as that of Rosas, the same style of dress has been worn since the time of Abraham. . . .

Analysis and Review Questions

1. How does Sarmiento characterize the Argentine wars for independence?
2. To what key internal division does Sarmiento link his "civilization versus barbarism" duality?
3. What evidence does Sarmiento use in assessing Argentine barbarism? What does Sarmiento's evidence tell you of his own prejudices?
4. What symbols do Argentines use in their politics?
5. To what extent does Sarmiento draw parallels between political symbolism and the civilization-barbarism issue? How does he use language to persuade his readers?

---

caciques: Leaders of indigenous communities.

CANUDOS: MILLENARIANISM IN LATE-NINETEENTH-CENTURY BRAZIL

About the Document

Despite claims of "color-blindness," Brazilians, like the rest of their Latin American counterparts, tended to view and interpret their society in racial terms. Brazilians' flirtation with European positivism and scientific racism exacerbated their biases. Several years after the fall of the Brazilian monarchy in 1889, a millenarian backlands rebellion involving mixed-blood inhabitants of the northeastern interior provided the new republic with a new "voice from below" as well as its first serious challenge. As the inhabitants of Canudos delivered unexpected setbacks to the Brazilian military, which recently had defeated several plots to restore the monarchy, public interest in the conflict grew accordingly. A journalist by training, Euclides da Cunha did more than report the news—he interpreted it through a lens shaped by the social and political biases of his time. As a fervent supporter of the republican regime, da Cunha grew increasingly critical of Canudos as the conflict wore on. This excerpt is from his classic *Os Sertões*.

Image 23.2 Inhabitants of Canudos

The Document

How a Monster Is Formed

And so there appeared in Baía the somber anchorite with hair down to his shoulders, a long tangled beard, an emaciated face, and a piercing eye—a monstrous being clad in a blue canvas garment and leaning on the classic staff which is used to stay the pilgrim's tottering steps.

What his life had been over so long a period of time, no one knows. An aged caboclo, captured in Canudos in the last days of the campaign, had something to tell me about this, but he was very vague and could give no exact dates or specific details. He had known Antonio Maciel in the backlands of Pernambuco, a year or two after the latter had left Crato. From what this witness told me, I gathered that, while still a youth, Antonio Maciel had made a vivid impression upon the imagination of the sertanejos. He had come there a vagabond, without any fixed destination, and he never referred to his past. His conversation was made up of short phrases and an occasional monosyllable. From one stop to the next he went, seemingly careless as to what direction he took, indifferent to danger, taking no thought of his life, eating little or nothing, and now and again sleeping out in the open, along the roadside, as if in fulfillment of a rude and prolonged penance.

It is not surprising, then, if to these simple folk he became a fantastic apparition, with something unprepossessing about him; nor is it strange if, when this singular old man of a little more than thirty years drew near the farmhouses of the tropeiros,° the festive guitars at once stopped strumming and the improvisations ceased. This was only natural. Filthy and battered in appearance, clad in his threadbare garment and silent as a ghost, he would spring up suddenly out of the plains, peopled by hobgoblins. Then he would pass on, bound for other places, leaving the superstitious backwoodsmen in a daze. And so it was, in the end, he came to dominate them without seeking to do so.

tropeiros: Mule drivers.

In the midst of a primitive society which, by its own ethnic qualities and through the malevolent influence of the holy missions, found it easier to comprehend life in the form of incomprehensible miracles, this man's mysterious way of living was bound to surround him with a more than ordinary amount of prestige, which merely served to aggravate his delirious temperament. All the legends and conjectures which sprang up about him were a propitious soil for the growth of his own hallucinations. His insanity therewith became externalized. The intense admiration and the absolute respect which were accorded him gradually led to his becoming the unconditional arbiter in all misunderstandings and disputes, the favored Counselor in all decisions. The multitude thus spared him an agonizing quest in search of his own emotional state, all the effort, the anguish-laden questionings, the entire process of delirious introspection such as ordinarily accompanies the evolution of madness in sickly brains. The multitude created him, refashioning him in its own image. It broadened his life immeasurably by impelling him into those errors that were common two thousand years ago. The people needed someone to translate for them their own vague idealizations, someone to guide them in the mysterious paths of heaven.

And so the evangelist arose, a monstrous being, but an automaton. This man who swayed the masses was but a puppet. Passive as a shade, he moved them. When all is said, he was doing no more than to condense the obscurantism of three separate races. And he grew in stature until he was projected into History. . . .

He looked upon the Republic with an evil eye and consistently preached rebellion against the new laws. From 1893 on he assumed an entirely new and combative attitude. This was due to an incident of no great moment in itself. The autonomy of the municipalities having been decreed, the chambers of the various localities in the interior of Baía had posted up on the traditional bulletin boards, taking the place of newspapers, the regulations governing the collection of taxes and the like. Antonio Conselheiro was in Bom Conselho at the time this novel procedure was instituted. He did not like the new taxes and planned an immediate retaliation. On a day of the fair he gathered the people and, amid seditious cries and noisy demonstrations, had them make a bonfire of the bulletin boards in the public square. And, raising his voice above this "audo-da-fé," which the authorities out of weakness had failed to prevent, he began openly preaching insurrection against the laws of the country. Then, realizing the gravity of his offense, he left town, taking the Monte Santo Road, to the north.

Why Not Preach Against the Republic?

He preached against the Republic, there is no denying that. This antagonism was an inevitable derivative of his mystic exacerbation, a variant of his religious delirium that was forced upon him. Yet he did not display the faintest trace of a political intuition; for your jagunço is quite as inapt at understanding the republican form of government as he is the constitutional monarchy. Both to him are abstractions, beyond the reach of his intelligence. He is instinctively opposed to both of them, since he is in that phase of evolution in which the only rule he can conceive is that of a priestly or a warrior chieftain.

We must insist upon this point: the war of Canudos marked an ebb, a backward flow, in our history. What we had to face here was the unlooked-for resurrection, under arms, of an old society, a dead society, galvanized into life by a madman. We were not acquainted with this society; it was not possible for us to have been acquainted with it.

The adventurers of the seventeenth century, it is true, would encounter in it conditions with which they were familiar, just as the visionaries of the Middle Ages would be at home among the *demonopaths* of Varzenis or the Stundists of Russia; for these epidemic psychoses make their appearance in all ages and in all places, as obvious anachronisms, inevitable contrasts in the uneven evolution of the peoples—contrasts which become especially evident at a time when a broad movement is vigorously impelling the backward peoples toward a higher and civilized way of life. We then behold the exaggerated Perfectionists breaking through the triumphant industrialism of North America, or the somber *Stürmisch* sect, inexplicably inspired by the genius of Klopstock, sharing the cradle of the German renascence.

.... Instead, we looked at it from the narrow-minded point of view of partisan politics. In the presence of these monstrous aberrations, we had a revealing fit of consternation; and, with an intrepidity that was worthy of a better cause, we proceeded to put them down with bayonets, thereby causing history to repeat itself, as we made yet another inglorious incursion into these unfortunate regions, opening up once more the grass-grown trails of the bandeiras.

In the backlands agitator, whose revolt was a phase of rebellion against the natural order of things, we beheld a serious adversary, a mighty foeman representing a regime that we had done away with, one who was capable of overthrowing our nascent institutions.

Analysis and Review Questions

1. How does da Cunha characterize backland society and its peoples?
2. What are da Cunha's impressions of the Counselor?
3. According to da Cunha, what were the motivations guiding the residents of Canudos, as they came into conflict with other Brazilians?
4. What kinds of biases—political, social, racial, etc.—do you detect in da Cunha's account of what took place?
5. In assessing the Canudos movement, what important questions remain unasked? How might they reveal a different perspective than that of da Cunha?

WEB LINKS

Selections from Longman World History—Primary Sources and Case Studies
http://longmanworldhistory.com
The following additional case studies can be found on the Web site.
Case Study 23.1, From Monarchs to Masons: Mexico's Changing Political Arena
Case Study 23.2, Brothers in Arms: Comparative Politics and Revolution
Case Study 23.3, Juxtaposition: Race and Identity in Nineteenth-Century South America

Background on Nineteenth-Century Latin American Revolutions

http://www.emayzine.com/lectures/bourbo~1.htm
This site addresses the role of the Bourbon Reforms—implemented in the 1760s—
in triggering several Andean colonial rebellions, arguably the first tentative steps toward
independence.

Revolutions from Below and Reactions from Above

http://www.newadvent.org/cathen/10565b.htm
Extensive biography of Morelos and the revolution he led. This site addresses some of
the key issues that divided Mexicans during and after the independence process.

http://www.tamu.edu/ccbn/dewitt/morelos1.htm
Another extensive biography of Morelos, this one focusing almost entirely on his role
during the Mexican revolutions for independence.

http://www.mexconnect.com/mex_/history/jtuck/jtfathermorelos.html
Solid biographical overview of Miguel Hidalgo, the so-called "father" of Mexican independence and leader of the first revolution from below. This site covers Hidalgo's
background and early years as well as his involvement in the initial revolution.

http://lego70.tripod.com/mex/agustin1.htm
Brief overview of Iturbide's role in defeating the revolutions from below, then leading
Mexico to independence via the short-lived Plan of Iguala.

Sarmiento and the Age of Caudillos

http://www.britannica.com/eb/article?eu=115686&tocid=32702&query=caudillos
This site establishes the context for understanding the emergence of caudillos in
nineteenth-century Latin America. Addresses both the causes and the implications
of the political instability that both engendered and sustained caudillos.

http://www.encyclopedia.com/articles/11485.html
Brief biography of Sarmiento, complete with bibliography.

Canudos

http://www.brazilbrazil.com/canudos.html
Overview and timeline of the Canudos episode. This site contains illustrations and photos.

http://www.pcusa.org/pcusa/wmd/ywla/canudos.htm
Critical assessment of Canudos, including an examination of events leading up to the
settlement's foundation, the issues that sparked conflict between the government and
the town's inhabitants, and the role that da Cunha played in distorting the meaning of
what took place.

CHAPTER 24

East Asia Faces
Challenge and Crisis

Industrialization in the West led European powers such as Great Britain, France, Germany, and Italy to explore overseas markets vigorously. In East Asia, the Western values introduced by these nations collided with Eastern culture, causing significant transformation in the economic, cultural, and political landscape of East Asia. As a result, China and Japan, in particular, underwent tremendous changes during the second half of the nineteenth century. Such development soon made East Asia an important region in international relations in the twentieth century.

In China, the British effort to open the opium trade posed serious social, economic, and political problems for the Qing government. Under the Canton trade system, foreign merchants had to conduct business through Cohong, a Qing government-controlled middleman agent. The Chinese viewed merchants as the bottom of all social classes and gave little value to the commercial activities in the country, let alone foreign trade. The British tried to change the Chinese way of doing business and open China's market, forcing the Qing government to take action against foreign trade. The result was the Opium War between 1839 and 1842. When China lost the war, the British, followed by other European powers, imposed unequal treaties on China, and the game of dividing the country began. During the remaining decades of the nineteenth century, the Qing government made several unsuccessful attempts to introduce reforms and modernization. Despite the 1911 Revolution, which ended China's last imperial dynasty and proclaimed the new republic, China remained backward in industrialization.

The Western challenge in Japan, however, brought different results. When U.S. naval battle ships anchored outside of Tokyo Bay, the Tokugawa government, after heated debate, decided to work with, instead of fight against, the Americans. Japan willingly opened its door. Western ideas, modernization, a new constitution, and social reforms worked their way through the country successfully. The Meiji Reform of 1868 brought the downfall of Japan's last shogun, and, in its place, founded a modern government that would change the path of the country forever. Japan was on its way to becoming a modern society.

LIN ZEXU: LETTER TO QUEEN VICTORIA, 1839

About the Document

By the early 1800s, the opium trade dominated by British merchants produced millions of Chinese addicts. The opium trade increased steadily; between 1800 and 1821, 4,500 chests a year were shipped to and sold in China. In 1838 the number reached 40,000 chests. The result was a serious outflow of Chinese silver. The Qing government finally decided in 1838 to ban the opium trade, and Lin Zexu was appointed as imperial commissioner to supervise the operation. Lin arrived in Guangzhou in March 1839 and soon launched strong attacks on both addicts and smugglers. He also ordered confiscation of opium in foreign merchants' possession and burned as many as 21,306 chests.

   Lin's letter to Queen Victoria was sent during his anti-opium campaign. Lin asked Queen Victoria to stop the sale of opium from India to China. In response to British merchants' request for protection, the British fleet was on its way to Guangzhou. War was imminent.

The Document

   His Majesty the Emperor comforts and cherishes foreigners as well as Chinese: he loves all the people in the world without discrimination. Whenever profit is found, he wishes to share it with all men; whenever harm appears, he likewise will eliminate it on behalf of all of mankind. His heart is in fact the heart of the whole universe.

   Generally speaking, the succeeding rulers of your honorable country have been respectful and obedient. Time and again they have sent petitions to China, saying: "We are grateful to His Majesty the Emperor for the impartial and favorable treatment he has granted to the citizens of my country who have come to China to trade," etc. I am pleased to learn that you, as the ruler of your honorable country, are thoroughly familiar with the principle of righteousness and are grateful for the favor that His Majesty the Emperor has bestowed upon your subjects. Because of this fact, the Celestial Empire,° following its traditional policy of treating foreigners with kindness, has been doubly considerate towards the people from England. You have traded in China for almost 200 years, and as a result, your country has become wealthy and prosperous.

   As this trade has lasted for a long time, there are bound to be unscrupulous as well as honest traders. Among the unscrupulous are those who bring opium to China to harm the Chinese; they succeed so well that this poison has spread far and wide in all the provinces. You, I hope, will certainly agree that people who pursue material gains to the great detriment of the welfare of others can be neither tolerated by Heaven nor endured by men. . . .

   Your country is more than 60,000 li° from China. The purpose of your ships in coming to China is to realize a large profit. Since this profit is realized in China and is in fact taken away from the Chinese people, how can foreigners return injury for the benefit they have received by sending this poison to harm their benefactors? They may not intend to harm others on purpose, but the fact remains that they are so obsessed with material gain that they have no concern whatever for the harm they can cause to

the Celestial Empire: China.
li: A Chinese unit of distance, approximately one-third of a mile or one-half of a kilometer.

others. Have they no conscience? I have heard that you strictly prohibit opium in your own country, indicating unmistakably that you know how harmful opium is. You do not wish opium to harm your own country, but you choose to bring that harm to other countries such as China. Why?

The products that originate from China are all useful items. They are good for food and other purposes and are easy to sell. Has China produced one item that is harmful to foreign countries? For instance, tea and rhubarb are so important to foreigners' livelihood that they have to consume them every day. Were China to concern herself only with her own advantage without showing any regard for other people's welfare, how could foreigners continue to live? Foreign products like woolen cloth and beiges rely on Chinese raw materials such as silk for their manufacturing. Had China sought only her own advantage, where would the foreigners' profit come from? The products that foreign countries need and have to import from China are too numerous to enumerate: from food products such as molasses, ginger, and cassia to useful necessities such as silk and porcelain. The imported goods from foreign countries, on the other hand, are merely playthings which can be easily dispensed with without causing any ill effect. Since we do not need these things really, what harm would come if we should decide to stop foreign trade altogether? The reason why we unhesitantly allow foreigners to ship out such Chinese products as tea and silk is that we feel that wherever there is an advantage, it should be shared by all the people in the world. . . .

I have heard that you are a kind, compassionate monarch. I am sure that you will not do to others what you yourself do not desire. I have also heard that you have instructed every British ship that sails for Canton not to bring any prohibited goods to China. It seems that your policy is as enlightened as it is proper. The fact that British ships have continued to bring opium to China results perhaps from the impossibility of making a thorough inspection of all of them owing to their large numbers. I am sending you this letter to reiterate the seriousness with which we enforce the law of the Celestial Empire and to make sure that merchants from your honorable country will not attempt to violate it again.

I have heard that the areas under your direct jurisdiction such as London, Scotland, and Ireland do not produce opium; it is produced instead in your Indian possessions such as Bengal, Madras, Bombay, Patna, and Malwa. In these possessions the English people not only plant opium poppies that stretch from one mountain to another but also open factories to manufacture this terrible drug. As months accumulate and years pass by, the poison they have produced increases in its wicked intensity, and its repugnant odor reaches as high as the sky. Heaven is furious with anger, and all the gods are moaning with pain! It is hereby suggested that you destroy and plow under all of these opium plants and grow food crops instead, while issuing an order to punish severely anyone who dares to plant opium poppies again. If you adopt this policy of love so as to produce good and exterminate evil, Heaven will protect you, and gods will bring you good fortune. Moreover, you will enjoy a long life and be rewarded with a multitude of children and grandchildren! In short, by taking this one measure, you can bring great happiness to others as well as yourself. Why do you not do it?

The right of foreigners to reside in China is a special favor granted by the Celestial Empire, and the profits they have made are those realized in China. As time passes by, some of them stay in China for a longer period than they do in their own country. For every government, past or present, one of its primary functions is to educate all the people living within its jurisdiction, foreigners as well as its own citizens, about the law and to punish them if they choose to violate it. Since a foreigner who goes to England to trade has to obey the English law, how can an Englishman not obey the Chinese law when he is physically within China? The present law calls for the imposition of the death sentence on any Chinese who has peddled or smoked opium. Since a Chinese could not peddle or smoke opium if foreigners had not brought it to China, it is clear that the true culprits of a Chinese's death as a result of an opium conviction are the opium traders from foreign countries. Being the cause of other people's death, why should they themselves be spared from capital punishment? A murderer of one person is subject to the death sentence; just imagine how many people opium has killed! This is the rationale behind the new law which says that any foreigner who brings opium to China will be sentenced to death by hanging or beheading. Our purpose is to eliminate this poison once and for all and to the benefit of all mankind. . . .

Our Celestial Empire towers over all other countries in virtue and possesses a power great and awesome enough to carry out its wishes. But we will not prosecute a person without warning him in advance; that is why we have made our law explicit and clear. If the merchants of your honorable country wish to enjoy trade with us on a permanent basis, they must fearfully observe our law by cutting off, once and for all, the supply of opium. Under no circumstance should they test our intention to enforce the law by deliberately violating it. You, as the ruler of your honorable country, should do your part to uncover the hidden and unmask the wicked. It is hoped that you will continue to enjoy your country and become more and more respectful and obeisant. How wonderful it is that we can all enjoy the blessing of peace!

Analysis and Review Questions

1. How does Lin view the right of foreigners to reside in China?
2. How does Lin see the different motives of Chinese and Europeans in conducting trade activities?
3. On what ground does Lin request Queen Victoria to order the end of the opium trade?
4. How does Lin understand the power of Queen Victoria?

THE TREATY OF NANJING

About the Document

The Treaty of Nanjing was signed on August 29, 1842, following the defeat of China in the Opium War. Of the 13 articles in the treaty, five on trade and diplomatic relations between China and the British government are significant. They compel China to:
1. Pay an indemnity of $21 million;
2. Abolish the Cohong monopolistic system of trade (thus ending the Canton trade system);
3. Open ports for trade and residence of British councils and merchants in Guangzhou (Canton), Xiamen (Amoy), Fuzhou (Foozhow), Ningbo (Ningpo), and Shanghai;
4. Cede Hong Kong island to Great Britain;
5. Establish a fixed tariff for imports and exports.

With the terms in the Treaty of Nanjing, the door of China was forced open, and the fate of this great empire also began to change. Following the example of Great Britain, a host of European powers, the United States, and Japan soon moved in to request "most-favored nation" status from the Chinese government. Thus, a treaty system was formed which tended to protect the interests of foreigners in China. During the late nineteenth century, the Chinese east coast was divided by foreign powers in different concessions in which foreign trading companies, foreign diplomats, and residents enjoyed tremendous privileges and immunities.

The 100 years since the Opium War were seen as "a century of humiliation" in modern Chinese history. It was not until 1943 that Great Britain and the United States decided to revoke their privileges in extraterritoriality.

The Document

[Ratifications exchanged at Hongkong, 26th June 1843.]

VICTORIA, by the Grace of God, Queen of the United Kingdom of Great Britain and Ireland, Defender of the Faith, etc., etc., etc. To All and Singular to whom these Presents shall come, Greeting! Whereas a Treaty between Us and Our Good Brother The Emperor of China, was concluded and signed, in the English and Chinese Languages, on board Our Ship the Cornwallis, at Nanking, on the Twenty-ninth day of August, in the Year of Our Lord One Thousand Eight Hundred and Forty-two, by the Plenipotentiaries° of Us and of Our said Good Brother, duly and respectively authorized for that purpose; which Treaty is hereunto annexed in Original.

Treaty

Her Majesty the Queen of the United Kingdom of Great Britain and Ireland, and His Majesty the Emperor of China, being desirous of putting an end to the misunderstandings and consequent hostilities which have arisen between the two Countries, have resolved to conclude a Treaty for that purpose, and have therefore named as their Plenipotentiaries, that is to say: Her Majesty the Queen of Great Britain and Ireland, HENRY POTTINGER, Bart., a Major General in the Service of the East India Company, etc., etc.; And His Imperial Majesty the Emperor of China, the High Commissioners KEYING, a Member of the Imperial House and Guardian of the Crown Prince and General of the Garrison of Canton; and ELEPOO, of Imperial Kindred, graciously permitted to wear the insignia of the first rank, and the distinction of Peacock's feather, lately Minister and Governor General etc., and now Lieutenant-General Commanding at Chapoo: Who, after having communicated to each other their respective Full Powers and found them to be in good and due form, have agreed upon and concluded, the following Articles:

Article I.

There shall henceforward be Peace and Friendship between Her Majesty the Queen of the United Kingdom of Great Britain and Ireland, and His Majesty the Emperor of China, and between their respective Subjects, who shall enjoy full security and protection for their persons and property within the Dominions of the other.

Plenipotentiaries: Diplomatic agents with power to transact business on behalf of others.

Article II.

His Majesty the Emperor of China agrees that British Subjects, with their families and establishments, shall be allowed to reside, for the purpose of carrying on their Mercantile pursuits, without molestation or restraint at the Cities and Towns of Canton, Amoy, Foochow-fu, Ningpo, and Shanghai, and Her Majesty the Queen of Great Britain, etc., will appoint Superintendents or Consular Officers, to reside at each of the above-named Cities or Towns, to be the medium of communication between the Chinese Authorities and the said Merchants, and to see that the just Duties and other Dues of the Chinese Government is hereafter provided for, are duly discharged by Her Britannic Majesty's Subjects.

Article III.

It being obviously necessary and desirable, that British Subjects should have some Port whereat they may careen and refit their Ships, when required, and keep Stores for that purpose, His Majesty the Emperor of China cedes to Her Majesty the Queen of Great Britain, etc., the Island of Hongkong, to be possessed in perpetuity by Her Britannic Majesty, Her Heirs and Successors, and to be governed by such Laws and Regulations as Her Majesty the Queen of Great Britain, etc., shall see fit to direct.

Article IV.

The Emperor of China agrees to pay the sum of Six Millions of Dollars as the value of Opium which was delivered up at Canton in the month of March 1839, as a Ransom for the lives of Her Britannic Majesty's Superintendent and Subjects, who had been imprisoned and threatened with death by the Chinese High Officers.

Article V.

The Government of China having compelled the British Merchants trading at Canton to deal exclusively with certain Chinese Merchants called Hong Merchants (or Cohong) who had been licensed by the Chinese Government for that purpose, the Emperor of China agrees to abolish that practice in future at all Ports where British Merchants may reside, and to permit them to carry on their mercantile transactions with whatever persons they please, and His Imperial Majesty further agrees to pay to the British Government the sum of Three Millions of Dollars, on account of Debts due to British Subjects by some of the said Hong Merchants (or Cohong), who have become insolvent, and who owe very large sums of money to Subjects of Her Britannic Majesty.

Article VI.

The Government of Her Britannic Majesty having been obliged to send out an Expedition to demand and obtain redress for the violent and unjust Proceedings of the Chinese High Authorities towards Her Britannic Majesty's Office and Subjects, the Emperor of China agrees to pay the sum of Twelve Millions of Dollars on account of the Expenses incurred, and Her Britannnic Majesty's Plenipotentiary voluntarily agrees, on behalf of Her Majesty, to deduct from the said amount of Twelve Millions of Dollars, any sums which may have been received by Her Majesty's combined Forces as Ransom for Cities and Towns in China, subsequent to the 1st day of August 1841.

In perpetuity: indefinitely.

Article VII.

It is agreed that the Total amount of Twenty-one Millions of Dollars, described in the three preceding Articles, shall be paid as follows:

Six Millions immediately.

Six Millions in 1843. That is: Three Millions on or before the 30th of the month of June, and Three Millions on or before the 31st of December.

Five Millions in 1844. That is: Two Millions and a Half on or before the 30th of June, and Two Millions and a on or before the 31st of December.

Four Millions in 1845. That is: Two Millions on or before the 30th of June, and Two Millions on or before the 31st of December; and it is further stipulated, that Interest at the rate of 5 per cent. per annum, shall be paid by the Government of China on any portions of the above sums that are not punctually discharged at the periods fixed.

Article VIII.

The Emperor of China agrees to release unconditionally all Subjects of her Britannic Majesty (whether Natives of Europe or India) who may be in confinement at this moment, in any part of the Chinese Empire.

Article IX.

The Emperor of China agrees to publish and promulgate, under His Imperial Sign Manual and Seal, a full and entire amnesty and act of indemnity, to all Subjects of China on account of their having resided under, or having had dealings and intercourse with, or having entered the Service of Her Britannic Majesty, or of Her Majesty's Officers, and His Imperial Majesty further engages to release all Chinese Subjects who may be at this moment in confinement for similar reasons.

Article X.

His Majesty the Emperor of China agrees to establish at all the Ports which are by the 2nd Article of this Treaty to be thrown open for the resort of British Merchants, a fair and regular Tariff of Export and Import Customs and other Dues, which Tariff shall be publicly notified and promulgated for general information, and the Emperor further engages, that when British Merchandise shall have once paid at any of the said Ports the regulated Customs and Dues agreeable to the Tariff, to be hereafter fixed, such Merchandise may be conveyed by Chinese Merchants, to any Province or City in the interior of the Empire of China. . .

Article XI.

It is agreed that Her Britannic Majesty's Chief High Officer in China shall correspond with the Chinese High Officers, both at the Capital and in the Provinces, under the term "Communication" [chinese characters]. The Subordinate British Officers and Chinese High Officers in the Provinces under the terms "Statement" [chinese characters] on the part of the former, and on the part of the latter "Declaration" [chinese characters], and the Subordinates of both Countries on a footing of perfect equality. Merchants and others not holding official situations and, therefore, not included in the above, on both sides, to use the term "Representation" [chinese characters] in all Papers addressed to, or intended for the notice of the respective Governments.

Article XII.

On the assent of the Emperor of China to this Treaty being received and the discharge of the first instalment of money, Her Britannic Majesty's Forces will retire from Nanking and the Grand Canal, and will no longer molest or stop the Trade of China. The Military Post at Chinhai will also be withdrawn, but the Islands of Koolangsoo and that of Chusan will continue to be held by Her Majesty's Forces until the money payments, and the arrangements for opening the Ports to British Merchants be completed.

Article XIII.

The Ratification of the Treaty by Her Majesty the Queen of Great Britain, etc., and His Majesty the Emperor of China shall be exchanged as soon as the great distance which separates England from China will admit; but in the meantime counterpart copies of it, signed and sealed by the Plenipotentiaries on behalf of their respective Sovereigns, shall be mutually delivered, and all its provisions and arrangements shall take effect.

Done at Nanking and Signed and Sealed by the Plenipotentiaries on board Her Britannic Majesty's ship Cornwall this twenty-ninth day of August, 1842, corresponding with the Chinese date, twenty-fourth day of the seventh month in the twenty-second Year of TAOU KWANG.

(L.S.) HENRY POTTINGER,
Her Majesty's Plenipotentiary.
Chinese Signatures (3).

We, having seen and considered the Treaty aforesaid, have approved, accepted, and confirmed the same in all and every one of its Articles and Clauses, as We do by these Presents approve, accept, confirm, and ratify it for Ourselves, Our Heirs, and Successors: Engaging and Promising upon Our Royal Word, that We will sincerely and faithfully perform and observe all and singular the things which are contained and expressed in the Treaty aforesaid, and that We will never suffer the same to be violated by anyone, or transgressed in any manner, as far as it lies in Our Power.

For the greater Testimony and Validity of all which, We have caused the Great Seal of Our United Kingdom of to be affixed to these Presents, which We have signed with Our Royal Hand.

Given at Our Court at Windsor Castle, the Twenty-eighth day of December, in the Year of Our Lord One Thousand Eight Hundred and Forty-two, and in the Sixth Year of Our Reign.

(Signed) VICTORIA R.

Analysis and Review Questions

Map 24.1
Treaty Ports and
the Boxer Rebellion
in China

1. How unequal are the terms in the Treaty of Nanjing?
2. What privileges are offered to the British in the treaty?
3. How important to the British trade activities in China is the opening of four more ports?
4. How do you understand the Chinese view of "a century of humiliation" as a result of the Opium War and the Treaty of Nanjing?

A Comic Dialogue, 1855

About the Document

After the arrival of American naval battle ships in Tokyo Bay in 1853, Japan opened its door. The Japanese view of the Americans, however, remained skeptical, and anti-American sentiment continued to grow despite the introduction of Western values into Japanese society. Conservative Japanese feared that Western ideology would destroy Japanese tradition and civilization.

In this comic dialogue, the conversation between the catfish, the symbol of the Japanese people, and Perry, reflects how East and West viewed and resisted each other.

Image 24.1
Japanese Woodcut
on Perry's Arrival

The Document

CATFISH: You stupid Americans have been making fun of us Japanese for the past two or three years. You have come and pushed us around too much. . . . Stop this useless talk of trade; we don't need it. We are sick of hearing the noisy calls of the candy sellers. Since we don't need you, hurry up and put your back to us. Fix your rudder and sail away at once.

AMERICA: What are you talking about, you stupid catfish! Mine is a country of benevolence and compassion. No matter what a person does, even if he is a laborer or a hunter, if he is benevolent he can become king. That's why many people want to come to my country. . . . But there is one thing which troubles us: we have too many people and not enough food to feed them. Therefore we have come to Japan to get rice, radishes and chickens; but you just say no, and have not given us anything. That's why we keep coming back.

CATFISH: Shut up, Perry. No matter how often you brag that your federation [*gasshú koku*] is a country of benevolence, if you don't have food you must be poor. If America had the buddha or the gods, then you would have a good harvest of the five grains. But since you don't, you have to depend upon piracy and steal your food. Knowing this, the gods of our country have gathered together and have caused a divine wind to blow to sink your ships and those of the Russians. For sure in the eleventh month of last year the gods struck out against your rudeness. I don't want to listen to any of your empty words.

AMERICA: You catfish! It is funny for you to speak like that, making up your own reasoning. Despite the fact that men can usually hold you down with a gourd, on the fourth day of the eleventh month you tried to send us away by shaking Shimazu and Numazu, but our American spirit remained unmoved.

CATFISH: You noisy[,] hairy barbarian! If you don't leave we'll bury you in mud!

AMERICA: Go ahead and try; I'll fight back with gun and bayonet.

PLASTERER: Both of you be quiet. If you are far away, listen carefully to my words; if you are close, look with your eyes and see the cracks in the warehouses. We are asked to patch up these cracks and holes, asked over and over again; we are asked to prop up the broken down walls; we are known for our fine work with the trowel. Everyone admires our work. We are thankful this time for the earthquake, but both of you try to resolve your differences without causing us any trouble. We don't want to see it; stop it!

Analysis and Review Questions

*Map 24.2
Japanese Colonial
Expansion to 1914*

1. What is the general view of the Americans in the dialogue?
2. How does the American brag about his culture?
3. What reasons does the American give for coming to Japan? Can these reasons be justified?
4. Find one sentence in the dialogue to describe Japanese anti-American sentiment.

WEB LINKS

Selections from Longman World History—Primary Sources and Case Studies

http://longmanworldhistory.com
The following additional readings and case studies can be found on the Web site.
Document 24.4, The Meiji Constitution
Case Study 24.1, How the East Views the West
Case Study 24.2, Different Responses to Westernization
Case Study 24.3, Two Perspectives on Westerners in East Asia

The Opium War

http://www.suite101.com/article.cfm/oriental_history/19388
Brief description of the issues surrounding opium trade between the British and the Chinese in the nineteenth century.

http://cyber.law.harvard.edu/ChinaDragon/opiumwar.html
Links to articles and other sites as well as a film on the Opium War.

http://serendipity.magnet.ch/wod/hongkong.html
Article from the July 10, 1997, *Worker's World* newspaper describing how the British took Hong Kong from China.

http://web.jjay.cuny.edu/~jobrien/reference/ob36.html
Painting of a naval battle during the Opium War; description of events leading to the war; and document from Captain Elliot, British Superintendent of Trade, to opium traders, March 27, 1839.

The Meiji Reform

http://www.japan-guide.com/e/e2130.html
Description of the Meiji Period, including links to related topics.

http://wgordon.web.wesleyan.edu/papers/jhist1.htm
Essay: "Tokugawa Period's Influence on Meiji Restoration."

http://www.uwosh.edu/home_pages/faculty_staff/earns/meiji.html
Detailed article: "Nagasaki in the Meiji Restoration: Choshu Loyalists and British Arms Merchants."

CHAPTER 25

South Asia:
Making of the British Raj

I ndia's Mughal Dynasty continued to rule much of the Indian subcontinent through the eighteenth and early nineteenth centuries, despite ongoing problems with corruption and inefficiency. Continuing oppression of Hindus by the Muslim administration distracted the government from the more important job of governing, and it also perpetuated long-standing animosities between Hindus and Muslims. Meanwhile, the weakness of the Mughal Empire and other local states was allowing Europeans increasing footholds and influence in the subcontinent.

By 1750 Britain's influence was on the rise, but by no means was Britain the only nation with influence. The French, Dutch, and Portuguese continued to maintain trading posts on the Indian Ocean coast. Certainly through the 1850s, European influence was primarily economic, exerted through trading agreements and monopolies. Britain's East India Company, especially, began to dominate mercantile activity in eastern India, in the province of Bengal. Nonetheless, local states, including the Mughal Empire, continued, at least in name, to rule much of India. By 1900, however, the unofficial and indirect rule of the East India Company had been nearly replaced with more direct colonial rule. India became one of Britain's most profitable and influential colonies.

*Map 25.1
(Interactive)
Growth of British
Control in India*

ARRIVAL OF THE BRITISH IN THE PUNJAB

About the Document

Indians were somewhat accustomed (by no means happily, in most cases) to being controlled by outsiders, so the arrival of the British did not have quite the immediate impact that it might have had elsewhere. Even after the arrival of the British, village life in India, as it had for centuries, continued to be dominated by traditional patterns of caste, leadership, and social norms. Caste rules branded Muslims, Christians, Sikhs, and others as outsiders, and most types of interaction were severely regulated for Hindus.

Life in the Punjab, a province of northwestern India, was somewhat different. There, the population included a high proportion of not only Hindus, but also Sikhs and Muslims. Everyday life was filled with contact with other groups, out of necessity. Not surprisingly, caste rules often were applied differently than they were in areas totally dominated by Hindus. In this selection from *Punjabi Century*, Prakash Tandon writes of both the caste system and the arrival of the British in the Punjab.

The Document

The Punjabis, as old people used to say, were puzzled at the first sight of the Englishmen because they had never seen any people look so implausible. They were used to Pathans, and some of their own people were fair, occasionally with light hair and grey eyes—we had a cousin with ginger hair and a skin that reddened instead of tanning, which he considered a great misfortune, as he was always compared to the posterior of a monkey! But never had they seen people so incredibly red-faced, and dressed in such quaint tight clothes displaying their bottoms so indecently. Never had they seen women who went about barefaced in equally incredible clothes, and spoke to strangers with the confidence of men. Their children they found unbelievably beautiful.

The villagers were, to begin with, frightened of the new conquerors. Women would hide their children. But fear soon gave way to curiosity and then to controversy. What were these Angrezi up to? Their ideas were quite unlike those of rulers in the past. They began by doing the oddest things, like consulting each peasant about the land he possessed and giving him a permanent title to it, with a fixed revenue which was remitted in years when crops were bad. The officers moved about freely, unguarded and without pomp and show. The visiting officials pitched their tents outside the villages, and held their office under a tree where anyone could approach them. Accompanied by just one or two persons they would ride on horseback for hours, inspecting and talking to people. Most of them had learned Punjabi well, some quite fluently. Their women, whom we soon began to call mem sahibs, also moved about freely, asking the village women and children questions. The officers and their wives had insatiable curiosity about our habits and customs and seemed never to tire of getting to know us. Their manners were strange but kindly and considerate, seldom hectoring or bullying. In their dress, manner or speech there was nothing of the rulers, as we were used to, and yet it was soon obvious that there was no authority lacking, and that they had a peppery temper.

I think what impressed our elders most, and what they still spoke about when I was young, was that in the past there had been rulers who were virtuous and mindful of the rayats welfare, but never a whole system of government that was bent to public good, with no apparent personal benefit to its officers. These and many other things at first intrigued the people, and later pleased them.

We Punjabis were fortunate in escaping the rule of the East India Company. . . . In this virgin field, with no regrets from the past, the government settled down to the task in which our family, like many others, was to play a small part, of building an administration; giving the province a new judiciary; for the first time a police; instituting land records and a revenue system; education department; building irrigation canals which changed deserts into granaries; and providing many other services that laid the foundation of a peaceful and prosperous countryside. It was a benevolent bureaucracy which gave much opportunity for building and therefore attracted men who liked pioneering under conditions of scope and power.

When I was at school our textbooks dividing Indian history into three periods, Hindu, Muslim and British, ended with a short chapter 'Angrezi Raj ki Barkaten'—

Blessings of the English Raj.° This was also a standard question in our examinations. There was a list of about a dozen blessings like law and order, irrigation canels, roads and bridges, schools, railways, telegraph and public health. In my generation these things were taken for granted, but my father used to explain that while he, too, was born in an era of peace, to his elders the new law and order really meant something. . . . The British solders [unlike other conquering soldiers] were simple, and instead of helping themselves paid fancy prices. If our generation began to be amused at the textbook blessings of the British Raj, my grandfather's generation took them seriously and praised them unreservedly. So did my father and his generation, at least to begin with.

At the time my father began his career, the service rules, like the Indian caste system, were clearly defined, well understood and fully accepted. You accepted them as the natural order of things. There were three grades in service, virtually like the Hindu castes, because entry was preordained and determined by birth. There was a grade for the British-born, which was the seniormost; followed by a middle grade for the locally born British, pure or mixed; and a junior grade for Indians, irrespective of their caste. Between the English-born and the Indian-born British we were unable to make a distinction. They all looked the same, spoke the same language and seemed to live alike. The difference was too subtle for us to appreciate. It could only be inferred that those who were born in England belonged to superior families and received better education than their local kinsmen and therefore were better qualified for superior posts; but strangely enough, the locally born talked of 'home' with the same nostalgia.

Analysis and Review Questions

1. What comment does Tandon offer about the clothing of the British?
2. Had any of the early British officials bothered to learn Punjabi, the local language? How might British knowledge of the language, or lack of it, have affected British colonial administration?
3. What were the three grades or levels in the civil service?
4. Do Tandon's relatives seem to be appreciative of the British?
5. List three of the developments brought by the British to the Punjab?

Image 25.1
The "Tiger
of Mysore"

THOMAS BABINGTON MACAULAY'S "MINUTE ON EDUCATION"

About the Document

As European influence increased in India, debates arose about the value of maintaining and encouraging the local traditional cultures. Some Europeans believed that Indian culture should be respected as an ancient and rich culture, while others believed it to be grossly inferior to Western culture. Often, those who supported efforts to maintain Indian culture were those who had lived and worked in India (usually as civil servants) and who had come to appreciate the great diversity of Indian civilization. These supporters were called "Orientalists." Those who believed Indian culture should be replaced by Western ideas and values

Raj: "Rule" or "reign," as in the British "Raj."

were often "utilitarians," or Englishmen who believed that people less fortunate could be "remade" into "better" people in the right environment. They believed that Western education in India would provide this "right" environment.

In the midst of the debate between these two groups in 1834, Thomas Babington Macaulay, a member of Parliament and one of the most noted British historians of the nineteenth century, wrote a report for the government called the "Minute on Education." He advocated a complete destruction of Indian civilization, and his opinion of Indian learning is made quite clear in this tract.

The Document

We have a fund to be employed as government shall direct for the intellectual improvement of the people of this country. The simple question is, what is the most useful way of employing it?

All parties seem to be agreed on one point, that the dialects commonly spoken among the natives of this part of India contain neither literary or scientific information, and are moreover so poor and rude that, until they are enriched from some other quarter, it will not be easy to translate any valuable work into them. It seems to be admitted on all sides that the intellectual improvement of those classes of the people who have the means of pursuing higher studies can at present be effected only by means of some language not vernacular amongst them.

What, then, shall that language be? One half of the Committee maintain that it should be English. The other half strongly recommend the Arabic and Sanskrit.° The whole question seems to me to be, which language is the best worth knowing?

I have no knowledge of either Sanskrit or Arabic. But I have done what I could to form a correct estimate of their value. I have read translations of the most celebrated Arabic and Sanskrit works. I have conversed both here and at home with the men distinguished by their proficiency in the Eastern tongues. I am quite ready to take the Oriental learning at the valuation of the Orientalists themselves. I have never found one among them who could deny that a single shelf of a good European library was worth the whole native literature of India and Arabia. The intrinsic superiority of the Western literature is, indeed, fully admitted by those members of the Committee who support the Oriental plan of education. . . .

It is said that the Sanskrit and Arabic are the languages in which the sacred books of a hundred millions of people are written, and that they are, on that account, entitled to peculiar encouragement. Assuredly it is the duty of the British government in India to be not only tolerant, but neutral on all religious questions. But to encourage the study of a literature admitted to be of small intrinsic value only because that literature inculcates the most serious errors on the most important subjects, is a course hardly reconcilable with reason, with morality, or even with that very neutrality which ought, as we all agree, to be sacredly preserved. It is confessed that a language is barren of useful knowledge. We are told to teach it because it is fruitful of monstrous superstitions. We are to teach false history, false astronomy, false medicine, because we find them in company with a false religion. We abstain, and I trust shall always abstain, from giving any public encouragement to those who are engaged in the work of converting natives to Christianity. And, while we act thus, can we reasonably and decently bribe men out of

Sanskrit: A classical Indian language, considered to be the language of Hinduism.

the revenues of the State to waste their youth in learning how they are to purify themselves after touching an ass, or what text of the Vedas they are to repeat to expiate the crime of killing a goat?

. . .

To sum up what I have said: I think it clear that we are free to employ our funds as we choose; that we ought to employ them in teaching what is best worth knowing; that English is better worth knowing than Sanskrit or Arabic; that the natives are desirous to be taught English, and are not desirous to be taught Sanskrit or Arabic; that neither as the languages of law, nor as the languages of religion, have the Sanskrit and Arabic any peculiar claim to our encouragement; that it is possible to make natives of this country thoroughly good English scholars, and that to this end our efforts ought to be directed.

In one point, I fully agree with the gentlemen to whose views I am opposed. I feel, with them, that it is impossible for us, with our limited means, to attempt to educate the body of the people. We must at present do our best to form a class who may be interpreters between us and the millions whom we govern; a class of persons, Indian in blood and colour, but English in taste, in opinions, in morals, and in intellect. To that class we may leave it to refine the vernacular dialects of the country, to enrich those dialects with terms of science borrowed from the Western nomenclature, and to render them by degrees fit vehicles for conveying knowledge to the great mass of the population.

Analysis and Review Questions

1. What does Macaulay have to say about the "literary or scientific" information found in the various Indian languages?
2. Does Macaulay actually state that English is better than either Sanskrit or Arabic? Explain.
3. Is there any advocacy here for broad public education? Explain.
4. Would you call Macaulay "racist"? Why or why not?
5. What sort of knowledge of Sanskrit and Arabic does Macaulay profess?

AN INDIAN NATIONALIST ON HINDU WOMEN AND EDUCATION

About the Document

Many Indian intellectuals began to reconcile themselves to British learning through the middle to late years of the nineteenth century. These individuals were often called "accomodationists" or "moderate" nationalists. Most of these scholars did not completely discount their own culture, but felt there was much to learn from the West, especially since India was increasingly influenced by the British and others. Others felt that learning Western ideas and attitudes could help to reinvigorate their own, usually Hindu, tradition.

Rammohun Roy was born around 1774 in Bengal, and enjoyed a varied education that included studying Persian and Sanskrit as well as Buddhism in Tibet. After he retired around age 40, he devoted himself to educational and social reform and began analyzing British culture and ideas (the first Indian scholar to do so seriously). Roy became a dedicated disciple of democracy and also of Western

Image 25.2
Indian Ruler
on Horseback

customs and thought, often analyzing his own Indian traditions through a Western looking-glass. Here, Roy discusses the position of women in Hindu society and also comments on an educational scheme put forth by the government.

The Document

Advocate. I alluded . . . to the real reason for our anxiety to persuade widows to follow their husbands, and for our endeavors to burn them pressed down with ropes: viz., that women are by nature of inferior understanding, without resolution, unworthy of trust, subject to passions, and void of virtuous knowledge; they, according to the precepts of the Sastra, are not allowed to marry again after the demise of their husbands, and consequently despair at once of all worldly pleasure; hence it is evident, that death to these unfortunate widows is preferable to existence, for the great difficulty which a widow may experience by living a purely ascetic life as prescribed by the Sastras is obvious; therefore if she do not perform Concremation [being burnt alive at her husband's cremation], it is probable that she may be guilty of such acts as may bring disgrace upon her paternal and maternal relations. . . .

Opponent. The reason you have now assigned for burning widows alive is indeed your true motive, as we are well aware; but the faults which you have imputed to women are not planted in their constitution by nature; it would be, therefore, grossly criminal to condemn that sex to death merely from precaution. By ascribing to them all sorts of improper conduct, you have indeed successfully persuaded the Hindoo community to look down upon them as contemptible and mischievous creatures, whence they have been subjected to constant miseries. I have, therefore, to offer a few remarks on this head.

Women are in general inferior to men in bodily strength and energy; consequently the male part of the community, taking advantage of their corporeal weakness, have denied to them those excellent merits that they are entitled to by nature, and afterwards they are apt to say that women are naturally incapable of acquiring those merits. . . .

As to their inferiority in point of understanding, when did you ever afford them a fair opportunity of exhibiting their natural capacity? How then can you accuse them of want of understanding? If, after instruction in knowledge and wisdom, a person cannot comprehend or retain what has been taught him, we may consider him as deficient; but as you keep women generally void of education and acquirements, you cannot, therefore, in justice pronounce on their inferiority.

Secondly. You charge them with want of resolution, at which I feel exceedingly surprised. For we constantly perceive, in a country where the name of death makes the male shudder, that the female, from her firmness of mind, offers to burn with the corpse of her deceased husband; and yet you accuse those women of deficiency in point of resolution.

Thirdly. With regard to their trustworthiness, let us look minutely into the conduct of both sexes, and we may be enabled to ascertain which of them is the most frequently guilty of betraying friends. If we enumerate such women in each village or town as have been deceived by men, and such men as have been betrayed by women, I presume that the number of the deceived women would be found ten times greater than that of the betrayed men. Men are, in general, able to read and write, and manage public affairs, by which means they easily promulgate such faults as women occasionally commit, but never consider as criminal the misconduct of men towards women. . . .

In the fourth place, with respect to their subjection to the passions, this may be judged of by the custom of marriage as to the respective sexes; for one man may marry two or three, sometimes even ten wives and upwards; while a woman, who marries but one husband, desires at his death to follow him, forsaking all worldly enjoyments, or to remain leading the austere life of an ascetic.

Fifthly. The accusation of their want of virtuous knowledge is an injustice. . . . How many Kulin . . . How many . . . Brahmans are there who marry ten or fifteen wives for the sake of money, that never see the greater number of them after the day of marriage, and visit others only three or four times in the course of their life. Still amongst those women, most, even without seeing or receiving any support from their husbands, living dependent on their fathers or brothers, and suffering much distress, continue to preserve their virtue. And when Brahmans, or those of other tribes, bring their wives to live with them, what misery do the women not suffer? At marriage the wife is recognized as half of her husband, but in after-conduct they are treated worse than inferior animals. For the woman is employed to do the work of a slave in the house, such as, in her turn, to clean the place very early in the morning, whether cold or wet, to scour the dishes, to wash the floor, to cook night and day, to prepare and serve food for her husband, father, mother-in-law, sisters-in-law, brothers-in-law, and friends and connections! . . . If in the preparation or serving up of the victuals they commit the smallest fault, what insult do they not receive from their husband, their mother-in-law, and the younger brothers of their husband? Should the husband acquire wealth, he indulges in criminal amours to her perfect knowledge and almost under her eyes, and does not see her perhaps once a month. As long as the husband is poor, she suffers every kind of trouble, and when he becomes rich, she is altogether heartbroken. . . . Where a husband takes two or three wives to live with him, they are subjected to mental miseries and constant quarrels. Even this distressed situation they virtuously endure. Sometimes it happens that the husband, from a preference for one of his wives, behaves cruelly to another. Amongst the lower classes, and those even of the better class who have not associated with good company, the wife, on the slightest fault, or even on bare suspicion of her misconduct, is chastised as a thief. . . . If, unable to bear such cruel usage, a wife leaves her husband's house to live separately from him, then the influence of the husband with the magisterial authority is generally sufficient to place her again in his hands; when, in revenge for her quitting him, he seizes every pretext to torment her in various ways, and sometimes even puts her privately to death. These are facts occurring every day, and not to be denied. What I lament is, that, seeing the women thus dependent and exposed to every misery, you feel for them no compassion that might exempt them from being tied down and burnt to death.

[Roy questioned the practice of keeping women uneducated. Here he comments on a new school in India.]

The establishment of a new Sangscrit School in Calcutta evinces the laudable desire of government to improve the Natives of India by Education—a blessing for which they must ever be grateful; and every well-wisher of the human race must be desirous that the efforts made to promote it should be guided by the most enlightened principles, so that the stream of intelligence may flow in the most useful channels.

While we looked forward with pleasing hope to the dawn of knowledge thus promised to the rising generation, our hearts were filled with mingled feelings of delight and gratitude; we already offered up thanks to Providence for inspiring the most generous and enlightened Nations of the West with the glorious ambition of planting in Asia the Arts and Sciences of modern Europe.

We find that the Government are establishing a Sangscrit school under Hindoo pandits to impart such knowledge as is already current in India. This seminary . . . can only be expected to load the minds of youth with grammatical niceties and metaphysical distinctions of little or no practicable use to the possessors or to society. The pupils will there acquire what was known two thousand years ago, with the addition of vain and empty subtleties since then produced by speculative men, such as is already commonly taught in all parts of India.

Analysis and Review Questions

Map 25.2
European Powers
in Southeast Asia

1. According to Roy, are women in any way naturally inferior?
2. How well educated were women in India?
3. How might a husband having multiple wives pose practical problems for the wives themselves?
4. Why is Roy critical of the government's plans for a Sanskrit school?
5. According to Roy, which is preferable, a poor husband or a rich husband?

AN INDIAN MUSLIM VISITS LONDON

About the Document

Muslims have always been a minority population in India, even during the Mughal Empire. Only around 20 percent of the population then had been Muslim. Nonetheless, in terms of culture, the Muslim population was never absorbed into the larger Hindu population. During the eighteenth and into the nineteenth century, there existed vibrant, active cultures and scholarship from both sides of the religious divide. While many Hindus tried to acclimate themselves to the arriving British, generally Muslims did not.

A notable exception to that general trend was Syed Ahmed Khan, born in 1817. Khan, like Rammohun Roy, welcomed British influence. He wished to show Muslims, usually hesitant to get too close to the British, that not only was this contact acceptable, it was a positive thing with only good results. Khan also wanted to prove to the British that protecting and aiding the Muslims in India was in their best interest. Khan had some success in each of these goals, though Muslims lagged behind Hindus in Western education and government service. Khan also visited London in 1869—a visit he writes about in one of the following documents. He also discusses the impact of Western education on Indian Muslims.

The Document

It is nearly six months since I arrived in London, and [I] have been unable to see many things I should have liked, been able to see a good deal, and have been in the society of lords and dukes at dinners and evening parties. Artisans and the common working-man I have seen in numbers, I have visited famous and spacious mansions, museums, engineering works, shipbuilding establishments, gun-foundries, ocean-telegraph companies which connect continents, vessels of war (in one of which I walked for miles, the Great Eastern steamship), have been present at the meetings of several societies, and have dined at clubs and private houses. The result of all this is, that although I do not absolve the English in India of discourtesy, and of looking upon the natives of that country as animals and beneath contempt, I think they do so from not understanding us; and I am afraid I must confess that they are not far wrong in their opinion of us. Without flattering the English, I can truly say that the natives of India, high and low, merchants and petty shopkeepers, educated and illiterate, when contrasted with the English in education, manners, and uprightness, are as like them as a dirty animal is to an able and handsome man. The English have reason for believing us in India to be imbecile brutes. Although my countrymen will consider this opinion of mine an extremely harsh one, and will wonder what they are deficient in, and in what the English excel, to cause me to write as I do, I maintain that they have no cause for wonder, as they are ignorant of everything here, which is really beyond imagination and conception. . . . I only remark on politeness, knowledge, good faith, cleanliness, skilled workmanship, accomplishments, and thoroughness, which are the results of education and civilisation. All good things, spiritual and worldly, which should be found in man, have been bestowed by the Almighty on Europe, and especially on England. By spiritual good things I mean that the English carry out all the details of the religion which they believe to be the true one, with a beauty and excellence which no other nation can compare with. This is entirely due to the education of the men and women . . . If Hindustanis can only attain to civilisation, it will probably, owing to its many excellent natural powers, become, if not the superior, at least the equal of England.

Look at this young girl Elizabeth Matthews [a servant in the house in which he was living], who, in spite of her poverty, invariably buys a half-penny paper called the "Echo" and reads it when at leisure. If she comes across a "Punch,"° in which there are pictures of women's manners and customs, she looks at them, and enjoys the editor's remarks thereon. All the shops have the names of their occupants written in front in splendid golden letters, and servants requiring anything have only to read and enter. Cabmen and coachmen keep a paper or a book under their seats and after taking the passenger to his destination, or in case the coach has to wait, they take out their newspaper and start reading.

Until the education of the masses is pushed on as it is here, it is impossible for a native to become civilised and honoured.

The cause of England's civilisation is that all the arts and sciences are in the language of the country. . . . Those who are really bent on improving and bettering India must remember that the only way of compassing this is by having the whole of the arts and sciences translated into their own language.

[From a letter to Mawlawi Tasadduq]

I have been accused by people, who do not understand, of being disloyal to the culture of Islam, even to Islam itself. There are men who say that I have become a Christian. All this I have drawn upon myself because I advocate the introduction of a new system of education which will not neglect the Islamic basis of our culture, nor, for that matter, the teaching of Islamic theology itself, but which will surely take account of the changed conditions in this land. Today there are no Muslim rulers to patronize those who are well versed in the old Arabic and Persian learning. The new rulers insist upon a knowledge of their language for all advancement in their services and in some of the independent professions like practising law as well. If the Muslims do not take to the system of education introduced by the British, they will not only remain a backward community but will sink lower and lower until there will be no hope of recovery left to them. Is this at all a pleasing prospect? . . .

The adoption of the new system of education does not mean the renunciation of Islam. It means its protection. We are justly proud of the achievements of our forefathers in the fields of learning and culture. We should, however, remember that these achievements were possible only because they were willing to act upon the teachings of the

Punch: An English magazine specializing in satire and commentary.

Prophet upon whom be peace and blessings of God. He said that knowledge is the heritage of the believer, and that he should acquire it wherever he can find it. He also said that the Muslims should seek knowledge even if they have to go to China to find it.... Islam, Islamic culture, and the Muslims themselves prospered as long as the Prophet was followed in respect of these teachings; when we ceased to take interest in the knowledge of others, we began to decline in every respect. Did the early Muslims not take to Greek learning avidly? Did this in any respect undermine their loyalty to Islam? ...

How can we remain true Muslims or serve Islam, if we sink into ignorance?

. . .

The Muslims have nothing to fear from the adoption of the new education if they simultaneously hold steadfast to their faith, because Islam is not irrational superstition; it is a rational religion which can march hand in hand with the growth of human knowledge. Any fear to the contrary betrays lack of faith in the truth of Islam.

Analysis and Review Questions

1. Does Khan seem to like London?
2. How do the "natives of India" stack up against the English?
3. What was so special about the servant girl, Elizabeth Matthews?
4. Why should Muslims undertake Western education, according to Khan?
5. Is Islam in any danger from Western education, according to Khan?

WEB LINKS

http://longmanworldhistory.com
The following additional readings and case studies can be found on the Web site.
Document 21.6, The Seneca Falls Convention
Document 25.5, The Indian Revolt
Case Study 25.1, Differing Views of Education in India
Case Study 25.2, A Hindu and a Muslim on Western Influence
Case Study 25.3, Calls for Women's Rights in Nineteenth Century India and the United States

http://www.123india.com
The site portrays itself as "India's Premier Portal" with good reason. Everything from current Indian news and online India chat to Indian search engines can be found here.

http://regiments.org/milhist/wars/19thcent/57india.htm
A mostly military history site dedicated to the British units involved in suppressing the Mutiny of 1857. Sections include campaigns, lists of units and soldiers, general overviews, and so on.

http://www.muslimindia.com/ahome.htm
Along with pages of more modern interest are history pages dealing with notable Indian Muslims, including Syed Ahmed Khan.

http://www.freeindia.org
A massive site, with large sections devoted to biographies of notable Indian gods and goddesses and leaders such as Rammohun Roy. Search engine focusing on Indian Web sites included as well.

CHAPTER 26

Africa:
The West Imposes

In 1750 only the coastal areas of Africa had experienced any consistent contact with Europeans. As most trade focused on the coasts of West and East Africa, Europeans had limited themselves to the establishment of trading companies and coastal outposts. Indeed, Europeans showed little real desire or ability to "conquer" parts of the continent. By the mid- to late nineteenth century, however, imperial rivalries and the Industrial Revolution, along with well-intentioned but often misguided humanitarian efforts, had combined to make the division of Africa into colonial possessions almost guaranteed.

Far from being passive participants, Africans frequently resisted European attempts at "civilizing" them and early on in the period were often dealt with as relative equals. By the end of the century, however, Africa, with the exceptions of independent Ethiopia and Liberia, had fallen under European domination. The speed at which Europeans conquered the continent would lay ruin to many African cultures and set the continent on a course with disaster less than a century later.

Map 26.1
The Beginning of
European Colonial
Rule in Africa

SLAVERY IN AFRICA BY MUNGO PARK

About the Document

During the late eighteenth and early nineteenth centuries in Europe, the scientific revolution and the Enlightenment were inspiring new attitudes and outlooks on the world. Educated Europeans were interested in what lay beyond their immediate horizon. It is no surprise, then, that this period marked the beginning of a new era of exploration and discovery, as European explorers delved deeper into areas of the world largely unknown to them. Underlying most, if not all, of these journeys, however, was the potential for economic gain for those who sponsored the travels.

One such explorer was Mungo Park, a Scotsman who traveled along the Gambia and Niger Rivers in West Africa from 1795 to 1797 and 1805 to 1806.

Park, who died on his second trip, was keenly aware that his purpose was to "scout out" economic potential. Nonetheless, Park's journals provide an insightful glimpse into life in West Africa. Abolitionists especially liked his commentary on slavery within Africa and quoted his writing to support their cause.

The Document

The slaves in Africa, I suppose, are nearly in the proportion of three to one to the free men. They claim no reward for their services except food and clothing, and are treated with kindness or severity, according to the good or bad disposition of their masters. Custom, however, has established certain rules with regard to the treatment of slaves, which it is thought dishonourable to violate. Thus, the domestic slaves, or such as are born in a man's own house, are treated with more lenity than those which are purchased with money. The authority of the master over the domestic slave, extends only to reasonable correction; for the master cannot sell his domestic without having first brought him to a public trial before the chief men of the place. But these restrictions on the power of the master extend not to the case of prisoners taken in war, nor to that of slaves purchased with money. All these unfortunate beings are considered as strangers and foreigners, who have no right to the protection of the law, and may be treated with severity, or sold to a stranger, according to the pleasure of their owners. There are, indeed, regular markets, where slaves of this description are bought and sold; and the value of a slave in the eye of an African purchaser, increases in proportion to his distance from his native kingdom; for when slaves are only a few days' journey from the place of their nativity, they frequently effect their escape; but when one or more kingdoms intervene, escape being more difficult, they are more readily reconciled to their situation. On this account, the unhappy slave is frequently transferred from one dealer to another, until he has lost all hopes of returning to his native kingdom. The slaves which are purchased by the Europeans on the coast are chiefly of this description; a few of them are collected in the petty wars, hereafter to be described, which take place near the coast; but by far the greater number are brought down in large caravans from the inland countries, of which many are unknown even by name to the Europeans. The slaves which are thus brought from the interior may be divided into two distinct classes; first, such as were slaves from their birth, having been born of enslaved mothers; secondly, such as were born free, but who afterwards, by whatever means, became slaves. Those of the first description are by far the most numerous; for prisoners taken in war (at least such as are taken in open and declared war, when one kingdom avows hostilities against another), are generally of this description.

Slaves of the second description generally become such by one or other of the following causes:—1. *Captivity*; 2. *Famine*; 3. *Insolvency*; 4. *Crimes*. A free man may, by the established customs of Africa, become a slave by being taken in war. War is, of all others, the most productive source, and was probably the origin of slavery.

Be this as it may, it is a known fact, that prisoners of war in Africa are the slaves of the conquerors; and when the weak or unsuccessful warrior begs for mercy beneath the uplifted spear of his opponent, he gives up at the same time his claim to liberty, and purchases his life at the expense of his freedom.

War, therefore, is certainly the most general and most productive source of slavery, and the desolations of war often (but not always) produce the second cause of slavery, famine, in which case a free man becomes a slave to avoid a greater calamity. During a great scarcity, which lasted for three years, in the countries of the Gambia, great numbers of people became slaves in this manner.

The third cause of slavery is insolvency. Of all the offences (if insolvency may be so called) to which the laws of Africa have affixed the punishment of slavery, this is the most common.

The fourth cause above enumerated is *the commission of crimes, on which the laws of the country affix slavery as a punishment*. In Africa, the only offences of this class are murder, adultery, and witchcraft; and I am happy to say that they did not appear to me to be common. In cases of murder, I was informed that the nearest relation of the deceased had it in his power, after conviction, either to kill the offender with his own hand, or sell him into slavery. When adultery occurs, it is generally left to the option of the person injured, either to sell the culprit, or accept such a ransom for him as he may think equivalent to the injury he has sustained. By witchcraft is meant pretended magic, by which the lives or healths of persons are affected; in other words, it is the administering of poison. No trial for this offence, however, came under my observation while I was in Africa, and I therefore suppose that the crime and its punishment occur but very seldom.

When a free man has become a slave by any one of the causes before mentioned, he generally continues so for life, and his children (if they are born of an enslaved mother) are brought up in the same state of servitude. There are, however, a few instances of slaves obtaining their freedom, and sometimes even with the consent of their masters; as by performing some singular piece of service, or by going to battle, and bringing home two slaves as a ransom; but the common way of regaining freedom is by escape; and when slaves have once set their minds on running away, they often succeed. Some of them will wait for years before an opportunity presents itself, and during that period show no signs of discontent. In general, it may be remarked, that slaves who come from a hilly country, and have been much accustomed to hunting and travel, are more apt to attempt their escape than such as are born in a flat country, and have been employed in cultivating the land.

[Regarding the Atlantic slave trade, Park says the following:]

How far it is maintained and supported by the slave traffic, which for two hundred years the nations of Europe have carried on with the natives of the coast, it is neither within my province nor in my power to explain. If my sentiments should be required concerning the effect which a discontinuance of that commerce would produce on the manners of the natives, I should have no hesitation in observing, that, in the present unenlightened state of their minds, my opinion is, the effect would neither be so extensive or beneficial as many wise and worthy persons fondly expect.

Analysis and Review Questions

1. What are the four most common ways for a person to become a slave?
2. If a person becomes a slave in one of these four ways, how long does he or she generally stay a slave?
3. Does Mungo Park appear to favor an end to the slave trade? Explain.
4. What two classes of slaves are brought to the coast from the interior?
5. Is Park's account objective? Does it indicate any bias, or is it "fair"?

AN AFRICAN PAMPHLETEER ATTACKS SLAVERY

About the Document

Though European writers, rather than non-white writers, tended to have the most significant impact on European attitudes toward slavery, there were nevertheless many former slaves who wrote compelling works that attacked the problem of slavery in Western society. In this era, one lesser-known writer of African heritage was Quobna Ottobah Cugoano. Cugoano's background is largely unknown, though he was born circa 1757 in what is today Ghana. He was sold into slavery by other locals at around 13 years of age and was sent to Grenada. His owner took him to England in 1772 where, through unknown means, he gained his freedom. Between 1787 and 1791, he spoke frequently at abolitionist meetings, calling for an end to slavery, and wrote several letters to London newspapers. He also published two books, but nothing is known of his whereabouts after 1791.

*Image 26.1
Yams as Sources
of Traditional
Power in West
Africa*

The excerpts that follow come from Cugoano's first book, *Thoughts and Sentiments on the Evil of Slavery*, published in 1787. Cugoano provides a clear and obvious challenge to English slavery based not only on Christian principles, but also on more worldly concepts, and asserts that slaves have the right and the obligation to rise up against their masters. Here, Cugoano attacks England and other nations for perpetuating the slave trade.

The Document

But whereas the people of Great-Britain having now acquired a greater share in that iniquitous commerce than all the rest together, they are the first that ought to set an example, lest they have to repent for their wickedness when it becomes too late; lest some impending calamity should speedily burst forth against them, and lest a just retribution for their enormous crimes, and a continuance in committing similar deeds of barbarity and injustice should involve them in ruin. For we may be assured that God will certainly avenge himself of such heinous transgressors of his law, and of all those planters and merchants, and of all others, who are the authors of the Africans' graves, severities, and cruel punishments, and no plea of any absolute necessity can possibly excuse them. And as the inhabitants of Great-Britain, and the inhabitants of the colonies, seem almost equally guilty of the oppression, there is great reason for both to dread the severe vengeance of Almighty God upon them, and upon all such notorious workers of wickedness; for it is evident that the legislature of Great-Britain patronises and encourages them, and shares in the infamous profits of the slavery of the Africans.

And even in that part of it carried on by the Liverpool and Bristol merchants, the many shocking and inhuman instances of their barbarity and cruelty are such, that every one that heareth thereof has reason to tremble, and cry out, *Should not the land tremble for this, and every one mourn that dwelleth therein*?

The vast carnage and murders committed by the British instigators of slavery, is attended with a very shocking, peculiar, and almost unheard of conception, according to the notion of the perpetrators of it; they either consider them as their own property, that they may do with as they please, in life or death; or that the taking away the life of a black man is of no more account than taking away the life of a beast.

Therefore let the inhabitants of any civilized nation determine, whether, if they were to be treated in the same manner that the Africans are, by various pirates, kidnappers, and slave-holders, and their wives, and their sons and daughters were to be robbed from them, or themselves violently taken away to a perpetual and intolerable slavery; or whether they would not think those robbers, who only took away their property, less injurious to them than the other. If they determine it so, as reason must tell every man, that himself is of more value than his property; then the executors of the laws of civilization ought to tremble at the inconsistency of passing judgment upon those whose crimes, in many cases, are less than what the whole legislature must be guilty of, when those of a far greater is encouraged and supported by it wherever slavery is tolerated by law, and, consequently, that slavery can no where be tolerated with any consistency to civilization and the laws of justice among men; but if it can maintain its ground, to have any place at all, it must be among a society of barbarians and thieves, and where the laws of their society is, for every one to catch what he can. Then, when theft and robbery become no crimes, the man-stealer and the conniving slave-holder might possibly get free.

But again let me observe, that whatever civilization the inhabitants of Great-Britain may enjoy among themselves, they have seldom maintained their own innocence in that great duty as a Christian nation towards others, and I may say, with respect to their African neighbours, or to any other wheresoever they may go by the way of commerce, they have not regarded them at all. And when they saw others robbing the Africans, and carrying them into captivity and slavery, they have neither helped them, not opposed their oppressors in the least. But instead thereof they have joined in combination against them with the rest of other profligate nations and people, to buy, enslave and make merchandize of them, because they found them helpless and fit to suit their own purpose, and are become the head carriers on of that iniquitous traffic. But the greater that any reformation and civilization is obtained by any nation, if they do not maintain righteousness, but carry on any course of wickedness and oppression, it makes them appear only the more inconsistent, and their tyranny and oppression the more conspicuous.

But why this diabolical traffic of slavery has not been abolished before now, and why it was introduced at all, as I have already enquired, must be greatly imputed to that powerful and pervading agency of infernal wickedness, which reigneth and prevaileth over the nations, and to that umbrageous image of iniquity established thereby.

I would hereby presume to offer the following considerations, as some outlines of a general reformation which ought to be established and carried on. And first, I would propose, that there ought to be days of mourning and fasting appointed, to make enquiry into that great and preeminent evil for many years past carried on against the Heathen nations, and the horrible iniquity of making merchandize of us, and cruelly enslaving the poor Africans; and that you might seek grace and repentance, and find mercy and forgiveness before God Omnipotent; and that he may give you wisdom and understanding to devise what ought to be done.

Secondly, I would propose that a total abolition of slavery should be made and proclaimed, and that an universal emancipation of slaves should begin from the date thereof, and be carried on in the following manner. That a proclamation should be caused to be made, setting forth the Antichristian unlawfulness of the slavery and commerce of the human species; and that it should be sent to all the courts and nations in Europe, to require their advice and assistance, and as they may find it unlawful to carry it on, let them whosoever will join to prohibit it.

And, thirdly, I would propose, that a fleet of some ships of war should be immediately sent to the coast of Africa, and particularly where the slave trade is carried on, with faithful men to direct that none should be brought from the coast of Africa without their own consent and the approbation of their friends, and to intercept all merchant ships that were bringing them away, until such a scrutiny was made, whatever nation they belonged to. And, I would suppose, if Great-Britain was to do any thing of this kind, that it would meet with the general approbation and assistance of other Christian nations; but whether it did or not, it could be very lawfully done at all the British forts and settlements on the coast of Africa.

These three preceding considerations may suffice at present to shew, that some plan might be adopted in such a manner as effectually to relieve the grievances and oppression of the Africans, and to bring great honour and blessings to that nation, and to all men whosoever would endeavour to promote so great good to mankind.

Analysis and Review Questions

*Map 26.2
(interactive)
Colonization
in Africa*

1. In what ways does Cugoano's attack on slavery have basis in Christian scripture?
2. Why does the author say that the slave trade has not already been abolished?
3. Outline the three propositions that Cugoano lays out for his "reformation" of slavery.
4. Which country does Cugoano say has the largest stake in the slave trade?
5. Which city's merchants seem to be most involved in the trade?

THE HISTORY OF MARY PRINCE

About the Document

The British slave trade was abolished in 1807, but the institution of slavery continued in British colonies until 1833. Abolitionists published treatises decrying the evils of slavery and the poor treatment of slaves, but relatively few accounts came from slaves or former slaves themselves. Even fewer testimonials came from female slaves.

The first such account published in Britain was *The History of Mary Prince*, published in 1831. Prince was born a slave in Bermuda in 1788, and, after several owners, she asked to be sold to the Wood family, which was setting off for Antigua. Subsequently, the Woods traveled to London with Mary Prince, where she soon asserted her legal right to freedom in Britain. Eventually, she made her way to the Anti-Slavery Society, Britain's premier antislavery organization. The secretary of the group suggested that Prince dictate her testimonial to a friend. With its moving and personal accounts of the harsh, degrading life of a Caribbean slave, the book caused a sensation when it was published.

The Document

At length the vendue master, who was to offer us for sale like sheep or cattle, arrived, and asked my mother which was the eldest. She said nothing, but pointed to me. He took me by the hand, and led me out into the middle of the street, and, turning me slowly round, exposed me to the view of those who attended the vendue. I was soon surrounded by strange men, who examined and handled me in the same manner that a butcher would a calf or a lamb he was about to purchase, and who talked about my shape and size in like words. I was then put up to sale. The bidding commenced at a few pounds, and gradually rose to fifty-seven, when I was knocked down to the highest bidder; and the people who stood by said that I had fetched a great sum for so young a slave.

I then saw my sisters led forth, and sold to different owners, so that we had not the sad satisfaction of being partners in bondage. When the sale was over, my mother hugged and kissed us, and mourned over us, begging of us to keep up a good heart, and do our duty to our new masters. It was a sad parting; one went one way, one another, and our poor mammy went home with nothing.

My new master was a Captain I—, who lived at Spanish Point.

Image 26.2
West African
Slave Market

[Mary was separated from her family and sent with her new master.]

It was night when I reached my new home.

Before I entered the house, two slave women, hired from another owner, who were at work in the yard, spoke to me, and asked who I belonged to? I replied, 'I am come to live here.'

When I went in, I stood up crying in a corner. Mrs I—came and took off my hat, and said in a rough voice, 'You are not come here to stand up in corners and cry, you are come here to work.'

The person I took the most notice of that night was a French Black called Hetty, whom my master took in privateering from another vessel, and made his slave. She was the most active woman I ever saw, and she was tasked to her utmost. A few minutes after my arrival she came in from milking the cows, and put the sweet-potatoes on for supper. She then fetched home the sheep, and penned them in the fold; drove home the cattle, and staked them about the pond side; fed and rubbed down my master's horse, and gave the hog and the fed cow their suppers; prepared the beds, and undressed the children, and laid them to sleep. She gave me my supper of potatoes and milk, and a blanket to sleep upon, which she spread for me in the passage before the door of Mrs I—'s chamber.

[That night, Mary heard Hetty being severely beaten.]

The next morning my mistress set about instructing me in my tasks. She taught me to do all sorts of household work; to wash and bake, pick cotton and wool, and wash floors, and cook. And she taught me (how can I ever forget it!) more things than these; she caused me to know the exact difference between the smart of the rope, the cart-whip, and the cow-skin, when applied to my naked body by her own cruel hand. And there was scarcely any punishment more dreadful than the blows I received on my face and head from her hard heavy fist. She was a fearful woman, and a savage mistress to her slaves. To strip me naked—to hang me up by the wrists and lay my flesh open with the cow-skin, was an ordinary punishment for even a slight offence. My mistress often robbed me too of the hours that belong to sleep. She used to sit up very late, frequently even until morning; and I had then to stand at a bench and wash during the greater part of the night, or pick wool and cotton; and often I have dropped down overcome by sleep and fatigue, till roused from a state of stupor by the whip, and forced to start up to my tasks.

Poor Hetty, my fellow slave, was very kind to me, and I used to call her my Aunt; but she led a most miserable life, and her death was hastened (at least the slaves all believed and said so,) by the dreadful chastisement she received from my master during her pregnancy. One of the cows had dragged the rope away from the stake to which

Hetty had fastened it, and got loose. My master flew into a terrible passion, and ordered the poor creature to be stripped quite naked, notwithstanding her pregnancy, and to be tied up to a tree in the yard. He then flogged her as hard as he could lick, both with the whip and cow-skin, till she was all over streaming with blood. He rested, and then beat her again and again. Her shrieks were terrible. The consequence was that poor Hetty was brought to bed before her time, and was delivered after severe labour of a dead child. Ere long her body and limbs swelled to a great size; and she lay on a mat in the kitchen, till the water burst out of her body and she died. All the slaves said that death was a good thing for poor Hetty; but I cried very much for her death. The manner of it filled me with horror.

One day a heavy squall of wind and rain came on suddenly, and my mistress sent me round the corner of the house to empty a large earthen jar. The jar was already cracked with an old deep crack that divided it in the middle, and in turning it upside down to empty it, it parted in my hand. I could not help the accident, but I was dreadfully frightened, looking forward to a severe punishment. I ran crying to my mistress, 'O mistress, the jar has come in two.' You have broken it, have you?' she replied; 'come directly here to me,' I came trembling: she stripped and flogged me long and severely with the cow-skin; as long as she had strength to use the lash, for she did not give over till she was quite tired. When my master came home at night, she told him of my fault; and oh, frightful! How he fell a swearing. After abusing me with every ill name he could think of, (too, too bad to speak in England,) and giving me several heavy blows with his hand, he said, 'I shall come home to-morrow morning at twelve, on purpose to give you a round hundred.' He kept his word—Oh sad for me! I cannot easily forget it. He tied me up upon a ladder, and gave me a hundred lashes with his own hand, and master Benjy stood by to count them for him. While my mistress went to bring him drink, there was a dreadful earthquake.

During the confusion I crawled away on my hands and knees, and laid myself down under the steps of the piazza, in front of the house. I was in a dreadful state—my body all blood and bruises, and I could not help moaning piteously. The other slaves, when they saw me, shook their heads and said, 'Poor child! Poor child!'—I lay there till the morning, careless of what might happen, for life was very weak in me, and I wished more than ever to die! But when we are very young, death always seems a great way off, and it would not come that night to me. The next morning I was forced by my master to rise and go about my usual work, though my body and limbs were so stiff and sore, that I could not move without the greatest pain. Nevertheless, even after all this severe punishment, I never heard the last of that jar; my mistress was always throwing it in my face.

After this I ran away and went to my mother, who was living with Mr. Richard Darrel. My poor mother was both grieved and glad to see me; grieved because I had been so ill used, and glad because she had not seen me for a long, long while. She dared not receive me into the house, but she hid me up in a hole in the rocks near, and brought me food at night, after everybody was asleep. My father, who lived at Crow-Lane, over the salt-water channel, last heard of my being hid up in the cavern, and he came and took me back to my master. Oh I was loth, loth to go back; but as there was no remedy, I was obliged to submit.

When we got home, my poor father said to Capt. I—, 'Sir, I am sorry that my child should be forced to run away from her owner; but the treatment she has received is enough to break her heart. The sight of her wounds has nearly broke mine. I entreat you, for the love of God, to forgive her for running away, and that you will be a kind master to her in future.' Capt. I—said I was used as well as I deserved, and that I ought to be punished for running away.

He did not, however, flog me that day. For five years after this I remained in his house, and almost daily received the same harsh treatment.

[Captain I. then sold Mary to a Mr. D.]

Mr. D—had a slave called old Daniel, whom he used to treat in the most cruel manner. Poor Daniel was lame in the hip, and could not keep up with the rest of the slaves; and our master would order him to be stripped and laid down on the ground, and have him beaten with a rod of rough briar till his skin was quite red and raw. He would then call for a bucket of salt, and fling upon the raw flesh till the man writhed on the ground like a worm, and screamed aloud with agony. This poor man's wounds were never healed, and I have often seen them full of maggots, which increased his torments to an intolerable degree. He was an object of pity and terror to the whole gang of slaves, and in his wretched case we saw, each of us, our own lot, if we should live to be as old.

Oh the horrors of slavery!—How the thought of it pains my heart! But the truth ought to be told of it; and what my eyes have seen I think it is my duty to relate; for few people in England know what slavery is. I have been a slave—I have felt what a slave feels, and I know what a slave knows, and I would have all the good people in England to know it too, that they may break our chains, and set us free.

Analysis and Review Questions

1. What are the differences between Mary's various owners?
2. Who was Hetty?
3. What led to Hetty's death?
4. Why do you think Mary's father returned Mary to her master after she ran away?
5. What seemed to be the usual punishment for Mary when she made a mistake?

MARY KINGSLEY AND THE BUBI OF FERNANDO PO

About the Document

It caused quite a stir when any explorer journeyed to Africa and returned to tell of his exploits, but it was even more sensational when the explorer was a woman. The best known of the European women travelers to Africa was Mary Kingsley. Kingsley's father had been a doctor who fancied traveling, and, when her parents died, she decided she would follow suit. In 1893 she made her first visit to West Africa. Her first journey included stops at notable West African ports, such as Freetown, and time in the Congo. For various reasons, Kingsley did not publish an account of this first sojourn.

In 1894, however, Kingsley set off from Liverpool, England, for a second voyage. This journey included more stops along the West African coast and considerable time spent on the island of Fernando Po where she wrote extensively on the Bubi, the local inhabitants. In her detailed accounts of local customs and culture, Kingsley displays both typical and atypical European attitudes toward non-westerners.

The Document

Having discoursed at large on the various incomers to Fernando Po° we may next turn to the natives, properly so-called, the Bubi. These people, although presenting a series of interesting problems to the ethnologist, both from their insular position, and their differentiation from any of the mainland peoples, are still but little known. To a great extent this has arisen from their exclusiveness, and their total lack of enthusiasm in trade matters, a thing that differentiates them more than any other characteristic from the mainlanders, who, young and old, men and women, regard trade as the great affair of life, take to it as soon as they can toddle, and don't even leave it off at death, according to their own accounts of the way the spirits of distinguished traders still dabble and interfere in market matters. But it is otherwise with the Bubi. A little rum, a few beads, and finish—then he will turn the rest of his attention to catching porcupines, or the beautiful little gazelles, gray on the back and white underneath, with which the island abounds. And what time he may have on hand after this, he spends in building houses and making himself hats. It is only his utterly spare moments that he employs in making just sufficient palm oil from the rich supply of nuts at his command to get that rum and those beads of his.

You must not, however, imagine that the Bubi is neglectful of his personal appearance. In his way he is quite a dandy. But his idea of decoration goes in the direction of a plaster of "tola" pomatum over his body, and above all a hat. This hat may be an antique European one, or a bound-round handkerchief, but it is more frequently a confection of native manufacture, and great taste and variety is displayed in its make. They are of plaited palm leaf—that's all you can safely generalise regarding them—for sometimes they have broad brims, sometimes narrow, sometimes no brims at all. So, too, with the crown. Sometimes it is thick and domed, sometimes non-existent, the wearer's hair aglow with red-tail parrots' feathers sticking up where the crown should be. As a general rule these hats are much adorned with oddments of birds' plumes, and one chief I knew had quite a Regent-street Dolly Varden creation which he used to affix to his wool in a most intelligent way with bonnet-pins made of wood. These hats are also a peculiarity of the Bubi, for none of the mainlanders care a row of pins for hats, except "for dandy," to wear occasionally, whereas the Bubi wears his perpetually, although he has by no means the same amount of sun to guard against owing to the glorious forests of his island. I am told there is a certain sound reason in his devotion for his hat, and that is that it acts as a protection against a beautiful but poisonous green tree snake that abounds on Fernando Po, whose habit it is to hang, upside down, from the trees. If the snake strikes the hat instead of the head when the wearer is out hunting, why so much the better for the wearer.

For earrings the Bubi wears pieces of wood stuck through the lobe of the ear, and although this is not a decorative habit still it is less undecorative than that of certain mainland friends of mine in this region, who wear large and necessarily dripping lumps of fat in their ears and in their hair. His neck is hung round with jujus on strings—bits of the backbones of pythons, teeth, feathers, and antelope horns—and round his upper arm are bracelets, preferably made of ivory got from the mainland, for celluloid bracelets carefully imported for his benefit he refuses to look at. Often also these bracelets are made of beads, or a circlet of leaves, and when on the war-path an armlet of twisted grass is always worn by the men. Men and women alike wear armlets, and in

---

Fernando Po: Island off the coast of modern-day Cameroon, today part of Equatorial Guinea and known as Bioko; former slave-trading outpost and base for Europeans. Home of the Bubi.

the case of the women they seem to be put on when young, for you see puffs of flesh growing out from between them. They are also not entirely for decoration, serving commonly as pockets, for under them in the case of men is stuck a knife, and in the case of women a tobacco pipe, a well-coloured clay. Leglets of similar construction are worn just under the knee on the right leg, while around the body you see belts of tshibbu, small pieces cut from Achatectonia shells, which form the native currency of the island. These shells are also made into veils worn by the women at their wedding.

The main interest of the Bubi's life lies in hunting, for he is more of a sportsman than the majority of mainlanders. He has not any big game to deal with, unless we except pythons—which attain a great size on the island—and crocodiles; but of the little gazelles, small monkeys, porcupines, and squirrels he has a large supply, and in the rivers a very pretty otter (*Lutra poensis*) with yellow brown fur often quite golden underneath; a creature which is, I believe, identical with the Angola otter.

The Bubis also fish, mostly by basket traps, but they are not experts either in this or in canoe management. Their chief sea-shore sport is hunting for the eggs of the turtles who lay in the sand from August to October.

Their domestic animals are the usual African list; cats, dogs, sheep, goats, and poultry.

For West Africans their agriculture is of a fairly high description—the noteworthy point about it, however, is the absence of manioc. Manioc is grown on Fernando Po, but only by the Portos. The Bubi cultivated plants are yams (*Dioscorea alata*), koko (*Colocasia esculenta*)—the taro of the South Seas, and plantains. Their farms are well kept, particularly those in the grass districts by San Carlos Bay. The yams of the Cordillera districts are the best flavoured, but those of the east coast the largest. Palm-oil is used for domestic purposes in the usual ways, and palm wine both fresh and fermented is the ordinary native drink. Rum is held in high esteem, but used in a general way in moderation as a cordial and a treat, for the Bubi is, like the rest of the West African natives, by no means an habitual drunkard. Gin he dislikes.

Physically the Bubis are a fairly well-formed race of medium height; they are decidedly inferior to the Benga or the Krus, but quite on a level with the Effiks. The women indeed are very comely: their colour is bronze and their skin the skin of the Bantu. Beards are not uncommon among the men, and these give their faces possibly more than anything else, a different look to the faces of the Effiks or the Duallas.

But the most remarkable instance of inferiority the Bubis display is their ignorance regarding methods of working iron. I do not know that iron in a native state is found on Fernando Po, but scrap-iron they have been in touch with for some hundreds of years. The mainlanders are all cognisant of native methods of working iron, although many tribes of them now depend entirely on European trade for their supply of knives, &c., and this difference between them and the Bubis would seem to indicate that the migration of the latter to the island must have taken place at a fairly remote period, a period before the iron-working tribes came down to the coast.

The spears used by this interesting people are even to this day made entirely of wood, and have such a Polynesian look about them that I intend some time or other to bring some home and experiment on that learned Polynesian-culture-expert, Baron von Hügel, with them:—intellectually experiment, not physically, pray understand.

The pottery has a very early-man look about it, but in this it does not differ much from that of the mainland, which is quite as poor, and similarly made without a wheel, and sun-baked. Those pots of the Bubis I have seen have, however, not had the pattern (any sort of pattern does, and it need not be carefully done) that runs round mainland pots to "keep their souls in"—*i.e.* to prevent their breaking up on their own account.

Their basket-work is of a superior order: the baskets they make to hold the semi-fluid palm oil are excellent, and will hold water like a basin, but I am in doubt whether this art is original, or imported by the Portuguese runaway slaves, for they put me very much in mind of those made by my old friends the Kabinders, from whom a good many of those slaves were recruited.

Analysis and Review Questions

1. What does Kingsley mean when she speaks of the "exclusiveness" of the Bubi?
2. What does Kingsley point out as the clearest indicator of the Bubi's supposed inferiority?
3. What is *Dioscorea alata*?
4. What was the safety value of the hats that the Bubi wore?
5. Does Kingsley seem favorably inclined toward the Bubi? Why or why not?

WEB LINKS

http://longmanworldhistory.com
The following additional readings and case studies can be found on the Web site.
Document 5.2, Aristotle on Slavery
Document 26.4, H. M. Stanley in Uganda
Case Study 26.1, Stanley and Kingsley on Africa
Case Study 26.2, Two Accounts of Slavery
Case Study 26.3, Slavery Through Time

http://www.spartacus.schoolnet.co.uk/slavery.htm
Includes slave accounts, descriptions of important antislavery legislation passed in the United States and Great Britain, and information about abolitionists on both sides of the Atlantic.

http://www.robinsonresearch.com/AFRICA/index.htm
A large site with mostly information on modern Africa, but includes a historical section with information on notable European explorers of Africa.

CHAPTER 27

The Middle East in the Age of European Expansion, 1750–1914

In the Middle East, the period from 1750 to 1914 was marked by two independent but interrelated historical processes that had their greatest impact on the Ottoman Empire, but also shaped the Qajar Empire of Iran. Social transformation related to changing political power, shifting trade patterns, introduction of new crops and agricultural technology, and growing trade with Europe interacted with political and cultural change in response to European military and economic expansion in the eighteenth and nineteenth centuries. By the eighteenth century, the Ottoman state system had grown more decentralized, with ever greater autonomy being exercised by provincial governors, tax farmers, and local urban commercial and religious elites. At the same time, diplomatic and commercial ties between European powers and the Ottoman Empire increased, as Europeans expanded their control of world markets and trade.

Technological developments, especially in warfare, led to an increasing imbalance of power between the European powers and the Ottomans, which was strikingly demonstrated by the 1798 French invasion of Egypt. Throughout the nineteenth century, Ottoman and Iranian statesmen and intellectuals worked to address the causes of the relative strength of Europe and weakness of their own states through a series of administrative, financial, judicial, economic, and cultural reforms. The reforms were aimed initially at strengthening the bureaucracy and military, at centralizing administration, and at reducing the autonomy of provincial elites. At the same time, the reforms helped create a new class of intellectuals, often trained in the West and familiar with the new intellectual trends emerging in post-Enlightenment Europe. At first employed by the state, but increasingly critical of its shortcomings, these intellectuals became vocal opponents of what they saw as autocracy, backwardness, and inertia, and they blamed their own governments and religious leaders for failing to meet the challenge of the West.

In 1908 a secret organization comprising military and civilian opponents of the regime of Abdülhamid II, the Committee of Union and Progress (CUP), known in the West as the Young Turks, staged a widely popular coup and

Map 27.1
The Decline of the Ottoman Empire

promised a new era of political freedom, equality, and protection of citizens' rights. In 1912 a group within the CUP staged another coup, using its power to attempt to stifle dissent and separatist movements within the Ottoman Empire. In 1914 the Ottoman Empire, led by Cemal, Talaat, and Enver Pashas, entered World War I on the German side.

THE WILLIAM KNOX D'ARCY OIL CONCESSION IN PERSIA, MAY 29, 1901

About the Document

By the early twentieth century, states in the Middle East had begun the practice of granting concessions to foreign companies for the development of a variety of enterprises, from banking, insurance, and postal service, to railroads, processing of commodities, and mineral and oil exploration and exploitation. The concessions, such as the 1889 Reuter Concession granted by Iran's Nasir al-Din Shah (1848–1896) or the 1901 D'Arcy Concession, granted by his successor Muzaffer al-Din Shah (1896–1907), were based on the standard practice of granting exclusive access in return for investment and the supply of technology and expertise by the concessionaire.

William Knox D'Arcy, an Australian entrepreneur, received the drilling rights to nearly all of Iran for 60 years. In 1908 he discovered oil in southwest Iran and formed the Anglo-Persian Oil Company with mostly British capital to exploit the concession. On the eve of World War I, the British government became the major investor in the oil company as a means to ensure a steady flow of petroleum for the British navy. The D'Arcy Concession served as a model for most similar concessions until the end of World War II, when Middle Eastern states began to demand and receive a greater share of the profits and more control over production and pricing policies.

Map 27.2
The Persian
Gulf Region,
c. 1900

The Document

Between the Government of His Imperial Majesty the Shah of Persia, of the one part, and William Knox d'Arcy, of independent means, residing in London at No. 42, Grosvenor Square (hereinafter called "the Concessionnaire"), of the other part;

The following has by these presents been agreed on and arranged—viz.:

ART. 1. The Government of His Imperial Majesty the Shah grants to the concessionnaire by these presents a special and exclusive privilege to search for, obtain, exploit, develop, render suitable for trade, carry away and sell natural gas petroleum, asphalt and ozokerite° throughout the whole extent of the Persian Empire for a term of sixty years as from the date of these presents.

---

ozokerite: A colorless or whitish by-product of petroleum used mostly to make candles. At the time of the D'Arcy Concession, petroleum was used mostly for the production of kerosene, industrial lubricants, medicines, and other household products. The Middle East produced a tiny percentage of the world's petroleum, most of which came from Baku on the Caspian Sea. The true significance of Middle Eastern oil reserves became apparent only after World War I with the boom in the use of internal combustion engines for transportation and industry.

ART. 2. This privilege shall comprise the exclusive right of laying the pipe-lines necessary from the deposits where there may be found one or several of the said products up to the Persian Gulf, as also the necessary distributing branches. It shall also comprise the right of constructing and maintaining all and any wells, reservoirs, stations and pump services, accumulation services and distribution services, factories and other works and arrangements that may be deemed necessary.

ART. 3. The Imperial Persian Government grants gratuitously to the concessionnaire all uncultivated lands belonging to the State which the concessionnaire's engineers may deem necessary for the construction of the whole or any part of the above-mentioned works. As for cultivated lands belonging to the State, the concessionnaire must purchase them at the fair and current price of the province. . . .

. . .

ART. 7. All lands granted by these presents to the concessionnaire or that may be acquired by him in the manner provided for in Articles 3 and 4 of these presents, as also all products exported, shall be free of all imposts and taxes during the term of the present concession. All material and apparatuses necessary for the exploration, working and development of the deposits, and for the construction and development of the pipelines, shall enter Persia° free of all taxes and Custom-House duties.

ART. 8. The concessionnaire shall immediately send out to Persia and at his own cost one or several experts with a view to their exploring the region in which there exist, as he believes, the said products, and, in the event of the report of the expert being in the opinion of the concessionnaire of a satisfactory nature, the latter shall immediately send to Persia and at his own cost all the technical staff necessary, with the working plant and machinery required for boring and sinking wells and ascertaining the value of the property. . . .

. . .

ART. 10. It shall be stipulated in the contract between the concessionnaire, of the one part, and the company, of the other part, that the latter is, within the term of one month as from the date of the formation of the first exploitation company, to pay the Imperial Persian Government the sum of £20,000 sterling in cash, and an additional sum of £20,000 sterling in paid-up shares of the first company founded by virtue of the foregoing article. It shall also pay the said Government annually a sum equal to 16 per cent of the annual net profits of any company or companies that may be formed in accordance with the said article. . . .

. . .

ART. 12. The workmen employed in the service of the company shall be subject to His Imperial Majesty the Shah, except the technical staff, such as the managers, engineers, borers and foremen. . . .

. . .

Persia: English derivation of the word *Fars*, or Parsumash, the name of a province in southwestern Iran considered the birthplace of the Persian monarchy and its expansion as a major power during the Achaemenid period (seventh to fourth centuries B.C.E.). In 1935 Reza Shah Pahlavi decreed that the name of the country should be changed from Persia to Iran, meaning the land of the Aryans, an ancient people that included the Achaemenids.

ART. 15. On the expiration of the term of the present concession, all materials, buildings and apparatuses then used by the company for the exploitation of its industry shall become the property of the said Government, and the company shall have no right to any indemnity in this connection.

. . .

ART. 17. In the event of there arising between the parties to the present concession any dispute or difference in respect of its interpretation or the rights or responsibilities of one or the other of the parties therefrom resulting, such dispute or difference shall be submitted to two arbitrators at Teheran, one of whom shall be named by each of the parties, and to an umpire who shall be appointed by the arbitrators before they proceed to arbitrate. The decision of the arbitrators or, in the event of the latter disagreeing, that of the umpire shall be final. . . .

Analysis and Review Questions

1. According to the concession, what privileges does the concessionaire acquire, for what purpose, and for how long?
2. What will the concessionaire provide at his own cost to carry out the concession, and what will the government provide?
3. How much will the concessionaire pay the government, and how will the profits be divided between the concessionaire and the government?
4. What does this concession say about the relative balance of power between the Europeans and Iranians? Who would seem to derive the most benefit from the terms of the concession, and why?
5. What does the concession reveal about the extent of industrial development in Iran in 1901? Why is the Iranian government dependent on a foreign company to explore and exploit its oil reserves?

Image 27.2
Young Turks Overthrow
Abdülhamid, 1908

THE YOUNG TURK REVOLUTION, 1908

About the Document

Halide Edib Ady'var (1884–1964) is best known as a prominent spokesperson for women's rights and an ardent supporter of the Turkish nationalist movement following World War I. Educated at the American-run Istanbul Women's College, Halide Edib authored several novels and two volumes of memoirs, covering the period from her childhood through the foundation of the Turkish Republic in 1923. After her husband, Adnan Ady'var, ran afoul of the regime of Mustafa Kemal Atatürk, Halide Edib spent the late 1920s and 1930s living, teaching, and writing in Europe, the United States, and India, before returning to Turkey following Atatürk's death.

The Document

On the morning of July 11, 1908, I was sitting in the spacious hall of Antigone, with my old friends from Beshiktash, Auntie Peyker and her husband Hamdi Effendi. Their son was the young officer who had escaped to Europe and joined the Young Turks, and they often came to me to talk of him and to get his letters, for they corresponded with him through an American friend of mine. They had no hope of ever seeing their son alive. Hamidian rule had a finality and inevitability which made one almost laugh at the idea that it could be changed by a few pamphlets published occasionally in Paris and sent to Constantinople in secret.

I well remember the silence before Salih Zeki Bey came into the hall with the morning paper open in his hands. Granny, who lived with me at the time, was peacefully settled on the corner sofa.

Salih Zeki Bey walked slowly, his eyes on the first page of the paper, and with a strange look of surprise on his face. Then he read aloud the imperial communiqué of four lines. The cringing praise of the sultan was even more exaggerated than usual, but the communiqué was written in concise terms and said that his Majesty the sultan was to restore the constitution of 1876.

As we listened in the old-fashioned hall, with the wide stretch of wonderful blue sea expanding behind a line of dark green pines, consternation overcame us.

The old pair sat in silence, the tears rolling down their wrinkled cheeks. Laconic as were those lines, they transfigured the minds of these old people with the radiant hope that they might see their son again. Granny, who hardly understood the meaning, looked over her spectacles as she asked:

"What does it mean, Halide?"

What did it mean? I hardly realized that a long scene of heaven and hell was to be enacted in the smothered land of Turkey and that I was to be called to act, to suffer, to knock my foolish young head against the realities of life, struggling endlessly, watching the interminable tragedy to its bitter end. This was to be my education in life after my education in school.

But now to return to our little group. The subject seemed alien and hard to discuss. The word "constitution," after its exile from the dictionary, was now suddenly used again in an imperial communiqué. The indestructibility of thought is marvelous; it is always there, blind to individual suffering and cost, boring its way from mind to mind, leaping large gaps and periods; but triumphant always, it marches on regardless of time, ceaselessly developing and maturing in the mind of man. . . .

What was the effect of this thunderbolt in the city of Istamboul? How would the city act, or how had it already acted? These were the enigmas we tried to solve that morning.

It was Hussein Jahid who brought us the news in the evening. The city had looked hesitatingly at the constitution so suddenly and simply announced. The people gathered at street corners and tried to talk in undertones, but there was a feeling of uncertainty, even of distrust, a vague questioning as to the meaning of this sudden change; some went so far as to take it for a trap in which to catch the people of Istamboul. Hussein Jahid had written enthusiastic editorials for "Sabah" and "Ikdam," the two prominent papers of the capital, for the next morning.

We had a sleepless night, sometimes talking but mostly thinking. I wandered restlessly in the large hall, walking out into the warm July night that was so sweet and balmy. Something invisible and new in the air haunted us. We had queer dreams and visions about the terror and blood which accompany revolutions, but we did not allow them utterance.

The words "equality, liberty, justice, and fraternity" sounded most strange. Fraternity was added on account of the Christians. The great ideals of Tanzimat, expressed as the Union of the Elements, had taken this familiar form. There had never been a more passionate desire in the peoples of Turkey to love each other, to work for the realization of this new Turkey, where a free government and a free life was to start.

Poor granny was restless. "No good comes out of new things. What you call constitution was given at the time of Midhat Pasha,° and he lost his head for it," she said.

In the evening of July 12, Hussein Jahid brought us news from the city once more. Usually so impassive and calm, he also seemed affected by the enthusiasm of the city. The papers might have been printed on gold-leaf, so high were the prices paid for them. People were embracing each other in the streets in mad rejoicing. Hussein Juhid smilingly added, "I had to wash my face well in the evening, for hundreds who did not know me from Adam, hundreds whom I have never seen, kissed me as I walked down the road of the Sublime Porte;° the ugly sides of revolution, vengeance and murder, will not stain ours."

The next day I went down to see Istamboul. The scene on the bridge caught me at once. There was a sea of men and women all cockaded in red and white, flowing like a vast human tide from one side to the other. The tradition of centuries seemed to have lost its effect. There was no such thing as sex or personal feeling. Men and women in a common wave of enthusiasm moved on, radiating something extraordinary, laughing, weeping in such intense emotion that human deficiency and ugliness were for the time completely obliterated. Thousands swayed and moved on. Before each official building there was an enormous crowd calling to the minister to come out and take the oath of allegiance to the new régime.

As I drove along the Sublime Porte the butchers of Istamboul were leaving its austere portals in their white chemises. They also had come to get assurance from the highest that this new joy was to be safeguarded and that they, the butchers, also were going to share in this great task.

In three days the whole empire had caught the fever of ecstasy. No one seemed clear about its meaning. The news of the change had come from Saloniki through several young officers whose names were shouted as its symbol. To the crowd the change in its clearest sense spelled the pulling down of a régime which meant oppression, corruption, and tyranny, while the new, whatever it was, spelled happiness and freedom.

I went down to the city twice that week and came back stirred to the very depths of my being. The motley rabble, the lowest pariahs, were going about in a sublime

Midhat Pasha: Ahmet Şefik Midhat Paşa (1822–1884) was the son of a cleric and entered the Ottoman civil service as an apprentice. He distinguished himself during the *Tanzimat* period as an energetic and capable provincial administrator, first in Bulgaria, then in Baghdad. Although he was never fully accepted as an equal by other high-ranking Ottoman statesmen, his successes at the provincial level eventually led to his appointment as Grand Vizier (roughly, Chief Minister) under Sultan Abdülaziz. When Abdülaziz opposed additional reforms, Midhat Paşa played a prominent role in deposing him in 1876 and in creating and implementing a constitution. After Abdülaziz was killed, his successor, Abdülhamit II, promised to adhere to the constitution. A year later, he used the war against Russia as an excuse to abrogate the constitution and close the new Ottoman parliament. Suspecting, but unable to prove that Midhat Paşa played a role in the death of Abdülaziz, Abdülhamid exiled him to Arabia, then had him murdered in 1884.

Sublime Porte: A term referring to a building in Istanbul that housed the offices of the Grand Vizier in the seventeenth and eighteenth centuries and the Ottoman cabinet after 1838. When Sultan Mahmut II (1808–1839) reorganized the Ottoman central administration along European lines, a new consultative body resembling a cabinet was headquartered in the building used by the Grand Vizier, the *Bab-i Ali*, or Sublime Porte. Throughout the remainder of the Ottoman period (through the early 1920s), commercial and diplomatic contacts with European governments were centered in the Sublime Porte; hence, Europeans came to use the term to refer to the Ottoman government as a whole.

emotion, with tears running down their unwashed faces, the shopkeepers joining the procession without any concern for their goods. There seemed to be no thieves and no criminals. Dr. Riza Tewfik and Selim Sirry paraded their handsome figures on horseback, solving the judicial difficulties of the people with long speeches. It looked like the millennium.

Analysis and Review Questions

1. How does Halide Edib portray the regime of Abdülhamid?
2. How does the author characterize the public reaction to the news of the restoration of the constitution? Why was the reaction so strong?
3. What were the public's expectations from the Young Turk revolution and restoration of the constitution?
4. What impact did the event have on the interaction between men and women, and between Muslims and non-Muslims? What accounts for this impact?
5. How does Halide Edib's account of the reaction to the Young Turk Revolution of 1908 compare with Tevfik Fikret's account of the Young Turk's coup of 1912?

RELIGIOUS MINORITIES IN THE MIDDLE EAST

About the Document

Mirza Husayn-i Hamdani represents a form of religious opposition in the late-nineteenth and early-twentieth-century Middle East. Mirza Husayn writes from the perspective of a minority religious sect, the *Baha'is*. The *Baha'is* emerged in the 1840s in Iran as followers of Sayyid Ali Muhammad Shirazi, a mystic who claimed to be the *Bab*, or gate, to salvation. Denounced as a heretic by the Shiite clergy and considered a political danger by Nasir al-Din Shah (1848–1896), Ali Muhammad was executed in 1850. Thousands of his followers continued to follow and spread his teachings in Iran and around the world, despite sometimes vicious repression.

The Document

. . . Such is the influence which the [Persian Shi'ah°] clergy enjoy, and so great is their power in every department of the state, that they have nullified the sovereign's authority in exactly the same way as they have destroyed all but the name of religion and law. . . . The King cannot issue any command or take any step opposed to their

---

Shi'ah: One of two major branches of Islam, the other being Sunni or Sunnite. The Shi'ah were partisans of Ali ibn Abu Talib, believing that upon the death of the Prophet Muhammad (c. 570–632), political and spiritual leadership of the Muslim community should pass to a blood relative (cousin) and his descendants, who were proclaimed Imams. The majority, "The Sunni," opted to accept the leader Abu Bakr, an early convert to Islam, as the Caliph (deputy of the Prophet), leading to a split along doctrinal as well as political lines.

views, and they imagine that he exists but to maintain their authority and to give effect to their decisions. Thus should any governor or minister, however powerful, issue any order or take any steps to secure the well-being of those subject to him, or to promote the national prosperity, without first consulting them, they will, by a mere hint, incite the people of his province or city to harass, vex, and thwart him till they have driven him out . . . at no previous time have any clergy possessed such power as is now wielded by the mullas of Persia, who regard themselves as the representatives of the Imams, and call their kings "dogs of the Imams' threshold." . . . On the return of His Majesty the King [Nasr al-Din Shah] from Europe [in 1873] they not only clamoured for the dismissal of the Prime Minister, circulating false reports of his atheism, but also prevented the introduction of railways, which would have greatly conduced to the prosperity of the country and the freedom of the people. . . .

Did not the territory of this same Persia once extend eastwards to Transoxanis° and the mountains of Thibet [*sic*] and China, westwards to the river Euphrates, southwards to the Gulf of Oman, and northwards to the Aral Mountains? . . . All the kings of the earth rendered homage to the monarchs of the Achaemenian dynasty (559–330 B.C.E.] and were as naught beside them, just as at the present day Persia is as naught beside the nations of Europe, but is like a dismissed governor or a cancelled edict, heeded by none. This abasement is the outcome of the learning of these divines, these upholders of religion and law, and the result of their undue power and influence. By the troubles which they have stirred up Persia has been made desolate and reduced to a few empoverished and deserted provinces, the total revenue derived from which at the present day only amounts to seven crores (of tumans) [between a million and a million and a half pounds sterling in 1890], and even of this, were the taxes fairly levied, not half would come into the royal treasury.

Shame on the people of Persia for their lack of spirit! By God, they have not a spark of patriotic or manly feeling; they have grown habituated to cowardice, falsehood, and flattery; they acquiesce in tyranny and oppression, and, relinquishing the position of free agents, have become mere passive instruments in the hands of the clergy! Do they forget that in days of yore their glory and honour, their wealth and prosperity, were the envy of all peoples? Do they not ask themselves why they have now become a byword amongst the nations for abject misery, meanness, and baseness? Moreover did they not once excel all mankind in every art, trade, and handicraft? . . . Do they never reflect why it is that their science is now restricted to such things as purifications, washing the orifices of the body, dyeing the beard, clipping the moustache, disputing about payment of tithes and alms, atonement for wrongs, Imam's money, and the like, for the determination of which things even it does not suffice? Yet so heedless are they that they do not perceive that most of these divines originally spring from the rustic population or the scum of the towns. They enter our cities and colleges with a smock and a staff, and feet full of sores encased in coarse socks and canvas shoes. There, by the alms and votive offerings of the people, by begging from this one and that one, by prayers and fastings paid for at the rate of two

---

Transoxanis: The land beyond the Oxus, or Amu Darya, River, which flows northwest along the current border of Uzbekistan and Turkmenistan into the Aral Sea in Central Asia. In the early Muslim period, the Amu Darya marked the northeastern limit of the conquests of the Umayyad Dynasty (661–750). Beyond the river lived nomadic Turkic people who were recruited by the Umayyads and Abbasid Dynasty (750–1258) to serve in their military. In the Qajar period (1779–1921) Transoxiana was the border of the Iranian state.

tumans a year, by reading through the whole Kuran for a kran, and by fees obtained for the performance of devotions, they manage to live in extreme wretchedness and poverty. After reading a few books, learning Arabic, filling their minds with all manner of doubts, hesitations, and vain scruples, and developing their obsolete superstitions and prejudices, they leave college, take their seats in the chair of the Law and the Imàmate, and forthwith become the absolute arbiters and lawgivers of the nation, the controllers of all men's lands and possessions, the owners of horses, mules, gold, and silver. They then think themselves entitled to set their feet on the necks of all mankind, to lord it over the noble, to maintain troops of horses and retinues of servants, to claim to be the (vice-regents) of the Imam, to receive his tithes, and to make atonements for wrong. They account themselves the most noble amongst all creatures and the most perfect, the generality of men as "like cattle," and the common folk as "even more astray." They become dead men's heirs, consumers of endowments, and collectors of tithes and "thirds," and usurp the station of "the One, the Dominant" "to whom belongeth dominion." . . .

Most people, however, have not sufficient sense to perceive from what sources all these luxuries, powers, shops, villages, lands, aqueducts, possessions, and moneys which the clergy possess are derived. Have they skill in working mines? No. Do they traffic in the merchandise of India, China, America, or Europe? No. Do they traverse land and sea, or cultivate fields which lie waste? No. Have they amassed their wealth by the discovery of new arts? No . . . Such being the case, what folly it is to take as guides men so notoriously evil and hypocritical, to follow their opinions, to be governed by their decisions, to cringe to them, flatter them, beseech their favour, and reckon them, forsooth, as the repositories of learning!

Analysis and Review Questions

Image 27.1
Women and Children
Workers in an Ottoman
Textile Mill, 1878

1. How does Mirza Husayn portray the political influence of the Shiite clergy (ulama), and what kind of influence do they have over the Shah of Iran's policies? Why does he oppose this influence?

2. What has been the result of the Shiite ulama's influence, according to Mirza Husayn? Why do the people support the ulama over the Shah?

3. How does Mirza Husayn portray the Shiite ulama in terms of their education, lifestyle, and piety? Why does he use this portrayal, and how does it support his own argument?

4. How does Mirza Husayn portray the Iranian people? Why does he express shame in the people?

5. What solutions, if any, does Mirza Husayn put forth to overcome the problems of Iran? Who does he believe should lead Iran into the future, and why?

POLITICAL OPPOSITION IN THE OTTOMAN EMPIRE

About the Document

Tevfik Fikret (1867–1915) was born in Istanbul, the son of an Ottoman bureaucrat. Educated at the Galatasaray Lycée, Tevfik Fikret made a career as a writer, poet, and newspaper editor. In 1896 he became editor of *Servet-i Fünun* (The

Wealth of Sciences), which published highly symbolic poetry critical of the regime of Abdülhamid II in abstruse terms, and he remained a powerful critic of both state oppression and religious control of the state. Following the Young Turk Revolution, he coedited the newspaper *Tanin* (The Echo).

FROM THE WRITINGS OF TEVFIK FIKRET

The Document

> The meal which, gentlemen, trembling waits
> To be devoured, is—the life of this nation,
> This land of pain, this land of agony!
> But gulp it down without hesitation.
>
> The meal is served, eat, gentlemen, eat
> Till it makes you gag, till you feel replete!
>
> You are hungry, gentlemen, your faces tell,
> Eat while you may, for tomorrow, who knows?
> The fleshpots welcome you with pride,
> The spoils of victory are yours!
>
> The meal is served, eat, gentlemen, eat
> Till it makes you gag, till you feel replete!
>
> Count your visible assets now,
> Rank, luxury, glory, blessings galore,
> The wedding, the bride, the mansion, the palace,
> All easily yours, and many more.
>
> The meal is served, eat, gentlemen, eat
> Till it makes you gag, till you feel replete!
>
> Though size impede digestion, think
> Of sweet revenge, of proud display!
> Give lustre to this dining-board:
> Head, brain, lung morsels in bloody array.
>
> The meal is served, eat, gentlemen, eat
> Till it makes you gag, till you feel replete!
>
> For this poor land will give its life,
> Hope, fortune, dreams, all that's in sight,
> Its daily comfort, its heart's desire.
> Dine, give no thought to wrong and right!
>
> The meal is served, eat, gentlemen, eat
> Till it makes you gag, till you feel replete!
>
> The crops may fail, have one last bite,
> The crackling hearth may turn to ash,
> While stomachs are strong and the soup is hot
> Scramble to fill your calabash!
>
> The meal is served, eat, gentlemen, eat
> Till it makes you gag, till you feel replete!

Analysis and Review Questions

1. Who are the "gentlemen" Tevfik Fikret is addressing in his poem? What tone does he use to address them in the poem, and how does the tone serve to emphasize his point?

2. What is the meal that Tevfik Fikret is inviting the "gentlemen" to eat? What does it consist of, and who has supplied the meal?

3. What attitude does Tevfik Fikret reflect toward the "gentlemen" he is inviting to dine? What does he imply will happen to the diners?

4. What role do the people play in this poem? Does Tevfik Fikret call on the people to resist?

5. What does Tevfik Fikret think the result will be if the "gentlemen" eat the meal he offers them? Do you agree with him? Why or why not?

WEB LINKS

Selections from Longman World History—Primary Sources and Case Studies

http://longmanworldhistory.com
The following additional readings and case studies can be found on the Web site.
Document 24.4, The Meiji Constitution, 1889
Document 27.1, Reform of the State as an Imperial Project: The Hatti-i Serif of Gülhane, November 3, 1839
Document 27.2, A British View of Egyptian Agriculture, 1840
Case Study 27.1, The Middle East Enters the World Economy
Case Study 27.2, Religious and Secular Opposition Within the Middle East
Case Study 27.3, Comparison Between the Hatt-i Serif of Gülhane and the Meiji Constitution

General Information on Muslim History and Societies

http://www.fordham.edu/halsall/islam/islamsbook.html
Fordham University, Internet *Islamic History Sourcebook.* A good source for primary documents on Islamic history from the Medieval to modern period.

http://menic.utexas.edu/menic.html
The Middle East Network Information Center at the Center for Middle Eastern Studies, the University of Texas. A very useful site, with links organized by country and subject.

http://www.columbia.edu/cu/lweb/indiv/mideast/cuvlm/
Columbia University Library, Middle East Studies Internet Resources. A Web site featuring links to bibliographical sources, including other libraries and collections.

Web Sites on Middle Eastern Literature

http://www.distinguishedwomen.com/subject/literat.html

A Web site featuring links on prominent women writers around the world. Also contains subdivisions on prominent women in other fields of endeavor.

http://www.cs.rpi.edu/~sibel/poetry/tevfik_fikret.html
A very useful Web site constructed by a student at Rensselaer Polytechnic Institute, which also contains links to other Turkish literary figures.

Web Sites on Petroleum in the pre-World War I Middle East

http://www.bp.com/
Web site of British Petroleum, the former Anglo-Persian Oil Company, with information on the history of the company and its current global operations.

http://www.mountmorgan.com/D'Arcy.htm
Web site of Mount Morgan, Queensland, Australia, where Wm. Knox D'Arcy made his fortune in mining, before gaining the concession to explore for oil in Persia. The Web site presents a brief overview of D'Arcy and his career.

ALL *MEN* ARE CREATED EQUAL?

THE DECLARATION OF INDEPENDENCE

About the Document

The English colonies in America had changed greatly since the founding of Jamestown in 1607. As time passed, the 13 colonies along the Atlantic coast developed economic, social, and political ideas that differed from those in England. A growing feud developed as the colonies strained for more economic and political freedom, while England passed a series of acts designed to bring the colonies under direct imperial control, especially through taxation and mercantilism. The colonists, who felt they were being mistreated since they had no direct representation in the English government, resisted through boycotts of British goods, repeated protests, and violence. Incident after incident finally brought the colonists to arms against the British in April 1775.

Colonial leaders who gathered in Philadelphia at the Second Continental Congress now faced a crisis of conscience: declare independence from Britain and face certain warfare or continue their protests for more rights as Englishmen. King George III decided for them by declaring all the American colonies in open rebellion. In June 1776 a five-person committee was selected to draft a declaration highlighting the colonists' grievances and proclaiming their independence. Thomas Jefferson served as principal author, and his document contained many ideas from the Enlightenment, especially John Locke's contract theory of government. Since the British government had failed to guarantee the natural rights of all its citizens, the colonists asserted their right to change their government and declare independence from what Jefferson called "absolute tyranny." The Congress adopted the statement on July 4, 1776.

The Document

WHEN in the Course of human Events, it becomes necessary for one People to dissolve the Political Bands which have connected them with another, and to assume among the Powers of the Earth, the separate and equal Station to which the Laws of Nature and of Nature's God entitle them, a decent Respect to the Opinions of Mankind requires that they should declare the causes which impel them to the Separation.

WE hold these Truths to be self-evident, that all Men are created equal, that they are endowed by their Creator with certain unalienable Rights,° that among these are Life, Liberty and the Pursuit of Happiness—That to secure these Rights, Governments are instituted among Men, deriving their just Powers from the Consent of the Governed, that whenever any Form of Government becomes destructive of these Ends, it is the Right of the People to alter or to abolish it, and to institute new Government, laying its Foundation on such Principles, and organizing its Powers in such Form, as to them shall seem most likely to effect their Safety and Happiness. Prudence, indeed, will dictate that Governments long established should not be changed for light and transient Causes; and accordingly all Experience hath shewn, that Mankind are more disposed to suffer, while Evils are sufferable, than to right themselves by abolishing the Forms to which they are accustomed. But when a long Train of Abuses and Usurpations, pursuing invariably the same Object, evinces a Design to reduce them under absolute Despotism, it is their Right, it is their Duty, to throw off such Government, and to provide new Guards for their future Security. Such has been the patient Sufferance of these Colonies; and such is now the Necessity which constrains them to alter their former Systems of Government. The History of the present King of Great-Britain is a History of repeated Injuries and Usurpations, all having in direct Object the Establishment of an absolute Tyranny over these States. To prove this, let Facts be submitted to a candid World.

HE has refused his Assent to Laws, the most wholesome and necessary for the public Good.

HE has forbidden his Governors to pass Laws of immediate and pressing Importance, unless suspended in their Operation till his Assent should be obtained; and when so suspended, he has utterly neglected to attend to them.

HE has refused to pass other Laws for the Accommodation of large Districts of People, unless those People would relinquish the Right of Representation in the Legislature, a Right inestimable to them, and formidable to Tyrants only.

HE has called together Legislative Bodies at Places unusual, uncomfortable, and distant from the Depository of their public Records, for the sole Purpose of fatiguing them into Compliance with his Measures.

HE has dissolved Representative Houses repeatedly, for opposing with manly Firmness his Invasions on the Rights of the People.

HE has refused for a long Time, after such Dissolutions, to cause others to be elected; whereby the Legislative Powers, incapable of the Annihilation, have returned to the People at large for their exercise; the State remaining in the mean time exposed to all the Dangers of Invasion from without, and the Convulsions within.

HE has endeavoured to prevent the Population of these States; for that Purpose obstructing the Laws for Naturalization of Foreigners; refusing to pass others to encourage their Migrations hither, and raising the Conditions of new Appropriations of Lands.

HE has obstructed the Administration of Justice, by refusing his Assent to Laws for establishing Judiciary Powers.

HE has made Judges dependent on his Will alone, for the Tenure of their Offices, and the Amount and Payment of their Salaries.

---

unalienable Rights: Jefferson borrowed this idea directly from John Locke's philosophy. Locke felt that humanity's natural rights included life, liberty, and property. Jefferson changed property to "the pursuit of happiness."

HE has erected a Multitude of new Offices, and sent hither Swarms of Officers to harrass our People, and eat out their Substance.

HE has kept among us, in Times of Peace, Standing Armies, without the consent of our Legislatures.

HE has affected to render the Military independent of and superior to the Civil Power.

HE has combined with others to subject us to a Jurisdiction foreign to our Constitution, and unacknowledged by our Laws; giving his Assent to their Acts of pretended Legislation:

FOR quartering large Bodies of Armed Troops among us;

FOR protecting them, by a mock Trial, from Punishment for any Murders which they should commit on the Inhabitants of these States:

FOR cutting off our Trade with all Parts of the World:

FOR imposing Taxes on us without our Consent:

FOR depriving us, in many Cases, of the Benefits of Trial by Jury:

FOR transporting us beyond Seas to be tried for pretended Offences:

FOR abolishing the free System of English Laws in a neighbouring Province, establishing therein an arbitrary Government, and enlarging its Boundaries, so as to render it at once an Example and fit Instrument for introducing the same absolute Rules into these Colonies:

FOR taking away our Charters, abolishing our most valuable Laws, and altering fundamentally the Forms of our Governments:

FOR suspending our own Legislatures, and declaring themselves invested with Power to legislate for us in all Cases whatsoever.

HE has abdicated Government here, by declaring us out of his Protection and waging War against us.

HE has plundered our Seas, ravaged our Coasts, burnt our Towns, and destroyed the Lives of our People.

HE is, at this Time, transporting large Armies of foreign Mercenaries to compleat the Works of Death, Desolation, and Tyranny, already begun with circumstances of Cruelty and Perfidy, scarcely paralleled in the most barbarous Ages, and totally unworthy the Head of a civilized Nation.

HE has constrained our fellow Citizens taken Captive on the high Seas to bear Arms against their Country, to become the Executioners of their Friends and Brethren, or to fall themselves by their Hands.

HE has excited domestic Insurrections amongst us, and has endeavoured to bring on the Inhabitants of our Frontiers, the merciless Indian Savages, whose known Rule of Warfare, is an undistinguished Destruction, of all Ages, Sexes and Conditions.

IN every stage of these Oppressions we have Petitioned for Redress in the most humble Terms: Our repeated Petitions have been answered only by repeated Injury. A Prince, whose Character is thus marked by every act which may define a Tyrant, is unfit to be the Ruler of a free People.

NOR have we been wanting in Attentions to our British Brethren. We have warned them from Time to Time of Attempts by their Legislature to extend an unwarrantable Jurisdiction over us. We have reminded them of the Circumstances of our Emigration and Settlement here. We have appealed to their native Justice and Magnanimity, and we have conjured them by the Ties of our common Kindred to disavow these Usurpations, which, would inevitably interrupt our Connections and Correspondence. They too have been deaf to the Voice of Justice and of Consanguinity. We must, therefore, acquiesce in the Necessity, which denounces our Separation, and hold them, as we hold the rest of Mankind, Enemies in War, in Peace, Friends.

WE, therefore, the Representatives of the UNITED STATES OF AMERICA, in GENERAL CONGRESS, Assembled, appealing to the Supreme Judge of the World for the Rectitude of our Intentions, do, in the Name, and by Authority of the good People of these Colonies, solemnly Publish and Declare, That these United Colonies are, and of Right ought to be, FREE AND INDEPENDENT STATES; that they are absolved from all Allegiance to the British Crown, and that all political Connection between them and the State of Great-Britain, is and ought to be totally dissolved; and that as FREE AND INDEPENDENT STATES, they have full Power to levy War, conclude Peace, contract Alliances, establish Commerce, and to do all other Acts and Things which INDEPENDENT STATES may of right do. And for the support of this Declaration, with a firm Reliance on the Protection of divine Providence, we mutually pledge to each other our Lives, our Fortunes, and our sacred Honor.

THE SENECA FALLS CONVENTION

About the Document

The 1848 Seneca Falls Convention is often regarded as the beginning of the feminist movement in America. However, the idea for the convention may have originated in the 1840 World Anti-Slavery Convention in London where women, despite their efforts to rid the world of slavery, were not allowed to speak and were forced to sit behind a partition.

Elizabeth Cady Stanton, who attended the meeting in London, was repulsed by the treatment women received and began to refine her anger into a statement based on Thomas Jefferson's Declaration of Independence. The draft was first proposed before the 300 participants at the Seneca Falls Convention in July 1848. This first meeting, and the proposals found in the Declaration of Sentiments, would provide a framework for the struggle of women to achieve equal rights and the right to vote.

The Document

THE DECLARATION OF SENTIMENTS OF THE SENECA FALLS CONVENTION

When, in the course of human events, it becomes necessary for one portion of the family of man to assume among the people of the earth a position different from that which they have hitherto occupied, but one to which the laws of nature and of nature's God entitle them, a decent respect to the opinions of mankind requires that they should declare the causes that impel them to such a course.

We hold these truths to be self-evident: that all men and women are created equal; that they are endowed by their Creator with certain inalienable rights; that among these are life, liberty, and the pursuit of happiness; that to secure these rights governments are instituted, deriving their just powers from the consent of the governed. Whenever any form of government becomes destructive of these ends, it is the right of those who suffer from it to refuse allegiance to it, and to insist upon the institution of a new government, laying its foundation on such principles, and organizing its powers in such form, as to them shall seem most likely to effect their safety and happiness. Prudence, indeed, will dictate that governments long established should not be changed for light and transient causes; and accordingly all experience hath shown that mankind are more disposed to suffer, while evils are sufferable, than to right themselves by abolishing the forms to which they are accustomed. But when a long train of abuses and usurpations, pursuing invariably the same object, evinces a design to reduce them under absolute despotism, it is their duty to throw off such government, and to provide new guards for their future security. Such has been the patient sufferance of the women under this government, and such is now the necessity which constrains them to demand the equal station to which they are entitled. The history of mankind is a history of repeated injuries and usurpations on the part of man toward woman, having in direct object the establishment of an absolute tyranny over her. To prove this, let facts be submitted to a candid world.

He has never permitted her to exercise her inalienable right to the elective franchise.

He has compelled her to submit to laws, in the formation of which she had no voice.

He has withheld from her rights which are given to the most ignorant and degraded men—both natives and foreigners.

Having deprived her of this first right of a citizen, the elective franchise, thereby leaving her without representation in the halls of legislation, he has oppressed her on all sides.

He has made her, if married, in the eye of the law, civilly dead.

He has taken from her all right in property, even to the wages she earns.

He has made her, morally, an irresponsible being, as she can commit many crimes with impunity, provided they be done in the presence of her husband. In the covenant of marriage, she is compelled to promise obedience to her husband, he becoming, to all intents and purposes, her master—the law giving him power to deprive her of her liberty, and to administer chastisement.

He has so framed the laws of divorce, as to what shall be the proper causes, and in case of separation, to whom the guardianship of the children shall be given, as to be wholly regardless of the happiness of women—the law, in all cases, going upon a false supposition of the supremacy of man, and giving all power into his hands.

After depriving her of all rights as a married woman, if single, and the owner of property, he has taxed her to support a government which recognizes her only when her property can be made profitable to it.

He has monopolized nearly all the profitable employments, and from those she is permitted to follow, she receives but a scanty remuneration. He closes against her all the avenues to wealth and distinction which he considers most honorable to himself. As a teacher of theology, medicine, or law, she is not known.

He has denied her the facilities for obtaining a thorough education, all colleges being closed against her.

He allows her in church, as well as state, but a subordinate position, claiming apostolic authority for her exclusion from the ministry, and, with some exceptions, from any public participation in the affairs of the church.

He has created a false public sentiment by giving to the world a different code of morals for men and women, by which moral delinquencies which exclude women from society, are not only tolerated, but deemed of little account in man.

He has usurped the prerogative of Jehovah himself, claiming it as his right to assign for her a sphere of action, when that belongs to her conscience and to her God.

He has endeavored, in every way that he could, to destroy her confidence in her own powers, to lessen her self-respect, and to make her willing to lead a dependent and abject life.

Now, in view of this entire disfranchisement of one-half the people of this country, their social and religious degradation—in view of the unjust laws above mentioned, and because women do feel themselves aggrieved, oppressed, and fraudulently deprived of their most sacred rights, we insist that they have immediate admission to all the rights and privileges which belong to them as citizens of the United States.

Analysis and Review Questions

1. In comparing the two documents, what is the first major difference you notice?
2. List the three most powerful accusations of men listed by the Seneca Falls statement.
3. How many of the issues raised have been resolved in
   a. The Declaration of Independence?
   b. The Declaration of Sentiments?
4. Does the Social Contract apply to individuals, or only to nations?

CHAPTER 28

The Modern West Emerges

C ivilization's progression into the modern age has brought astounding change and advancement. The Industrial Revolution brought new industry, new techniques, and new opportunities. Unfortunately, many of these advancements played a role in two of the most cataclysmic events in our civilization's history: the two World Wars. Despite these problems, the human race rebounded, and some of the problems were addressed. Others still require our attention, and our future could depend on how we remember these past mistakes.

The selections that follow reflect some of the dark points in modern history, including the effects of the two World Wars, an economic collapse, and the horrific effects of science applied to warfare. Some selections, though, offer rays of hope and demonstrate our attempts to right past wrongs.

WILFRED OWEN, "DULCE ET DECORUM EST"

About the Document

The Great War, as many refer to the conflict between 1914 and 1918, was a bloody contest heavily influenced by the Industrial Revolution. Death and destruction became efficient, as machine guns, tanks, poison gas, and airplanes were introduced into the battlefield. On the Western Front, trenches dominated the front lines that stretched through France and into Belgium.

Soldiers involved in this conflict spent their time in misery and hopelessness. Some expressed their feelings through writing. Wilfred Owen (1893–1918) volunteered for service in the British Army in 1915. As an officer, he served with distinction. Wounded in June 1917 and sent to a hospital near Edinburgh, Owen met Siegfried Sassoon, another war poet, who encouraged Owen to continue his writing. Owen returned to France in August 1918, won the Military Cross in October, and was killed in action on November 4, 1918, one week before the Armistice. In the selection below, Owen bitterly mocks the wastefulness of war by casting doubt on the Latin proverb "Dulce et decorum est pro patria mori," meaning "It is sweet and honorable to die for one's country."

Map 28.1
World War I

The Document

DULCE ET DECORUM EST

Bent double, like old beggars under sacks,
Knock-kneed, coughing like hags, we cursed through sludge,
Till on the haunting flares we turned our backs
And towards our distant rest began to trudge.
Men marched asleep. Many had lost their boots
But limped on, blood-shod. All went lame; all blind;
Drunk with fatigue; deaf even to the hoots
Of disappointed tired, outstripped Five-Nines that dropped behind.

GAS!° Gas! Quick, boys!—An ecstasy of fumbling,
Fitting the clumsy helmets just in time;
But someone still was yelling out and stumbling,
And floundering like a man in fire or lime. . . .
Dim, through the misty panes and thick green light
As under a green sea, I saw him drowning.

In all my dreams, before my helpless sight,
He plunges at me, guttering, choking, drowning.

If in some smothering dreams you too could pace
Behind the wagon that we flung him in,
And watch the white eyes writhing in his face,
His hanging face, like a devil's sick of sin;
If you could hear, at every jolt, the blood
Come gargling from the froth-corrupted lungs,
Obscene as cancer, bitter as the cud
Of vile, incurable sores on innocent tongues,
My friend, you would not tell with such high zest
To children ardent for some desperate glory,
The old Lie: Dulce et decorum est
Pro patria mori.

Map 28.2
(Interactive)
The Division of
Germany and Austria

Analysis and Review Questions

1. Describe the life of the soldiers in the trenches.
2. Describe the gas attack. What happens to the soldier who fails to get his protective equipment on in time?
3. What is the mood of the poem?
4. How effective is the use of the Latin proverb in the last line of the poem?
5. What message about war is Owen trying to get the reader to understand?

Gas: The battlefields of World War I saw the first use of poison gas. This poem describes a gas attack—probably mustard gas, which blinded and blistered all exposed flesh, and, if inhaled, stripped off the mucous membranes of bronchial tubes causing bleeding and ultimately death.

THE GREAT DEPRESSION: AN ORAL ACCOUNT

About the Document

No one incident from the catastrophic Great Depression can sum up the misery, hopelessness, and fear felt by those who lived through it. From 1928 until the outbreak of World War II, most Western nations suffered from a sagging economy due to America's financial collapse. President Herbert Hoover was reluctant to offer any direct governmental assistance to those suffering, including veterans of World War I.

In response, as many as 20,000 veterans staged the Bonus March on Washington, D.C., to protest their situation and petition Congress and the President for an early payment of their service bonus of $1,000, which was scheduled to be paid in 1945. They received little sympathy from the government, including President Hoover, who ordered the veterans to be dispersed from the city. In the oral history that follows, one witness describes how those orders were carried out.

The Document

The soldiers were walking the streets, the fellas who had fought for democracy in Germany. They thought they should get the bonus right then and there because they needed the money. A fella by the name of Waters, I think, got up the idea of these ex-soldiers would go to Washington, make the kind of trip the hoboes made with Coxey° in 1898, they would be able to get the government to come through.

D. C. Webb organized a group from Bughouse Square to go on this bonus march. Not having been in the army—I was too young for World War I and too old for World War II (laughs)—I was wondering if I would be a legitimate marcher. But the ten or fifteen other fellas were all soldiers, and they thought it would be O.K. for me to go. Webb said, "Come along, you're a pretty good bum." (Laughs.)

We went down to the railyards and grabbed a freight train. . . .

Sometimes there'd be fifty, sixty people in a boxcar. We'd just be sprawled out on the floor. The toilet . . . you had to hold it till you got a division point. (Laughs.) That's generally a hundred miles. You didn't carry food with you. You had to bum the town. It was beggary on a grand scale.

In one town, D. C. Webb got up on the bandstand and made a speech. We passed the hat, even, among the local citizenry. The money was used to buy cigarettes for the boys. Townspeople, they were very sympathetic.

There was none of this hatred you see now when strange people come to town, or strangers come to a neighborhood. They resent it, I don't know why. That's one of the things about the Depression. There was more camaraderie than there is now. . . .

When we got to Washington, there was quite a few ex-servicemen there before us. There was no arrangements for housing. Most of the men that had wives and children

---

Coxey: The U.S. economic depression of 1893 was extremely severe—as many as one million Americans were unemployed, and over 8,000 businesses failed. In 1894 Jacob S. Coxey, an Ohio businessman, organized a march of unemployed workers to Washington, D.C., to present relief demands to Congress, including work relief and public works jobs for the unemployed. Congress took no action on these demands.

were living in Hooverville. This was across the Potomac River—what was known as Anacostia Flats. They had set up housing there, made of cardboard and of all kinds. I don't know how they managed to get their food. Most other contingents was along Pennsylvania Avenue.

They were tearing down a lot of buildings along that street, where they were going to do some renewal, build some federal buildings. A lot of ex-servicemen just sort of turned them into barracks. They just sorta bunked there. Garages that were vacant, they took over. Had no respect for private property. They didn't even ask permission of the owners. They didn't even know who the hell the owners was.

They had come to petition Hoover, to give them the bonus before it was due. And Hoover refused this. He told them they couldn't get it because it would make the country go broke. They would hold midnight vigils around the White House and march around the White House in shifts.

The question was now: How were they going to get them out of Washington? They were ordered out four or five times, and they refused. The police chief was called to send them out, but he [General Pelham D. Glassford] refused. I also heard that the marine commander, who was called to bring out the marines, also refused. Finally, the one they did get to shove these bedraggled ex-servicemen out of Washington was none other than the great MacArthur.°

The picture I'll always remember . . . here is MacArthur coming down Pennsylvania Avenue. And, believe me, ladies and gentlemen, he came on a white horse. He was riding a white horse. Behind him were tanks, troops of the regular army.

This was really a riot that wasn't a riot, in a way. When these ex-soldiers wouldn't move, they'd poke them with their bayonets, and hit them on the head with the butt of a rifle. First, they had a hell of a time getting them out of the buildings they were in. Like a sit-in.

They managed to get them out. A big colored soldier, about six feet tall, had a big American flag he was carrying. He was one of the bonus marchers. He turned to one of the soldiers who was pushing him along, saying: "Get along there, you big black bastard." That was it. He turned and said, "Don't try to push me. I fought for this flag. I fought for this flag in France and I'm gonna fight for it here on Pennsylvania Avenue." The soldier hit him on the side of the legs with the bayonet. I think he was injured. But I don't know if he was sent to the hospital.

This was the beginning of a riot, in a way. These soldiers were pushing these people. They didn't want to move, but they were pushing them anyway.

As night fell, they crossed the Potomac. They were given orders to get out of Anacostia Flats, and they refused. The soldiers set those shanties on fire. They were practically smoked out. I saw it from a distance. I could see the pandemonium. The fires were something like the fires you see nowadays that are started in these ghettoes. But they weren't started by the people that live there.

The soldiers threw tear gas at them and vomiting gas. It was one assignment they reluctantly took on. They were younger than the marchers. It was like sons attacking their

---

MacArthur: President Hoover and Secretary of War Patrick Hurley ordered then Army Chief of Staff Douglas MacArthur to remove the protestors from Pennsylvania Avenue. MacArthur quickly accomplished his task but then continued to remove protestors from all of the downtown area and destroyed the marchers' camp at Anacostia. Other participants in this operation included MacArthur's assistant, Major Dwight David Eisenhower, and Major George S. Patton. All three men would go on to fame in World War II.

fathers. The next day the newspapers deplored the fact and so forth, but they realized the necessity of getting these men off. Because they were causing a health hazard to the city. MacArthur was looked upon as a hero.

And so the bonus marchers straggled back to the various places they came from. And without their bonus.

Analysis and Review Questions

1. What was the purpose of the Bonus March, and who participated?
2. Why do you think President Hoover ordered the veterans to be removed?
3. What happened to the black veteran who was protesting? What his response to being forced out?
4. Since the author tells us that he was not a veteran, do you think he was an effective witness?
5. Who was responsible for the removal of the veterans?

THE HOLOCAUST: MEMOIRS FROM THE COMMANDANT OF AUSCHWITZ

About the Document

Image 28.2
Liberating the
Concentration
Camps

The Holocaust, the systematic slaughter of over six million European Jews during World War II, was the most horrific aspect of the Nazi reign in Germany. The origins of the Holocaust were as early as 1935, with the passage of the Nuremberg Laws, which strictly regulated Jewish involvement in German society. The laws prevented Jews from government service, intermarriage with other (non-Jewish) Germans, or holding public office. By January 1942 Nazi leaders were openly discussing the "Final Solution": a removal of European Jews through any means necessary, including extermination.

The Nazi government removed many Jews from their towns and villages and placed them in concentration camps located in various parts of Europe. The most infamous of these was Auschwitz, located in German-occupied Poland. On arrival, Jews unfit for work were immediately exterminated; others were spared only to be worked to death in forced labor camps. The selection that follows is from the Commandant of Auschwitz, Rudolf Hess, who wrote his memoirs while in prison after the war. He was executed for his crimes in 1947.

The Document

In the spring of 1942 the first transports of Jews, all earmarked for extermination, arrived from Upper Silesia.

They were taken from the detraining platform to the "cottage"—to bunker I—across the meadows where later building site II was located. The transport was conducted by Aumeier and Palitzisch and some of the block leaders. They talked with the Jews about general topics, inquiring concerning their qualifications and trades, with a view to misleading them. On arrival at the "cottage," they were told to undress. At first they went calmly into the rooms where they were supposed to be disinfected. But some of them showed signs of alarm, and spoke of death by suffocation and of annihilation. A sort of panic set in at once. Immediately all the Jews still outside were pushed into the chambers, and the doors were screwed shut. With subsequent transports the difficult individuals were picked out early and most carefully supervised. At the first signs of unrest, those responsible were unobtrusively led behind the building and killed with a small-caliber gun, that was inaudible to the others. The presence and calm behavior of the Special Detachment [of *Sonderkommandos*] served to reassure those who were worried or who suspected what was about to happen. A further calming effect was obtained by members of the Special Detachment accompanying them into the rooms and remaining with them until the last moment, while an SS man also stood in the doorway until the end.

It was most important that the whole business of arriving and undressing should take place in an atmosphere of the greatest possible calm. People reluctant to take off their clothes had to be helped by those of their companions who had already undressed, or by men of the Special Detachment.

The refractory ones were calmed down and encouraged to undress. The prisoners of the Special Detachment also saw to it that the process of undressing was carried out quickly, so that the victims would have little time to wonder what was happening. . .

Many of the women hid their babies among the piles of clothing. The men of the Special Detachment were particularly on the lookout for this, and would speak words of encouragement to the woman until they had persuaded her to take the child with her. The women believed that the disinfectant might be bad for their smaller children, hence their efforts to conceal them.

The smaller children usually cried because of the strangeness of being undressed in this fashion, but when their mothers or members of the Special Detachment comforted them, they became calm and entered the gas chambers, playing or joking with one another and carrying their toys.

I noticed that women who either guessed or knew what awaited them nevertheless found the courage to joke with the children to encourage them, despite the mortal terror visible in their own eyes.

One woman approached me as she walked past and, pointing to her four children who were manfully helping the smallest ones over the rough ground, whispered:

"How can you bring yourself to kill such beautiful, darling children? Have you no heart at all?"

One old man, as he passed by me, hissed:

"Germany will pay a heavy penance for this mass murder of the Jews."

His eyes glowed with hatred as he said this. Nevertheless he walked calmly into the gas chamber, without worrying about the others.

One young woman caught my attention particularly as she ran busily hither and thither, helping the smallest children and the old women to undress. During the selection she had had two small children with her, and her agitated behavior and appearance had brought her to my notice at once. She did not look in the least like a Jewess. Now her children were no longer with her. She waited until the end, helping the women who were not undressed and who had several children with them, encouraging them and calming the children. She went with the very last ones into the gas chamber. Standing in the doorway, she said:

"I knew all the time that we were being brought to Auschwitz to be gassed. When the selection took place I avoided being put with the able-bodied ones, as I wished to look after the children. I wanted to go through it all, fully conscious of what was happening. I hope that it will be quick. Goodbye!"

From time to time women would suddenly give the most terrible shrieks while undressing, or tear their hair, or scream like maniacs. These were immediately led away behind the building and shot in the back of the neck with a small-caliber weapon.

It sometimes happened that, as the men of the Special Detachment left the gas chamber, the women would suddenly realize what was happening, and would call down every imaginable curse upon our heads.

I remember, too, a woman who tried to throw her children out of the gas chamber, just as the door was closing. Weeping, she called out:

"At least let my precious children live."

There were many such shattering scenes, which affected all who witnessed them.

During the spring of 1942 hundreds of vigorous men and women walked all unsuspecting to their death in the gas chambers, under the blossom-laden fruit trees of the "cottage" orchard. This picture of death in the midst of life remains with me to this day.

The process of selection, which took place on the unloading platforms, was in itself rich in incident.

The breaking up of families, and the separation of the men from the women and children, caused much agitation and spread anxiety throughout the whole transport. This was increased by the further separation from the others of those capable of work. Families wished at all costs to remain together. Those who had been selected ran back to rejoin their relations. Mothers with children cried to join their husbands, or old people attempted to find those of their children who had been selected for work, and who had been led away.

Often the confusion was so great that the selections had to be begun all over again. The limited area of standing room did not permit better sorting arrangements. All attempts to pacify these agitated mobs were useless. It was often necessary to use force to restore order.

As I have already frequently said, the Jews have strongly developed family feelings. They stick together like limpets . . .

Then the bodies had to be taken from the gas chambers, and after the gold teeth had been extracted, and the hair cut off, they had to be dragged to the pits or to the crematoria. Then the fires in the pits had to be stoked, the surplus fat drained off, and the mountain of burning corpses constantly turned over so that the draught might fan the flames . . .

It happened repeatedly that Jews of the Special Detachment would come upon the bodies of close relatives among the corpses, and even among the living as they entered the gas chambers. They were obviously affected by this, but it never led to any incident.

Analysis and Review Questions

1. How did Hess and the Nazis view the Jews? Does he ever refer to them with any emotion?
2. What role did the Sonderkommandos, or Special Detachment troops, play in the process?
3. What do you feel was the most horrifying experience faced by the Jews in the camp?
4. What happened to the bodies after the gassing process?
5. How does Hess seem to view the process? Does he see it as horrible, or does he view it with pride, especially in terms of the efficiency of the process?

Image 28.1
The Technology of War

AN EYEWITNESS TO HIROSHIMA

About the Document

The war effort surrounding World War II brought about surprising scientific advancement. Jet propulsion, radar, and sonar all trace their origins back to the conflict, as does nuclear fission. The American effort to develop an atomic bomb, code-named the Manhattan Project, began in earnest in 1942 under the military direction of General Leslie R. Groves. Groves gathered together a group of scientists, physicists, and engineers to construct a bomb that derived its explosive power from the splitting of atoms rather than a chemical reaction. They successfully created three nuclear weapons (code-named Trinity) and exploded the first bomb in May 1945 in New Mexico.

The remaining two bombs were sent to Tinian Island to be used against Japan, which still remained at war with the United States. President Truman, faced with the choice of either invading the Japanese home islands in an all-out assault or using the new weapon, decided that the atomic bombs should be used despite the enormous loss of civilian life. On August 6, 1945, the first bomb exploded over the city of Hiroshima. Three days later, on August 9, the second bomb exploded over Nagasaki. Total casualties may never be known due to the effects of radiation, but most figures indicate that more than 200,000 Japanese were either killed or injured. These devastating losses contributed to the Japanese surrender on August 15, 1945. The selection that follows is from Father John A. Siemes, professor of modern philosophy at Tokyo's Catholic University and an eyewitness to the first explosion in Hiroshima.

The Document

Up to August 6th, occasional bombs, which did no great damage, had fallen on Hiroshima. Many cities roundabout, one after the other, were destroyed, but Hiroshima itself remained protected. There were almost daily observation planes over the city but none of them dropped a bomb. The citizens wondered why they alone had remained undisturbed for so long a time. There were fantastic rumors that the enemy had something special in mind for this city, but no one dreamed that the end would come in such a fashion as on the morning of August 6th.

August 6th began in a bright, clear, summer morning. About seven o'clock, there was an air raid alarm which we had heard almost every day and a few planes appeared over the city. No one paid any attention and at about eight o'clock, the all-clear was sounded. I am sitting in my room at the Novitiate of the Society of Jesus in Nagatsuke; during the past half year, the philosophical and theological section of our Mission had been evacuated to this place from Tokyo. The Novitiate is situated approximately two kilometers from Hiroshima, half-way up the sides of a broad valley which stretches from the town at sea level into this mountainous hinterland, and through which courses a river. From my window, I have a wonderful view down the valley to the edge of the city.

Suddenly—the time is approximately 8:14—the whole valley is filled by a garish light which resembles the magnesium light used in photography, and I am conscious of a wave of heat. I jump to the window to find out the cause of this remarkable phenomenon, but I see nothing more than that brilliant yellow light. As I make for the door, it doesn't occur to me that the light might have something to do with enemy planes. On the way from the window, I hear a moderately loud explosion which seems to come from a distance and, at the same time, the windows are broken in with a loud crash. There has been an interval of perhaps ten seconds since the flash of light. I am sprayed by fragments of glass. The entire window frame has been forced into the room. I realize now that a bomb has burst and I am under the impression that it exploded directly over our house or in the immediate vicinity.

I am bleeding from cuts about the hands and head. I attempt to get out of the door. It has been forced outwards by the air pressure and has become jammed. I force an opening in the door by means of repeated blows with my hands and feet and come to a broad hallway from which open the various rooms. Everything is in a state of confusion. All windows are broken and all the doors are forced inwards. The bookshelves in the hallway have tumbled down. I do not note a second explosion and the fliers seem to have gone on. Most of my colleagues have been injured by fragments of glass. A few are bleeding but none has been seriously injured. All of us have been fortunate since it is now apparent that the wall of my room opposite the window has been lacerated by long fragments of glass.

We proceed to the front of the house to see where the bomb has landed. There is no evidence, however, of a bomb crater; but the southeast section of the house is very severely damaged. Not a door nor a window remains. The blast of air had penetrated the entire house from the southeast, but the house still stands. It is constructed in a Japanese style with a wooden framework, but has been greatly strengthened by the labor of our Brother Gropper as is frequently done in Japanese homes. Only along the front of the chapel which adjoins the house, three supports have given way (it has been made in the manner of Japanese temple, entirely out of wood).

Down in the valley, perhaps one kilometer toward the city from us, several peasant homes are on fire and the woods on the opposite side of the valley are aflame. A few of us go over to help control the flames. While we are attempting to put things in order, a storm comes up and it begins to rain. Over the city, clouds of smoke are rising and I hear a few slight explosions. I come to the conclusion that an incendiary bomb with an especially strong explosive action has gone off down in the valley. A few of us saw three planes at great altitude over the city at the time of the explosion. I, myself, saw no aircraft whatsoever.

Perhaps a half-hour after the explosion, a procession of people begins to stream up the valley from the city. The crowd thickens continuously. A few come up the road to our house. We give them first aid and bring them into the chapel, which we have in the meantime cleaned and cleared of wreckage, and put them to rest on the straw mats which constitute the floor of Japanese houses. A few display horrible wounds of the extremities and back. The small quantity of fat which we possessed during this time of war was soon used up in the care of the burns. Father Rektor who, before taking holy orders, had studied medicine, ministers to the injured, but our bandages and drugs are soon gone. We must be content with cleansing the wounds.

More and more of the injured come to us. The least injured drag the more seriously wounded. There are wounded soldiers, and mothers carrying burned children in their arms. From the houses of the farmers in the valley comes word: "Our houses are full of wounded and dying. Can you help, at least by taking the worst cases?" The wounded come from the sections at the edge of the city. They saw the bright light, their houses collapsed and buried the inmates in their rooms. Those that were in the open suffered instantaneous burns, particularly on the lightly clothed or un-clothed parts of the body. Numerous fires sprang up which soon consumed the entire district. We now conclude that the epicenter of the explosion was at the edge of the city near the Jokogawa Station, three kilometers away from us. We are concerned about Father Kopp who that same morning, went to hold Mass at the Sisters of the Poor, who have a home for children at the edge of the city. He had not returned as yet.

Toward noon, our large chapel and library are filled with the seriously injured. The procession of refugees from the city continues. Finally, about one o'clock, Father Kopp returns, together with the Sisters. Their house and the entire district where they live has burned to the ground. Father Kopp is bleeding about the head and neck, and he has a large burn on the right palm. He was standing in front of the nunnery ready to go home. All of a sudden, he became aware of the light, felt the wave of heat and a large blister formed on his hand. The windows were torn out by the blast. He thought that the bomb had fallen in his immediate vicinity. The nunnery, also a wooden structure made by our Brother Gropper, still remained but soon it is noted that the house is as good as lost because the fire, which had begun at many points in the neighborhood, sweeps closer and closer, and water is not available. There is still time to rescue certain things from the house and to bury them in an open spot. Then the house is swept by flame, and they fight their way back to us along the shore of the river and through the burning streets.

Soon comes news that the entire city has been destroyed by the explosion and that it is on fire.

Analysis and Review Questions

1. What were some of the immediate effects of the nuclear explosion?
2. How prepared are the priests or the population for this explosion?
3. Do you think Father Siemes is a reliable witness? Why or why not?
4. What are some of the problems faced by the priests after the blast?
5. How effective do you think the detonation of the atomic bomb was in driving Japan to surrender?

WEB LINKS

Selections from Longman World History—Primary Sources and Case Studies

http://longmanworldhistory.com
The following additional readings and case studies can be found on the Web site.
Document 28.5, United Nations: Universal Declaration of Human Rights
Document 28.6, President Harry S. Truman: The Truman Doctrine
Document 28.7, A Turkish Officer Describes the Armenian Massacres
Case Study 28.1, Oral History vs. Memoirs
Case Study 28.2, Human Rights
Case Study 28.3, Genocide

World War I

Trenches on the Web
http://www.worldwarI.com/
Comprehensive site that offers visitors access to a reference library, discussion forums, and other interactive areas to further understanding of the soldier's experience during the war. This site also serves as the home page for the Great War Society.

Great Depression

America from the Great Depression to World War II: Photographs from the FSA–OWI, 1935–1945
http://memory.loc.gov/ammem/Fsowhome.html
The Library of Congress index to photographs taken by the Farm Security Administration and the Office of War Information during the years of the Great Depression. These images catalog the everyday struggles of Americans during the economic crisis. Over 112,000 black-and-white photographs and 1,600 color photographs are available.

Holocaust

United States Holocaust Memorial Museum
http://www.ushmm.org/
Excellent source for students and scholars to explore the Holocaust. Has links to online exhibitions, learning materials, and research materials.

Human Rights

Amnesty International
http://www.amnesty.org/
Nonprofit watchdog organization dedicated to upholding human rights through-out the globe. Provides visitors with potential human rights trouble areas, reports of potential human rights abuses, and offers resources to pressure various governments to free prisoners of conscience.

Cold War

Cold War Museum
http://coldwar.org/
Site provides visitors with online exhibitions broken down by decade. Trivia Game, discussion forum, and educational resources available to the student.

CHAPTER 29

Russia and Eastern Europe: The Dream Becomes a Nightmare

From 1917 to 1991, Soviet Russia underwent an unprecedented transformation from a backward, agricultural, peasant society into an industrial, technological, and military superpower. The cost of that transformation was also unprecedented: an environmental and demographic disaster so intense that one American scholar has described it as "catastroika." No other country has ever undertaken such a radical transformation so rapidly. The degradation of the environment in Russia has never been seen before in an industrialized civilization.

The first two documents of this chapter demonstrate the extreme sense of urgency that early Soviet leaders, fearful of external threats and heedless of domestic demographic and environmental costs, felt in driving industrialization forward. The third document presents the continuation of this vision by the last Soviet leader, despite the setbacks reality dealt in the late Soviet period. The final document provides a first look at the devastating costs and consequences of the seven decades of Soviet power.

While this chapter focuses primarily on the territory of the former Soviet Union, it is critical to recall that similar policies, with similar results, were implemented in each of the states of the former Soviet bloc in Eastern Europe as well.

LENIN CALLS FOR ELECTRIFICATION OF ALL RUSSIA

About the Document

Having successfully taken power, escaped German conquest, and gained victory over the Whites in the Russian Civil War, Lenin recognized in 1920 the critical state of Bolshevik Russia's economy. In this address to the Eighth All-Russia Congress of Soviets, Lenin delivers a stark, realistic portrayal of conditions in the Russian countryside and the attitudes of Russia's peasantry toward Soviet power. He calls on the assembled delegates to approve the regime's plan for the electrification of Russia and to pursue the plan's implementation with the same fervor and dedication that led to Red Victory in the Civil War.

Lenin offers an intriguing view of the necessity both to convince and coerce elements of the population into supporting the electrification plan. In an eerie foreshadowing of Stalin's central theme, Lenin cites the hostility of the capitalist world toward the land of the Soviets to add urgency to his message.

The Document

The essential feature of the present political situation is that we are now passing through a crucial period of transition, something of a zigzag transition from war to economic development. This has occurred before, but not on such a wide scale. This should constantly remind us of what the general political tasks of the Soviet government are, and what constitutes the particular feature of this transition. The dictatorship of the proletariat has been successful because it has been able to combine compulsion with persuasion. The dictatorship of the proletariat does not fear any resort to compulsion and to the most severe, decisive and ruthless forms of coercion by the state. The advanced class, the class most oppressed by capitalism, is entitled to use compulsion, because it is doing so in the interests of the working and exploited people, and because it possesses means of compulsion and persuasion such as no former classes ever possessed, although they had incomparably greater material facilities for propaganda and agitation than we have. . . .

. . . Now ask yourselves whether we at present have the condition for the rapid and unequivocal success that we had during the war, the condition of the masses being drawn into the work. Are the members of the trade unions and the majority of the non-Party people convinced that our new methods and our great tasks of economic development are necessary? Are they as convinced of this as they were of the necessity of devoting everything to the war, of sacrificing everything for the sake of victory on the war front? If the question is presented in that way, you will be compelled to answer that they are certainly not. They are far from being as fully convinced of this as they should be.

War was a matter which people understood and were used to for hundreds and thousands of years. The acts of violence and brutality formerly committed by the landowners were so obvious that it was easy to convince the people; it was not difficult to convince even the peasants of the richer grain regions, who are least connected with industry, that we were waging war in the interests of the working people, and it was therefore possible to arouse almost universal enthusiasm. It will be more difficult to get the peasant masses and the members of the trade unions to understand these tasks now, to get them to understand that we cannot go on living in the old way, that however firmly capitalist exploitation has been implanted in the course of decades, it must be overcome. We must get everybody to understand that Russia belongs to us, and that only we, the masses of workers and peasants, can by our activities and our strict labour discipline remould the old economic conditions of existence and put a great economic plan into practice. There can be no salvation apart from this. We are lagging behind the capitalist powers and shall continue to lag behind them; we shall be defeated if we do not succeed in restoring our economy. . . .

We have been completely successful in the military sphere, and we must now prepare to achieve similar successes in tasks which are more difficult and which demand enthusiasm and self-sacrifice from the vast majority of workers and peasants. The conviction that the new tasks are necessary must be instilled in hundreds of millions of people who from generation to generation have lived in a state of slavery and oppression and whose every initiative has been suppressed. We must convince the millions of workers who belong to trade unions but who are still not politically conscious and are unaccustomed to regarding themselves as masters. They must be organised, not to resist the government but to support and develop the measures of their workers' government and to carry them out to the full. This transition will be accompanied by difficulties. . . .

The necessity of organising production propaganda on a nation-wide scale follows from the special features of the political situation. It is equally necessary to the working class, the trade unions, and the peasantry. It is absolutely essential to our state apparatus, which we have used far from enough for this purpose. We have a thousand times more knowledge, book knowledge, of how to run industry and how to interest the masses than is being applied in practice. We must see to it that literally every member of the trade unions becomes interested in production, and remembers that only by increasing production and raising labour productivity will Soviet Russia be in a state to win. Only in this way will Soviet Russia be able to shorten by about ten years the period of the frightful conditions she is now experiencing, the hunger and cold she is now suffering. If we do not understand this task, we may all perish, because we shall have to retreat owing to the weakness of our apparatus, since, after a short respite, the capitalists may at any moment renew the war, while we shall not be in a state to continue it. . . .

Our country has been and still is a country of small peasants, and the transition to communism is far more difficult for us than it would be under any other conditions. To accomplish this transition, the peasants' participation in it must be ten times as much as in the war. The war could demand, and was bound to demand, part of the adult male population. However, our country, a land of peasants which is still in a state of exhaustion, has to mobilise the entire male and female population of workers and peasants without exception. It is not difficult to convince us Communists, workers in the Land Departments, that state labour conscription is necessary. In the discussion of the bill of December 14, which has been submitted for your consideration, I hope that on this point there will not be even a shadow of difference in principle. We must realise that there is another difficulty, that of convincing the non-Party peasants. The peasants are not socialists. To base our socialist plans on the assumption that they are would be building on sand; it would mean that we do not understand our tasks and that, during these three years, we have not learnt to adjust our programmes and carry out our new undertakings with due account of the poverty and often squalor that surround us. . . .

Every non-Party peasant must be made to understand this undoubted truth, and we are sure that he will understand it. He has not lived through these last six painful and difficult years in vain. He is not like the pre-war muzhik. He has suffered severely, has done a lot of thinking, and has borne many political and economic hardships that have induced him to give up a good deal of their old habits. It seems to me that he already realises that he cannot live in the old way, that he must live in a different way. All our means of propaganda, all the resources of the state, all our educational facilities and all our Party resources and reserves must be devoted in full force to convincing the non-Party peasant. . . .

Comrades, here is what I particularly want to bring home to you now that we have turned from the phase of war to economic development. In a country of small peasants, our chief and basic task is to be able to resort to state compulsion in order to raise the level of peasant farming, beginning with measures that are absolutely essential, urgent and fully intelligible and comprehensible to the peasant. . . . And unless we succeed, unless we achieve a practical and massive improvement in small-scale peasant farming, there is no salvation for us. . . . we cannot go on starving and freezing endlessly, for then we shall be overthrown in the next period of wars. This is a state matter; it concerns the interests of our state. Whoever reveals the least weakness, the least slackness in this matter, is an out-and-out criminal towards the workers' and peasants' government; he is helping the landowner and the capitalist. And the landowner and the capitalist have their armies nearby, holding them in readiness to launch against us the instant they see us weakening. . . .

We admit that we are in debt to the peasant. We have had grain from him in return for paper money, and have taken it from him on credit. We must repay that debt, and we shall do so when we have restored our industry. To restore it we need a surplus of agricultural products. That is why the agrarian bill is important, not only because we must secure practical results, but also because around it, as on a focal point, are grouped hundreds of decisions and legislative measures of the Soviet government. . . .

. . . There can be no socialist country, no state with a workers' and peasants' government unless, by the joint efforts of the workers and peasants, it can accumulate a stock of food sufficient to guarantee the subsistence of the workers engaged in industry and to make it possible to send tens and hundreds of thousands of workers wherever the Soviet government deems it necessary. Without this there can be nothing but empty talk. Food stocks are the real basis of the economic system. In this we have achieved a signal success. Having achieved this success and with such a reserve, we can set about restoring our economy. We know that these successes have been achieved at the cost of tremendous privation, hunger and lack of cattle fodder among the peasants, which may become still more acute. We know that the year of drought increased the hardships and privations of the peasants to an unparalleled extent. We therefore lay prime stress on the measures of assistance contained in the bill I have referred to. We regard stocks of food as a fund for the restoration of industry, as a fund for helping the peasants. Without such a fund the state power is nothing. Without such a fund socialist policy is but a pious wish. . . .

We must introduce more machines everywhere, and resort to machine technology as widely as possible. . . . We have produced these machines; . . . We have made the machines required for the new method, but we have made them badly. If we send our people abroad, with the establishment of trade with foreign countries, with even the existing semi-legal trade relations, the machines designed by our inventors could be made properly there. The number of these machines and the success gained in this field by the Chief Peat Committee and the Supreme Council of the National Economy will serve as a measure of all our economic achievements. . . .

I now come to the last item—the question of electrification, which stands on the agenda of the Congress. You are to hear a report on this subject. I think that we are witnessing a momentous change, one which in any case marks the beginning of important successes for the Soviets. Henceforth the rostrum at All-Russia Congresses will be mounted, not only by politicians and administrators but also by engineers and agronomists. This marks the beginning of that very happy time when politics will recede into the background, when politics will be discussed less often and at shorter length, and engineers and agronomists will do most of the talking. . . .

We have, no doubt, learnt politics; here we stand as firm as a rock. But things are bad as far as economic matters are concerned. Henceforth, less politics will be the best politics. Bring more engineers and agronomists to the fore, learn from them, keep an eye on their work, and turn our congresses and conferences, not into propaganda meetings but into bodies that will verify our economic achievements, bodies in which we can really learn the business of economic development.

You will hear the report of the State Electrification Commission, which was set up in conformity with the decision of the All-Russia Central Executive Committee of February 7, 1920. . . . Without a plan of electrification, we cannot undertake any real constructive work. When we discuss the restoration of agriculture, industry and transport, and their harmonious co-ordination, we are obliged to discuss a broad economic plan. We must adopt a definite plan. . . . We need it as a first draft, which will be submitted to the whole of Russia as a great economic plan designed for a period of not less than ten years and indicating how Russia is to be placed on the real economic basis required for communism. What was one of the most powerful incentives that multiplied our strength and our energies to a tremendous degree when we fought and won on the war front? It was the realisation of danger. Everybody asked whether it was possible that the landowners and capitalists might return to Russia. And the reply was that it was. We therefore multiplied our efforts a hundredfold, and we were victorious.

Take the economic front, and ask whether capitalism can be restored economically in Russia. We have combated the Sukharevka black market. The other day, just prior to the opening of the All-Russia Congress of Soviets, this not very pleasant institution was closed down by the Moscow Soviet of Workers' and Red Army Deputies. (Applause.) . . . The sinister thing is the "Sukharevka" that resides in the heart and behaviour of every petty proprietor. This is the "Sukharevka" that must be closed down. That "Sukharevka" is the basis of capitalism. While it exists, the capitalists may return to Russia and may grow stronger than we are. That must be clearly realised. . . . Anyone who has carefully observed life in the Countryside, as compared with life in the cities, knows that we have not torn up the roots of capitalism and have not undermined the foundation, the basis, of the internal enemy. The latter depends on small-scale production, and there is only one way of undermining it, namely, to place the economy of the country, including agriculture, on a new technical basis, that of modern large-scale production. Only electricity provides that basis.

Communism is Soviet power plus the electrification of the whole country. Otherwise the country will remain a small-peasant country, and we must clearly realise that. We are weaker than capitalism, not only on the world scale, but also within the country. That is common knowledge. We have realised it, and we shall see to it that the economic basis is transformed from a small-peasant basis into a large-scale industrial basis. Only when the country has been electrified, and industry, agriculture and transport have been placed on the technical basis of modern large-scale industry, only then shall we be fully victorious.

We have already drawn up a preliminary plan for the electrification of the country; two hundred of our best scientific and technical men have worked on it. We have a plan which gives us estimates of materials and finances covering a long period of years, not less than a decade. This plan indicates how many million barrels of cement and how many million bricks we shall require for the purpose of electrification. To accomplish the task of electrification from the financial point of view, the estimates are between 1,000 and 1,200 million gold rubles. You know that we are far from being able to meet this sum from our gold reserves. Our stock of foodstuffs is not very large either. We must therefore meet the expenditure indicated in these estimates by means of concessions, in accordance with the plan I have mentioned. You will see the calculation showing how the restoration of our industry and our transport is being planned on this basis.

I recently had occasion to attend a peasant festival held in Volokolamsk Uyezd, a remote part of Moscow Gubernia, where the peasants have electric lighting. A meeting was arranged in the street, and one of the peasants came forward and began to make a speech welcoming this new event in the lives of the peasants. "We peasants were unenlightened," he said, "and now light has appeared among us, an 'unnatural light, which will light up our peasant darkness'." For my part, these words did not surprise me. Of course, to the non-Party peasant masses electric light is an "unnatural" light; but what we consider unnatural is that the peasants and workers should have lived for hundreds and thousands of years in such backwardness, poverty and oppression under the yoke of the landowners and the capitalists. You cannot emerge from this darkness very rapidly. What we must now try is to convert every electric power station we build into a stronghold of enlightenment to be used to make the masses electricity-conscious, so to speak. . . . To carry out the electrification plan we may need a period of ten or twenty years to effect the changes that will preclude any return to capitalism. This will be an example of rapid social development without precedent anywhere in the world. The plan must be carried out at all costs, and its deadline brought nearer.

This is the first time that we have set about economic work in such a fashion that, besides separate plans which have arisen in separate sections of industry as, for instance, in the transport system and have been brought into other branches of industry, we now have an all-over plan calculated for a number of years. This is hard work, designed to bring about the victory of communism.

It should, however, be realised and remembered that we cannot carry out electrification with the illiterates we have. Our commission will endeavour to stamp out illiteracy—but that is not enough. It has done a good deal compared with the past, but it was done little compared with what has to be done. Besides literacy, we need cultured, enlightened and educated working people; the majority of the peasants must be made fully aware of the tasks awaiting us. . . .

Our best men, our economic experts, have accomplished the task we set them of drawing up a plan for the electrification of Russia and the restoration of her economy. We must now see to it that the workers and peasants should realise how great and difficult this task is, how it must be approached and tackled.

We must see to it that every factory and every electric power station becomes a centre of enlightenment; if Russia is covered with a dense network of electric power stations and powerful technical installations, our communist economic development will become a model for a future socialist Europe and Asia. (*Stormy and prolonged applause.*)

Analysis and Review Questions

1. Why did Lenin believe that the Bolsheviks had to modernize Russia rapidly?
2. How did Lenin view the relationship between the bulk of the Russian people and the Bolshevik regime?
3. What role should education play in the modernization process, according to Lenin?
4. Why did Lenin see electrification of the entire country as such an urgent necessity?
5. What time frame did Lenin consider appropriate for completion of the modernization process?

Image 29.1
Red Square
Military Parade

STALIN DEMANDS RAPID INDUSTRIALIZATION OF THE USSR

About the Document

Stalin consolidated his leadership of the Soviet Union by the end of 1927. He immediately turned to the industrialization of the nation with the first Five-Year Plan, which began in November 1928. The plan called for the gradual, voluntary collectivization of Soviet agriculture, yet Stalin began forcing farmers into collectives within a year of the plan's start. Despite a temporary retreat from coercion in the spring of 1930 (peasant resistance to coercion had endangered the spring planting), Stalin continued forcing peasants into collective farms throughout the 1930s. Against this backdrop of violence in the countryside, the industrialization drive continued.

The following document presents Stalin's views on the contemporary problems of the ongoing industrialization process early in 1931. Speaking to a group of what we would now call "business executives," Stalin sets forth the challenge to complete the industrialization of the country within a decade. His reasons include foreign and domestic concerns, and draw on both Russian nationalism and proletarian internationalism as critical factors.

The Document

About ten years ago a slogan was issued: "Since Communists do not yet properly understand the technique of production, since they have yet to learn the art of management, let the old technicians and engineers—the experts—carry on production, and you, Communists, do not interfere with the technique of the business; but, while not interfering, study technique, study the art of management tirelessly, in order later on, together with the experts who are loyal to us, to become true managers of production, true masters of the business." Such was the slogan. But what actually happened? The second part of this formula was cast aside, for it is harder to study than to sign papers; and the first part of the formula was vulgarised: non-interference was interpreted to mean refraining from studying the technique of production. The result has been nonsense, harmful and dangerous nonsense, which the sooner we discard the better.

Life itself has more than once warned us that all was not well in this field. The Shakhty affair was the first grave warning. The Shakhty affair showed that the Party organisations and the trade unions lacked revolutionary vigilance. It showed that our business executives were disgracefully backward in technical knowledge; that some of the old engineers and technicians, working without supervision, rather easily go over to wrecking° activities, especially as they are constantly being besieged by "offers" from our enemies abroad.

The second warning was the "Industrial Party" trial.

Of course, the underlying cause of wrecking activities is the class struggle. Of course, the class enemy furiously resists the socialist offensive. This alone, however, is not an adequate explanation for the luxuriant growth of wrecking activities.

---

wrecking: The deliberate sabotage of Soviet policy, especially of economic programs, became known as "wrecking." Criminal charges of "wrecking" were often levied against former Tsarist specialists in the 1920s and 1930s, and any failure of any Soviet economic program was generally blamed on "wreckers."

How is it that wrecking activities assumed such wide dimensions? Who is to blame for this? We are to blame. Had we handled the business of managing production differently, had we started much earlier to learn the technique of the business, to master technique, had we more frequently and efficiently intervened in the management of production, the wreckers would not have succeeded in doing so much damage.

We must ourselves become experts, masters of the business; we must turn to technical science—such was the lesson life itself was teaching us. But neither the first warning nor even the second brought about the necessary change. It is time, high time that we turned towards technique. It is time to discard the old slogan, the obsolete slogan of non-interference in technique, and ourselves become specialists, experts, complete masters of our economic affairs.

It is frequently asked: Why have we not one-man management?° We do not have it and we shall not get it until we have mastered technique. Until there are among us Bolsheviks a sufficient number of people thoroughly familiar with technique, economy and finance, we shall not have real one-man management. You can write as many resolutions as you please, take as many vows as you please, but, unless you master the technique, economy and finance of the mill, factory or mine, nothing will come of it, there will be no one-man management.

Hence, the task is for us to master technique ourselves, to become masters of the business ourselves. This is the sole guarantee that our plans will be carried out in full, and that one-man management will be established.

This, of course, is no easy matter; but it can certainly be accomplished. Science, technical experience, knowledge, are all things that can be acquired. We may not have them today, but tomorrow we shall. The main thing is to have the passionate Bolshevik desire to master technique, to master the science of production. Everything can be achieved, everything can be overcome, if there is a passionate desire for it.

It is sometimes asked whether it is not possible to slow down the tempo somewhat, to put a check on the movement. No, comrades, it is not possible! The tempo must not be reduced! On the contrary, we must increase it as much as is within our powers and possibilities. This is dictated to us by our obligations to the workers and peasants of the U.S.S.R. This is dictated to us by our obligations to the working class of the whole world.

To slacken the tempo would mean falling behind. And those who fall behind get beaten. But we do not want to be beaten. No, we refuse to be beaten! One feature of the history of old Russia was the continual beatings she suffered because of her backwardness. She was beaten by the Mongol khans. She was beaten by the Turkish beys. She was beaten by the Swedish feudal lords. She was beaten by the Polish and Lithuanian gentry. She was beaten by the British and French capitalists. She was beaten by the Japanese barons. All beat her—because of her backwardness, because of her military backwardness, cultural backwardness, political backwardness, industrial backwardness, agricultural backwardness. They beat her because to do so was profitable and could be done with impunity. You remember the words of the pre-revolutionary poet: "You are poor and abundant, mighty and impotent, Mother Russia." Those gentlemen were

---

one-man management: Any time a non-Bolshevik specialist led a unit of industry or of the military, a reliable political overseer (at various times referred to as a "commissar" or *zampolit*) supervised his work and loyalty. This dual chain of command often came under fire in both economic and military spheres as inefficient and counterproductive. Those who criticized the dual system called for "one-man management" as their panacea to correct managerial problems.

quite familiar with the verses of the old poet. They beat her, saying: "You are abundant," so one can enrich oneself at your expense. They beat her, saying: "You are poor and impotent," so you can be beaten and plundered with impunity. Such is the law of the exploiters—to beat the backward and the weak. It is the jungle law of capitalism. You are backward, you are weak—therefore you are wrong; hence you can be beaten and enslaved. You are mighty—therefore you are right; hence we must be wary of you.

That is why we must no longer lag behind.

In the past we had no fatherland, nor could we have had one. But now that we have overthrown capitalism and power is in our hands, in the hands of the people, we have a fatherland, and we will uphold its independence. Do you want our socialist fatherland to be beaten and to lose its independence? If you do not want this, you must put an end to its backwardness in the shortest possible time and develop a genuine Bolshevik tempo in building up its socialist economy. There is no other way. That is why Lenin said on the eve of the October Revolution: "Either perish, or overtake and outstrip the advanced capitalist countries."

We are fifty or a hundred years behind the advanced countries. We must make good this distance in ten years. Either we do it, or we shall go under.

That is what our obligations to the workers and peasants of the U.S.S.R. dictate to us.

But we have yet other, more serious and more important, obligations. They are our obligations to the world proletariat. They coincide with our obligations to the workers and peasants of the U.S.S.R. But we place them higher. The working class of the U.S.S.R. is part of the world working class. We achieved victory not solely through the efforts of the working class of the U.S.S.R., but also thanks to the support of the working class of the world. Without this support we would have been torn to pieces long ago. It is said that our country is the shock brigade of the proletariat of all countries. That is well said. But it imposes very serious obligations upon us. Why does the international proletariat support us? How did we merit this support? By the fact that we were the first to hurl ourselves into the battle against capitalism, we were the first to establish working-class state power, we were the first to begin building socialism. By the fact that we are engaged on a cause which, if successful, will transform the whole world and free the entire working class. But what is needed for success? The elimination of our backwardness, the development of a high Bolshevik tempo of construction. We must march forward in such a way that the working class of the whole world, looking at us, may say: There you have my advanced detachment, my shock brigade, my working-class state power, my fatherland; they are engaged on their cause, our cause, and they are working well; let us support them against the capitalists and promote the cause of the world revolution. Must we not justify the hopes of the world's working class, must we not fulfil our obligations to them? Yes, we must if we do not want to utterly disgrace ourselves.

Such are our obligations, internal and international.

As you see, they dictate to us a Bolshevik tempo of development.

I will not say that we have accomplished nothing in regard to management of production during these years. In fact, we have accomplished a good deal. We have doubled our industrial output compared with the pre-war level. We have created the largest-scale agricultural production in the world. But we could have accomplished still more if we had tried during this period really to master production, the technique of production, the financial and economic side of it.

In ten years at most we must make good the distance that separates us from the advanced capitalist countries. We have all the "objective" possibilities for this. The only thing lacking is the ability to make proper use of these possibilities. And that depends on us. *Only* on us! It is time we learned to make use of these possibilities. It is time to put an end to the rotten line of non-interference in production. It is time to adopt a new line, one corresponding to the present period—the line of *interfering in everything*. If you are a factory manager—interfere in all the affairs of the factory, look into everything, let nothing escape you, learn and learn again. Bolsheviks must master technique. It is time Bolsheviks themselves became experts. In the period of reconstruction, technique decides everything. And a business executive who does not want to study technique, who does not want to master technique, is a joke and not an executive.

It is said that it is hard to master technique. That is not true! There are no fortresses that Bolsheviks cannot capture. We have solved a number of most difficult problems. We have overthrown capitalism. We have assumed power. We have built up a huge socialist industry. We have transferred the middle peasants on to the path of socialism. We have already accomplished what is most important from the point of view of construction. What remains to be done is not so much: to study technique, to master science. And when we have done that we shall develop a tempo of which we dare not even dream at present.

And we shall do it if we really want to.

Analysis and Review Questions

1. What did Stalin see as the role of education in the industrialization process?
2. How did Stalin view the relationship between Russian nationalism and international socialism?
3. Why did Stalin consider industrialization to be so urgent for Russia?
4. To what root cause did Stalin attribute "wrecking"?
5. How did Stalin view the relationship between the bulk of the Soviet people and the regime?

Map 29.2
The Cold War
Military Stand-Off

MIKHAIL GORBACHEV ON THE NEED FOR ECONOMIC REFORM

About the Document

Mikhail Gorbachev became the leader of the USSR in March 1985 and immediately launched into the reform of Soviet economic and social policy. Calling for the restructuring (*perestroika*) of the socialist economy and for increased openness (*glasnost*) in Soviet society, Gorbachev admitted that the USSR had fallen behind in its economic competition with the West.

In this document, Gorbachev lays out some specific steps that the leaders of the USSR's economy must take to revitalize the socialist system. He also defines bureaucracy as the "enemy" of Soviet progress and the "people" as the repository of wisdom and initiative. He lauds Soviet advancements in scientific theories and Soviet development—if not widespread application—of modern techniques in manufacturing and production.

The Document

In carrying out a radical economic reform, it was important to preclude the repetition of the past mistakes which in the 1950s, 1960s and 1970s doomed to failure our attempts to change the system of economic management. At the same time, those attempts proved to be incomplete and inconsistent for they emphasized certain issues, while ignoring others. Speaking frankly, the solutions that were offered then were not radical, they were halfway measures, which not infrequently missed the essence of the matter.

I would say that the concept of economic reform, which we submitted to the June Plenary Meeting, is of an all-embracing, comprehensive character. It provides for fundamental changes in every area, including the transfer of enterprises to complete cost accounting, a radical transformation of the centralized management of the economy, fundamental changes in planning, a reform of the price formation system and of the financial and crediting mechanism, and the restructuring of foreign economic ties. It also provides for the creation of new organizational structures of management, for the all-round development of the democratic foundations of management, and for the broad introduction of the self-management principles.

There is an inner logic in any complex process, and it reflects interrelationships between certain measures, between certain concrete steps. A natural question arose before us: Where to begin! What is the starting point in restructuring management?

In our planned economy, it would seem logical, at first sight, to start restructuring from the centre, to determine the structure and functions of central economic bodies, then go over to the middle management level, and then, finally, to enterprises and amalgamations, the primary level. That might be correct from the viewpoint of abstract logic, but reality and accumulated experience dictated a different approach and a different logic: we should start with enterprises and amalgamations, the main link in the economic chain. We should start with finding the most effective economic model for them, then create the optimum economic conditions, extend and consolidate their rights, and only on that basis introduce fundamental changes in the activity of all higher echelons of economic management.

As we determined that sequence of the restructuring effort, we bore in mind that it is there, at enterprises and amalgamations, that the main economic processes are taking place, that material values are being created, and scientific and technological ideas are materializing. It is the work collective that gives a tangible shape to economic and social relations, and it is in the work collective that personal, collective and social interests of people are interlinked. The work collective largely determines the social and political atmosphere countrywide.

We also took into consideration our past experience, in which repeated attempts to reform the upper management levels without support from below were unsuccessful because of the stubborn resistance of the management apparatus, which did not want to part with its numerous rights and prerogatives. We have recently encountered that resistance, and still encounter it now. Here too, as in all other areas of restructuring, we must combine what comes from above with the movement from below, i.e., give the restructuring effort a profoundly democratic nature.

What is the main shortcoming of the old economic machinery?

It is above all the lack of inner stimuli for self-development. Indeed, through the system of plan indices, the enterprise receives assignments and resources. Practically all expenses are covered, sales of products are essentially guaranteed and, most importantly, the employees' incomes do not depend on the end results of the collective's work: the fulfilment of contract commitments, production quality and profits. Such a mechanism is likely to produce medium or even poor quality work, whether we like it or not. How can the economy advance if it creates preferential conditions for backward enterprises and penalizes the foremost ones?

We can no longer run our affairs like that. The new economic mechanism must put matters right. It must become a powerful lever, a motivating force for resourceful quality performance. Every enterprise must proceed from real social demands to determine production and sales plans for itself. Those plans must be based not on numerous detailed assignments set by higher bodies, but on direct orders placed by government organizations, self-accounting enterprises and trade firms for specific products of appropriate quantity and quality. Enterprises must be put in such conditions as to encourage economic competition for the best satisfaction of consumer demands and employees' incomes must strictly depend on end production results, on profits.

We included all these principles of economic management and its specific forms in the draft Law on the State Enterprise (Amalgamation) which was discussed nationwide in work collectives, at meetings of workers and trade-union locals, and in the media. The draft law evoked the interest of the entire nation. The people felt that their opinion was needed. A special group of government officials, scientists and representatives of various state agencies considered the submitted proposals, amendments and additions. Everything that was rational and reasonable was included and considerably improved it.

Most corrections were meant to extend the work collective's rights. The general demand was not to retreat under the influence of inertia, but to go on firmly. It was felt that the new law should not be overburdened by numerous instructions which could emasculate it and bring it to a standstill. The USSR Supreme Soviet has adopted the law which will enter into force on 1 January 1988.

True, the press carried some proposals which went outside our system. There was an opinion, for instance, that we ought to give up planned economy and sanction unemployment. We cannot permit this, however, since we aim to strengthen socialism, not replace it with a different system. What is offered to us from the West, from a different economy, is unacceptable to us. We are sure that if we really put into effect the potential of socialism, if we adhere to its basic principles, if we take fully into consideration human interests and use the benefits of a planned economy, socialism can achieve much more than capitalism.

We attach primary importance to the Law on the State Enterprise in our economic reform. We use it as a yardstick for our other steps and measures. We consider them from the point of view of how fully they conform to this law and contribute to its practical implementation.

The June Plenary Meeting of the CPSU Central Committee, its decisions, and the "Basic Provisions for Radical Restructuring of Economic Management" it adopted, are, in effect, completing the construction of a modern *model* of socialist economy to meet the challenge of the present stage of national development.

The Plenary Meeting and the session of the Supreme Soviet of the USSR that followed it developed and consolidated the policy of promoting the people's active involvement in economic and production processes, closely combining the interests of the state with those of the individual and the work collective, and of making the Soviet working people the true master.

Of course, we will still have things to complete or, perhaps, re-do. No society can ever have any system of economic management replaced overnight by a different, even a more advanced one, as if it were a kind of mechanical contrivance. We will have to adjust a dynamic and flexible mechanism sensitive to changes in production and capable of being constantly modernized, accepting what is advanced and rejecting what has outlived itself. The main danger here is stopping the belief that since decisions have been taken they will always be relevant in their present form.

By drawing up a program for a radical economic reform, we have laid the foundations for a full-scale offensive, this time in every area of the process of accelerating and extending the restructuring. The decisions taken provide the organizational and economic prerequisites for attaining the targets of the current five-year plan and the long-term objectives up to the year 2000. The task now in hand is to bring the new machinery of economic management into full operation competently and without delay.

This is, perhaps, the most crucial moment in the restructuring of the economy and management. The stage of constructive work has started. Now everything must be translated into reality. The emphasis now is on actually doing what we have concentrated our efforts for—and that is the hallmark of this juncture.

On to Full Cost Accounting!

The essence of what we plan to do throughout the country is to replace predominantly administrative methods by predominantly economic methods. That we must have full cost accounting° is quite clear to the Soviet leadership.

True, there are some obstacles. Two of them, at least, are large. The first is that we have to do this in the context of the already endorsed five-year plan, that is, make it fit in. This particular aspect has a serious effect on the process of transition. So what are we to do, after all: stick to the five-year plan or drop it? There is only one answer to this question: we must reach the five-year-plan targets! This is an extremely difficult five-year-plan period: extensive forward-looking research is being conducted, great structural changes are taking place, many social issues are being resolved, and, along with all that, many innovations must be introduced in the course of this period. These are trying times for the factory managers: they have a heavy burden of problems that have built up and at the same time they have to change over to self-financing.

Another obstacle is that some of the more important components of the new management mechanism are not yet ready and will not be put into effect at once. It will take two or three years to prepare a reform of price formation and of the finance and crediting mechanism, and five to six years to go over to wholesale trade in the means of production. A lot has still to be decided about determining the functions of ministries, the reorganization of territorial administration, and the reduction of personnel.

Therefore we shall have a very complicated transition period, during which both the old and the newly introduced mechanisms will coexist. But full cost accounting will be introduced without delay. We will energetically follow this path gaining experience in the process. We will try out and test everything.

Whenever I meet people working in industry or even ministers, I tell them: never flinch; search and try things out. The people have so much wisdom and so keen a sense of responsibility that you can and must act boldly and confidently. Well, suppose we make mistakes. So what? It is better to rectify them than sit and wait.

full cost accounting: The notion that supply and demand should be allowed to determine the prices of finished goods produced by Soviet enterprises contradicted the traditional central planning scheme by which prices had been determined. Gorbachev used "full cost accounting" as a euphemism for the introduction of some market elements into the Soviet planned economy.

A New Concept of Centralism

In the course of perestroika a new concept of democratic centralism° is taking shape. It is important to have its two sides correctly balanced, bearing in mind that at different stages different aspects will be highlighted.

The situation now stands as follows: there are many people who are calling for stronger centralism. Balance sheets, proportions, the need for incomes to correspond to the mass of commodities and volume of services, structural policies, state finances, defense—all these require a firm centralized principle. All our republics and all our peoples should feel that they are placed in equal conditions and have equal opportunities for development. In this lies the guarantee of Soviet society's stability. That is why we do not want to weaken the role of the center, because otherwise we would lose the advantages of the planned economy.

At the same time, one cannot fail to see that the central authorities are overburdened with minor work. We will relieve them of current duties, for, by dealing with them, they lose sight of strategic matters.

Much of what we justly criticized at the January and June Plenary Meetings is due in the first place to omissions at the center: it could not sense dangerous trends in time, failed to find solutions to new problems, etc. All reorganization of the central apparatus and its functions, I repeat, will be strictly matched against the Law on the State Enterprise. Centralism in the conditions of perestroika has nothing in common with bureaucratic regulation of the many-faceted life of production, scientific and design collectives. We have yet to divide the functions of the center and localities, to change the essence of ministries' work, and their very purpose.

We are contemplating democratizing planning. This means that plan-making—not formal but actual—will begin within enterprises and work collectives. It is they who will be planning the production of their output, on the basis of social needs expressed in target figures and government contracts and on direct economic contract ties with consumers.

In short, the advantages of planning will be increasingly combined with stimulating factors of the socialist market. But all this will take place within the mainstream of socialist goals and principles of management.

The broadening of the rights and economic autonomy of enterprises, the changing of the functions of central economic and sectoral departments and the transition from predominantly administrative methods to mainly economic methods of management call for radical changes in the managerial structure.

Earlier, the improvement of management was often accompanied by the establishment of new organizational elements, which resulted in the swelling of the apparatus, its becoming bulky, unwieldy and bureaucratic. We realize that the rates of economic restructuring are in no small degree held back by the bulky nature and inadequate efficiency of the management apparatus. So we intend to make heavy cuts in the managerial apparatus and, when necessary, will simplify its structure and enlarge sectoral ministries. We already have some experience of doing this. For example, agriculture and the processing of its produce were managed in our country by seven all-Union ministries and departments. We amalgamated all these departments into Gosagroprom, at the same time cutting their managerial staff by almost half. In another case, we chose to enlarge some ministries by merging them. This is how we will proceed in [the] future, taking each case on its individual merits.

democratic centralism: At the Tenth Party Congress in 1921, factions amongst the Bolshevik Party were officially banned. Party members remained theoretically free to discuss issues and offer alternatives for policies that had not yet been officially approved or implemented (*democratic*). But once a decision had been taken and the Party had adopted a policy, all members were expected to support it (*centralism*).

It is now clear to everyone that given the present scale of the economy, no ministerial or departmental apparatus, however qualified, can take upon itself the solution of absolutely every question, nor can it replace the thought and initiative of work collectives. Redistribution of rights between the central departments and the enterprises is not proceeding smoothly. The apparatus of the ministries and ministers themselves are unwilling to give up the habit of deciding minor matters themselves. They are used to that practice, which makes it so much easier for them. Any transfer of rights from the center to the localities is, in general painful, although, I repeat, the necessity of this is obvious to all, to both ministers and staff. They realize that this action benefits the cause, but, nevertheless, narrow departmental and sometimes group interests are put above those of society and the people.

There is one more way of perfecting economic management. Experience shows that there is potential for achieving maximum efficiency at the points where industries meet. But to expect that the State Planning Committee will be able to trace all intersectoral links and choose an optimum variant is to harbor an illusion. The ministries are even less in a position to do so. It was this that put on the agenda the question of setting up agencies to manage large economic complexes. As can be seen, the management system will undergo great changes. We intend to act resolutely, but also in a balanced way, without unnecessary fuss.

Goal: World Technological Standards

While restructuring our planning and economic activities and extending the rights of the enterprises, we have also tackled the questions of scientific and technological progress. The branches that are in the forefront of this progress are being lent additional financial and material support. To this end a target-oriented national program has been mapped out, and funds allocated.

During the Twelfth Five-Year-Plan period, we will renew the greater part of fixed assets in machine-building. The amount set aside for these purposes will be almost double that spent in the previous five years.

Analysis of industry's performance has shown mistakes in the investment policy. For many years our policy had been to build more and more enterprises. The construction of workshops and administrative buildings absorbed vast sums. The existing enterprises, meanwhile, remained at the same technological level. Of course, if good use is made of everything available in two or three shifts, the targets of the Twelfth Five-Year Plan can be met using the existing equipment. But obsolescent equipment would in one way or another drag us backward, since it would mean we would be unable to put out modern products. Old machinery must be given up. This is why we are so drastically changing our structural and investment policies.

In 1983, I visited ZIL. It was a time of active preparations for the modernization of that plant, one of the first such projects of the Soviet automotive industry. In 1985, I again visited ZIL and asked how modernization had progressed. It turned out that sights had been set on the average technological level, with reliance on equipment made five to seven years earlier. One could not, therefore, expect substantial advances in technology. Besides, a larger workforce would be required. Focusing on outdated technology does not lead to appreciable intensification of production; it merely consolidates the time-lag. As it transpired, the collective had come up with another, more advanced version, but it had not been supported and work on it had been discontinued. We backed the decision of the plant collective to go back to this plan for the ZIL modernization. A new plan for retooling has been drawn up, and is being successfully implemented. ZIL will become a really modern enterprise.

Generally speaking, drastic changes in technology and equipment take time. As we say, "Moscow was not built in a day." If we had set the task of deciding everything at one go, we would have had to modernize production by using outmoded, obsolescent equipment. It would have been tantamount to marking time.

Then we took a look at what equipment we had and whether it met world standards. It was discovered that only a lesser part of it was on that level. The conclusion suggested itself: rather than preserve our technological backwardness for many years, we would do better to pass through the pains of developing new equipment now and then, through advances in machine-building, make a breakthrough to the newest technologies. That "then" does not necessarily imply a remote future. No, structural modernization of Soviet machine-building must be combined with vast efforts to turn the scientific potential to good account. This is the most vital and urgent task for us, even a top priority. We have found ourselves in this situation technologically because we underestimated our scientific potential and placed too great a reliance on external ties.

As I see it, we accepted the policy of *détente* with too radiant hopes; I would say, too trustingly. Many thought it would be irreversible and open up unbounded possibilities, in particular for expanding trade and economic relations with the West. We even discontinued some of our research and technological developments, hoping for the international division of labor, and thinking that some machines would be more advantageous to buy than to manufacture at home. But what happened in reality? We were seriously punished for our *naïveté*. There came a period of embargoes, boycotts, bans, restrictions, intimidation of those trading with us, etc. Some Western politicians even publicly anticipated the collapse of the Soviet system. But they ranted in vain.

Certainly, we have drawn the necessary conclusions, started the necessary research and development and the production of what we once proposed to purchase, so Western firms will ultimately be the losers. Incidentally, I think all this noise about bans and restrictions is aimed not only against the USSR, but also, in very large measure, against rival non-American firms.

On the whole, the various US "sanctions" and "embargoes" and other bans helped clarify a great deal. As they say, every cloud has a silver lining. We have drawn lessons from the decisions taken by the US and some other Western countries to refuse to sell the Soviet Union advanced technology. That is perhaps why we are now experiencing a real boom in the fields of information science, computer technology and other areas of science and technology.

We decided to put a firm end to the "import scourge," as our economic executives call it. To these ends we are putting into operation the great potential of our science and mechanical engineering.

It is a paradox that many achievements of Soviet scientists were introduced in the West more quickly than in our own country, for instance, rotary conveyor lines. We were also slow in another case. We were the first to invent continuous steel casting. What came of it? Now eighty percent of the steel produced in some countries is cast by our method, but much less, in our country. The path in our country from a scientific discovery to its introduction in production is too long. This enables enterprising foreign industrials to make money out of our ideas. Of course, such a situation does not suit us. There must be reciprocity in exchanges. Evidently, the situation is going to change. And, indeed, of late it has.

Considerable work is being done to invigorate scientific and technological progress. We are launching target-oriented programs, prompting work collectives and economic and other scientists to work in a creative way, and have organized twenty-two inter-sectoral research and technological complexes headed by leading scientists. The priority of the day is, as I said, the development of Soviet mechanical engineering. The June 1986 Plenary Meeting of the CPSU Central Committee proposed a program for radical modernization in mechanical engineering. It set a target unprecedented in the history of Soviet industry, that of reaching in the next six to seven years world standards as regards major machinery, equipment and instruments. The emphasis, it was decided, would be placed on machine tool-building, instrument-making, electronics and electrical engineering. The iron-and-steel and chemical industries are also being modernized on a wide scale.

Wishful thinking is a most dangerous occupation. And yet all the changes under way hold out much promise. Recently, I visited the town of Zelenograd not far from Moscow, where some research organizations and enterprises of the electronics industry are concentrated. I was gratified to hear scientists and specialists say that in a number of fields we are not trailing behind or even keeping level with the US, but are ahead in some ways. So the West's technological arrogance has proved of benefit to us. The task now, which is no less difficult, is to translate these results into practice.

Analysis and Review Questions

1. What did Gorbachev define as the major obstacle to economic improvement?
2. How did Gorbachev view the relationship between the bulk of the Soviet people and the regime?
3. What relationship did Gorbachev view as appropriate between the Soviet Union and other nations?
4. According to Gorbachev, from where should the impetus for improving the Soviet economy come?
5. What should the relationship be between Soviet industrial enterprises and the central planning authorities, in Gorbachev's view?

Image 29.2
Statue of Lenin Toppled
During Soviet Collapse

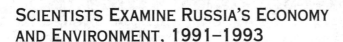

SCIENTISTS EXAMINE RUSSIA'S ECONOMY AND ENVIRONMENT, 1991–1993

About the Document

When the Soviet Union disintegrated in 1991, for the first time, Russian and outside observers could openly analyze and discuss the consequences of the country's industrialization. Only then did the other side of Russia's frenetic transformation in the twentieth century begin to become clear.

In 1995 the first surveys of Russian scientific analyses of the state of the Russian environment were published in Moscow. The following document includes excerpts from the introduction to an atlas of over 300 maps designed to graphically portray environmental and demographic problems directly related to the industrialization drive. It discusses the country's economic situation in 1993 and summarizes problems with radioactivity and air and water pollution throughout the Russian Federation.

The Document

2.2.2. The Current Economic Situation, A. S. Martynov, V. G. Vinogradov, A. V. Denisov, A. N. Yelokhin and A. A. Sorogin

The economic situation in Russia in 1991–1993 can be simply characterized as a crisis. In this part of the Atlas, indicators are shown which illustrate mostly the process of the disintegration of the economic system while touching upon the standard of living and social mood of the population.

The fall of output from the beginning of reforms enables us to identify the regions in which the highest intensity of socially significant changes occurred. It is completely unimportant whether these changes are linked only to the disintegration of the old structures, or if they occurred simultaneously with the growth of new economic relations. Both translated at social and household levels into an uncomfortable feeling among the people (loss of jobs, changes of jobs, learning new specialties at a mature age, erratic work schedules, etc.). On a mass scale, all these processes led to an accumulation of social stress, losses in the material guarantees of the standard of living, and reductions in expenditures for health care. At the regional level, the situation was aggravated by reductions in expenditures for municipal health care systems (when output drops, tax receipts decrease); for the individual, medicines become inaccessible, the system of preventive measures disintegrated, and chronic diseases were neglected. On the other hand, the decline in production in most cases almost meant an overall reduction of emissions into the air and of discharges of contaminated water.

Purely economic factors such as the level of debts of enterprises to banks, suppliers and consumers relative to the financial assets of enterprises have serious ecological and social consequences. The regions having the greatest financial difficulties are those in which industries do not occupy a monopolistic position in the markets of Russia (mostly agricultural). The same reason explains the relatively [sic] well-being of some Siberian regions which produce raw materials, while Kamchatka oblast, which does not have any significant raw materials, is experiencing full financial collapse.

Financial difficulties cause problems of supplying industry with necessary spare parts, resources and maintenance. Enterprise indebtedness leads to unstable salary payments to their workforce, which consequently leads to social instability and stress. In particular, there is a correlation between those areas where enterprises are experiencing financial problems and areas where results from the referendum of April 25, 1993 and the elections of December 12, 1993 were unfavorable to the authorities.

But the greatest danger for the people working at enterprises in economic disarray, as well as for the environment, arises when enterprises continue to work using worn-out equipment, do not perform preventive maintenance, violating work regimes and regulations, and use of inappropriate raw materials due to breakdowns in supply.

Less obvious, but no less important for the health of the population is the overall breakdown of social services, including medicines, which is a consequence of the financial difficulties of enterprises. This process will have the most serious consequences in Siberia and the Far East, where due to the uncompleted developmental processes in these regions, the infrastructure of the cities and especially of the workers' settlements, depends on the industrial enterprises.

The maps showing the rate of industrial accidents in the regions of Russia show the relationship of its growth to the simultaneous reduction in the volume of output.

The level of danger of accidents and losses connected with them are growing. The very "age" of these industrial centers represents a set of factors which lead to a high accident rate. Those "centers" which were created and intensively developed in the years before and during the war, such as the Urals, the Kuzbass, and Tula have reached the period of extreme aging of their capital stock. Similarly, work on very worn-out equipment, explains the high accident rates in such poorly developed regions as Kalmykiya and Tuva. The grave financial situation of enterprises, among a number of factors, determines the level of accidents in the North Caucasus.

The greatest accident rate increase in 1992–1993 occurred in those regions which have highly developed metallurgical and chemical industries, while in the northern and Siberian mining regions it was decreasing or at best increasing at a lower rate. Due to economic disarray, the number of skilled personnel in large industry has declined as competent cadres departed. . . .

The significance of a poorly developed infrastructure is much clearer in the materials on Emergency Situations (ES) . . . Given equal industrial activity, ecological and ecologically-significant emergency situations occur less often in industrially developed centers, than in less developed regions. Given the weakness of the systems for prevention and clean-up of accidents, even a small accident may develop ecological consequences, and threaten to become an Emergency Situation.

This situation reflects a mutual compensation in the increased frequency of Emergency Situations and in reduced production activity. Murmansk and Astrakhan oblasts can be pointed to as dangerous places. Nonetheless, one also should note the steadily increasing, but not yet maximal level frequency of Emergency Situations in the entire Lower Volga region. This region has ecologically dangerous industries but a considerable potential for further development during the post-crisis period. This potential is based on a combination of freed-up reserves from military sites and plants, a good transportation infrastructure, the lack of acute ethnic conflicts, successful implementation of agricultural reforms ("setting up new farmers"), an intensive concentration of migrants from Central Asia, and a returning German population which has a strong work ethic along with a very probable investment support from Germany. In the aggregate, these factors can provide a steady increase in industrial activity in this region which, taking into account the frequency of Emergency Situations, may create serious ecological safety problems.

2.2.3. Radiation Danger, V. A. Rikunov

2.2.3.1. Radioactively Dangerous Places

The radiation danger in individual regions of Russia is determined by the activity of a large number of enterprises involved in mining, processing and storing of radioactive materials, nuclear fuel production, and nuclear power plants operation. . . .

. . . on the Nuclear Submarines withdrawn from operation ("retired" nuclear submarines), the fixed length of reactor service time running out, the established periods of active zones operation were exceeded, equipment inspection not carried out, periodic radiochemical analysis of the heat-transfer device not scheduled, and the state of individual zones at the time of withdrawal from operation of the nuclear submarines was characterized as "inadmissible". The submarines have actually been converted into floating spent nuclear fuel repositories. Their technical condition is unsatisfactory and they may sink.

By December 31, 1993, 96 nuclear submarines were retired from operation, of which, 54 from the Northern Fleet, and 42 from the Pacific Fleet, the "active zones" (nuclear engine compartments) were unloaded from 36 nuclear submarines (Northern Fleet - 17, Pacific Fleet - 19). Sixty nuclear submarines loaded with nuclear fuel remain afloat (9 of which are located in the territory of Severodvinsk city). When the decision was made to remove nuclear submarines from operation, the basic requirement aimed at assuring nuclear safety is the obligatory unloading of the "active zones" or their further utilization. This requirement is not being carried out. Reserve capacity for storing spent nuclear fuel from the Navy is almost exhausted and their technical condition does not correspond to modern normative requirements. Moreover, their radiation situation is unsatisfactory.

2.2.3.2. Radioactive Wastes

The storage and disposal of radioactive waste products is one of the most serious problems in nuclear power plant operation and of using radiation sources. Map 2.47 shows how full are the radioactive waste depositories belonging to the nuclear power stations, nuclear research installations and in some "Radon" Special Combines repositories. The burying of radioactive waste products in the seas adjacent to the territory of Russia is an extremely acute problem. . . .

In reality, the Navy does not have any technical means for reprocessing liquid and solid radioactive waste products. . . . The practice of discharging liquid radioactive waste into the sea continues; for example, in 1993, discharge of liquid radioactive waste took place in the Sea of Japan. The greatest potential radio-ecological danger comes from the nuclear submarine reactors and the "screen assembly" of the Lenin nuclear ice-breaker with its nuclear fuel still not unloaded thrown into the shallow waters of the Novaya Zemlya archipelago in the Karsk Sea.

2.2.3.3. Accidents and Operational Incidents

. . . The aggravation of the criminal situation, emergence of a "black" market for ionized radiation sources and marketable radionucleides increases the possibility for theft, and unauthorized dismantling of [radioactively] dangerous equipment.

2.2.3.4. Radioactive Pollution

The most noticeable threats for radiation safety still arise from the pollution caused as a result of the accident at the Chernobyl Nuclear Power Plant and the explosion at the "Mayak" radio-chemistry plant. . . .

2.2.4. Air Pollution

2.2.4.1. Emission of Pollutants, A. S. Martynov and V. G. Vinogradov

Statistics on the emissions of the pollutants into the air reflect mainly the ecological inefficiency of rather large enterprises . . .

The trends in the level of industrial emissions during the period from 1991 to 1993 are linked to the development pattern of the crisis in the economy of the country. Preservation of output levels and the concomitant air pollution is a specific feature of the highly monopolized heavy industry enterprises. In 1993, the index of the specific pollutants of a plant was decisively determined by the placement of the large heavy industry centers. But it has been the less developed and technologically backward industries which first cut down their production, while the giants have preserved their output levels. . . .

The situation is most dangerous (in descending order) in Tomsk, Komi, Chelyabinsk, Orenburg, Vologodsk, Murmansk and Sverdlovsk oblasts.

Comparison of the lists of these potentially dangerous regions due to specific emissions into the air and water discharges into reservoirs indicates the following pattern: Eight regions which are actively transforming the structure of output are on the list of dangerous water pollution. Irkutsk oblast is the only one among these regions which has preserved their product mix, but only at its very end. As regards air pollution, regions with different strategies of development are proportionally represented in the list of dangerous regions. This feature is linked to the process of de-industrialization. Large discharges into the general purpose sewage system are a specific feature of medium-sized and small enterprises, while it is precisely the big enterprises which have traditionally been the major air polluters. This leads to a relative undercounting of emissions into the air in those regions where deindustrialization and splitting up of enterprises occurs.

The strategy of preserving current industrial production in large industrial centers is highly dangerous for air pollution. According to official statistics, the total level of air pollution and its tendency to grow are understated (compared with water pollution), especially in regions suffering from the recession and changes in its output structure.

2.2.4.2. Air Pollution in Cities, E. Yu. Bezuglaya

. . . At present, regular observations are undertaken in 292 cities at 760 stations of the concentrations of the suspended particles (dust), sulfur dioxide, nitrogen oxide and dioxide, carbon monoxide, benzo(a)pyrene and many other substances.

The results of these observations which have been carried out during the past four years (1989–1992) show that since 1991 the worsening economic situation and the general decline of production, the closure of enterprises, has led to decreasing emissions of pollutants into the air of the cities and some decrease in their admixture. But still the level of air pollution remains high. The annual average concentrations of suspended particles, nitrogen dioxide, formaldehyde and benzo(a)pyrene in many cities exceed the Maximum Allowable Concentrations (MAC) established for populated places in Russia, as well as World Health Organization (WHO) standards in 230 cities. . . .

The maximal concentrations of many substances exceed MAC by 5 times in more than 150 cities and 10 times in 86 cities. The number of people experiencing the influence of 5 times the MAC value, is 54.9 million persons and 10 times the MAC value, 40.1 million persons. More than 66 million persons live in places where the average level of pollution is higher than the MAC value.

2.2.5. The Use and Contamination of Water, Yu. A. Bobrov

In 1993, the largest amount of water drawn from natural sources was in Moscow, Leningrad and Rostov oblasts, in Dagestan and in Krasnodarsk and Stavropol krays. The total collection of water from natural sources decreased in 1993 compared with 1991 and 1992, which may be connected to the fall in output and the decrease of electric power generation. . . .

For some regions, as compared to 1992, the total discharge of contaminated waste water into the natural water sites supply decreased. Nevertheless, the analysis of the current situation of supplying water to the population, including drinkable water, shows that this situation is unfavorable in practically all regions of the country. . . .

Compared to 1992, the discharge of contaminated waste water into natural water sites decreased in 1993 by an average of 17%. . . .

The amount of discharged waste water in 1993 exceeded the 1992 level by more than 140%. Such trends were visible in Voronezh and Tyumen oblasts and in Buryatiya. In Dagestan, the increase in waste water discharge exceeded 1200%. In Sverdlovsk, Chelyabinsk, Yaroslavl, Smolensk, Tula, Tambov, Ulyanovsk, Amur and Chita oblasts, as well as in Primorskiy kray, the waste water discharge level was no more than 140% of the 1992 level. On the whole, the situation has improved, compared to 1991.

When analyzing the discharge of waste water per unit of output (per 1000 rubles), one can easily see that more than 50% of water collected for production needs returns as dirty drainage. The ratio of contaminated waste water discharge in 1992 and 1993 did not differ by much. . . .

The collection of water per capita for industrial and drinking needs in 1993 compared to that in 1992 practically did not change. It should be noted, that for urban dwellers, the minimum value of this index was three times higher than for the whole population, including the rural population.

Supplying the population with high quality drinking water in conditions of the deterioration of the general ecological situation is one of the most critical issues. Even without a profound analysis of the current state of water supply for the population, it is clear that the situation is not very good.

A significant amount of drinking water (more than 20% of the total volume, according to data for 1992) is not used for its designated purpose, but for different production needs (industry, municipal economy, etc.). . . . In 1993, the quality of drinking water supplied to the population practically remained at the 1991 level, although in many regions it worsened due to real economic difficulties and the worsening of the ecological situation.

In all, about 50% of the population of Russia continues drinking water which does not correspond to hygienic requirements according to a wide spectrum of water quality indicators. . . .

About one-third of the whole amount of pollutants carried into water sources by surface and storm sewers from regions containing unsanitary populated places, agricultural sites, and arable lands that influence the seasonal worsening of the quality of drinking water, especially noticeable during the period of spring floods, and noticeable annually in major cities, including Moscow.

The situation of drinking water quality is also unsatisfactory, especially in the countryside. Sixty-eight percent of the population (47% of populated places), use centralized water supplies. Fifty-nine percent of the rural population uses water from common wells. . . .

In some regions, people have to use imported water due to insufficient amounts available from their own water sources. The highest consumption of imported water takes place in Sakha (Yakutiya (97%), Kalmykiya (30%), Kamchatka (19%), and Magadan (6%) oblasts and in Stavropol kray (10%).

The main locations in southern Russia are the Kuban river and its tributaries Laba, Belaya, and Urupa. In a number of sections, the quality of water is not up to hygienic standards. The leading indicators of contamination of the waters of the Kuban river basin are organic substances, oil products, phenols and the level of bacterial pollution. The specific indicators of contamination of this region are heavy metals, toxic chemicals, and the nitrogen-containing compounds.

Map 29.1
(Interactive)
Break up of the
Soviet Union

The rivers of the Arctic basin of Siberia also experience a considerable anthropogenic burden. . . . The Tom' river basin serves as a gigantic collector of the waste waters of most cities, settlements and industrial enterprises of Kemerovo oblast. The scale of contamination of the Tom' river is so high, that any expected self-cleaning does not occur even 300 kilometers downstream from the city of Kemerovo.

Analysis and Review Questions

1. How do the scientists view the relationship between central and regional authorities in Russia?
2. Why were extant Russian laws on environmental protection not being implemented?
3. What factors are cited as causing the improvement of environmental conditions in some regions?
4. What principal causes of Russian water pollution are discussed?
5. What relationship is noted between the economic crisis and the public health crisis?

WEB LINKS

Selections from Longman World History—Primary Sources and Case Studies

http://longmanworldhistory.com
The following additional readings and case studies can be found on the Web site.
Document 29.3, Nikita Khrushchev Challenges the West to Disarm and Advance World Prosperity
Case Study 29.1, Lenin, 1920, vs Stalin, 1931
Case Study 29.2, Lenin, 1920, vs Khrushchev, 1960
Case Study 29.3, Gorbachev, 1987, vs Lenin, 1920, and Stalin, 1931

Russian History

http://www.departments.bucknell.edu/russian/history.html
Includes links to a discussion group and numerous sites dealing with all aspects of Russian history.

http://www.marxists.org/history/ussr/
Devoted to Marxist and early Soviet history; includes a sound archive, a photo and map archive, and many links.

Russian and Soviet Technology

http://web.mit.edu/slava/guide/
Virtual guide to the history of Russian and Soviet science and technology. Includes links to news, archives, courses, journals, institutions, etc.

Pollution/Health/Demographic Concerns

http://www.rand.org/publications/IP/IP162

Informative, statistic-based discussion of population issues, health care, and labor problems in Russia.

CHAPTER 30

Twentieth–Century Latin America

To understand modern Latin America, one must be able to understand the dramatic changes that have taken place in the various countries of Central and South America. Latin America is difficult to understand because it is a region of contrasts despite the shared language of Spanish (with the exception of Portuguese in Brazil and scattered pockets of Indian languages). Since its European discovery in 1492, Latin America has strained to free itself from its colonial bindings, and this struggle for independence has had a dramatic political impact on the region. Revolutions and tumultuous politics have plagued this region like no other, and outside influences like conservatism, fascism, Marxism, and corporatism have left their mark on the political landscape. Latin American nations have tried desperately to enter the world market and overcome the poverty that has often been associated with the region. Industrialization has brought many Latin American nations into modernity, but at a cost to the workers who labor in poor conditions. Further complicating Latin American history is its neighbor to the north—the United States—that has, from time to time, meddled in its economic and political affairs, occasionally causing great animosity.

The complexities of Latin American history lead many North Americans to view the region with disdain or lack of interest. It must be remembered, however, that Latin American influence has made its way into North America—the 2000 census demonstrated that the Hispanic peoples are the fastest growing minority group in the United States. An understanding of the region's history and culture will be a necessary tool in the future. With further study, students may realize that Latin American nations share many of the same problems, successes, and hopes with their own nation.

Map 30.1
Central
America Today

PLAN DE AYALA

About the Document

Porfirio Díaz, dictator of Mexico from 1876 until 1910, brought economic advancement and stability to the Mexican government at the expense of individual and political liberty. His economic policies benefited the wealthy of Mexico, but placed the individual laborer and the rural farmer at a great disadvantage. Díaz controlled politics with an iron fist, so he was not worried about the presidential election scheduled for 1910. The dictator intended to rig the results, if necessary, to ensure a sizeable victory. However, he underestimated the growing strength of his opponent, Francisco Madero. Although Díaz won the election, it galvanized the opposition against his leadership and led to the Mexican Revolution.

After the election, Díaz arrested his political opponent, hoping to remove him from view and calm the nation. However, many citizens rallied to Madero's cause and demanded his release. Díaz and the military were unsuccessful in destroying the opposition forces, and the dictator fled Mexico in 1911, leaving Madero to claim victory.

Despite eradicating Díaz's dictatorship, Madero still had not satisfied all the demands of the peasants and farmers. Emiliano Zapata, a mestizo leader of guerilla forces from the southern area of Morelos, had initially sided with Madero due to his promise of land reform, but became dissatisfied when little action was taken. Zapata broke with Madero and issued his own plan of action, the Plan de Ayala, which contained promises of land reform. Zapata's followers, the Zapatistas, survived repeated attacks by Madero's forces and began to seize lands from large landowners in the south. Zapata and his followers continued their fight through the successive governments of Victoriano Huerta and Venustio Carranza. Zapata continued to fight for the reforms proposed in the Plan de Ayala until one of Carranza's followers assassinated Zapata in 1919. Zapatas' ideas live on among bands of his followers, who make their presence known through various guerrilla actions.

The Document

This is the platform for liberation proposed by the Sons of the State of Morelos, affiliated with the Insurgent Army. It seems to fulfill the Plan of San Luis,° the document issued by Francisco Madero after Porfirio Díaz stole the 1910 election.

We who undersign, constituted in a revolutionary junta to sustain and carry out the promises which the revolution of November 20, 1910 just past, made to the country, declare solemnly before the face of the civilized world which judges us and before the nation to which we belong and which we call [*amamos*, "love"], propositions which we have formulated to end the tyranny which oppresses us and redeem the fatherland from the dictatorships which are imposed on us, which [propositions] are determined in the following plan:

. . .

5. The Revolutionary Junta of the State of Morelos will admit no transactions or compromises until it achieves the overthrow of the dictatorial elements of Porfirio Díaz and Francisco I. Madero, for the nation is tired of false men and traitors who make promises like liberators and who on arriving in power forget them and constitute themselves as tyrants.

6. As an additional part of the plan we invoke, we give notice: that [regarding] the fields, timber, and water which the landlords, *científicos*, or bosses have usurped, the pueblos or citizens who have the titles corresponding to those properties will immediately enter into possession of that real estate of which they have been despoiled by the bad faith

Plan of San Luis: Document issued by Francisco Madero after Porfirio Díaz stole the 1910 election. Madero, virtually in exile, called for Mexican citizens to nullify the election and take up arms against the government.

Most scholars argue that the date of the Declaration, November 20, 1910, is the start of the Mexican revolution.

of our oppressors, maintaining at any cost with arms in hand the mentioned possession; and the usurpers who consider themselves with a right to them [those properties] will deduce it before the special tribunals which will be established on the triumph of the revolution.

7. In virtue of the fact that the immense majority of Mexican pueblos and citizens are owners of no more than the land they walk on, suffering the horrors of poverty without being able to improve their social condition in any way or to dedicate themselves to Industry or Agriculture, because lands, timber, and water are monopolized in a few hands, for this cause there will be expropriated the third part of those monopolies from the powerful proprietors of them, with prior indemnization, in order that the pueblos and citizens of Mexico may obtain ejidos, colonies, and foundations for pueblos, or fields for sowing or laboring, and the Mexicans' lack of prosperity and well-being may improve in all and for all.

8. [Regarding] The landlords, científicos, or bosses who oppose the present plan directly or indirectly, their goods will be nationalized and the two third parts which [otherwise would] belong to them will go for indemnizations of war, pensions for widows and orphans of the victims who succumb in the struggle for the present plan.

9. In order to execute the procedures regarding the properties aforementioned, the laws of disamortization and nationalization will be applied as they fit, for serving us as norm and example can be those laws put in force by the immortal Juarez on ecclesiastical properties, which punished the despots and conservatives who in every time have tried to impose on us the ignominious yoke of oppression and backwardness.

. . .

14. If President Madero and other dictatorial elements of the present and former regime want to avoid the immense misfortunes which afflict the fatherland, and [if they] possess true sentiments of love for it, let them make immediate renunciation of the posts they occupy and with that they will with something staunch the grave wounds which they have opened in the bosom of the fatherland, since, if they do not do so, on their heads will fall the blood and the anathema of our brothers.

15. Mexicans: consider that the cunning and bad faith of one man is shedding blood in a scandalous manner, because he is incapable of governing; consider that his system of government is choking the fatherland and trampling with the brute force of bayonets on our institutions; and thus, as we raised up our weapons to elevate him to power, we again raise them up against him for defaulting on his promises to the Mexican people and for having betrayed the revolution initiated by him, we are not personalists, we are partisans of principles and not of men!

Mexican People, support this plan with arms in hand and you will make the prosperity and well-being of the fatherland.

Ayala, November 25, 1911
Liberty, Justice, and Law

Analysis and Review Questions

1. What is the main goal behind the Plan de Ayala? How will it be achieved?
2. Whom does the plan blame for the failure of the revolution thus far?
3. Who is blamed for the economic problems of the common citizens and the farmers? Do you agree?
4. Could you support this plan if you were a poor farmer? An urban laborer? A wealthy landowner? Why or why not?

JUAN PERÓN AND POST-WAR POPULISM

About the Document

In 1943 a military coup removed Ramon Castillo from power in Argentina. Immediately, the military instituted a plan to improve Argentina's economy by reducing its reliance on foreign markets and improving its own industrial base. The military thought that organized labor unions hindered industrial development. A young Col. Juan Domingo Perón disputed this, and from his post as Minister of Labor and Welfare, supported the working classes.

After his election to the presidency in 1946, Perón sought to further develop the Argentine economy. His wife, Eva Duarte Perón, served as his liaison to the workers and was beloved by Argentines for her social justice and women's suffrage campaigns. Unfortunately for Juan Perón, the Argentine economy sagged from 1948 until his downfall in 1955. Perón's relationship with labor and the common people suffered after Eva's death in 1952 from cancer. Finally, Perón lost the support of the military that had brought him to power and popularity before making another comeback. Included below is a brief outline of Perón's economic beliefs.

Image 30.1
Juan and Eva Perón

The Document

2. Objectives

From today onwards we shall industrialize the country so that our work may be done by Argentine workers and so that they may earn what foreign workers earned before. This is what industrialization means to us. To accomplish this cycle we shall complete and intensify the economic cycle of production and consumption, we shall produce more, and value that production in view of our own industrialization and commerce, avoiding exploitation and increasing the consumption. When this cycle is closed, we shall be able to provide our country with 80 or 90 per cent of our production and we shall only export 10 or 20 per cent, because it is necessary to convince ourselves that the money of a man from Catamarca or Santiago del Estero is worth as much as that of the English, Americans or Japanese. All this problem is in itself simple if one tries to solve it, but it gets complicated when one cannot or does not want to solve it. We have our orientation clearly defined and a plan of action that will take us directly to the achievement of the objectives we are looking for. (July 30th, 1947)

3. Everything Should Be Argentine

Foundations have already been laid for the national tin-plate factory—an article of trade which is taking too long in getting to our country—in which the containers we need to export our production in will be manufactured. Due to the lack of a factory of tin-plate containers, the Republic has lost many thousands of millions of pesos; and we have not had any tin-plate factory before because certain foreigners that negotiated with our food production, objected to it. But in the future we shall have the containers that our production requires, the ships necessary to transport it, and those who in previous times commanded here as if they were in their own land, we will have to submit and receive our products canned by Argentine hands, transported by Argentine railways and taken to Europe by Argentine ships. (March 2nd, 1947)

Analysis and Review Questions

1. What does Perón mean by a "closed cycle"? Why is that so important to the Argentine economy?
2. Perón used the tin-plate factory as an example of what he hoped to accomplish. According to Perón, what should the future of the Argentine economy look like?
3. What will be the role of the working classes? Why were good relations with them so important to Perón?

*Image 30.2
Soviet Deputy
Premier in Cuba*

FIDEL CASTRO DEFENDS THE REVOLUTION

About the Document

The Cuban Revolution of 1959 not only had a tremendous impact on the lives of the Cuban people, but also proved to be one of the most pivotal moments in modern international relations. Fulgencio Batista dominated Cuban politics as a strongman from 1933 to 1940, as president from 1940 to 1944, and after 1952, as dictator. Many Cubans were dissatisfied with Batista's policies, including a lawyer named Fidel Castro, who began to organize an armed uprising to overthrow the government. In July 1953, Castro and his revolutionaries failed in an attempt to seize Moncado Barracks. Castro was put on trial where, in his defense, he delivered his "History Will Absolve Me" speech. He was later imprisoned in a penal colony until his release in 1955.

Castro then recruited other revolutionaries to join with him in another attempt to overthrow the government. His force was unsuccessful in creating a revolution in 1956, and they retreated to the mountains of Cuba. Over the next two years, Castro built his forces from disenchanted peasants, employees, and teachers. He was seen by the outside world, including the United States, as a hero struggling against a corrupt dictatorship. The Eisenhower Administration cut off arms shipments to the Batista government in 1958, hoping to help Castro's revolution, but seemed unaware of Castro's leftist leanings. Many of Castro's most trusted aides, including Ernesto "Che" Guevara, were Marxists and had encouraged Castro to create a Marxist state. In December 1958, Castro defeated Batista's forces and, by January 1959, had placed himself at the head of the Cuban government.

Early in 1959, the United States attempted to reign in Castro, but he responded by nationalizing industries in Cuba that had long been dominated by U.S. companies, including Standard Oil, IT&T, and United Fruit. Monetary losses to these and other American companies were staggering, and the United States began a policy of trying to remove Castro from power. The failed Bay of Pigs invasion in 1961 was a huge embarrassment to John F. Kennedy's administration, and Cuba became a flashpoint for U.S.–U.S.S.R. Cold War confrontations. To this day, Cuba remains a sore point in American foreign policy and continues to be the focus of an economic embargo. Despite this, Castro has solidified his power and remains one of the last-standing Communist dictators who emerged during the Cold War.

The selection below is from Castro's impassioned defense in 1953. The "History Will Absolve Me" speech outlines what Castro was fighting for in his attempt to overthrow the Batista government and what changes he would have made if he had been successful in 1953.

The Document

I stated that the second consideration on which we based our chances for success was one of social order because we were sure of the people's support. When we speak of the people we do not mean the comfortable ones, the conservative elements of the nation, who welcome any regime of oppression, any dictatorship, any despotism, prostrating themselves before the master of the moment until they grind their foreheads into the ground. When we speak of struggle, the people means the vast unredeemed masses, to whom all make promises and whom all deceive; we mean the people who yearn for a better, more dignified and more just nation; who are moved by ancestral aspirations of justice, for they have suffered injustice and mockery generation after generation; . . .

The people we counted on in our struggle were these:

Seven hundred thousand Cubans without work, who desire to earn their daily bread honestly without having to emigrate in search of a livelihood.

Five hundred thousand farm labourers inhabiting miserable shacks (*bohíos*), who work four months of the year and starve during the rest, sharing their misery with their children; who have not an inch of land to till, and whose existence would move any heart not made of stone.

Four hundred thousand industrial labourers and stevedores whose retirement funds have been embezzled, whose benefits are being taken away, whose homes are wretched quarters, whose salaries pass from the hands of the boss to those of the moneylender (*garrotero*), whose future is a pay reduction and dismissal, whose life is eternal work and whose only rest is in the tomb.

One hundred thousand small farmers who live and die working on land that is not theirs, looking at it with sadness as Moses looked at the promised land, to die without ever owning it; who, like feudal serfs, have to pay for the use of their parcel of land by giving up a portion of its products; who cannot love it, improve it, beautify it, nor plant a lemon or an orange tree on it, because they never know when a sheriff will come with the rural guard to evict them from it.

Thirty thousand teachers and professors who are so devoted, dedicated and necessary to the better destiny of future generations and who are so badly treated and paid.

Twenty thousand small business men, weighted down by debts, ruined by the crisis and harangued by a plague of grafting and venal officials.

Ten thousand young professionals: doctors, engineers, lawyers, veterinarians, school teachers, dentists, pharmacists, newspapermen, painters, sculptors, etc., who come forth from school with their degrees, anxious to work and full of hope, only to find themselves at a dead end with all doors closed, and where no ear hears their clamour or supplication.

These are the people, the ones who know misfortune and, therefore, are caable of fighting with limitless courage!

To the people whose desperate roads through life have been paved with the bricks of betrayals and false promises, we were not going to say: 'We will eventually give you what you need,' but rather—'Here you have it, fight for it with all your might, so that liberty and happiness may be yours!'

In the brief of this case, the five revolutionary laws that would have been proclaimed immediately after the capture of the Moncada Barracks and would have been broadcasted to the nation by radio should be recorded. It is possible that Colonel Chaviano may deliberately have destroyed these documents, but even if he has done so I remember them.

The First Revolutionary Law would have returned power to the people and proclaimed the Constitution of 1940 the supreme Law of the State, until such time as the people should decide to modify or change it. And, in order to effect its implementation and punish those who had violated it, there being no organization for holding elections to accomplish this, the revolutionary movement, as the momentous incarnation of this sovereignty, the only source of legitimate power, would have assumed all the faculties inherent in it, except that of modifying the Constitution itself: in other words, it would have assumed the legislative, executive and judicial powers.

. . .

The Second Revolutionary Law would have granted property, non-mortgageable and non-transferable, to all planters, non-quota planters, lessees, share-croppers, and squatters who hold parcels of five caballerías° of land or less, and the State would indemnify the former owners on the basis of the rental which they would have received for these parcels over a period of ten years.

The Third Revolutionary Law would have granted workers and employees the right to share thirty per cent of the profits of all the large industrial, mercantile and mining enterprises, including the sugar mills. The strictly agricultural enterprises would be exempt in consideration of other agrarian laws which would be implemented.

The Fourth Revolutionary Law would have granted all planters the right to share fifty-five per cent of the sugar production and a minimum quota of forty thousand arrobas° for all small planters who have been established for three or more years.

The Fifth Revolutionary Law would have ordered the confiscation of all holdings and ill-gotten gains of those who had committed frauds during previous regimes, as well as the holdings and ill-gotten gains of all their legatees and heirs. To implement this, special courts with full powers would gain access to all records of all corporations registered or operating in this country, in order to investigate concealed funds of illegal origin, and to request that foreign governments extradite persons and attach holdings rightfully belonging to the Cuban people. Half of the property recovered would be used to subsidize retirement funds for workers and the other half would be used for hospitals, asylums and charitable organizations.

Furthermore, it was to be declared that Cuban policy in the Americas would be one of close solidarity with the democratic peoples of this continent, and that those politically persecuted by bloody tyrants oppressing our sister nations would find generous asylum, brotherhood and bread in the land of Martí; not the persecution, hunger and treason they find today. Cuba should be the bulwark of liberty and not a shameful link in the chain of despotism.

These laws would have been proclaimed immediately, as soon as the upheavals were ended and prior to a detailed and far-reaching study. They would have been

---

caballerías: Approximately 33⅓ acres of land.
arrobas: A unit of weight equivalent to approximately 25 pounds.

followed by another series of laws and fundamental measures, such as the Agrarian Reform, the integral Reform of Education, electric power nationalization of the trust and the telephone trust, refund to the people of the illegal excessive rates this company has charged, and payment to the Treasury of all taxes brazenly evaded in the past.

Analysis and Review Questions

1. Who were the people Castro counted on in his failed revolution of 1953? Do you think these same people were responsible for his success in 1959?
2. Do the five revolutionary changes proposed by Castro seem all that revolutionary? Have you seen these proposals before?
3. Which one of the revolutionary changes do you think was the most popular with the Cuban people?
4. What does Castro say would follow the implementation of the five revolutionary laws? How important were these things to Cuba?

CAMILO TORRES AND LIBERATION THEOLOGY

About the Document

Map 30.2
South America Today

Latin America in the 1940s and 1950s experienced tremendous industrialization and economic development, which helped countries like Argentina and Mexico become more economically independent. Unfortunately, these shifts also benefited the upper and middle classes at the expense of the working classes and farmers, who labored in poverty. Within the Catholic Church, changes were taking place as well. The working clergy, parish priests, and nuns, who ministered in the slums of the cities and poor rural areas, felt that the Church needed to return to its roots and become a body that defended the poor. Even within the Church hierarchy, some bishops had taken a favorable view of socialism as a means for the oppressed in Latin America to overcome their economic limitations. Liberation Theology was born, and it incorporated a Marxist economic view with traditional Church views on religion. Priests and nuns took these new views to the poor and established grassroots communities within the slums and countryside that incorporated Bible study with discussions of how to implement political and social change.

The life of Camilo Torres exemplified this movement within the Church. Born to an aristocratic Colombian family in 1929, Torres entered the priesthood and became an excellent scholar and minister. He watched as the Colombian government continued its repression of liberals and ignored the problems in the slums and countryside. Torres became disenchanted when peaceful means failed to bring any relief to the poor in his homeland and joined with the Army of National Liberation, a communist-led guerrilla group that sought the overthrow of the government. He was killed in action in 1966.

The selection below is a brief explanation of how Torres felt that socialism and Christianity could be combined.

The Document

Because of the traditional relations between Christians and Marxists, and between the Church and the Communist party, it is quite likely that erroneous suspicions and suppositions will arise regarding the relations of Christians and Marxists within the United Front, and of a priest and the Communist Party.

This is why I want to clarify to the Colombian people my relations with the Communist Party and its position within the United Front.

I have said that I am a revolutionary as a Colombian, as a sociologist, as a Christian, and as a priest. I believe that there are elements within the Communist Party which are genuinely revolutionary. Consequently, I cannot be anti-Communist either as a Colombian, as a sociologist, as a Christian, or as a priest.

I am not anti-Communist as a Colombian because anti-Communism in my country is best on persecuting the dissatisfied, whether they be Communist or not, who in the main are poor people.

I am not an anti-Communist as a sociologist because the Communist proposals to combat poverty, hunger, illiteracy, and lack of housing and public service are effective and scientific.

I am not an anti-Communist as a Christian because I believe that anti-Communism condemns the whole of Communism, without acknowledging that there is some justice in its cause, as well as injustice. By condemning the whole we condemn the just and the unjust, and this is anti-Christian.

I am not anti-Communist as a priest because whether the Communists realize it or not, there are within their ranks some authentic Christians. If they are working in good faith, they might well be the recipients of sanctifying grace. Should this be true, and should they love their neighbor, they would be saved. My role as a priest, even though I am not exercising its prerogatives externally, is to lead all men to God. The most effective way to do this is to get men to serve the people in keeping with their conscience.

I do not intend to proselytize among the Communists and to try to get them to accept the dogma and teaching of the Catholic Church. I do want all men to act in accordance with their conscience, to look in earnest for the truth, and to love their neighbor effectively.

The Communists must be fully aware of the fact that I will not join their ranks, that I am not nor will I ever be a Communist, either as a Colombian, as a sociologist, as a Christian, or as a priest.

Yet I am disposed to fight with them for common objectives: against the oligarchy and the domination of the United States, and for the takeover of power by the popular class.

I do not want public opinion to identify me with the Communists. This is why in all my public appearances I have wanted to be surrounded not only by the Communists but by all revolutionaries, be they independent or followers of other movements. . . .

Once the popular class assumes power, with the help of all revolutionaries, then our people will be ready to discuss the religious orientation they should give their lives.

Poland is an example of how socialism can be established without destroying what is essential to Christianity. As a Polish priest once said: "As Christians we have the obligation of contributing to the construction of a socialist state so long as we are allowed to adore God as we wish."

Analysis and Review Questions

1. What are the four ways that Torres identifies himself as a revolutionary? Which of these reasons is the most important?
2. Does Torres intend on becoming a Communist? Why or why not?
3. Why is Torres fighting with the Communists?
4. Is his argument convincing? Could you justify a combination of religion and violence?

Web Links

Selections from Longman World History—Primary Sources and Case Studies

http://longmanworldhistory.com
The following additional readings and case studies can be found on the Web site.
Document 30.5, Brazil's Constitution of 1988
Document 30.6, John F. Kennedy and Cuba
Document 30.7, Pope John Paul II: Address before the Puebla Conference
Document 30.8, Chico Mendes on the Rainforest
Case Study 30.1, The Cold War and Cuba
Case Study 30.2, Liberation Theology Challenged
Case Study 30.3, The Rainforest

Mexican Revolution

http://nt2.ec.man.ac.uk/multimedia/Mexican%20Revolution.htm
This site is supported by the University of Manchester and the ERA Consortium. It contains case studies that explore the transformation of rural societies during the twentieth century. This section of the site contains a thorough discussion of the Mexican Revolution, the people involved, and its impact on rural societies.

http://www.netdotcom.com/revmexpc/default.htm
Collection of postcards depicting various leaders of the Mexican Revolution with brief biographical sketches.

Juan and Eva Perón

http://www.evitaperon.org
Site dedicated to the memory of Eva Perón. Contains her biography, a collection of photographs, and a discussion of her lasting impact.

Cuban Revolution

http://www.geocities.com/Hollywood/8702/che.html
The Che Guevara information archive has links to a biography of the Argentine-Cuban revolutionary leader and full-text newspaper articles with photos relating to his activities.

http://www.marxists.org
Site contains texts of major speeches given by Fidel Castro and Che Guevara.

http://www.lanic.utexas.edu/la/cb/cuba
University of Texas' Latin American Network Information Center provides links to
major sites dedicated to the history, culture, and governments of Latin America countries. This link provides numerous links to other sites for further exploration.

Liberation Theology

http://www.visi.com/~contra_m//cm/features/cm08_theolib.html
Excellent discussion of the history and development of Liberation Theology. Contains
discussions of papal documents that address Liberation Theology, major proponents in
Latin America, and a thorough history of the development of the beliefs.

The Environment

http://www.chicomendes.com
Site dedicated to the work of rainforest preservation pioneered by Chico Mendes.
Slides, photos, and documents are available.

http://www.pbs.org/journeyintoamazonia
From the PBS series, this site has numerous resources detailing the importance of the
rainforest.

CHAPTER 31

East Asia and the Pacific Rim in the Twentieth Century

At the dawn of the twentieth century, East Asia emerged as a challenging force in the face of a changing world. During the progress of the century, East Asia went through two major world wars and several regional conflicts that reshaped its geographic politics and brought about significant economic developments in the Pacific. Meiji Reforms in the late nineteenth century gave Japan a rich country and a strong military. This big power status, unfortunately, led to the rise of militarism and, eventually, the destruction of the country at the end of World War II. Japan, however, managed a comeback and, with the strong support of the United States, rejoined the international community.

The century following the Opium War was turbulent for China. It brought imperial partition, fighting warlords, civil war, and finally Communist takeover of mainland China in 1949. This last event made China a major partner of the Soviet Union against the United States in the Cold War.

Korea, once a unified country of "morning calm," suffered Japanese colonial rule between 1910 and 1945. The post-World War II settlement of a partitioned Korea led to the outbreak of the Korean War, and the Armistice Agreement, following three years of fierce fighting and unyielding negotiations, only ensured that the Korean Peninsula remained divided.

The second half of the twentieth century, however, witnessed dramatic changes in these three major countries. Japan's economic miracles earned it a leading position in international economic development. Communist China began to introduce reforms after U.S. President Nixon's visit in 1972, and has achieved tremendous results. South Korea joined Taiwan, Singapore, and Hong Kong to become one of the Four Little Dragons of the Asian economy. Although by the end of the twentieth century, North Korea seemed to be the last Communist stronghold, dialogues between South and North Koreans have been progressing positively, leading to the recent Summit Accord in June 2000. The unification of Korea is no longer impossible.

With economic accomplishments came the attempts at political reforms. In both South Korea and Taiwan, democratization proved to be successful. China experienced a setback in 1989, but has been trying to find its way out of the confusion.

East Asia has drawn the world's strong attention. Soon, a new terminology came into use: the Pacific Rim, which included countries on both sides of the Pacific in an economically active and politically sensitive circle. With the end of the Cold War, the role of the United States in the Pacific started to change. The Pacific region is an open-ended frontier, with great potential and unlimited boundaries.

CHINA'S ONE-CHILD FAMILY POLICY

About the Document

In the early 1970s, the Chinese government announced that China's population reached one billion. In order to control population growth, the Chinese government worked out a strategy, known as the one-child family policy, which was applicable to all couples getting married and preparing to have a child. The policy regulates that the newly wedded couple is allowed to have only one child, and any ensuing pregnancy will have to be terminated by abortion. In order to encourage citizens to comply with the birth-planning policy, the government also provided benefits such as free medical care for both the parents and the one child, free education for the one child, and other incentives at the workplace for the parents. Penalties for not abiding by the rule lead to fines, demotions, being fired, laid off, or removed from Communist Party membership. The policy has become compulsory, with various measures to reinforce it.

Map 31.1
China in Civil War
and Revolution

The major barrier for a smooth implementation of the one-child family policy has been the traditional Chinese concept of having the male heir to continue the family name. The policy has been working more effectively in urban areas than in rural areas, largely because employment for the urban population imposes pressures on them to observe the policy. The rural population, on the other hand, relies exclusively on a family-centered work force in the field, especially the male laborers. Therefore, a female child is not desirable, and having one will compel the family to have the second, or the third, until they have a male.

The following document is the version from Sichuan Province—the most populated province in China. The document is closely identified with the version from the Central Committee of the Chinese government in terms of regulations and rules.

The Document

Sichuan Provincial Birth-Planning Rules

ARTICLE 1

   To practice birth planning, exercise control over the population, and improve the quality of the population so that population growth would be suited to economic and social development plans, these regulations are enacted in accordance with the People's Republic of China (PRC) Constitution, PRC Marriage Law, and relevant regulations of the state, and in connection with Sichuan's actual realities.

ARTICLE 2

Both husband and wife have the duty to practice birth planning.

. . .

ARTICLE 6

Late marriage and late births are encouraged.

Late marriage means that both men and women are married three years later than the lawful age [of 20 for women and 22 for men]. Late births mean births by women aged 24 and above.

ARTICLE 7

Births should occur in a planned manner.

Each couple is encouraged to give birth to one child.

No births must occur without marriage.

ARTICLE 8

Couples who can meet the following requirements may have a second child:

1. The first child has a nonhereditary disease and cannot become a normal laborer;
2. Marriage between an only son and an only daughter;
3. In the rural areas, the groom moves to the house of the bride, who is an only daughter, after marriage;
4. Only sons and daughters of martyrs in rural areas;
5. Disabled demobilized soldiers in rural areas with Merit Citation Class II, A;
6. Those in rural areas who were disabled while on duty and are equivalent to the disabled demobilized soldiers with Merit Citation Class II, A;
7. The person is the only one of several brothers in rural areas who is capable of having children;
8. In the rural areas, the husband or wife is the only son or daughter for two generations;
9. In the rural areas of the Pengzhou mountain counties and the mountain townships (not including the flatland, hilly land, and valleys) within the basin approved by the cities (prefectures) of the economic construction zone, families with only daughters that have labor shortages;
10. In the rural areas of the remote mountain areas in Pengzhou mountain counties, families with only sons and daughters; and
11. Both husband and wife are returned overseas Chinese who have settled down in Sichuan.

ARTICLE 9

Couples who have no children many years after marriage, but the wife has become pregnant after adopting a child, may give birth to a child.

ARTICLE 10

Those who can meet one of the following requirements may have a second child:

1. A widower or widow remarries and before the remarriage, the widower or widow has fewer than two children, while the spouse has no children; and

2. Husband or wife who remarries after a divorce and before the remarriage, one side has only one child, while the other has no children.

ARTICLE 11

For those who can meet the requirements of Articles 8, 9, and 10 and who want to bear children, both husband and wife should submit an application, which will be examined and brought into line with birth planning by the departments at the county level responsible for birth planning work. Second births should occur after an interval of four years.

. . .

ARTICLE 23

Those who refuse education and give birth to children not covered by the plan will be fined from the month the child is born. The wages or annual income of both husband and wife will be decreased by ten to twenty percent for seven years; the total sum deducted should not be less than five hundred yuan. Those who give birth to another child after the birth permitted according to Articles 8, 9, and 10 of these regulations will be fined at a minimum of eight hundred yuan. A heavy fine will be imposed on those giving births not covered by the plan.

Regarding pregnancy not covered by the plan, both husband and wife will be imposed a fine of twenty to thirty yuan a month during the period of pregnancy. If the pregnancy is terminated, the fine imposed will be returned.

The fine imposed will be used for birth planning work only. The provincial birth planning committee and finance department will work out use and management methods.

ARTICLE 24

If those giving births not covered by the plan are cadres and staff members, apart from imposing a fine, the units where they work should also apply disciplinary sanctions according to the seriousness of the case.

ARTICLE 25

Those who have received certificates for only children and are allowed to give birth to a second child should return their certificates and will no longer get rewards and preferential treatment from the month they are allowed to give birth to a second child. Those who give birth to another child without approval, apart from the measures stipulated in Articles 23 and 24, will no longer get rewards and preferential treatment for only children and must return the certificates and health care benefits for only children.

ARTICLE 26

Regarding doctors, nurses, and working personnel in charge of birth planning work and marriage registration and state functionaries who violate these regulations, practice fraud, and accept bribes, the units where they work or the higher level competent departments should educate them through criticisms and disciplinary sanctions. If their practices constitute an offense, the judicial organs will investigate and affix the responsibility for the offense according to law.

Persons holding direct responsibility for accidents in ligation operations due to negligence will be handled according to relevant regulations.

ARTICLE 27

Regarding those who insult, threaten, and beat doctors, nurses, and working personnel in charge of birth planning work or use other methods to obstruct birth planning, the public security organs will handle the cases in light of the "PRC Regulations Concerning Public Security Management and Punishment." If the practices constitute an offense, the judicial organs will investigate and affix the responsibility for the offense according to law.

ARTICLE 28

Drowning, abandoning, selling, and maltreatment of girl babies and their mothers are prohibited. Regarding those involved in any of these practices, the units where they work or the leading organs concerned should educate them through criticisms and disciplinary sanction in light of the seriousness of the case. If their practices constitute an offense, the judicial organs will investigate and affix the responsibility for the offense according to law.

Illegal removal of intrauterine devices is prohibited. In addition to confiscating the income obtained from illegally taking out the intrauterine device, a fine of over five hundred yuan will be imposed. A heavy fine will be imposed on those who commit the offense repeatedly. The judicial organs will, according to law, investigate and affix the responsibility for injuries and deaths caused therefrom.

*Image 31.1
Tradition vs.
Modernity*

Analysis and Review Questions

1. What are the major reasons given by the Chinese government to promote the one-child family policy?
2. Under what conditions can a couple have a second child without paying the fine?
3. What practices are prohibited?
4. How does the government encourage the Chinese citizens to adhere to the policy?
5. What are the major punishments for violating the policy?

NORTH AND SOUTH KOREAN ACCORD, JUNE 2000

About the Document

The legacy of the Korean War was a divided peninsula and a long-term hostility between people who used to share a unified country. The war also created two different states that have gone in opposite directions in their political and economic development.

With the end of the Cold War and economic reforms in the Pacific, South Korea has emerged as one of the Four Little Dragons in the region, while North Korea remains isolated from the rest of the international community. The Korean families, separated by the war and the 1953 cease-fire, have been longing for union and dialogue. In the 1980s, exchange programs of family visits and communication between the South and North gradually began taking place.

The summit between leaders of South Korea and North Korea in June 2000 was a historic event that marked a step toward unification of the peninsula and further cooperation. Most importantly, the Koreans are going to resolve the issue of unification among themselves, through cooperation and understanding.

The Document

Upholding the lofty wishes of the Korean people yearning for peaceful reunification of the fatherland, President Kim Dae-jung of the Republic of (South) Korea and Kim Jong II, chairman of the National Defense Commission of the Democratic Peoples' Republic of (North) Korea, held a historic meeting and summit talks on June 13–15, 2000. Noting that the meeting and talks held for the first time in the divided Korean history carry grave significance in promoting mutual understanding and developing South-North relations and achieving peaceful, national reunification, the top leaders of South and North Korea declared as follows:

(1) The South and North, as masters of national unification, will join hands in efforts to resolve the issue of national unification independently.

(2) Acknowledging common elements in the South's proposal for a consideration and the North's proposal for a federation of lower stage, the South and the North agreed to promote reunification.

(3) The South and North will exchange groups of dispersed family members and their relatives around Aug. 15 and resolve as soon as possible humanitarian issues, including the repatriation° of communist prisoners.

(4) The South and North will pursue a balanced development of their national economies and build mutual trust by accelerating exchange in the social, cultural, sports, health and environmental sectors.

(5) In order to put these agreements into practice, the South and North will hold a dialogue between government authorities at an early date. President Kim Dae-jung cordially invited National Defense Commission chairman Kim Jong II to visit Seoul and he agreed to do that at an appropriate time.

Analysis and Review Questions

1. What is the main goal for both the South and North Korean people in the summit?
2. What are the major differences between North Korea and South Korea?
3. Given the fact that both the United States (under the United Nations banner) and China were involved in the Korean War, why are these two powers not included in this accord?
4. How important is this accord to the future cooperation of both South and North Korea?

Vietnamese Declaration of Independence

About the Document

After World War II, European colonial empires began to disintegrate. Nationalist movements either emerged or gained momentum in India, Africa, and the Middle East, with leaders such as Kwame Nkrumah in Ghana and Gandhi in India providing inspiration far beyond their nations' borders. The situation in Vietnam was similar, yet at the same time, unique.

repatriation: To send a person (e.g. a prisoner of war) back to his or her own country.

For 100 years, Vietnam had been French Indochina. A productive agricultural colony, Vietnam was occupied by Japanese forces in World War II. The administration of the colony was left for the most part in the hands of the Vichy French colonial government, but the Japanese took direct control in the waning months of the war. With Japan's surrender, the Viet Minh, Vietnam's communist nationalist movement, asserted itself. In September 1945, the Viet Minh leader, Ho Chi Minh, issued a Vietnamese declaration of independence, that established the Democratic Republic of Vietnam. Over 20 years of struggle followed before Vietnam emerged as an independent, truly sovereign nation.

The Document

"All men are created equal. They are endowed by their Creator with certain inalienable rights, among these are Life, Liberty, and the pursuit of Happiness."

This immortal statement was made in the Declaration of Independence of the United States of America in 1776. In a broader sense, this means: All the peoples on the earth are equal from birth, all the peoples have a right to live, to be happy and free.

The Declaration of the French Revolution made in 1791 on the Rights of Man and the Citizen also states: "All men are born free and with equal rights, and must always remain free and have equal rights." Those are undeniable truths.

Nevertheless, for more than eighty years, the French imperialists, abusing the standard of Liberty, Equality, and Fraternity, have violated our Fatherland and oppressed our fellow-citizens. They have acted contrary to the ideals of humanity and justice. In the field of politics, they have deprived our people of every democratic liberty.

They have enforced inhuman laws; they have set up three distinct political regimes in the North, the Center and the South of Vietnam in order to wreck our national unity and prevent our people from being united.

They have built more prisons than schools. They have mercilessly slain our patriots—they have drowned our uprisings in rivers of blood. They have fettered public opinion; they have practiced obscurantism against our people. To weaken our race they have forced us to use opium and alcohol.

In the fields of economics, they have fleeced us to the backbone, impoverished our people, and devastated our land.

They have robbed us of our rice fields, our mines, our forests, and our raw materials. They have monopolised the issuing of bank-notes and the export trade.

They have invented numerous unjustifiable taxes and reduced our people, especially our peasantry, to a state of extreme poverty.

They have hampered the prospering of our national bourgeoisie; they have mercilessly exploited our workers.

In the autumn of 1940, when the Japanese Fascists violated Indochina's territory to establish new bases in their fight against the Allies, the French imperialists went down on their bended knees and handed over our country to them.

Thus, from that date, our people were subjected to the double yoke of the French and the Japanese. Their sufferings and miseries increased. The result was that from the end of last year to the beginning of this year, from Quang Tri province to the North of Vietnam, more than two million of our fellow-citizens died from starvation. On March 9, the French troops were disarmed by the Japanese. The French colonialists either fled or surrendered, showing that not only were they incapable of "protecting" us, but that, in the span of five years, they had twice sold our country to the Japanese.

On several occasions before March 9, the Vietminh League urged the French to ally themselves with it against the Japanese. Instead of agreeing to this proposal, the French colonialists so intensified their terrorist activities against the Vietminh members that before fleeing they massacred a great number of our political prisoners detained at Yen Bai and Cao Bang.

Not withstanding all this, our fellow-citizens have always manifested toward the French a tolerant and humane attitude. Even after the Japanese putsch° of March 1945, the Vietminh League helped many Frenchmen to cross the frontier, rescued some of them from Japanese jails, and protected French lives and property.

From the autumn of 1940, our country had in fact ceased to be a French colony and had become a Japanese possession.

After the Japanese had surrendered to the Allies, our whole people rose to regain our national sovereignty and to found the Democratic Republic of Vietnam.

The truth is that we have wrested our independence from the Japanese and not from the French.

The French have fled, the Japanese have capitulated, Emperor Bao Dai has abdicated. Our people have broken the chains which for nearly a century have fettered them and have won independence for the Fatherland. Our people at the same time have overthrown the monarchic regime that has reigned supreme for dozens of centuries. In its place has been established the present Democratic Republic.

For these reasons, we, members of the Provisional Government, representing the whole Vietnamese people, declare that from now on we break off all relations of a colonial character with France; we repeal all the international obligation that France has so far subscribed to on behalf of Vietnam and we abolish all the special rights the French have unlawfully acquired in our Fatherland.

The whole Vietnamese people, animated by a common purpose, are determined to fight to the bitter end against any attempt by the French colonialists to reconquer their country.

We are convinced that the Allied nations which at Tehran and San Francisco have acknowledged the principles of self-determination and equality of nations, will not refuse to acknowledge the independence of Vietnam.

A people who have courageously opposed French domination for more than eighty years, a people who have fought side by side with the Allies against the Fascists during these last years, such a people must be free and independent.

For these reasons, we, members of the Provisional Government of the Democratic Republic of Vietnam, solemnly declare to the world that Vietnam has the right to be a free and independent country and in fact it is so already. The entire Vietnamese people are determined to mobilize all their physical and mental strength, to sacrifice their lives and property in order to safeguard their independence and liberty.

Analysis and Review Questions

1. What problems of French rule does Ho mention?
2. Have the French made much effort to build up Vietnam's educational system?

putsch: A sudden uprising.

3. What happened on March 9, 1941?

4. Why does Ho say, "We wrested our independence from the Japanese and not from the French"?

5. Why do you think Ho started out his declaration with words from the U.S. Declaration of Independence?

WEB LINKS

Selections from Longman World History—Primary Sources and Case Studies

http://longmanworldhistory.com

The following additional readings and case studies can be found on the Web site.

Document 24.2, The Treaty of Nanjing

Document 24.4, The Meiji Constitution, 1889

Document 31.1, The Constitution of Japan, 1947

Document 31.2, The Shanghai Communique, 1972

Case Study 31.1, The Constitution of Japan, Two Versions

Case Study 31.2, China vs. Foreign Powers in Two Treaties

Case Study 31.3, Eastern Tradition vs. Western Culture

The Pacific Rim

http://www.prf.com/

This is a place where readers can find top leaders from the region voicing their opinions on political, economic, and other emerging issues. This site also provides updated information for recent or upcoming conferences.

http://www.apecsec.org.sg/

Site of Asia–Pacific Economic Cooperation (APEC) that includes information about all its member nations in the region.

http://www.pecc.org/

This is the official site for the U.S. National Committee for the Pacific Economic Corporation Council, which "combines the knowledge and resources of businesses, research institutions, and government agencies to develop new strategies for Asia-Pacific economic cooperation."

South Korea

http://www.mofat.go.kr/ko/index.mof

The official site of the South Korean Ministry of Foreign Affairs and Trade, with information on foreign policy, trade activities, treaties, and related events.

http://www.photius.com/wfb/wfb1999/korea_south/korea_south_economy.html

This site focuses on the economic development of South Korea.

The Korean War

http://korea50.army.mil

The official site of the U.S. Army for the special occasion of the fiftieth anniversary of the Korean War. It offers historical background, pictures, current events, and other topics relating to the activities surrounding the anniversary between 2000 and 2003.

Japan

http://irpslibrary.ucsd.edu/irpsJapanRelated.html
A site that leads to other links on Japan, including its government, trade unions, financial institutions, etc.

http://liberty.uc.wlu.edu/~msmitka/garland/garland_vol_5.html
A short bibliography on postwar Japanese economic development.

http://www.jinjapan.org/today/econo/econo_1.html
This essay discusses Japan's postwar economic development.

http://www.askasia.org/frclasrm/readings/r000128.htm
An essay on the Japanese family.

China

http://libraries.ucsd.edu/EastAsia/ChinaBusEcon.html
A resource guide from the International Relations and Pacific Studies Library on China's business and economy.

http://axe.acadiau.ca/~043638z/one-child

http://www.tulane.edu/~rouxbee/kids99/china1.html
Both links are about China's one-child policy.

http://207.238.152.36/CATALOG/WP/1995/95-6.htm
A discussion on China's economic reforms and their impact on international development.

http://afe.easia.columbia.edu/teachingaids/china/for_pol/tai_us.htm
Information on Taiwan and U.S.–China relations.

CHAPTER 32

South Asia:
Freedom and State-Building
in India and Pakistan

B ritish rule in India had remained largely unchallenged throughout most of
the nineteenth century. The major Indian nationalist leaders tended to be
quite moderate, generally stressing the benefits of Westernization and British rule.

   As the twentieth century wore on, however, it became apparent to the
British that their control over South Asia was not going to be permanent. Nationalist leaders, both Hindu and Muslim, had emerged and were calling for an end
to the Raj. For decades, Hindus and Muslims had been somewhat united against
the British, putting aside many of their differences for the good of India as they
imagined it. But it soon became clear that the two sides, with a long history of
animosity and suspicion, were not likely to come together again to govern a free
India. Because of this division, the journey for India immediately after independence in 1947 would not be a smooth one. Almost immediately, what had been
British India split into Hindu-dominated India and Muslim-controlled Pakistan.

Map 32.1
(Interactive)
South Asia

GANDHI SPEAKS AGAINST THE PARTITION OF INDIA

About the Document

Despite its leaders' high hopes for a peaceful transition from British colony to independent nation, India had no such luck. There had been no real consensus
among nationalist leaders about the new nation's relationship with Britain, and
tensions between Hindus and Muslims had long existed. These tensions had been
partially smoothed over by the desire to expel the British, but almost immediately
upon independence in 1947, they returned to the surface. Some more extreme
leaders on both sides of the issue had called for separate countries for the two
groups, but many Indian leaders pleaded against division in favor of unity.

   The most well-known Indian nationalist was Mohandas Gandhi (1869–1948).
Gandhi was the dominant force in the Indian National Congress (the main

239

nationalist organization) through much of the early twentieth century and remained in many ways India's guiding light until his assassination in 1948.

Image 32.1
Nehru

Gandhi had always worked diligently to pull together Hindus and Muslims and believed that a successful nation included both. While many Hindus supported Gandhi's efforts toward Muslims, it was in fact a Hindu, upset with his conciliatory approach, who eventually murdered him. In this series of quotes, Gandhi pleads for a unified India.

The Document

Image 32.2
Gandhi

[The demand for Pakistan] as put forth by the Moslem League is un-Islamic and I have not hesitated to call it sinful. Islam stands for unity and the brotherhood of mankind, not for disrupting the oneness of the human family. Therefore, those who want to divide India into possibly warring groups are enemies alike of India and Islam. They may cut me to pieces but they cannot make me subscribe to something which I consider to be wrong.

A friend from Eastern Pakistan asks how can I declare myself an inhabitant of undivided India when it is cut into two, and when to be of one part excludes you from the other? Whatever the legal pundits may say, they cannot dominate the mind of man. Who can prevent the friend from declaring himself as a citizen of the world even though legally he is not, and though he may be, as he will be, prevented from entering many States under their laws? Legal status should not worry a man who has not reduced himself to the state of a machine as many of us have. So long as the moral condition is sound, there is no warrant for anxiety. What every one of us has to guard against is the harboring of ill-will against a State or its people....

In actual life, it is impossible to separate us into two nations. We are not two nations. Every Moslem will have a Hindu name if he goes back far enough in his family history. Every Moslem is merely a Hindu who has accepted Islam. That does not create nationality....We in India have a common culture. In the North, Hindi and Urdu are understood by both Hindus and Moslems. In Madras, Hindus and Moslems speak Tamil, and in Bengal, they both speak Bengali and neither Hindi nor Urdu. When communal riots take place, they are always provoked by incidents over cows and by religious processions. That means that it is our superstitions that create the trouble and not our separate nationalities.

...We must not cease to aspire, in spite of [the] wild talk, to befriend all Moslems and hold them fast as prisoners of our love.

[If] India is divided she will be lost forever. Therefore ... if India is to remain undivided, Hindus and Moslems must live together in brotherly love, not in hostile camps organized either for defensive action or retaliation....

Analysis and Review Questions

1. Why does Gandhi call the idea of a separate Pakistan "sinful"?
2. What common languages do Hindus and Muslims share in northern India?
3. What common language is shared in Bengal?
4. Does it appear that there are any circumstances under which Gandhi would accept the separation of the two groups?

Jinnah, the "Father" of Pakistan

About the Document

Mohammed Ali Jinnah (1875–1948) is usually considered the founder of Pakistan, much like Gandhi is considered the father of modern India. Like many other nationalist leaders, Jinnah earned a law degree in England and returned to practice in India. Unlike many other Muslim leaders, he played an active role in the Hindu-dominated Indian National Congress. Later, he also joined a new Muslim league and pushed for acceptance of a British proposal that guaranteed a certain number of Muslim seats to India's legislature.

Jinnah did not subscribe to Gandhi's belief that Hindus and Muslims could get along sufficiently to maintain peace, nor his emphasis on nonviolent resistance. As Britain prepared to withdraw, Jinnah pledged to fight for Muslim rights and also began a serious call for a separate Muslim state. Faced with escalating religious violence, the last British viceroy, Lord Mountbatten, agreed to partition India into Muslim- and Hindu-dominated regions. Jinnah became Pakistan's first prime minister and put forth his view of Pakistan as a modern, if religiously focused, state. He died in late 1948, after more than a year of dealing with major crises, but in mid-1947 he had laid out his image of the new Pakistan.

The Document

I cordially thank you, with the utmost sincerity, for the honour you have conferred upon me—the greatest honour that is possible for this Sovereign Assembly to confer—by electing me as your first President. I also thank those leaders who have spoken in appreciation of my services and their personal references to me. I sincerely hope that with your support and your co-operation we shall make this Constituent Assembly an example to the world. The Constituent Assembly has got two main functions to perform. The first is the very onerous and responsible task of framing our future Constitution of Pakistan and the second of functioning as a full and complete Sovereign body as the Federal Legislature of Pakistan. We have to do the best we can in adopting a provisional constitution for the Federal Legislature of Pakistan. You know really that not only we ourselves are wondering but, I think, the whole world is wondering at this unprecedented cyclonic revolution which has brought about the plan of creating and establishing two independent Sovereign Dominions in this sub-continent. As it is, it has been unprecedented; there is no parallel in the history of the world. This mighty sub-continent with all kinds of inhabitants has been brought under a plan which is titanic, unknown, unparalleled. And what is very important with regard to it is that we have achieved it peacefully and by means of an evolution of the greatest possible character.

Dealing with our first function in this Assembly, I cannot make any well-considered pronouncement at this moment, but I shall say a few things as they occur to me. The first and the foremost thing that I would like to emphasise is this—remember that you are now a Sovereign Legislative body and you have got all the powers. It, therefore, places on you the gravest responsibility as to how you should take your decisions. The first observation that I would like to make is this: You will no doubt agree with me that the first duty of a Government is to maintain law and order, so that the life, property and religious beliefs of its subjects are fully protected by the State. . . .

I know there are people who do not quite agree with the division of India and the partition of the Punjab and Bengal. Much has been said against it, but now that it has been accepted, it is the duty of everyone of us to loyally abide by it and honourably act according to the agreement which is now final and binding on all. But you must remember, as I have said, that this mighty revolution that has taken place is unprecedented. One can quite understand the feeling that exists between the two communities wherever one community is in majority and the other is in minority. But the question is, whether, it was possible or practicable to act otherwise than what has been done. A division had to take place. On both sides, in Hindustan and Pakistan, there are sections of people who may not agree with it, who may not like it, but in my judgment there was no other solution and I am sure future history will record its verdict in favour of it. And what is more it will be proved by actual experience as we go on that that was the only solution of India's constitutional problem. Any idea of a United India could never have worked and in my judgment it would have led us to terrific disaster. May be that view is correct; may be it is not; that remains to be seen. All the same, in this division it was impossible to avoid the question of minorities being in one Dominion or the other. Now that was unavoidable. There is no other solution. Now what shall we do? Now, if we want to make this great State of Pakistan happy and prosperous we should wholly and solely concentrate on the well-being of the people, and especially of the masses and the poor. If you will work in co-operation, forgetting the past, burying the hatchet you are bound to succeed. If you change your past and work together in a spirit that every one of you, no matter to what community he belongs, no matter what relations he had with you in the past, no matter what is his colour, caste or creed, is first, second, and last a citizen of this State with equal rights, privileges and obligations, there will be no end to the progress you will make.

I cannot emphasise it too much. We should begin to work in that spirit and in course of time all these angularities of the majority and minority communities, the Hindu community and the Muslim community—because even as regards Muslims you have Pathans, Punjabis, Shias, Sunnis and so on and among the Hindus you have Brahmans, Visahnavas, Khatris, also Bengalees, Madrasis, and so on—will vanish. Indeed if you ask me this has been the biggest hindrance in the way of India to attain the freedom and independence and but for this we would have been free peoples long long ago. No power can hold another nation, and specially a nation of 400 million souls in subjection; nobody could have conquered you, and even if it had happened, nobody could have continued its hold on you for any length of time but for this. Therefore, we must learn a lesson from this. You are free; you are free to go to your temples, you are free to go to your mosques or to any other places of worship in this State of Pakistan. You may belong to any religion or caste or creed—that has nothing to do with the business of the State. As you know, history shows that in England conditions, some time ago, were much worse than those prevailing in India today. The Roman Catholics and the Protestants persecuted each other. Even now there are some States in existence where there are discriminations made and bars imposed against a particular class. Thank God, we are not starting in those days. We are starting in the days when there is no discrimination, no distinction between one community and another, no discrimination between one caste or creed and another. We are starting with this fundamental principle that we are all citizens and equal citizens of one State. The people of England in course of time had to face the realities of the situation and had to discharge the responsibilities and burdens placed upon them by the government of their country and they went through that fire step by step. Today, you might say with justice that Roman Catholics and Protestants do not exist; what exists now is that every man is a citizen, an equal citizen of Great Britain and they are all members of the Nation.

Now, I think we should keep that in front of us as our ideal and you will find that in course of time Hindus would cease to be Hindus and Muslims would cease to be Muslims, not in the religious sense, because that is the personal faith of each individual, but in the political sense as citizens of the State.

Well, gentlemen, I do not wish to take up any more of your time and thank you again for the honour you have done to me. I shall always be guided by the principles of justice and fair-play without any, as is put in the political language, prejudice or ill-will, in other words, partiality or favouritism. My guiding principle will be justice and complete impartiality, and I am sure that with your support and co-operation, I can look forward to Pakistan becoming one of the greatest Nations of the world.

Analysis and Review Questions

1. To what does Jinnah liken the conflicts between Hindus and Muslims?
2. Does it appear that Pakistan will respect religious differences and freedoms?
3. What does Jinnah have to say about the caste system?
4. What are the two main responsibilities of the Constituent Assembly?
5. What is the primary duty of a government, according to Jinnah?

THE TANDON FAMILY AT PARTITION

About the Document

Despite the protests of figures such as Gandhi, the partition of British India into the independent nations of Pakistan and India had become necessary due to the increasing inter-sect rioting and violence common in 1946 and 1947. Southern India, with a fairly insignificant Muslim population, felt little immediate impact from the split, but this was not the case in the north. Most Muslims lived in the northern provinces such as the Punjab. Both Indian and Pakistani leaders pledged to treat minority religious practitioners fairly and equitably. After partition, however, violence quickly returned, as Hindus attacked Muslims still in India, and Muslims harassed Hindus in Pakistani territory. What followed were two mass migrations, wherein Muslims migrated out of India and into the territories designated for Pakistan, and Hindus fled into India from Pakistan.

The partition was especially traumatic for those involved in the migrations. Many were forced out of the homes and occupations their families had maintained for centuries, while others initially refused to leave and were rarely safe for long. Prakash Tandon writes in *Punjabi Century* about some of his family's experiences during this period.

The Document

Dear Prakash,
    Come and get us out before it is too late.

While the fading paper flags of the independence celebrations were still waving, the horror of partition broke on us suddenly one day when a post-card arrived from Uncle Dwarka Prashad. It contained this single line.

With my younger brother, who was also settled in Bombay, I had discounted the first rumours, while Government tried to tone down the press hand-outs. No one wanted to spoil the music of freedom still in the air. But every day the news became graver, and uncle's post-card told us that the end had come.

In June of 1947, when partition was announced, most Hindus and Sikhs had accepted it fatalistically. 'We have lived under the Muslims before, then under the Sikhs and the British, and if we are now back under Muslim rule, so what? We shall manage somehow, as we have managed before. Nowadays governments are different, they give you some rights, they have to listen to the people!' Fortified by such arguments, people decided to stay where they were and face the change.

In July things began to look menacing, but few thought of leaving. There were sporadic attacks on Hindus and Sikhs, but they were mostly looked upon as signs of another riot. The turn had come of the Punjab, where people during the war years had prided themselves on living in peace while the rest of the country shook with the ugly outburst of Hindu-Muslim violence. As things worsened, father wrote to say that he considered it pointless to leave the house. Even if there was real trouble he would be safe, because he had so many Muslim friends and neighbours. Who would want to harm an old man, semi-paralysed by a stroke? Besides, he was so comfortable with his faithful Chattar Singh, who was on such good terms with everybody, Hindus, Muslims and Sikhs alike, to look after him.

In August law and order of ninety years came to an end. Elementary civil protection, taken for granted the week before, ceased. Chattar Singh felt that his own family would prove a burden if he suddenly had to leave; and to take care of father would be an added problem. So he appealed frantically to our neighbours to persuade father to go away for a while, till things improved. He was going to move his wife and children to the safety of Amritsar, now across the border. My elder brother wired from Bihar that father must leave, and reluctantly he agreed, whereupon Chattar Singh hurriedly packed him off. Many others were sending their women and children and old people away. Like everyone else, father thought he was only going for a short time, till the riots subsided.

Uncle Dwarka Prashad had remarried some years after Savitri's death and had permanently settled in Gujrat.

Uncle had always been tough and fearless, and easily persuaded to fight. He was greatly respected by all communities, and most of his practice came from Muslim litigants in the district. Everyone assured him that he could safely stay, no one would touch him and his family. He wanted to believe in their assurances even as he saw the trickle of exodus gather volume. These others thought it wise to go away for a while; they would all return when everything was calm again. The thought that this was a going away for ever never crossed anybody's mind. A calamity might cause temporary uprooting, but afterwards you came back to what had always been your home.

One day, a train crammed with two thousand refugees came from the more predominantly Muslim areas of Jhelum and beyond. At Gujrat station the train was stopped, and the Muslims from the neighbourhood, excited by the news of violence in East Punjab, began to attack and loot. There was indescribable carnage. Several hours later the train moved on, filled with a bloody mess of corpses, without a soul alive. At Amritsar, when the train with its load of dead arrived, they took revenge on a trainload of Muslim refugees. Six million Hindus and Sikhs from the West Punjab began to move in one dense mass towards safety, and from the east of the border a similar mass movement was under way in the opposite direction.

Muslim friends came to uncle late one night and said with tears in their eyes that they were unable to offer him protection any longer. The family must move at once, before dawn! Dwarka Prashad now saw it only too well that they had to go away, not for a few days, but for ever. He had in fact been expecting it since the day of the massacre at the station, but the problem had been how to get out; and it was then that he had sent the post-card.

His friends rushed to an Indian military evacuation convoy that had arrived the same evening, and brought a truck. They heaved a sigh of relief as uncle and his family, with two suitcases and a few blankets, drove away. On the Grand Trunk Road their truck joined an unending line of military and civil trucks and cars, bullock carts and tongas, people on horseback, and carried on shoulders. In its long history of over a thousand years this road had never seen such a migration.

As dawn was breaking, they caught the last view of Gujrat through the shisham trees by the road.

Partition changed the course of many lives which would otherwise have run in their familiar channels.

AT PARTITION we three brothers were already scattered outside the Punjab.

For us there was no more Punjab. Many refugees settled in East Punjab, but to us and many others, it was all over when the West Punjab went, and home was now where we earned our living. Those amongst the refugees who did not find an immediate footing in the East Punjab went all over India. One could not help admiring their courage and enterprise. Simple people, who had probably never been further than fifty miles away from their homes, set off in all directions and landed up in places they had never heard of.

My younger brother and I decided to forget the Punjab and regard Bombay as our home. We built two small houses next to each other, at the foot of Pali Hill in an area of largely Christian population. We had already lived in this area for a number of years and made many friends. Now, instinctively, we began to throw the roots deeper, and soon we were invited to their weddings and christenings and attended their funerals. They found our Punjabi ways, or Indian ways, as they called them, quaint. Our children went to the local schools where they learned English while they spoke Hindi at home. They never learned Punjabi.

Analysis and Review Questions

1. Which relative does Prakash Tandon primarily speak of in this excerpt?
2. Where do Tandon and his younger brother finally settle?
3. Why didn't Tandon's father wish to leave the Punjab at first?
4. What happened to the train full of Hindu refugees as it was passing through a Muslim-dominated area?
5. After partition, what did many Punjabis say was the reason they planned on staying in their homes?

WOMEN IN KARIMPUR, INDIA

About the Document

The twentieth century was a period of profound change for South Asia. The development of a nationalist movement in India helped speed up the process of decolonization for the British there, and the partition of British India ultimately led to the emergence of three primary nations—India, Pakistan, and Bangladesh, which was originally East Pakistan—and other smaller ones, such as Bhutan. Yet for many people in the Indian countryside living traditional lifestyles, the change from British to "Indian" rule had relatively little effect on most aspects of life until late in the century.

India portrayed itself as a new, modern state, preaching equality and opportunity for all, regardless of background or gender. Overall, however, the status of women remained (and in some ways, remains today) as it always had: respected, perhaps, but in no way equal.

In 1930 William and Charlotte Wiser went to live in and study a village called Karimpur in northern India; they wrote about their experiences in *Behind Mud Walls*. Mrs. Wiser returned to the village in the 1960s and 1970s, and Susan Wadley returned in 1984; their subsequent accounts provide an unusual look at change over time in a traditional village. While the 1980s saw tremendous possibilities emerge for many poorer citizens, women actually began to be excluded from many economic undertakings due to industrial development. The following selections illustrate how the status of women has changed over the last century in rural India.

The Document

As we go through the village, we are no longer conscious of mud walls, but of the life going on before and behind them. Before them, in the lanes, children skip and turn somersaults, farmers feed their animals, and craftsmen work at their trades. Behind them, further protected by the cattle rooms, are the women and small children in the family courtyards. Women of families of serving castes are obliged to go out for a part of each day, to the houses of employers, carrying water or grinding grain. But in every home where it is possible, the women and smaller children of the family—be it large or small—spend their lives in the family courtyard.

The men regard this courtyard as the women's realm, and chaff the man who spends much time there. In their own courtyards, the women go about their work scolding, laughing, chaffing, grumbling, without reserve. But the instant a man of the family enters they become self-conscious, covering (or making a pretense at covering) their faces, bowing their heads, and in every way emphasizing their sex and their role as subordinates. In families where economic pressure compels a woman to venture beyond her own mud walls, she goes cowering along the lanes, managing to keep her face hidden while balancing the jars of water or baskets of refuse which she must carry. In her own back lane, if she is of humble caste and if the menfolk are away in the fields, she is freer, but still ready to hide herself or her face if outsiders pass by. She is never quite at ease until she gains her own doorway.

Patience and service were required of the Memsahiba° before she was freely welcomed behind the mud walls. When she had finally convinced them that in every way she was made like themselves, their curiosity waned and a normal level of companionship was found.

But in normal times, there is the mental relaxation of following the topics of interest to women limited in outlook to their own households. Round and round the same circle they move—babies, husbands, food, physical ailments, all interwoven with their simple faith in spiritdom. Affairs of state are unimportant. When newspapers were headlined with the passing of the Sarda Bill, in 1929 (prohibiting marriages of males less than eighteen and females less than fourteen years old), the Memsahiba tried to interest the women in its significance, with indifferent response. On the same day there was a back-page item, reporting a rumor that locusts had devoured a baby in a district some distance from ours. Immediately interest was aroused. A mother losing her baby—this was within their grasp.

Babies are longed for, and greatly loved when they arrive. No one considers himself too busy, or too dignified to stop a moment to enjoy the antics of his youngest. The natural kindliness of village folk leads one to expect the same attitude toward all children. But the spirit of caste has so permeated their lives that they are indifferent toward children outside their own brotherhood, especially toward the children of untouchables. It still distresses us to see a grandmother of caste suddenly change from proud smiles to vindictive shouts because some untouchable toddler has innocently ventured near her grandchild.

Like mothers everywhere, those of our village thrill at the dependence of the new little lives on themselves. They prolong the pleasure of this dependence as long as possible, without the knowledge that it might be harmful to the child. A mother is proud of the fact that her baby of two refuses all food but her milk. At the same time she is distraught because the child is languid, emaciated, and steadily losing.

As girls grow older, their work and interests draw them more closely to their mothers. As the time of marriage approaches, with the dread of a mother-in-law, a girl clings to her mother as her strongest ally. The boys, as soon as they are able, desert the women's quarters for the fields and the companionship of the men. It is a period when a mother faces the realization that she is no longer needed.

It would be unfair to the joint family, which has much in its favor economically, to accuse it of disallowing love and companionship between husbands and wives. Such companionship would be possible, if there were less emphasis on sex. As it is, a woman performs her duty to her husband, satisfying his elemental needs, while she lavishes more and more of her love on her children. In the smaller homes, where the walls surround a single family, there is more natural relationship. With no older women present constantly to remind husband and wife of their respective roles, they work together for the good of their little family, without excessive consciousness of sex. In such courtyards, the wife may draw her scarf closely over her face when her husband enters and do his bidding without question, but she is free to talk with him alone. Even while he eats and she stands nearby ready to supply his wants, she may tell him about the baby's latest prank.

If a wife resents her husband's abuse of his control, as sometimes happens, she has a means of escape without scandal. As long as her father's house is maintained by one of her male relatives, she is free to return to it for visits of indefinite length.

Memsahiba: A European married woman.

[Charlotte Wiser returns to Karimpur in 1960, and notes the changes in the lives of the women there.]

There are few changes to report in the lives of the women of the village. The one radical change is in their style of dress. The women who must go out to work, either in their fields or in the households of others, still wear the traditional long, very full, colored skirts, with head scarves of a different color, and short blouses with sleeves. Those who remain in their own courtyards, or step out briefly to visit neighbors, have changed to what are known as dhotis.° The men have always worn *dhotis*, some short, some well below the knees. Town women have worn, and still wear, saris,° the draped gowns noted for their graceful lines. The *dhotis* now adopted by the village women are a cross between the two, longer and wider than those worn by the men and plainer and scantier than *saris*. Aside from this innovation, the women's world—the courtyard—is unchanged. The women of our village seem more at home in the setting of the Familiar than in the New.

[In 1984, Susan Wadley returned to the village and provided another update.]

Both men and women in Karimpur had benefited from increased education, although male levels of education had grown more markedly than female. Education, particularly for girls at all ages and for sons past fifth grade, was not evenly spread through the village. For the poor, school was still a luxury many could not afford, even for sons.

Despite increased education among females, most Karimpur° women felt girls were sufficiently educated if they were able "to write a letter home if there is trouble in their in-laws." The result was that poor and landless daughters either did not attend school or attended only through second or third grade. In addition, because educated girls required larger dowries as families sought to find comparably educated mates for them, educating a girl was often economically detrimental to a family.

Birth control was known to most Karimpur residents, but many women had no access to it. Birth control, like other forms of female health care, was unavailable unless permission was sought from husbands and/or mothers-in-law. Further, the method most strongly advocated by the Indian government was sterilization, particularly of women.

What was most troublesome was the increasing disparity between male and female child deaths in certain groups. Poor women in Karimpur were attempting to ensure family welfare by using high fertility and sex-specific child mortality to maximize the number of surviving males. More sons and fewer daughters optimized a family's welfare: dowries were saved, more income was generated, and sons remained with the family after marriage.

Karimpur mothers, especially the poor, verbalized little clear son preference, often saying, "Whatever Bhagvan [God] gives, we will have." Behaviorally, however, preferences were being shown.

Karimpur residents were blatant in their discrimination against female children. Births of daughters were not celebrated unless it was the first child born to that woman, and sometimes not even then. None of the birth songs honored the birth of a daughter.

---

dhoti: A longer garment worn traditionally by men, and generally less ornamental than saris.
saris: A typically lightweight women's garment worn wrapped around the body.
Karimpur: The village in India that is the subject of *Behind Mud Walls.*

Analysis and Review Questions

1. What was the Sarda Bill?
2. This selection is almost completely about women. In Nehru's "Declaration of Independence," is there any mention of what role women are to play in an independent India?
3. Would you say from this reading that women seem to accept their traditional roles in the village, or not?
4. What changes do you see for women in Karimpur from 1930 to 1984?
5. In 1984 what was still a mark of an "educated" young woman in Karimpur?

Map 32.2
Asia
2000

WEB LINKS

Selections from Longman World History—Primary Sources and Case Studies

http://longmanworldhistory.com
The following additional readings and case studies can be found on the Web site.
Document 32.1, Indian Declaration of Independence
At a 1930 meeting of the Congress of Lahore, a nationalist organization, Jawaharlal Nehru issued what has been called an "Indian Declaration of Independence."
Case Study 32.1, The Partition of India

General Information on India

http://www.indnet.org
Includes all sorts of information, from images on Indian postage stamps to statistics on South Asian immigration to the United States.

Other Information on India

http://www.123india.com
The site portrays itself as "India's Premier Portal," and there is some truth to the statement. Everything from current Indian news and online India chat to Indian search engines can be found here.

Behind Mud Walls

http://www.maxwell.syr.edu/southasiacenter/karimpur/
Susan Wadley, who added to the Wisers' accounts in *Behind Mud Walls*, helped with this site, which consists of many original images taken by the Wisers. This site provides an excellent view into Indian village life.

Gandhi

http://www.mahatma.org.in
The official site for the Mahatma Gandhi Foundation, dedicated to carrying on his nonviolent legacy. Includes photos, quotes from and about Gandhi, and more.

Indian Film and Culture

http://www.bollywoodonweb.com
A site dedicated to the world's largest film industry. Any aspect of Indian cinema and music is well covered here.

CHAPTER **33**

Twentieth Century Africa: From Colonies to Countries

*Map 33.1
New Nations
in Africa*

n 1900 sub-Saharan Africa, only Ethiopia and Liberia could be considered truly independent countries. Acquiring independence was far from easy for most African nations, and it was not completed in some until the 1970s. South Africa did not free itself from a white-minority dominated government until the 1990s.

To understand modern Africa and its multitudes of problems, we must take a look at the crucial twentieth century. The emergence of African nationalism, which encouraged independence movements, is of paramount importance. In some nations, relatively peaceful protest was enough to gain freedom, while in others, violent civil war was needed. Also key to an understanding of Africa is a study of the perpetuation of the repressive white-controlled administration in South Africa. The story of this century is one of tragedy, struggle, disappointment, and yet promise for Africa.

THE WRETCHED OF THE EARTH

About the Document

Many of the African nationalists of the later nineteenth century and early twentieth century preferred an accommodationist stance toward their colonial masters. Many were Western-educated and believed that Western influence was often a positive factor in their societies and lives. As time went on, however, many rejected these attitudes—some simply rejected the accommodation, while others openly advocated a violent overthrow of colonial regimes.

Frantz Fanon was born in the West Indies in 1925 and educated in France. He fought for the French in World War II and then returned to medical school to become a psychiatrist. Later, he was appointed head of the mental health department at an Algerian hospital.

Algeria became a trouble spot for the French in the 1950s, and Fanon saw firsthand the psychological effects of civil war on members of all sides. Finally, he resigned from the hospital to support the rebels, and it is from his writing that his fame comes. Fanon's *Wretched of the Earth*, as well as his other works critical of colonial rule, became influential in colonies around the world and inspired many independence movements.

250

The Document

National liberation, national renaissance, the restoration of nationhood to the people, commonwealth: whatever may be the headings used or the new formulas introduced, decolonisation is always a violent phenomenon. At whatever level we study it—relationships between individuals, new names for sports clubs, the human admixture at cocktail parties, in the police, on the directing boards of national or private banks—decolonisation is quite simply the replacing of a certain "species" of men by another "species" of men. Without any period of transition, there is a total, complete and absolute substitution. . . . Decolonisation, which sets out to change the order of the world, is, obviously, a programme of complete disorder. . . .

Decolonisation is the meeting of two forces, opposed to each other by their very nature, which in fact owe their originality to that sort of substantification which results from and is nourished by the situation in the colonies. Their first encounter was marked by violence and their existence together—that is to say the exploitation of the native by the settler—was carried on by dint of a great array of bayonets and cannon. The settler and the native are old acquaintances. In fact, the settler is right when he speaks of knowing "them" well. . . .

. . . The settler owes the fact of his very existence, that is to say his property, to the colonial system.

Decolonisation never takes place un-noticed, for it influences individuals and modifies them fundamentally. It transforms spectators crushed with their inessentiality into privileged actors, with the grandiose glare of history's floodlights upon them. It brings a natural rhythm into existence, introduced by new men, and with it a new language and a new humanity.

In decolonisation, there is therefore the need of a complete calling in question of the colonial situation. If we wish to describe it precisely, we might find it in the well-known words: "The last shall be first and the first last." Decolonisation is the putting into practice of this sentence. That is why, if we try to describe it, all decolonisation is successful.

The naked truth of decolonisation evokes for us the searing bullets and blood-stained knives which emanate from it. For if the last shall be first, this will only come to pass after a murderous and decisive struggle between the two protagonists. . . . The colonial world is a world divided into compartments. It is probably unnecessary to re-call the existence of native quarters and European quarters, of schools for natives and schools for Europeans; in the same way we need not recall Apartheid in South Africa. Yet, if we examine closely this system of compartments, we will at least be able to re-veal the lines of force it implies. This approach to the colonial world, its ordering and its geographical lay-out will allow us to mark out the lines on which a decolonised society will be reorganised.

The colonial world is a world cut in two. The dividing line, the frontiers are shown by barracks and police stations. In the colonies it is the policeman and the sol-dier who are the official, instituted go-betweens, the spokesmen of the settler and his rule of oppression. In capitalist societies the educational system, whether lay or cleri-cal, the structure of moral reflexes handed down from father to son, the exemplary honesty of workers who are given a medal after fifty years of good and loyal service, and the affection which springs from harmonious relations and good behaviour—all these esthetic expressions of respect for the established order serve to create around the exploited person an atmosphere of submission and of inhibition which lightens the task of policing considerably. In the capitalist countries a multitude of moral teachers, counsellors and "bewilderers" separate the exploited from those in power. In the colonial countries, on the contrary, the policeman and the soldier, by their immediate presence and their frequent and direct action maintain contact with the native and advise him by means of rifle-butts and napalm not to budge. It is obvious here that the agents of government speak the language of pure force.

The violence which has ruled over the ordering of the colonial world, which has ceaselessly drummed the rhythm for the destruction of native social forms and broken up without reserve the systems of reference of the economy, the customs of dress and external life, that same violence will be claimed and taken over by the native at the moment when, deciding to embody history in his own person, he surges into the forbidden quarters. To wreck the colonial world is henceforward a mental picture of action which is very clear, very easy to understand and which may be assumed by each one of the individuals which constitute the colonised people.

But it so happens that for the colonised people this violence, because it constitutes their only work, invests their characters with positive and creative qualities. The practice of violence binds them together as a whole, since each individual forms a violent link in the great chain, a part of the great organism of violence which has surged upwards in reaction to the settler's violence in the beginning.... The armed struggle mobilises the people; that is to say, it throws them in one way and in one direction.

The mobilisation of the masses, when it arises out of the war of liberation, introduces into each man's consciousness the ideas of a common cause, of a national destiny and of a collective history.

We have said that the native's violence unifies the people. By its very structure, colonialism is separatist and regionalist. Colonialism does not simply state the existence of tribes; it also re-inforces it and separates them.... Violence is in action all-inclusive and national. It follows that it is closely involved in the liquidation of regionalism and of tribalism....°

At the level of individuals, violence is a cleansing force. It frees the native from his inferiority complex and from his despair and inaction; it makes him fearless and restores his self-respect. Even if the armed struggle has been symbolic and the nation is demobilised through a rapid movement of decolonisation, the people have the time to see that the liberation has been the business of each and all and that the leader has no special merit. From thence comes that type of aggressive reticence with regard to the machinery of protocol which young governments quickly show. When the people have taken violent part in the national liberation they will allow no one to set themselves up as "liberators." They show themselves to be jealous of the results of their action and take good care not to place their future, their destiny or the fate of their country in the hands of a living god. Yesterday they were completely irresponsible; today they mean to understand everything and make all decisions. Illuminated by violence, the consciousness of the people rebels against any pacification. From now on the demagogues, the opportunists and the magicians have a difficult task. The action which has thrown them into a hand-to-hand struggle confers upon the masses a voracious taste for the concrete. The attempt at mystification becomes, in the long run, practically impossible.

---

tribalism: A form of tribal nationalism or consciousness based on a narrow group identity that can hinder the development of a wider national identity.

Analysis and Review Questions

1. According to Fanon, violence is a "cleansing force" at what level?
2. Does Fanon seem to be an advocate of violence overall?
3. What are the two compartments of the colonial world, according to Fanon?
4. Why don't people accept "liberators"?
5. Does Fanon seem similar to any figures in American history from the last 50 years?

Image 33.1
Kwame Nkhrumah

A LIBERAL WHITE JOURNALIST ON APARTHEID

About the Document

As the nations of sub-Saharan Africa slowly, but steadily, gained freedom from the colonial powers, the semi-independent country of South Africa remained clouded with the oppressive system of apartheid. Under Europeans, southern Africa had a history of various racial tensions, but no systematic and deliberate system of repression had previously existed.

Donald Woods was a white South African journalist. Through much of his early adult life, he harbored many of the same prejudices as many other whites in his country, but in the early 1970s, he became involved in the struggle for equality. Woods wrote an acclaimed biography of Steve Biko, the noted black student leader murdered while in police custody. This excerpt from Woods' autobiography discusses the journalist's experiences working for social equality of blacks in South Africa, first in a chess club, then through sports.

The Document

Wendy and I had become friendly with Rob and Hildur Amato, who started a non-racial theatre group, and through them we met for the first time blacks who spoke as social equals with whom we became friendly. It was exciting to see barriers broken down, even within a small circle like a theatre group. To get round the law their plays were staged on private property and no admission charge was made, playgoers contributing to a "voluntary collection" which hadn't been legislated against in the race laws. I decided to try to achieve in chess, cricket and rugby what Rob was doing in theatre. . . .

[Woods joined a chess club.]

. . . There were no black members, and when I proposed that membership should be open to all races only one member, an elderly Afrikaner, objected. Elected to the committee, I started bringing black chess players to the club, and when the old man objected the committee told him he was welcome to leave the club if he didn't like it. Several other players didn't like it, in fact, but tolerated it rather than lose their chess.

I knew that multinational companies operating in the area were under pressure from their head offices overseas to promote black welfare and were given budgeted allowances to do this, so I went to all of them, collecting money to be made available to the chess club provided it was fully integrated. . . .

[This club became the first fully integrated chess club in South Africa.]

Heartened by the success of the chess club integration, in which we contravened the apartheid laws regularly, gradually gaining public acceptance by printing pictures of tournament play, I decided to try the same approach to integrate club cricket. Working with Kemal Casoojee, who headed the local chapter of the non-racial South African Cricket Board of Control, or SACBOC, I became involved with black cricketers in the area. There was a lot of talent, and Kemal and I formed the provocatively named Rainbow Cricket Club, selecting such good players that on playing merit we were able to apply for first-league status. This threw the local white cricket administrators into a panic. Our star team had three blacks, two Indians, three coloureds and three whites, and the white cricket authorities refused our application on the grounds that multiracial cricket was illegal. . . .

. . . While the Afrikaner Nationalist government might turn a blind eye to an integrated chess club, rather than suffer adverse publicity overseas for closing it, a mass-following sport like cricket was something else. It concerned the country's entire "way of life." In those years I also became involved with the rugby body trying to do in rugby what SACBOC aimed to do in cricket. This was the non-racial South African Rugby Union, and its task was the hardest because rugby was almost a religion with South African whites, especially Afrikaners.

I had told Koornhof [the Minister of Sport] about our Rainbow Cricket Club and he had said: "Yes, man, go ahead and tell the white officials that although it's against the law we'll turn a blind eye to it. I can't say it publicly but tell them I say it privately—that provided there's no fuss and no big bloody headlines screaming all over the place they can just go ahead." But the white officials of the Border Cricket Association were too scared to take a chance. Their president, Leigh Warren, dug in his heels. "It's all very well for Koornhof to say this privately and unofficially," he said. "But *we* have to break the laws, not him. If the police here prosecute us it is *our* cricket clubs that lose their liquor licences." I flew to Johannesburg and told Koornhof that Warren and the other white officials wouldn't go ahead without permission from him in writing. Koornhof was alarmed. "Hell, man, I can't put that officially. I can't give you a letter telling them officially to break my Government's laws." I said: "Well, they won't do a thing without your written permission." Dr Koornhof looked unhappy. "What about an informal message on the back of a cigarette packet?" I asked him. "That isn't official, but it's in writing, isn't it?" I said. "*Ja*, I suppose so," he replied. I pulled out a packet of cigarettes, and on the cardboard back of it scrawled out a message to "L. Warren, Border Cricket Union" certifying that it was in order to admit the Rainbow Cricket Club to the Border League, then held it out to Dr Koornhof. He smiled and signed. When I got back to East London Kemal said he wanted it recorded in the SACBOC minutes that cricket in the Eastern Cape had been integrated on the back of my cigarette packet.

We became the first region in the country to stage a non-racial league cricket game. Kemal and I were tense as the teams arrived, because the local police and populace didn't know about the cigarette packet deal, and in the *Dispatch* a restrained preview of the match had been published without stress on its non-racial nature. However, anyone could realize by the team-names—Njokweni and Mbatani were unmistakably African names and Pillay was an unmistakably Indian name—that it was no ordinary match. A bigger crowd than usual turned up to see the strange sight on one of our big-league cricket grounds of black, coloured and Indian players in one team-huddle out in the middle.

Afterwards, an official of the Department of Sport came to see me and pointed out that the Rainbow team's participation in the league was illegal. I reached into my pocket and pulled out the cigarette box signed by Koornhof. His eyes widened with astonishment. "Jesus!" he exclaimed, taking it from me to examine the ministerial signature more closely. "We have nothing about this from our Department," he said, nonplussed. "Well, phone your Minister," I said. "Or if you prefer to cause less embarrassment all round, phone his secretary, Mr Beyers Hoek, who was present when this was signed." He phoned Hoek, who mumbled some departmental jargon about "elements of the policy being under review," and advised the local East London office to "assist Mr Woods and the other cricket officials" pending further explanations from the Minister himself. The official told me this in tones of awe, after which our team felt able to arrive at designated grounds to fulfil their fixtures without risking arrest.

[Later, Woods is arrested and banned from visiting non-white areas and from gathering with others, including his chess club matches.]

One of the early problems of the banning was communicating the full extent of the restrictions to the children. They were used to bringing schoolfriends home, and couldn't at first grasp that I couldn't be in a room with them if their friends were present. I, or the friend, or the children, would have to leave the room. It was even more awkward with close friends. . . . We would have to "split up" between the lounge and television room, although we often relaxed this to the extent of sitting near enough to each other in adjoining areas such as the lounge and hallway to carry on a general conversation.

An amusing example of this restriction came when I decided to test the outer parameters of the banning orders within the first few days. I went to Colonel van der Merwe and said: "Colonel, I'm still captain of the East London Chess Club—am I no longer allowed to play chess at the club on Monday evenings?" "Certainly not," he replied. "Of course you may not attend a club or gathering of any kind." But I was ready for this, and said: "You misunderstand me, Colonel. I know I am not allowed to attend the chess club in the normal way any more, but I can make special arrangements to play my league matches in a separate room. How can that be breaking the ban if I'm with only one other person in a separate room at the club?" He frowned and puzzled the matter over, leafing through the restriction documents, then he looked up and said: "I can find no specific objection to such an arrangement—but don't drink tea or coffee while you're playing." "Don't drink tea or coffee?" I asked. "What's that all about?" "Common social purpose," he replied, looking through the documents again. "The restrictions are not only there to prevent conspiring against the State, they're also aimed at preventing any common social purpose. You can be in a separate room at your chess club if there's only your opponent present, but if you drink tea or coffee that will mean it's a common social purpose with other members elsewhere in the club, because they will also be drinking tea or coffee."

Analysis and Review Questions

1. Why was the government more upset about integrating cricket as opposed to chess?
2. What sort of note did Koornhof give to Woods to help allow the cricket game?
3. What was the reaction of the chess club when Woods introduced black players?
4. What couldn't Woods do when he was banned?
5. Who was Kemal Casoojee?

*Image 33.2
Voters Waiting to
Vote in South
Africa's First Open
Election, 1994*

WORLD BANK–SUPPORTED DAY CARE PROGRAMS IN UGANDA

About the Document

The International Monetary Fund (IMF) and the World Bank were created by the United Nations partially to help foster development in Third World countries. Though each organization is often surrounded with controversy over their programs and the loans they make to poor nations, there is no denying that programs sponsored by these organizations can have profound impacts on poor countries.

Independent from Great Britain in 1962, Uganda almost immediately had problems with political stability. After a decade of chaos in the 1970s under dictator Idi Amin, Uganda continued to struggle with the problem. Finally, during the 1990s, internal strife and insurgency declined (though they remain important concerns), allowing the government to focus increasingly on social policies and economic growth.

Today, Uganda struggles with many of the same issues plaguing other Third World nations: poverty, illiteracy, human rights violations, and environmental problems. But the World Bank, along with many other international social organizations, has been supporting programs in Uganda to help overcome some of the nagging dilemmas. The following program, a community-based child day care and health service arrangement, was funded largely by World Bank contributions.

The Document

Community-based Mother–Child Day Care Center Services (MCDCCS) provide modern, affordable child care for working mothers living in the slums and rural trading areas of Uganda. The target group are poor, disheartened, and homeless mothers who cannot afford to pay for regular child-care services and who are not reached by national programs that aim to address the needs of women and girl children.

Using an integrated approach, the centers also offer a variety of programs to help these women. Programs include:

Formal and non-formal education for women (e.g., literacy courses)

Breastfeeding counseling

Family planning counseling and services

Promotion of safe motherhood

Public health education for children (hygiene and nutrition) and mothers

Campaigns for free immunization and universal primary education

Assistance with health issues and immunization

Promotion of gender equality, and the education and special needs of girl children

Enforcement of positive child-rearing practices

Training of child-care workers to reach certificate level

Creation of employment opportunities for mothers through income-generating projects and micro-credit facilities.

Those facilities are, for many women, the only way to cover their social, domestic, and business expansion needs and to pay school fees or for prompt medical treatment for their children.

[The following provides some cultural context for the programs.]

In many African countries, including Uganda, men strive to show their worth by fathering as many children as possible. This is particularly true for the unemployed, low-income working class. Uganda's illiteracy rate is high, and studies reveal that the number of educated and self-sufficient women is comparatively low. Thus, the overwhelming majority of women in Uganda today are not only illiterate but poor, frustrated, and helpless. They carry the burden of childbearing and child-rearing, often with little or no financial support. High illiteracy and birthrates remain a problem that is stalling the productivity and potentials of many poor women.

[The following details the general approach.]

In 1997 the Ugandan Government introduced Universal Primary Education (UPE), beginning with four children per family and with plans to cover all Uganda's children in the near future. This proposal has good intentions to benefit girl children; however, their traditional role at home and in the workplace makes it almost impossible for them to attend school from early ages without interruption. Several other government-launched programs directly related to the advancement of women in Uganda don't reach the poorest and most marginalized women and mothers, because they are not in a position to take advantage of those programs.

The program aims to improve the condition of young children by empowering mothers to become economically productive and less ignorant. When poor women are liberated from constant child care and become involved in financial activities, the future of their children is safer, healthier, and more productive, and girl children are freed from their surrogate mother role in caring for younger siblings.

A breakthrough can be made only if women and family issues are addressed as a whole taking the specific needs of women into account who are targeted by the program. When low-cost, high-quality child-care services are provided for children ranging in age from a few days to more than 10 years old, mothers can become economically self-reliant, and thus provide better for their children's basic needs.

In contrast to traditional Ugandan child-care centers, which are expensive and provide services for children aged 3 and older, the MCDCCS centers are geared toward children aged 0–3. The general approach is integrated and holistic, addressing issues such as child health, family planning, gender issues, and the special needs of the girl child. In addition to providing a safe environment for children and educating the mothers, the centers train caregivers and teachers and generate employment opportunities for women through small-scale income-generating projects and micro-credit schemes. This is an important step toward increasing women's independence and helping them reach a position in which they can negotiate greater control over family planning and birthrates, safe motherhood, and curbing of sexually transmitted diseases. . . .

[The following discusses implementation of the program.]

The three current centers are wholly oriented toward serving the mother's needs. Locations close to the workplace (e.g., the market) make it feasible for mothers to leave their children at the centers from 6:30 a.m. to 6:30 p.m. If the child is younger than one year old, the mother is required to come in periodically for breastfeeding. Hourly drop-off arrangements and after-school care for older children also are provided. The centers help mothers acquire immunization cards, which are required for all children, and keep track of immunization records.

Over time, the centers have become special places for both mothers and children. They have become focal points for learning, teaching, and relaxing—places where women can openly discuss their major concerns of daily life.

Some important findings follow:

Between 1987 and 1999, more than 900 mothers used MCDCCS services and about 6,600 children benefited from the program.

Children who start at the age of a few days to one year old show much better performance results in all aspects of child development and skill learning than children who came to the centers at the age of 3+ years.

Infant mortality among MCDCCS children is extremely low (3 children out of all 6,600).

The growing demand for family planning services has led to a decrease in the number of very young children (less than a year old) in the centers from a daily average of 25 in 1987 to 4 in 1999.

As women are liberated from child-care duties, they can become economically active. The mother's ability to pay the monthly fees for childcare services promptly is a direct indicator of the reduction of poverty. Despite the fact that fees increased 10-fold between 1987 and 1999, the number of MCDCCS mothers who paid promptly rose from 20% to 50% during that period.

Mothers who attend the centers' programs soon become agents of positive change within their home community and workplace. Community-level indicators for program evaluation and monitoring indicators include:

Increase in the number of women who request family planning services

Improved weight and overall health status of children who attend the centers

Decrease in infant and child mortality rates

Improved social habits of women and children

Increase in school readiness and thus school attendance, especially for girls

Increase in literacy rate of girls

Decrease in population growth rate

Decrease in rate of sexually transmitted disease

Increase in immunization coverage

Increase in gross national product

The project generates money by:

Collecting small fees from the mothers for child-care services. As the potential for economic productivity increases, they are expected to pay higher fees.

Engaging in income-generating activities, such as poultry (selling eggs and hens) and pig farms

Operating small farms and gardens for subsistence-level production of local fruits and vegetables

Charging fees for training services

Renting out the main hall of the centers for special events

The project itself provides employment possibilities for unemployed mothers who use the centers' child-care services. An average of 60 workers per month, mostly mothers, are employed to run the three current centers and the related income-generating projects.

[The project received new funding to:]

Improve and update the three existing centers

Expand services by starting three new centers

Increase income-generating potentials by producing children's books and teaching material and expanding farm production

Increase local capacity—through training, supervision, improved teaching material, performance assessments, and evaluation—to provide high-quality child-care services

Introduce new elements, such as music and computer equipment and skills

Launch a major marketing campaign (posters and radio, newspaper, and TV announcements) to create awareness of child development issues related to health and education in the early years

[Basic principles leading to success:]

Follow a holistic approach to combat the causes of poverty, not the symptoms.

Design programs to meet the very specific needs of one of the poorest and most marginalized groups in Uganda: illiterate and excluded women in slum areas.

Combine the early child development agenda and parent education with job creation and income-generating activities in a unique and creative way.

Make the programs community-based and adjust them to the mothers' needs.

Allow flexibility in providing education and health programs on demand.

Monitor the children's growth and motor and cognitive development.

Have a wide range of spill-over effects, because they establish a linkage between non-formal education for women, health education, and family planning with other national health and immunization campaigns.

Alleviate poverty from the grassroots level through empowerment.

[Future outlook:]

With six centers, the project plans to become financially sustainable by expanding its income-generating activities, providing professional training for teachers and caregivers, and enhancing the ability of mothers to pay higher fees for child care.

However, the project's vision is to have a broader influence on public policy by raising awareness in communities and eventually achieving nationwide impact. For these steps, financial support and technical assistance are needed from national and international agencies.

One of the center's programs that has not reached out to the majority of MCDCCS women is literacy. The mothers' key objective is survival; beyond that, they rely on the center's services to enable them to increase the profits from their business. They cannot imagine spending precious time studying. The mothers also point out that, because they are now able to educate their children, the children can read and write for them if the need arises. As long as women are poor and struggling for survival they will not consider literacy a priority. Only the establishment of day care centers on a massive scale will make it possible for girl children to start their education early. In the long run, this will help to reduce the number of illiterate women in Uganda dramatically.

Analysis and Review Questions

1. What does MCDCCS stand for?
2. How does the program generate money?
3. What do men tend to do in many African societies to prove their worth?
4. What contrast was made between traditional Ugandan day care centers and those in the program?
5. Does this program seem at all similar to programs that exist in Western countries, such as the United States?

WEB LINKS

http://longmanworldhistory.com
The following additional readings and case studies can be found on the Web site.
Document 31.5, Vietnamese Declaration of Independence
Document 32.1, Indian Declaration of Independence
Document 33.2, Kwame Nkrumah on African Unity
Case Study 33.1, Frantz Fanon and Ho Chi Minh Speak Out Against Imperialism
Case Study 33.2, Frantz Fanon and Nehru's Indian Declaration of Independence

http://www.gov.za/index.html
Site includes not only specifics about the South African government, but also sections on history, the ending of apartheid, tourism, and other topics. Links to the official government pages of other southern African nations are included.

http://allafrica.com
Included in this comprehensive site are links to top current news stories, topical pages on subjects ranging from sports to the environment, and an African search engine.

http://www.sas.upenn.edu/African_Studies/AS.html
Site of the African Studies Center at the University of Pennsylvania. The section of online resources includes a multimedia archive, K–12 resources, country-specific page links, and a bulletin board.

http://www.africanconservation.com
Includes a country-by-country analysis of environmental and conservation initiatives.

http://africafocus.library.wisc.edu
Sponsored by the African Studies Program at the University of Wisconsin–Madison, these pages include over 3,000 contemporary images and sound clips from most of Africa.

CHAPTER 34

The Middle East in the Twentieth Century

The twentieth century saw the division of empires into sovereign nation-states, unequal efforts at economic development, and struggles to define authentic cultural experiences that confront the needs of the modern world while preserving traditions and beliefs of people around the world. In the Middle East, the 600-year-old Ottoman Empire collapsed after its defeat in World War I. The Arab lands of the Empire fell under European control, either directly—in the form of League of Nations Mandates—or indirectly—through treaties that gave the European powers significant control over borders, militaries, finances, and natural resources. In Anatolia, a group of former Ottoman officers led a successful struggle for Turkish independence, then abolished the Ottoman dynasty and declared Turkey a secular republic. In Iran, the Qajar Dynasty fell to the upstart Reza Shah, who declared his own Pahlavi Dynasty in 1925 and began a series of reforms aimed at strengthening the central state against provincial, tribal, and religious elites. Eventually, the reforms would fail to create a democratic, egalitarian, or just society, and in 1979 the Pahlavis went the way of other dynasties brought down by popular revolution.

Following World War II, British and French influence in the Middle East waned, as the United States increased ties with the region in an effort to maintain access to petroleum and thwart Soviet influence. Just as the Arab countries began to assert their sovereignty, they were faced with the creation of Israel, a state most Arabs viewed as an extension of European imperialism. Every decade since the 1940s has brought a major military confrontation between Israel and its Arab neighbors. But with the collapse of the Soviet Union, the apparent end of the Cold War, and the creation of a coalition of Arab states allied against Iraq in the Gulf War, peace suddenly seemed to be a real possibility, as Israel and the PLO signed an interim agreement to negotiate solutions to all outstanding tensions.

Map 34.1
The Middle East
in the 1920s

THE SIX ARROWS OF KEMALISM: THE PRINCIPLES OF THE REPUBLICAN PEOPLE'S PARTY (RPP), 1935

About the Document

Following the Ottoman defeat in World War I, a group of Turkish nationalists regrouped in eastern Anatolia to begin a struggle against Allied and Greek occupation of Anatolia. The nationalists, led by Mustafa Kemal (Atatürk), Ismet° (Inonü), Kazym° (Karabekir) and other former Ottoman officers, created a parliament in their headquarters, Ankara, and vested sovereignty in the Grand National Assembly. In 1923, along with declaring the Turkish Republic, Mustafa Kemal led the creation of a political party, the People's Party (later Republican People's Party, or RPP), which dominated Turkish politics until its defeat by the Democrat Party in 1950. Throughout the 1920s, the People's Party was the center of politics, and two experiments, in 1924 and 1929, with the formation of an opposition party ended unsuccessfully. In response to the impact of the Great Depression and expressions of popular discontent with single-party rule, party leaders decided in 1931 to articulate a set of guiding principles, or arrows, of the RPP. The following selection was published following the fourth party congress in 1935.

The Document

Adopted by the Fourth Grand Congress of the Party, May 1935

Introduction

The fundamental ideas that constitute the basis of the Program of the Republican Party of the People are evident in the acts and realizations which have taken place from the beginning of our Revolution until today.

On the other hand, the main ideas have been formulated in the general principles of the Statutes of the Party, adopted also by the Grand Congress of the Party in 1927, as

---

Ismet: Mustafa Ismet (Inonü, 1884–1972), popularly known as Ismet Pasha, trained at the Ottoman War College before serving as an officer in World War I. Following the war, he joined the nationalist cause, was named commander of the nationalist forces in 1920, and led Turkish troops to major victories over the Greeks at Inonü, in western Anatolia. In 1922 through 1923 he led the Turkish negotiations at Lausanne, which recognized the independence and sovereignty of the Ankara government. From 1923 to 1937, he served almost continuously as Prime Minister of the Turkish Republic. Following the death of Atatürk in 1938, Inonü became the second president of Turkey, a position he held until the RPP's electoral defeat in 1950. He remained in the Grand National Assembly, serving as prime minister in the early 1960s, until his retirement in 1971.

Kazym: Kâzym Karabekir (1882–1948) was trained at the Ottoman War College. Kâzym Pasha served as commander of the Caucasian front in World War I. Following the war, he was one of the first Ottoman commanders to begin gathering support for nationalist defense of Anatolia. After accepting the overall leadership of Mustafa Kemal, Karabekir continued to serve as commander of the nationalist forces on the eastern front and defeated Armenian efforts to form an independent state in 1920. Karabekir eventually clashed with Atatürk over the latter's control in the RPP and the National Assembly and was arrested and tried for conspiracy to assassinate Atatürk in 1926. Acquitted, Karabekir retired from public life until Atatürk's death in 1938, when Ismet Inonü asked him to take a seat in the Assembly.

well as in the Declaration published on the occasion of the elections to the Grand National Assembly° in 1931.

The main lines of our intentions, not only for a few years, but for the future as well, are here put together in a compact form. All of these principles which are the fundamentals of the Party constitute Kamâlism.°

Part I

Principles

1—The Fatherland
2—The Nation
3—The Constitution of the State
4—The Public Rights

1—THE FATHERLAND. The Fatherland is the sacred country within our present political boundaries, where the Turkish Nation lives with its ancient and illustrious history, and with its past glories still living in the depths of its soil.

The Fatherland is a Unity which does not accept separation under any circumstance.

2—THE NATION. The Nation is the political Unit composed of citizens bound together with the bonds of language, culture and ideal.

3—CONSTITUTIONAL ORGANIZATION OF THE STATE. Turkey is a nationalist, populist, *étatist*, secular [*laïque*], and revolutionary Republic.

The form of administration of the Turkish nation is based on the principle of the unity of power. There is only one Sovereignty, and it belongs to the nation without restriction or condition.

The Grand National Assembly exercises the right of sovereignty in the name of the nation. The legislative authority and the executive power are embodied in the Grand National Assembly. The Assembly exercises its legislative power itself. It leaves its executive authority to the President of the Republic, elected from among its members, and to the Council of Ministers appointed by him. The courts in Turkey are independent.

The Party is convinced that this is the most suitable of all State organizations.

4—PUBLIC RIGHTS.

(a) It is one of the important principles of our Party to safeguard the individual and social rights of liberty, of equality, of inviolabilty, and of property. These rights are within the bounds of the State's authority. The activity of the individuals and of legal persons shall not be in contradiction with the interests of the public. Laws are made in accordance with this principle.

(b) The Party does not make any distinction between men and women in giving rights and duties to citizens.

Grand National Assembly: Grand National Assembly (Türkiye Büyük Millet Meclisi). The parliament of the Turkish Republic was first convened in Ankara on April 23, 1920, during the Turkish War of Independence. Among its first acts were to name Mustafa Kemal (Atatürk), president of the Assembly, and to proclaim itself the sole legitimate representative of the entire Turkish nation in the struggle against Allied and Greek occupation forces and the government of the Ottoman Sultan.

Kamâlism: Kamâlism (Kemalism). Named after Mustafa Kemal Atatürk, Kamalism is the ideological underpinning of a series of legal, political, economic, and cultural reforms carried out during Atatürk's presidency, from 1923 through 1938 and after. The reforms include the six arrows, or guiding principles of republicanism, nationalism, secularism, populism, reformism, and statism.

(c) The Law on the election of deputies shall be renewed. We find it more suitable to the real requirements of democracy to leave the citizen free to elect electors whom he knows well and trusts, in accordance with the general conditions of our country. The election of the deputies shall take place in this manner.

Part II

The Essential Characteristics of the Republican Party of the People

5—The Republican Party of the People is: (a) Republican (b) Nationalist (c) Populist (d) *Étatist* (e) Secular (f) Revolutionary.

(a) The Party is convinced that the Republic is the form of government which represents and realizes most safely the ideal of national sovereignty. With this un-shakable conviction, the Party defends, with all its means, the Republic against all danger.

(b) The Party considers it essential to preserve the special character and the entirely independent identity of the Turkish social community in the sense explained in Art. 2. The Party follows, in the meantime, a way parallel to and in harmony with all the modern nations in the way of progress and development, and in international contacts and relations.

(c) The source of Will and Sovereignty is the Nation. The Party considers it an important principle that this Will and Sovereignty be used to regulate the proper fulfillment of the mutual duties of the citizen to the State and of the State to the citizen.

We consider the individuals who accept an absolute equality before the Law, and who recognize no privileges for any individual, family, class, or community, to be of the people and for the people (populist).

It is one of our main principles to consider the people of the Turkish Republic, not as composed of different classes, but as a community divided into various professions according to the requirements of the division of labor for the individual and social life of the Turkish people.

The farmers, handicraftsmen, laborers and workmen, people exercising free professions, industrialists, merchants, and public servants are the main groups of work constituting the Turkish community. The functioning of each of these groups is essential to the life and happiness of the others and of the community.

The aims of our Party, with this principle, are to secure social order and solidarity instead of class conflict, and to establish harmony of interests. The benefits are to be proportionate to the aptitude to the amount of work.

(d) Although considering private work and activity a basic idea, it is one of our main principles to interest the State actively in matters where the general and vital interests of the nation are in question, especially in the economic field, in order to lead the nation and the country to prosperity in as short a time as possible.

The interest of the State in economic matters is to be an actual builder, as well as to encourage private enterprises, and also to regulate and control the work that is being done.

The determination of the economic matters to be undertaken by the State depends upon the requirements of the greatest public interest of the nation. If the enterprise, which the State itself decides to undertake actively as a result of this necessity, is in the hands of private entrepreneurs, its appropriation shall, each time, depend upon the enactment of a law, which will indicate the way in which the State shall indemnify the loss sustained by the private enterprise as a result of this appropriation. In the estimation of the loss the possibility of future earnings shall not be taken into consideration.

(e) The Party considers it a principle to have the laws, regulations, and methods in the administration of the State prepared and applied in conformity with the needs of the world and on the basis of the fundamentals and methods provided for modern civilization by Science and Technique.

As the conception of religion is a matter of conscience, the Party considers it to be one of the chief factors of the success of our nation in contemporary progress, to separate ideas of religion from politics, and from the affairs of the world and of the State.

(f) The Party does not consider itself bound by progressive and evolutionary principles in finding measures in the State administration. The Party holds it essential to remain faithful to the principles born of revolutions which our nation has made with great sacrifices, and to defend these principles which have since been elaborated.

Analysis and Review Questions

1. How does the document define the Turkish nation? What is the connection between the nation and the fatherland?
2. What are the six characteristics, or arrows, of the RPP? Why does the party reject the notion of class division or conflict in Turkish society? In whose interest does the party claim to serve?
3. According to the fourth principle, *étatism*, what role should the Turkish state play in the economy, and why? How does this principle affect views of the role of private enterprise?
4. How does the document define secularism? Why does the party advocate secularism?
5. Compare this document with the Hatt-i Şerif of Gühane (1839) of Sultan Abdülmecid I in Chapter 27. In what ways are the two documents similar and different, in terms of defining the rights and obligations of citizens, and in terms of the role of the state in economic and cultural matters?

THE SAUDI-ARAMCO "50/50" AGREEMENT, DECEMBER 30, 1950

About the Document

In 1933 a consortium of American oil companies, led by Standard Oil of California, signed a concession with the Saudi Arabian government of King Abd al-Aziz ibn Saud° (r. 1902–1953) to explore for petroleum in the eastern provinces of the

King Abd al-Aziz ibn Saud: Founder of the modern state of Saudi Arabia, ibn Saud built his kingdom following World War I on the pillars of family alliances and Wahabbism, a puritanical form of Islam that emerged in eastern Arabia in the eighteenth century. After capturing Riyadh and overcoming the al-Rashid family, ibn Saud turned his efforts to conquest of the Hejaz, the territory in western Arabia containing the holy cities of Mecca and Medina. By 1929 ibn Saud was using the title King. Since the early 1930s, the cornerstone of Saudi foreign policy has been close relations with the United States—in part as a way to balance American and British interests in the region's oil. In 1945 on his way back from Yalta, Franklin Roosevelt met with ibn Saud, setting the groundwork for a military and economic alliance that has survived ever since.

kingdom. In 1938 the company discovered oil and began exporting small quantities. Following World War II, global demand for oil increased dramatically, and with the demand, the Saudi government's royalties rose from less than $5 million to more than $50 million in four years. After learning that the company, renamed Aramco (Arab-American Oil Company), in 1944 paid more in U.S. taxes than in royalties, and following a trend developing in Venezuela and Iran, the Saudi government requested, then demanded, renegotiation of the division of royalties. The resulting agreement between Aramco and the Saudi government, also known as the "50/50" Agreement, set the precedent of equal sharing of income from petroleum in the Middle East, and paved the way to nationalization of petroleum reserves. Following the 1973 Arab-Israeli war, the Arab members of OPEC° (the Organization of Petroleum Exporting Countries) imposed an embargo against Western supporters of Israel, resulting in the first of a series of price increases that transformed the world oil market. In 1938, Saudi Arabia produced 1,400 barrels of oil daily. By 1999, the amount was close to 8,000,000 barrels per day, about 12 percent of the world's total production, with an annual value of $46.5 billion. Saudi Arabia is estimated to have about 262.8 billion barrels of crude oil reserves, about 25 percent of the world's total.

The Document

Agreement concluded on 30 December 1950 between the government of the Sa'udi Arab Kingdom, hereinafter called "the Government," represented by His Excellency al-Shaykh 'Abdallah al-Sulayman al-Hamdan, Minister of Finance, and The Arabian American Oil Company, hereinafter called "Aramco," represented by F. A. Davies, its Executive Vice-President and Senior Resident Officer in the Sa'udi Arab Kingdom.

Whereas, the Government for a period of many months has been seeking additional revenue from Aramco, has held views different from those of Aramco on many long-standing interpretations of Aramco's concession and other agreements, and has made many claims and exactions which Aramco has contested as contrary to Aramco's concessionary rights and immunities; and

Whereas, the Government by letter of 20 August 1950 demanded amendment of certain conditions of Aramco's concession and other outstanding agreements and on 5 September 1950 submitted some thirteen points for discussion; and

OPEC, Organization of Petroleum Exporting Countries: As late as the 1950s, world oil production and pricing was dominated by the major international oil companies, which set prices unilaterally. In September 1960, in an effort to take control of pricing and production, the governments of Venezuela, Saudi Arabia, Iran, Iraq, and Kuwait agreed to create OPEC. Since then, OPEC has grown to 11 countries: the original five, plus Algeria, Indonesia, Libya, Nigeria, Qatar, and the United Arab Emirates. Following the October 1973 Arab-Israeli war, the Arab members of OPEC imposed an embargo against countries that had supported Israel. As a result, gasoline shortages hit Europe and the United States, and the global price of oil quadrupled. After another price increase following the Iranian Revolution of 1979, oil prices stabilized, and OPEC producers split over strategy, with one group favoring cuts in production to keep prices high, and the other favoring higher production in order to keep prices lower to stimulate steady demand. Today, OPEC countries account for about 78 percent of the world's known crude oil reserves, and about 41 percent of the world's crude oil production. Saudi Arabia is the largest producer, itself accounting for roughly 25 percent of the world's total reserves, and 12 percent of production.

Whereas, the Government on 4 November 1950 and on 27 December 1950 promulgated income tax decrees providing, among other things, for the taxation of business profits within the Sa'udi Arab Kingdom; and

Whereas, both the Government and Aramco recognize the necessity for resolving all matters in dispute so that Aramco may proceed with the development of oil resources in areas of Aramco's concession in full agreement with and having full cooperation from the Government;

Now, therefore, it is hereby agreed as follows:

1. Anything in article 21 in Aramco's concessionary agreement [of 29 May 1933] notwithstanding, Aramco submits to the income taxes provided in royal decrees, . . . it being understood that:

a. In no case shall the total of taxes, royalties, rentals and exactions of the Government for any year exceed fifty per cent (50%) of the gross income of Aramco, after such gross income has been reduced by Aramco's cost of operation, including losses and depreciation, and by income taxes, if any, payable to any foreign country but not reduced by any taxes, royalties, rentals, or other exactions of the Government for such year; and

b. In all other respects Aramco's exemptions and immunities set forth in article 21 of the concession agreement shall continue in full force and effect.

2. It is further understood that:

a. Aramco shall have the option to pay the taxes . . . in the currencies of the Sa'udi Arab Kingdom or in other currencies in the proportions in which Aramco receives such currencies from its sales.

b. The term "exactions of the Government" as herein used shall include, among other things, the amount of all fees and charges for services rendered to Aramco in excess of the cost of such services and all duties on imports by Aramco for Aramco, for its service organizations and for the use and benefit of Aramco employees and of such organizations, except duties on food and items imported by Aramco for sale in its canteens.

3. The Government recognizes the continuing nature of the provisions of articles 1 and 2 of this agreement, and agrees that the new arrangement described therein constitutes a complete satisfaction of all outstanding claims and demands of the Government with respect both to the past and to the future; the Government agrees that Aramco may continue to conduct its operations in accordance with the Aramco concessionary agreements in the same manner as in the past.

4. The following are examples of the effect of article 3:

a. The demands of the Government's letter of 20 August 1950, and the Government's points for discussion of 5 September 1950, are fully satisfied.

b. Aramco's practices of using the English ton of 2,240 pounds in computation of royalties, selecting the locations for royalty gauging, taking natural salt for use in Aramco's operations, and using crude oil, gas, and petroleum products free of royalty in Aramco's operations and facilities in Sa'udi Arabia, are in accordance with the terms of the concessionary agreement.

c. The Government agrees that Aramco may gauge and deliver oil to the Trans-Arabian Pipe Line Company at al-Qaysumah.

d. The Jiddah radio agreement of 6 March 1949 is in full force and effect.

These articles in no way limit the all-inclusive generality of article 3.

6. The free gasoline and kerosene that shall be offered the Government pursuant to article 8 of the Supplemental Agreement dated 31 May 1939 is hereby increased commencing 1 January 1951 to two million six hundred and fifty thousand (2,650,000) American gallons of gasoline per annum and to two hundred thousand (200,000)

American gallons of kerosene per annum, all in bulk at Ras-al-Tannurah. Aramco agrees further to offer the Government commencing 1 January 1951 seven thousand five hundred (7,500) tons per annum of road asphalt at Ras-al-Tannurah, the said asphalt to be supplied in drums, provided that drums are available at reasonable cost. No royalty shall be payable on crude oil required for the manufacture of gasoline, kerosene and asphalt offered free by Aramco and taken by the Government. The costs of producing the said crude oil and of manufacturing the said free gasoline, kerosene, and asphalt shall be regarded as an expense of operations and not as an exaction within the meaning of article 2 (b) of this agreement. It is understood that all the said free gasoline, kerosene and asphalt is for the ordinary requirements of the Government and not for sale outside or inside of Sa'udi Arabia.

7. Aramco agrees, commencing 1 January 1951, to pay the Government seven hundred thousand dollars ($700,000.00) per annum toward the expenses, support and maintenance of representatives of the Government concerned with the administration of Aramco operations. The said amount of seven hundred thousand dollars ($700,000.00) shall be paid in equal installments in January, April, July and October of each year and shall be viewed as an expense of operations and not as an exaction within the meaning of article 2 (b) of this agreement. The Government accepts Aramco's undertaking to pay the said amount of seven hundred thousand dollars ($700,000.00) per annum as full satisfaction of all claims and demands for expenses, support and maintenance of representatives of the Government concerned with the administration of Aramco's operations, including all such representatives of the national, provincial and municipal governments, police, guards, guides, soldiers and officials of the customs, immigration and quarantine services. It is understood that the said payment without limiting the generality of the foregoing shall be in lieu of all claims for salaries, wages, expense, transport, free services, residence and construction of every description, and all payments and services otherwise accruing after 1 January 1951 pursuant to article 20 of Aramco's concessionary agreement.

8. Aramco confirms its policy of conducting its operations in accordance with first-class oil field practice and its accounting in accordance with generally recognized standards. The Government for its part confirms the Government's confidence in the management of Aramco in conducting Aramco's operations.

9. This agreement shall become effective on the date hereof and shall remain in full force and effect for the duration of the concessionary agreement.

Analysis and Review Questions

1. What are the major reasons for this agreement between Aramco and the Saudi Arabian government? Why was the old agreement no longer considered suitable?

2. According to the agreement, what does the company accept in the way of taxes, and what does the Saudi government accept in terms of limits on its own power over the company? What protection does the agreement give against nationalization of oil?

3. According to the agreement, why does Aramco agree to pay $700,000 per year to the Saudi government? What does the government agree to in return?

4. Does this agreement favor either the company or the Saudi government? Why would the company agree to pay higher royalties, and how could the Saudi

government have responded had the company refused to pay?

5. Compare this agreement with the D'Arcy Concession of 1901 in Chapter 27. In what ways are the two agreements similar and different? How do you account for the similarities and differences?

ISLAM AND THE STATE IN THE MIDDLE EAST: AYATOLLAH KHOMEINI'S VISION OF ISLAMIC GOVERNMENT

About the Document

*Image 34.1
Ayatollah
Khomeini*

Ayatollah Ruhollah Khomeini (1900–1989) was born in the Iranian city of Khomein, the son of a Shi'i cleric, and began his own study of religion at an early age. While studying at the Feyziyeh Medrese in Qom, Khomeini became known as an activist, although he refrained from engagement in political matters until the death of his mentor, Ayatollah Borujerdi in 1962. In June 1962 Khomeini was arrested for speaking publicly against Muhammad Reza Shah Pahlavi's (1941–1979) "White Revolution," a set of reforms aimed partly at decreasing the influence of the ulema° in Iran. After his exile in 1964, Khomeini settled in Najaf, Iraq, a center for Shi'i pilgrimages and learning, where he continued to denounce the Shah as an oppressor and puppet of the West. As an alternative to the monarchy, Khomeini developed his theory of *Velayet-e Faqih,* governance of the jurist, which he claimed was in accord with the example of Ali and the twelve Imams recognized by most Shi'is as the true leaders of the Muslim community. For Khomeini and his supporters, this was the only form of government that could meet the demands of the modern world while remaining in accord with the *Qur'an* and traditions of the Prophet Muhammad, since it would replace a secular monarchy with the authority of the highest ranking Shi'i ulema, the Ayatollahs. From his exile in Iraq, then Paris, Ayatollah Khomeini became the leading symbol and inspiration for opposition to the regime of the Shah. On January 31, 1979, Khomeini returned from exile in triumph, two weeks after the departure of the deposed Shah. For the next ten years he guided the Iranian Revolution and creation of the Islamic Republic, following his precepts of governance of the jurist. Ayatollah Khomeini died June 5, 1989.

The Document

Need for Executive Agencies

A collection of laws is not enough to reform society. For a law to be an element for reforming and making people happy, it requires an executive authority. This is why God, may He be praised, created on earth, in addition to the laws, a government and an executive and administrative agency. The great prophet, may God's prayers be upon him, headed all the executive agencies running the Moslem society. In addition to the tasks of conveying, explaining and detailing the laws and the regulations, he took care of implementing them until he brought the State of Islam into existence. In his time,

---

ulema: Plural of *alim,* meaning a religious scholar, judge, or theologian trained in a *medrese.*

the prophet was not content with legislating the penal code, for example, but also sought to implement it. He cut off hands, whipped and stoned. After the prophet, the tasks of the caliph were no less than those of the prophet. The appointment of a caliph was not for the sole purpose of explaining the laws but also for implementing them. This is the goal that endowed the caliphate° with importance and significance. The prophet, had he not appointed a caliph to succeed him, would have been considered to have failed to convey his message. The Moslems were new to Islam and were in direct need for somebody to implement the laws and to make God's will and orders the judge among people to secure their happiness in this world and in the hereafter. . . .

Need for Political Revolution

. . . The Shari'a and reason require us not to let governments have a free hand. The proof of this is evident. The persistence of these governments in their transgressions means obstructing the system and laws of Islam whereas there are numerous provisions that describe every non-Islamic system as a form of idolatry and a ruler or an authority in such a system as a false god. We are responsible for eliminating the traces of idolatry from our Moslem society and for keeping it away from our life. At the same time, we are responsible for preparing the right atmosphere for bringing up a faithful generation that destroys the thrones of false gods and destroys their illegal powers because corruption and deviation grow on their hands. This corruption must be wiped out and erased and the severest punishment must be inflicted upon those who cause it. In His venerable book, God describes Pharaoh as "a corrupter." Under the canopy of a pharonic rule that dominates and corrupts society rather than reform it, no faithful and pious person can live abiding by and preserving his faith and piety. Such a person has before him two paths, and no third to them: either be forced to commit sinful acts or rebel against and fight the rule of false gods, try to wipe out or at least reduce the impact of such a rule. We only have the second path open to us. We have no alternative but to work for destroying the corrupt and corrupting systems and to destroy the symbol of treason and the unjust among the rulers of peoples.

This is a duty that all Moslems wherever they may be are entrusted—a duty to create a victorious and triumphant Islamic political revolution.

Need for Islamic Unity

. . . The only means that we possess to unite the Moslem nation, to liberate its lands from the grip of the colonialists and to topple the agent governments of colonialism, is to seek to establish our Islamic government. The efforts of this government will be crowned with success when we become able to destroy the heads of treason, the idols, the human images and the false gods who disseminate injustice and corruption on earth.

The formation of a government is then for the purpose of preserving the unity of the Moslems after it is achieved. This was mentioned in the speech of Fatimah al-Zahra', may peace be upon her, when she said: ". . . In obeying us lies the nation's order, and our imamhood is a guarantee against division."

Need for Rescuing Wronged and Deprived

To achieve their unjust economic goals, the colonialists employed the help of their agents in our countries. As a result of this, there are hundreds of millions of starving

---

caliphate: Following the death of Muhammad, the majority of the Muslim community (Sunni) accepted the leadership of a caliph, or "deputy," as the rightful leader of the community. The title was used by the rulers of the Umayyad, Abbasid, and other Muslim dynasties, including the Ottomans (1300–1922), until the Turkish parliament voted to abolish the position in 1924.

people who lack the simplest health and educational means. On the other side, there are individuals with excessive wealth and broad corruption. The starving people are in a constant struggle to improve their conditions and to free themselves from the tyranny of the aggressive rulers. But the ruling minorities and their government agencies are also seeking to extinguish this struggle. On our part, we are entrusted to rescue the deprived and the wronged. We are instructed to help the wronged and to fight the oppressors, as the amir of the faithful ('Ali) instructed his two sons in his will: "Fight the tyrant and aid the wronged."

The Moslem ulema are entrusted to fight the greedy exploiters so that society may not have a deprived beggar and, on the other side, someone living in comfort and luxury and suffering from gluttony. The amir of the faithful ('Ali) says: "By Him Who split the seed and created the breeze, were it not for the presence of the Omnipresent, the presence of the proof of the existence of the Victory Giver, and were it not for God's instructions to the ulema not to condone the oppression of a tyrant nor the suffering of the wronged, I would let matters go unchecked and would get the end mixed up with the beginning and you would find this world of yours less significant to me than a goat's sneeze."

How can we stand nowadays to keep silent on a handful of exploiters and foreigners who dominate with the force of arms when these people have denied hundreds of millions of others the joy of enjoying the smallest degree of life's pleasures and blessings? The duty of the ulema and of all the Moslems is to put an end to this injustice and to seek to bring happiness to millions of peoples through destroying and eliminating the unjust governments and through establishing a sincere and active Moslem government.

Islamic System of Government

Distinction from Other Political Systems

The Islamic government is not similar to the well-known systems of government. It is not a despotic government in which the head of state dictates his opinion and tampers with the lives and property of the people. The prophet, may God's prayers be upon him, and 'Ali, the amir of the faithful, and the other imams had no power to tamper with people's property or with their lives. The Islamic government is not despotic but constitutional. However, it is not constitutional in the well-known sense of the word, which is represented in the parliamentary system or in the people's councils. It is constitutional in the sense that those in charge of affairs observe a number of conditions and rules underlined in the Koran and in the Sunna and represented in the necessity of observing the system and of applying the dictates and laws of Islam. This is why the Islamic government is the government of the divine law. The difference between the Islamic government and the constitutional governments, both monarchic and republican, lies in the fact that the people's representatives or the king's representatives are the ones who codify and legislate, whereas the power of legislation is confined to God, may He be praised, and nobody else has the right to legislate and nobody may rule by that which has not been given power by God. This is why Islam replaces the legislative council by a planning council that works to run the affairs and work of the ministries so that they may offer their services in all spheres. . . .

Yes, government in Islam means obeying the law and making it the judge. The powers given to the prophet, may God's peace and prayers be upon him, and to the legitimate rulers after him are powers derived from God. God ordered that the prophet and the rulers after him be obeyed: "Obey the prophet and those in charge among you." There is no place for opinions and whims in the government of Islam. The prophet, the imams and the people obey God's will and Shari'a.

The government of Islam is not monarchic, not a shahin-shahdom and not an empire, because Islam is above squandering and unjustly undermining the lives and property of people. This is why the government of Islam does not have the many big palaces, the servants, the royal courts, the crown prince courts and other trivial requirements that consume half or most of the country's resources and that the sultans and the emperors have. The life of the great prophet was a life of utter simplicity, even though the prophet was the head of the state, who ran and ruled it by himself. This method continued to a degree after him and until the Ommiads° seized power. The government of 'Ali ibn Abi Talib was a government of reform, as you know, and 'Ali lived a life of utter simplicity while managing a vast state in which Iran, Egypt, Hejaz and Yemen were mere provinces under his rule. I do not believe that any of our poor people can live the kind of life that the imam ('Ali) lived. When he had two cloaks, he gave the better one to Qanbar, his servant, and he wore the other. When he found extra material in his sleeves, he cut it off. Had this course continued until the present, people would have known the taste of happiness and the country's treasury would not have been plundered to be spent on fornication, abomination and the court's costs and expenditures. You know that most of the corrupt aspects of our society are due to the corruption of the ruling dynasty and the royal family. What is the legitimacy of these rulers who build houses of entertainment, corruption, fornication and abomination and who destroy houses which God ordered be raised and in which His name is mentioned? Were it not for what the court wastes and what it embezzles, the country's budget would not experience any deficit that forces the state to borrow from America and England, with all the humiliation and insult that accompany such borrowing. Has our oil decreased or have our minerals that are stored under this good earth run out? We possess everything and we would not need the help of America or of others if it were not for the costs of the court and for its wasteful use of the people's money. . . .

Qualifications of Ruler

The qualifications that must be available to the ruler emanate from the nature of the Islamic government. Regardless of the general qualifications, such as intelligence, maturity and a good sense of management, there are two important qualifications:

1. *Knowledge of Islamic Law*
2. *Justice*

A. In view of the fact that the Islamic government is a government of law, it is a must that the ruler of the Moslems be knowledgeable in the law, as the Hadith° says.

Ommiads: Dynasty founded in Damascus by Mu'awiyah (661–680 C.E.). In the generations following the death of Muhammad (d. 632 C.E.), the Umayyads led the conquest and creation of an empire stretching from Spain to western China, bringing millions into the Muslim community. The Umayyads began the process of creating a state, with legal and educational systems, and developing a distinctly Muslim form of culture, before being overthrown by the Abbasids.
Hadith: The collected sayings and actions attributed to the Prophet Muhammad; it is seen by Muslims as one of the guides (second in importance to the Qur'an) to correct behavior.

Whoever occupies a (public) post or carries out a certain task must know as much as he needs within the limits of his jurisdiction and the ruler must know more than everybody else. Our imams proved their worthiness of the people's trust by their early search for knowledge. What the Shiite ulema fault others for revolves mostly around the level of knowledge attained by our ulema—a standard that the others failed to rise to.

Knowledge of the law and of justice are among the most important mainstays of the imamate. If a person knows a lot about nature and its secrets and masters many arts but is ignorant of the law, then his knowledge does not qualify him for the caliphate and does not put him ahead of those who know the law and deal with justice. . . .

B. The ruler must have the highest degree of faith in the creed, good ethics, the sense of justice and freedom from sins, because whoever undertakes to set the strictures, to achieve the rights, and to organize the revenues and expenditures of the treasury house must not be unjust. God says in his precious book: "The unjust shall not have my support." Thus, if the ruler is not just, he cannot be trusted not to betray the trust and not to favor himself, his family and his relatives over the people. . . .

Rule of Jurisprudent

If a knowledgeable and just jurisprudent undertakes the task of forming the government, then he will run the social affairs that the prophet used to run and it is the duty of the people to listen to him and obey him.

This ruler will have as much control over running the people's administration, welfare and policy as the prophet and amir of the faithful had despite the special virtues and the traits that distinguished the prophet and the imam. Their virtues did not entitle them to contradict the instructions of the Shari'a or to dominate people with disregard to God's order. God has given the actual Islamic government that is supposed to be formed in the time of absence (of caliph 'Ali ibn Abi Talib) the same powers that he gave the prophet and the amir of the faithful in regard to ruling, justice and the settlement of disputes, the appointment of provincial rulers and officers, the collection of taxes and the development of the country. All that there is to the matter is that the appointment of the ruler at present depends on (finding) someone who has both knowledge and justice.

Analysis and Review Questions

1. According to Khomeini, what is the importance of the executive branch of government? Why is executive authority more vital to good government than legislative or judicial authority?
2. According to Khomeini, what role did the Prophet play in establishing executive authority in Muslim society?
3. According to Khomeini, what are the main causes of injustice? How can the people fight injustice, and what role should the ulema play in the people's struggle against injustice?
4. What does Khomeini mean when he says that Islamic government is constitutional? What is the difference between Islamic government and constitutional monarchies and republics?

5. Compare Khomeini's vision of the Shi'i ulema with that of Mirza Husayn-i Hamdani in Chapter 27. In what ways are their views similar and different? Who do they identify as the enemies of the people, and in what ways do their proposals for change overlap or diverge, and why?

ISRAEL-PLO DECLARATION OF PRINCIPLES ON INTERIM SELF-GOVERNMENT ARRANGEMENTS, SEPTEMBER 13, 1993

Image 34.2
Rabin and Arafat
Shake Hands at the
White House, 1993

About the Document

On September 13, 1993, Yasir Arafat,° chairman of the Palestine Liberation Organization (PLO)° and Yitzhak Rabin,° prime minister of Israel, met on the lawn of the White House to sign a historic accord between the Israelis and Palestinians. After the signing, Arafat extended his hand to Rabin, who hesi-

Yasir Arafat: Descending from an old and prominent Palestinian family, Arafat was born either in Jerusalem or Egypt, according to contrasting claims. After being educated as an engineer in Egypt and Europe, Arafat worked in Kuwait in the 1950s. In the late 1950s he formed al-Fatah, one of several Palestinian exile groups that advocated armed struggle against Israel. After the 1967 war, al-Fatah rose to prominence, and by 1969, Arafat was chairman of the PLO's Executive Committee, a position he has retained despite an airplane crash, military defeat, and several attempts to remove him from office or assassinate him. In 1974 Arafat addressed the United Nations General Assembly, and he has been the most enduring symbol of the Palestinian cause, despite at one time having been branded a terrorist by the Israeli and American governments and their allies.

Palestine Liberation Organization: In January 1964 Arab governments formed the PLO as a means of channeling Palestinian nationalism and controlling guerilla groups that had emerged to challenge Israel by force. Leadership in the organization was vested in the Palestine National Congress (PNC), which in turn elected a 15-member Executive Committee. In its Charter, the PNC called for the destruction of Israel and restoration of Palestinian sovereignty over all of the territory of the pre-1948 Palestine Mandate, a struggle that was given to the Palestine Liberation Army (PLA), the military wing of the PLO. Following the stunning failure of the Arab governments to protect Palestinian claims in the 1967 Arab-Israeli war, Palestinians gained control of the organization. Yasir Arafat came to dominate the Executive Committee, but his leadership has faced challenges from several directions, including the Popular Front for the Liberation of Palestine (PFLP), led by George Habash, and Hamas, which emerged following the destruction of the PLO's base in Lebanon in 1982. Another challenge to the PLO began in December 1987, with the *intifada*, a popular uprising in the West Bank and Gaza Strip that was organized within local communities without the direction of the PLO leadership. During the Gulf War of 1991, the Palestinians and the PLO supported Iraq, which resulted in the Gulf States cutting off their financial support for the organization. Facing severe financial problems and the danger of becoming irrelevant to the Palestinians in the Occupied Territories, the PLO leadership decided to seek a peace agreement with Israel that would give the PLO authority over at least parts of the West Bank and Gaza Strip.

Yitzhak Rabin: Born in Jerusalem, Rabin joined a branch of the Jewish Defense Force in 1941, during the British Mandate. Following the independence of Israel, he pursued a military career and was Commander in Chief during the 1967 Arab-Israeli war. In March 1973 Rabin was elected to the Israeli parliament, the Knesset, and succeeded Golda Meir as prime minister after her government collapsed due to scandals surrounding the 1973 war. Rabin himself resigned in 1977 due to intra-party feuding, economic troubles, and rumors of financial wrongdoing. He returned to the prime ministership in 1989, after the Labour Party defeated the conservative Likud coalition. After the Gulf War of 1991, Rabin led his government in negotiating a peace agreement with the PLO that would return parts of the Gaza Strip and West Bank to Palestinian sovereignty. Opposition to the Declaration of Principles remained fierce, and in 1995, following a peace rally in support of negotiations, Yitzhak Rabin was assassinated.

tated for some time before President Bill Clinton nudged him on the back then he shook Arafat's hand. The event, watched around the world, signaled the culmination of more than a year of secret and open negotiations between representatives of the PLO and the government of Israel. As the world was just learning, beginning in April 1992, Norwegian academics and diplomats with ties to both the PLO and the Israeli Labour Party had offered to act as intermediaries to bring together the two sides. Over several months, more than a dozen secret meetings were held in London and Norway. In August 1992 representatives of the PLO and Israel signed a declaration of principles, known as the Oslo Accord. The declaration, which formed the basis for subsequent negotiations, committed the PLO to removing the clause in its Charter calling for the destruction of Israel and renouncing the use of violence against Israelis, while Israel accepted the PLO as the legitimate representative of the Palestinian people—those living in the occupied West Bank and Gaza Strip, as well as those living in exile.

Although the compromises in the Oslo Accord were hotly contested by both Israeli and Palestinian opponents, Rabin and Arafat convinced their supporters that the risks of not having an accord were now greater than the risks of reaching a compromise. On September 13 the two leaders, longtime adversaries, met to show their commitment to replacing a decades-long struggle marked by violence with a new relationship based on mutual trust. On November 4, 1995, Yitzhak Rabin was assassinated by an opponent of the peace process. Confronting huge political, economic, and cultural barriers, the Israelis and Palestinians continue to struggle with the meaning and implications of the Declaration of Principles, which remains more a blueprint for future possibilities than a record of accomplishments.

The Document

ISRAEL-PLO DECLARATION OF PRINCIPLES ON INTERIM SELF-GOVERNMENT ARRANGEMENTS, SEPTEMBER 13, 1993

The Government of the State of Israel and the P.L.O. team (in the Jordanian-Palestinian delegation to the Middle East Peace Conference) (the "Palestinian Delegation"), representing the Palestinian people, agree that it is time to put an end to decades of confrontation and conflict, recognize their mutual legitimate and political rights, and strive to live in peaceful coexistence and mutual dignity and security and achieve a just, lasting and comprehensive peace settlement and historic reconciliation through the agreed political process. Accordingly, the two sides agree to the following principles:

Article I: Aim of the Negotiations

The aim of the Israeli–Palestinian negotiations within the current Middle East peace process is, among other things, to establish a Palestinian Interim Self-Government Authority, the elected Council (the "Council"), for the Palestinian people in the West Bank and the Gaza Strip, for a transitional period not exceeding five years, leading to a permanent settlement based on Security Council Resolutions 242 and 338.

It is understood that the interim arrangements are an integral part of the whole peace process and that the negotiations on the permanent status will lead to the implementation of Security Council Resolutions 242 and 338....

. . .

Article III: Elections

1. In order that the Palestinian people in the West Bank and Gaza Strip may govern themselves according to democratic principles, direct, free and general political elections will be held for the Council under agreed supervision and international observation, while the Palestinian police will ensure public order....

3. These elections will constitute a significant interim preparatory step toward the realization of the legitimate rights of the Palestinian people and their just requirements.

Article IV: Jurisdiction

Jurisdiction of the Council will cover West Bank and Gaza Strip territory, except for issues that will be negotiated in the permanent status negotiations. The two sides view the West Bank and the Gaza Strip as a single territorial unit, whose integrity will be preserved during the interim period.

Article V: Transitional Period and Permanent Status Negotiations

1. The five-year transitional period will begin upon the withdrawal from the Gaza Strip and Jericho area.

2. Permanent status negotiations will commence as soon as possible, but not later than the beginning of the third year of the interim period, between the Government of Israel and the Palestinian people representatives.

3. It is understood that these negotiations shall cover remaining issues, including: Jerusalem, refugees, settlements, security arrangements, borders, relations and cooperation with other neighbors, and other issues of common interest....

. . .

Article VI: Preparatory Transfer of Powers and Responsibilities

1. Upon the entry into force of this Declaration of Principles and the withdrawal from the Gaza Strip and the Jericho area, a transfer of authority from the Israeli military government and its Civil Administration to the authorised Palestinians for this task, as detailed herein, will commence. This transfer of authority will be of a preparatory nature until the inauguration of the Council.

2. Immediately after the entry into force of this Declaration of Principles and the withdrawal from the Gaza Strip and Jericho area, with the view to promoting economic development in the West Bank and Gaza Strip, authority will be transferred to the Palestinians on the following spheres: education and culture, health, social welfare, direct taxation, and tourism. The Palestinian side will commence in building the Palestinian police force, as agreed upon. Pending the inauguration of the Council, the two parties may negotiate the transfer of additional powers and responsibilities, as agreed upon.

Article VII: Interim Agreement

1. The Israeli and Palestinian delegations will negotiate an agreement on the interim period (the "Interim Agreement").

2. The Interim Agreement shall specify, among other things, the structure of the Council, the number of its members, and the transfer of powers and responsibilities from the Israeli military government and its Civil Administration to the Council. The Interim Agreement shall also specify the Council's executive authority, legislative

authority in accordance with Article IX below, and the independent Palestinian judicial organs.

3. The Interim Agreement shall include arrangements, to be implemented upon the inauguration of the Council, for the assumption by the Council of all of the powers and responsibilities transferred previously in accordance with Article VI above.

4. In order to enable the Council to promote economic growth, upon its inauguration, the Council will establish, among other things, a Palestinian Electricity Authority, a Gaza Sea Port Authority, a Palestinian Development Bank, a Palestinian Export Promotion Board, a Palestinian Environmental Authority, a Palestinian Land Authority and a Palestinian Water Administration Authority, and any other Authorities agreed upon, in accordance with the Interim Agreement that will specify their powers and responsibilities.

5. After the inauguration of the Council, the Civil Administration will be dissolved, and the Israeli military government will be withdrawn.

Article VIII: Public Order and Security

In order to guarantee public order and internal security for the Palestinians of the West Bank and the Gaza Strip, the Council will establish a strong police force, while Israel will continue to carry the responsibility for defending against external threats, as well as the responsibility for overall security of Israelis for the purpose of safeguarding their internal security and public order. . . .

Article XIII: Redeployment of Israeli Forces

1. After the entry into force of this Declaration of Principles, and not later than the eve of elections for the Council, a redeployment of Israeli military forces in the West Bank and the Gaza Strip will take place, in addition to withdrawal of Israeli forces carried out in accordance with Article XIV.

2. In redeploying its military forces, Israel will be guided by the principle that its military forces should be redeployed outside populated areas.

3. Further redeployments to specified locations will be gradually implemented commensurate with the assumption of responsibility for public order and internal security by the Palestinian police force pursuant to Article VIII above. . . .

Annex II: Protocol on Withdrawal of Israeli Forces from the Gaza Strip and Jericho Area

1. The two sides will conclude and sign within two months from the date of entry into force of this Declaration of Principles, an agreement on the withdrawal of Israeli military forces from the Gaza Strip and Jericho area. This agreement will include comprehensive arrangements to apply in the Gaza Strip and the Jericho area subsequent to the Israeli withdrawal.

2. Israel will implement an accelerated and scheduled withdrawal of Israeli military forces from the Gaza Strip and Jericho area, beginning immediately with the signing of the agreement on the Gaza Strip and Jericho area and to be completed within a period not exceeding four months after the signing of this agreement.

3. The above agreement will include, among other things:

a. Arrangements for a smooth and peaceful transfer of authority from the Israeli military government and its Civil Administration to the Palestinian representatives.

b. Structure, powers and responsibilities of the Palestinian authority in these areas, except: external security, settlements, Israelis, foreign relations, and other mutually agreed matters.

c. Arrangements for the assumption of internal security and public order by the Palestinian police force consisting of police officers recruited locally and from abroad holding Jordanian passports and Palestinian documents issued by Egypt. Those who will participate in the Palestinian police force coming from abroad should be trained as police and police officers.

d. A temporary international or foreign presence, as agreed upon.

e. Establishment of a joint Palestinian-Israeli Coordination and Cooperation Committee for mutual security purposes.

f. An economic development and stabilization program, including the establishment of an Emergency Fund, to encourage foreign investment, and financial and economic support. Both sides will coordinate and cooperate jointly and unilaterally with regional and international parties to support these aims.

g. Arrangements for a safe passage for persons and transportation between the Gaza Strip and Jericho area. . . .

Annex III: Protocol on Israeli-Palestinian Cooperation in Economic and Development Programs

The two sides agree to establish an Israeli-Palestinian continuing Committee for Economic Cooperation, focusing, among other things, on the following:

1. Cooperation in the field of water, including a Water Development Program. . . .

2. Cooperation in the field of electricity, including an Electricity Development Program. . . .

3. Cooperation in the field of energy, including an Energy Development Program. . . .

4. Cooperation in the field of finance, including a Financial Development and Action Program. . . .

5. Cooperation in the field of transport and communications. . . .

6. Cooperation in the field of trade, including studies, and Trade Promotion Programs. . . .

7. Cooperation in the field of industry, including Industrial Development Programs. . . .

8. A program for cooperation in, and regulation of, labor relations and cooperation in social welfare issues.

9. A Human Resources Development and Cooperation Plan. . . .

10. An Environmental Protection Plan, providing for joint and/or coordinated measures in this sphere.

11. A program for developing coordination and cooperation in the field of communication and media.

12. Any other programs of mutual interest.

Done at Washington, D.C., this thirteenth day of September, 1993.
For the Government of Israel   Shimon Peres
For the P.L.O.   Mahmud Abbas
Witnessed By:
The United States of America   Warren Christopher
The Russian Federation   Andrei Kozyrev

Analysis and Review Questions

1. What are the major reasons for the declaration, and what is the aim of negotiations?
2. What territories are covered by the declaration, and how will authority be transferred to the Palestinians? Who is to represent the Palestinians, and what will be the responsibilities of the Palestinian authority?
3. According to the agreement, who will be responsible for public order, security, and external relations? What limits does the declaration place on Israeli power

in the West Bank and Gaza Strip? What limits does the declaration place on Palestinian sovereignty in the West Bank and Gaza Strip?

4. What are the main forms of political and economic cooperation called for in the declaration? What types of civilian or military organizations are to achieve this cooperation?

5. In your view, what are the major strengths and weaknesses of the declaration? What issues seem to receive the most attention in the declaration? What political, economic, or social issues receive little or no attention in the declaration? If you were a negotiator, how would you strengthen the declaration?

Map 34.2
(Interactive) The
Modern Middle East

WEB LINKS

Selections from Longman World History—Primary Sources and Case Studies

http://longmanworldhistory.com
The following additional readings and case studies can be found on the Web site.
Document 27.3, The William Knox D'Arcy Oil Concession in Persia, May 29, 1901
Document 29.2, Stalin Demands Rapid Industrialization of the USSR
Document 34.2, The Search for Justice and Voices of Protest: Nâzim Hikmet and Nazik al-Mala'ika
Case Study 34.1, The Political Vision of Atatürk and Khomeini
Case Study 34.2, Two Petroleum Agreements
Case Study 34.3, Soviet and Turkish Plans for Industrialization

General Information on Muslim History and Societies

http://www.fordham.edu/halsall/islam/islamsbook.html
Fordham University, Internet *Islamic History Sourcebook.* A good source for primary documents on Islamic history from the Medieval to the modern period.

http://lcweb2.loc.gov/frd/cs/
Library of Congress, Research Division, Country Studies, with links for all countries in the Middle East. Each country study is subdivided into topics such as history, government, resources, and population.

http://menic.utexas.edu/menic.html
The Middle East Network Information Center at the Center for Middle Eastern Studies, the University of Texas. A very useful site, with links organized by country and subject.

http://www.columbia.edu/cu/lweb/indiv/mideast/cuvlm/
Columbia University Library, Middle East Studies Internet Resources. A Web site featuring links to bibliographical sources, including other libraries and collections.

Web Sites Related to Turkey

http://turkey.org/start.html
Official Web site of the Republic of Turkey.

http://www.tarihvakfi.org.tr/english/
Web site of the Turkish History Foundation, an independent organization supporting
the study of Ottoman and modern Turkish history, with good links to publications and
information about archival sources.

http://www.cc.columbia.edu/cu/tsa/ata/ata.html
A Web site with information and links related to Mustafa Kemal (Atatürk), the first
president of the Turkish Republic. This Web site is sponsored by the Turkish Students'
Association at Columbia University.

Petroleum in the Middle East

http://gulib.lausun.georgetown.edu/dept/speccoll/cl185.htm
Web site of the Aramco History Project at Georgetown University, with information
about the development of the oil industry in Saudi Arabia.

http://www.saudinf.com/main/d19.htm
Web site of Saudi Aramco, the Saudi state oil company created in 1988 to develop
Saudi petroleum products.

http://www.opec.org/
Offical Web site of the Organization of Petroleum Exporting Countries, OPEC, with
information about member countries and the global oil market.

Information on Iran and the Iranian Revolution

http://persia.org/khatami/
Official Web site of the president of Iran, Muhammad Khatami, with news and information about Iran as well as his political agenda.

http://www.ummah.net/
A Web site maintained by the Islamic Gateway World Wide Media Network, with
news and information geared toward a Muslim readership.

Web Sites Related to the Palestinian-Israeli Conflict

http://www.un.org/Depts/dpa/qpal/index.html
Official Web site of the United Nations, which includes a history of the conflict, rele-
vant UN resolutions and documents, and information about the current state of Israeli-
Palestinian relations.

http://www.mtholyoke.edu/acad/intrel/me.htm
A Web site maintained by the International Relations program at Mount Holyoke
College, with a historical overview and links to relevant documents.

http://israel.gov.il/eng/sub-TZRS-peace.asp
Official Web site of the Israeli government, presenting the Israeli perspective on the
conflict.

http://www.pna.org/
Official Web site of the Palestinian National Authority, with links to a number of ministries and official organizations.

THE CONSTITUTION OF JAPAN, TWO VERSIONS

Acomparison of the Meiji Constitution with the Japanese Constitution of 1947 illustrates Japan's transformation from a feudal society to a modern state, from an agrarian economy to an industrial country and from an emerging Asian power to a military disaster and, finally, to a nation again being redefined. Politically, the Western values and democracy introduced into the Meiji Constitution in the late nineteenth century gave Japan its first modern legal base to transform and reform. At the end of World War II, the new constitution helped rebuild a new Japan to lead the Pacific and the world.

THE MEIJI CONSTITUTION, 1889

About the Document

The Meiji Constitution is the most important part of the Meiji Reform that began in 1886. Leaders of the early Meiji period sent several embassies abroad to Europe and the United States to study the Western political institutions and economic system. In their effort to modernize their country, the reform-minded Japanese wrote their first modern constitution along the Prussian model, with the help of a German diplomat, Herman Roesler.

The Meiji Constitution turned out to be a blend of both modern and feudal elements for a Japan that was still in transition. On the one hand, the divine authority of the Japanese Emperor is defined as "sacred and inviolable." On the other hand, the Diet, a parliamentary organ, is established to distribute power between the House of Peers and the House of Representatives. The Constitution also guarantees a series of popular rights to the Japanese people, such as freedom of religion and speech, right to property, due process of law, etc.

The Meiji Constitution remained effective until the end of World War II, when Japan surrendered. It was replaced with the 1947 Constitution, which the Americans helped draft.

The Document

Chapter I: The Emperor

ARTICLE I

The Empire of Japan shall be reigned over and governed by a line of Emperors unbroken for ages eternal.

ARTICLE II

The Imperial Throne shall be succeeded to by Imperial male descendants, according to the provisions of the Imperial House Law.

ARTICLE III

The Emperor is sacred and inviolable.

ARTICLE IV

The Emperor is the head of the Empire, combining in Himself the rights of sovereignty, and exercises them, according to the provisions of the present Constitution.

ARTICLE V

The Emperor exercises the legislative power with the consent of the Imperial Diet.

ARTICLE VI

The Emperor gives sanction to laws and orders them to be promulgated and executed.

ARTICLE VII

The Emperor convokes the Imperial Diet, opens, closes, and prorogues (suspends) it, and dissolves the House of Representatives.

ARTICLE VIII

The Emperor, in consequence of an urgent necessity to maintain public safety or to avert public calamities, issues, when the Imperial Diet is not sitting, Imperial Ordinances in the place of law.

Such Imperial Ordinances are to be laid before the Imperial Diet at its next session, and when the Diet does not approve the said Ordinances, the government shall declare them to be invalid for the future.

. . .

ARTICLE X

The Emperor determines the organization of the different branches of the administration, and salaries of all civil and military officers, and appoints and dismisses the same. Exceptions especially provided for in the present Constitution or in other laws, shall be in accordance with the respective provisions (bearing thereon).

ARTICLE XI

The Emperor has the supreme command of the Army and Navy.

ARTICLE XII

The Emperor determines the organization and peace standing of the Army and Navy.

ARTICLE XIII

The Emperor declares war, makes peace, and concludes treaties.

ARTICLE XIV

The Emperor declares a state of siege. The conditions and effects of a state of siege shall be determined by law.

ARTICLE XV

The Emperor confers titles of nobility, rank, orders and other marks of honor.

ARTICLE XVI

The Emperor orders amnesty, pardon, commutation of punishments and rehabilitation.

. . .

Chapter II: Rights and Duties of Subjects

ARTICLE XVIII

The conditions necessary for being a Japanese subject shall be determined by law.

ARTICLE XIX

Japanese subjects may, according to qualifications determined in laws of Ordinances, be appointed to civil or military or any other public offices equally.

ARTICLE XX

Japanese subjects are amenable to service in the Army or Navy, according to the provisions of law.

ARTICLE XXI

Japanese subjects are amenable to the duty of paying taxes, according to the provisions of law.

ARTICLE XXII

Japanese subjects shall have the liberty of abode and of changing the same within the limits of the law.

ARTICLE XXIII

No Japanese subjects shall be arrested, detained, tried or punished, unless according to law.

ARTICLE XXIV

No Japanese subject shall be deprived of his right of being tried by the judges determined by law.

ARTICLE XXV

Except in the cases provided for in the law, the house of no Japanese subject shall be entered or searched without his consent.

Measures necessary to be taken for the public benefit shall be provided for by law.

ARTICLE XXVI

Except in the cases mentioned in the law, the secrecy of the letters of every Japanese subject shall remain inviolate.

ARTICLE XXVII

The right of property of every Japanese subject shall remain inviolate.

ARTICLE XXVIII

Japanese subjects shall, within limits not prejudicial to peace and order, and not antagonistic to their duties as subjects, enjoy freedom of religious belief.

ARTICLE XXIX

Japanese subjects shall, within the limits of law, enjoy the liberty of speech, writing, publication, public meetings and associations.

ARTICLE XXX

Japanese subjects may present petitions, by observing the proper forms of respect, and by complying with the rules specially provided for the same.

ARTICLE XXXI

The provisions contained in the present Chapter shall not affect the exercises of the powers appertaining to the Emperor, in times of war or in cases of a national emergency.

. . .

Chapter III: The Imperial Diet

ARTICLE XXXIII

The Imperial Diet shall consist of two Houses, a House of Peers and a House of Representatives.

ARTICLE XXXIV

The House of Peers shall, in accordance with the Ordinance concerning the House of Peers, be composed of the members of the Imperial Family, of the orders of nobility, and of those who have been nominated thereto by the Emperor.

ARTICLE XXXV

The House of Representatives shall be composed of Members elected by the people.

. . .

Chapter VI: Finance

ARTICLE LXII

The imposition of a new tax or the modification of the rates (of an existing one) shall be determined by law.

However, all such administrative fees or other revenue having the nature of compensation shall not fall within the category of the above clause.

The raising of natural loans and the contracting of other liabilities to the charge of the National Treasury, except those that are provided in the Budget, shall require the consent of the Imperial Diet.

ARTICLE LXIII

The taxes levied at present shall, in so far as they are not remodelled by a new law, be collected according to the old system.

ARTICLE LXIV

The expenditure and revenue of the State require the consent of the Imperial Diet by means of an annual Budget.

Any and all expenditures overpassing the appropriations set forth in the Titles and Paragraphs of the Budget, or that are not provided for in the Budget, shall subsequently require the approbation of the Imperial Diet.

ARTICLE LXV

The Budget shall be first laid before the House of Representatives.

ARTICLE LXVI

The expenditures of the Imperial House shall be defrayed every year out of the National Treasury, according to the present fixed amount for the same, and shall not require the consent thereto of the Imperial Diet, except in case an increase thereof is found necessary.

ARTICLE LXVII

Those already fixed expenditures based on the Constitution upon the powers appertaining to the Emperor, and such expenditures as may have arisen by the effect of law, or that appertain to the legal obligations of the Government, shall be neither rejectred nor reduced by the Imperial Diet without the concurrence of the Government.

ARTICLE LXXI

When the Imperial Diet has not voted on the Budget, or when the Budget has not been brought into actual existence, the Government shall carry out the Budget of the preceding year.

THE CONSTITUTION OF JAPAN, 1947

About the Document

Following Japan's surrender at the end of World War II, Allied occupation forces, known as the SCAP (Supreme Command of Allied Powers), began its task of remaking a new Japan that would be an American ally in the Pacific. The SCAP was responsible for drafting the new Constitution, which became effective when it was ratified by the Japanese Diet on May 3, 1947. The new Japanese Constitution gave new meaning to the Japanese Emperor as "the symbol of the State and . . . the unity of the people." A series of clauses provide universal suffrage, freedom, liberty, and other rights to the Japanese people. Article 9 renounces war, making sure that Japan is not allowed to keep regular military forces. The new Constitution would reshape Japan in all aspects.

The occupation of Japan ended in 1952. Under the new Constitution of 1947, Japan not only embarked on political reform, but made an economic leap forward. During the next three decades or so Japan became a synonym for high technology and new inventions. Asia and the Pacific now treat Japan as a model as more countries experience the democratic process and economic reforms.

The Document

We, the Japanese people, acting through our duly elected representatives in the National Diet, determined that we shall decree for ourselves and our posterity the fruits of peaceful cooperation with all nations and the blessings of liberty throughout this land, and resolved that never again shall we be visited with the horrors of war through the action of government, do proclaim that sovereign power resides with the people and do firmly establish this Constitution. Government is a sacred trust of the people, the authority for which is derived from the people, the powers of which are exercised by the representatives of the people, and the benefits of which are enjoyed by the people. This is a universal principle of mankind upon which this Constitution is founded. We reject and revoke all constitutions, laws, ordinances, and rescripts in conflict herewith.

We, the Japanese people, desire peace for all time and are deeply conscious of the high ideals controlling human relationship, and we have determined to preserve our security and existence, trusting in the justice and faith of the peace-loving peoples of the world. We desire to occupy an honored place in an international society striving for the preservation of peace, and the banishment of tyranny and slavery, oppression and intolerance for all time from the earth. We recognize that all peoples of the world have the right to live in peace, free from fear and want.

Chapter I. The Emperor

ARTICLE 1

The Emperor shall be the symbol of the State and of the unity of the people, deriving his position from the will of the people, with whom resides sovereign power.

ARTICLE 2

The Imperial Throne shall be dynastic and succeeded to in accordance with the Imperial House Law passed by the Diet.

ARTICLE 3

The advice and approval of the Cabinet shall be required for all acts of the Emperor in matters of state, and the Cabinet shall be responsible therefor.

ARTICLE 4

The Emperor shall perform only such acts in matters of state as are provided for in this Constitution and he shall not have powers related to government.

2. The Emperor may delegate the performance of his acts in matters of state as may be provided by law.

ARTICLE 5

When, in accordance with the Imperial House Law, a Regency is established, the Regent shall perform his acts in matters of state in the Emperor's name. In this case, paragraph one of the preceding article will be applicable.

ARTICLE 6

The Emperor shall appoint the Prime Minister as designated by the Diet.

2. The Emperor shall appoint the Chief Judge of the Supreme Court as designated by the Cabinet.

. . .

Chapter II. Renunciation of War

ARTICLE 9

Aspiring sincerely to an international peace based on justice and order, the Japanese people forever renounce war as a sovereign right of the nation and the threat or use of force as means of settling international disputes.

2. In order to accomplish the aim of the preceding paragraph, land, sea, and air forces, as well as other war potential, will never be maintained. The right of belligerency of the state will not be recognized.

Chapter III. Rights and Duties of the People

ARTICLE 10

The conditions necessary for being a Japanese national shall be determined by law.

ARTICLE 11

The people shall not be prevented from enjoying any of the fundamental human rights. These fundamental human rights guaranteed to the people of this Constitution shall be conferred upon the people of this and future generations as eternal and inviolate rights.

. . .

ARTICLE 13

All of the people shall be respected as individuals. Their right to life, liberty, and the pursuit of happiness shall, to the extent that it does not interfere with the public welfare, be the supreme consideration in legislation and in other governmental affairs.

ARTICLE 14

All of the people are equal under the law and there shall be no discrimination in political, economic, or social relations because of race, creed, sex, social status, or family origin.

ARTICLE 15

The people have the inalienable right to choose their public officials and to dismiss them.

2. All public officials are servants of the whole community and not of any group thereof.

3. Universal adult suffrage is guaranteed with regard to the election of public officials.

4. In all elections, secrecy of the ballot shall not be violated. A voter shall not be answerable, publicly or privately, for the choice he has made.

ARTICLE 16

Every person shall have the right of peaceful petition for the redress of damage, for the removal of public officials, for the enactment, repeal, or amendment of laws, ordinances, or regulations, and for other matters, nor shall any person be in any way discriminated against for sponsoring such a petition.

. . .

ARTICLE 18

No person shall be held in bondage of any kind. Involuntary servitude, except as punishment for crime, is prohibited.

ARTICLE 19

Freedom of thought and conscience shall not be violated.

ARTICLE 20

Freedom of religion is guaranteed to all. No religious organization shall receive any privileges from the State nor exercise any political authority.

2. No person shall be compelled to take part in any religious acts, celebration, rite, or practice.

3. The State and its organs shall refrain from religious education or any other religious activity.

ARTICLE 21

Freedom of assembly and association as well as speech, press, and all other forms of expression are guaranteed.

2. No censorship shall be maintained, nor shall the secrecy of any means of communication be violated.

. . .

ARTICLE 23

Academic freedom is guaranteed.

ARTICLE 24

Marriage shall be based only on the mutual consent of both sexes and it shall be maintained through mutual cooperation with the equal rights of husband and wife as a basis.

2. With regard to choice of spouse, property rights, inheritance, choice of domicile, divorce, and other matters pertaining to marriage and the family, laws shall be enacted from the standpoint of individual dignity and the essential equality of the sexes.

ARTICLE 25

All people shall have the right to maintain the minimum standards of wholesome and cultured living.

ARTICLE 26

All people shall have the right to receive an equal education correspondent to their ability, as provided by law.

ARTICLE 27

All people shall have the right and the obligation to work.

ARTICLE 28

The right of workers to organize and to bargain and act collectively is guaranteed.

ARTICLE 29

The right to own or hold property is inviolable.

ARTICLE 30

The people shall be liable to taxation as provided by law.

ARTICLE 31

No person shall be deprived of life or liberty, nor shall any other criminal penalty be imposed, except according to procedure established by law.

ARTICLE 32

No person shall be denied the right of access to the courts.

ARTICLE 33

No person shall be apprehended except upon warrant issued by a competent judicial officer which specifies the offense with which the person is charged, unless he is apprehended, the offense being committed.

ARTICLE 34

No person shall be arrested or detained without being at once informed of the charges against him or without the immediate privilege of counsel; nor shall he be detained without adequate cause; and upon demand of any person such cause must be immediately shown in open court in his presence and the presence of his counsel.

ARTICLE 35

The right of all persons to be secure in their homes, papers, and effects against entries, searches, and seizures shall not be impaired except upon warrant issued for adequate cause and particularly describing the place to be searched and things to be seized, or except as provided by Article 33.

ARTICLE 36

The infliction of torture by any public officer and cruel punishments are absolutely forbidden.

ARTICLE 37

In all criminal cases the accused shall enjoy the right to a speedy and public trial by an impartial tribunal.

2. At all times the accused shall have the assistance of competent counsel who shall, if the accused is unable to secure the same by his own efforts, be assigned to his use by the State.

ARTICLE 38

No person shall be compelled to testify against himself.

ARTICLE 39

No person shall be held criminally liable for an act which was lawful at the time it was committed, or of which he has been acquitted, nor shall he be placed in double jeopardy.

ARTICLE 40

Any person, in case he is acquitted after he has been arrested or detained, may sue the State for redress as provided by law.

Chapter IV. The Diet

ARTICLE 41

The Diet shall be the highest organ of state power, and shall be the sole law-making organ of the State.

ARTICLE 42

The Diet shall consist of two Houses, namely the House of Representatives and the House of Councillors.

ARTICLE 43

Both Houses shall consist of elected members, representative of all the people.

. . .

ARTICLE 51

Members of both Houses shall not be held liable outside the House for speeches, debates or votes cast inside the House.

ARTICLE 52

An ordinary session of the Diet shall be convoked once per year.

. . .

ARTICLE 57
Deliberation in each House shall be public. However, a secret meeting may be held where a majority of two-thirds or more of those members present passes a resolution therefor.

. . .

ARTICLE 59
A bill becomes a law on passage by both Houses, except as otherwise provided by the Constitution.

2. A bill which is passed by the House of Representatives, and upon which the House of Councillors makes a decision different from that of the House of Representatives, becomes a law when passed a second time by the House of Representatives by a majority of two-thirds or more of the members present.

. . .

Chapter V. The Cabinet

ARTICLE 65
Executive power shall be vested in the Cabinet.

ARTICLE 66
The Cabinet shall consist of the Prime Minister, who shall be its head, and other Ministers of State, as provided for by law.

2. The Prime Minister and other Ministers of State must be civilians.

3. The Cabinet, in the exercise of executive power, shall be collectively responsible to the Diet.

ARTICLE 67
The Prime Minister shall be designated from among the members of the Diet by a resolution of the Diet. This designation shall precede all other business.

. . .

Chapter VI. The Judiciary

ARTICLE 76
The whole judicial power is vested in a Supreme Court and in such inferior courts as are established by law.

. . .

ARTICLE 79
The Supreme Court shall consist of a Chief Judge and such number of judges as may be determined by law; all such judges excepting the Chief Judge shall be appointed by the Cabinet.

. . .

Chapter IX. Amendments

ARTICLE 96
Amendments to this Constitution shall be initiated by the Diet, through a concurring vote of two-thirds or more of all the members of each House and shall thereupon

be submitted to the people for ratification, which shall require the affirmative vote of a majority of all votes case thereon, at a special referendum or at such election as the Diet shall specify.

2. Amendments when so ratified shall immediately be promulgated by the Emperor in the name of the people, as an integral part of this Constitution.

Chapter X. Supreme Law

ARTICLE 97

The fundamental human rights by this Constitution guaranteed to the people of Japan are fruits of the age-old struggle of man to be free; they have survived the many exacting tests for durability and are conferred upon this and future generations in trust, to be held for all time inviolate.

ARTICLE 98

This Constitution shall be the supreme law of the nation and no law, ordinance, imperial rescript, or other act of government, or part thereof, contrary to the provisions hereof, shall have legal force or validity.

Analysis and Review Questions

1. Identify the different functions of the Japanese Emperor in both constitutions.
2. How different is the role of the Diet in the two constitutions?
3. What is the most controversial section in the 1947 Constitution?
4. How can we see the progress and transformation of Japan from an early modern society to a democratic and industrialized state?

Credits

2 Reprinted from *Luther's Works*, vol. 51, ed. John W. Doberstein. Copyright © 1959 Fortress Press. Used by permission of Augsburg Fortress.

7 Reprinted by permission of Oxford University Press from *Documents of the Christian Church*, 3rd ed., ed. Henry Bettenson, 364-67.

9 Reprinted from *The Political Works of James I* (1616), intro. Charles Howard McIlwain (Cambridge, MA.: Harvard University Press, 1918), 53-70.

14 *A King's Lessons in Statecraft: Louis XIV: Letters to His Heirs with Introduction and Notes,* by Jean Longnon, trans. Herbert Wilson (Port Washington, NY: Kennikat Press, 1970), 39-40, 48-51.

19 Reprinted with the permission of The Johns Hopkins University Press from *On the Revolutions: Nicholas Copernicus Complete Works*, by Nicholas Copernicus, ed. Jerzy Dobrzycki, trans., commentary by Edward Rosen, 3-5. © 1978 The Johns Hopkins University Press.

21 *An Ambassador's Report on The Ottoman Empire, 1555*, from *The Life and Letters of Ogier Ghiselin de Busbecq*, ed. C.T. Forster, F. H. B. Daniell, vol. I (London: C. K. Paul and Co., 1881).

23 Excerpted from *A Source Book for Russian History*, ed. G. Vernadsky, R. T. Fisher, Jr. Copyright © 1972 by Yale University Press. Reprinted by permission.

25 Reprinted with permission of Cambridge University Press from *On the Corruption of Morals in Russia*, by Prince M. M. Shcherbatov, ed., trans. A. Lentin. Copyright © 1969 by Cambridge University Press.

31 From *The Bernal Diaz Chronicles*, trans. Albert Idell. Copyright © 1956 by Albert Idell. Used by permission of Doubleday, a division of Random House.

31 Reprinted by permission of Beacon Press, Boston, from *The Broken Spears*, by Miguel Leon-Portilla. © 1962, 1990 by Miguel Leon-Portilla. Expanded and updated edition © 1992 by Miguel Leon-Portilla.

34 Reprinted by permission from *In Defense of the Indians*, by Bartolome de las Casas, ed., trans. Stafford Poole (Northern Illinois University Press, 1974).

36 Margaret Sayers Peden's translation of *La Respuesta a Sor Filotea*, the first translation of the work into the English language, was originally commissioned by a small independent New England press, Lime Rock Press, of Salisbury, CT. It appeared in 1982 in a limited edition entitled *A Woman of Genius: The Intellectual Autobiography of Sor Juana Inès de la Cruz*, with photographs by Gabriel North Seymour. Copyright © 1982 by Lime Rock Press, Inc. Reprinted with permission.

41 From *China in the Sixteenth Century*, by Matthew Ricci, trans. Louis J. Gallagher, S.J. Copyright 1942, 1953, renewed 1970 by Louis J. Gallagher, S.J.

44 Reprinted by permission from *Japan: A Documentary History*, trans., ed. David John Lu (Armonk, NY: M. E. Sharpe, 1997).

46 *East Asia: A New History*, 2nd ed., by Rhoads Murphey (Longman, 2001), 127.

50 *Readings in European History*, vol. II, ed. James Harvey Robinson (Boston: Ginn and Co. 1906), 333-35.

52 Reprinted with the permission of the publisher from *Sources of Indian Tradition*, ed. Theodore de Bary. © 1958 Columbia University Press.

55 *Akbar and the Jesuits*, trans., with introduction and notes by C.H. Payne (New York & London: Harper & Brothers, 1926), 211-13.

58 *The History of India as Told by Its Own Historians*, 8 vols., ed. Henry M. Elliot, John Dowson (London: Truebner, 1867-1877), vol. 7, 157-62.

62 "Description of a Voyage from Lisbon to the Island of Sao Thomë," from *Europeans in West Africa 1540–1560*, ed. John William Blake. Reprinted by permission of The Hakluyt Society.

66 From "A Defense of the African Slave Trade, 1740," *London Magazine*, 9 (1740), 493-94, in Elizabeth Donnan, *Documents Illustrative of the History of the Slave Trade to America* (Washington, DC: Carnegie Institution, 1930), II, 469-70.

Vol. II: Modern India and Pakistan, ed. Stephen Hay. © 1988 Columbia University Press.

156 *Thoughts and Sentiments on the Evil of Slavery*, by Quobna Ottoabah Cugoano (New York: Penguin, 1999).

162 *Travels in West Africa*, by Mary H. Kingsley (London: Macmillan, 1897).

166 *The Middle East and North Africa in World Politics: A Documentary Record*, vol. I, 2nd ed., ed. J. C. Hurewitz (Yale Univ. Press, 1975), 482-84.

168 *Memoirs of Halidè Edib,* by Halidè Edib Adivar (New York: Arno Press, 1926), 252-53, 256-59.

171 *The New History of Mirza Ali Muhammad, the Bab*, trans. E.G. Brown (Cambridge University Press, 1895), 180-85.

174 "Free Meal," by Tevfik Fikret, from *The Penguin Book of Turkish Verse*, trans. Nermin Menemencioglu (1978). Reprinted by permission of Osman Streater.

184 "Dulce et Decorum Est," by Wilfred Owen, as it appears in *Wilfred Owen: The Complete Poems and Fragments*, ed. Jon Stallworthy. © The Executors of Harold Owen's Estate, 1963 and 1983. Published by Chatto & Windus. Used by permission of the Random House Group Limited.

185 Reprinted by permission of Donadio & Olson, Inc. from *Hard Times,* by Studs Terkel. Copyright 1986 by Studs Terkel.

187 Reprinted by permission from *Commandant to Auschwitz,* by Rudolf Hoess (Wiedenfeld & Nicolson, Ltd.).

190 "Hiroshima—August 6th, 1945," by Father John A. Siemes, professor of modern philosophy, Tokyo Catholic University.

195 *V.I. Lenin: Collected Works,* Vol. 31, April-December 1920, ed., trans. Julius Katzer (Moscow: Progress Publishers, 1966), 496-518.

200 Reprinted by permission from *J. Stalin: Works July 1930–January 1934,* Vol. 13, by J. Stalin (London: Lawrence and Wishart, 1955).

204 Reprinted by permission of Harper-Collins Publishers, Inc. from *Perestroika,* by Mikhail Gorbachev, 84-95. Copyright © 1987 by Mikhail Gorbachev.

211 Reprinted by permission from *Environmental and Health Atlas of Russia*, ed. Murray Feshbach (1995).

219 Used by permission of Alfred A. Knopf, a division of Random House, from *Zapata and the Mexican Revolution*, by John Womack, Jr. Copyright © 1968 by John Womack, Jr.

221 *Pernûn Expounds His Doctrine*, by Juan Domingo Pernûn (Buenos Aires, 1948), 146-47, 149.

223 *History Will Absolve Me*, by Fidel Castro (London: Jonathon Cape, 1968).

226 Reprinted with permission from *Camilo Torres: His Life and His Message*, ed. John Alvarez Garcia, Christian Restrepo Call (Templegate Publishers, 1968).

230 Reprinted with the permission of The Free Press, a Division of Simon & Schuster, from *Chinese Civilization: A Sourcebook*, 2nd ed., by Patricia Buckley Ebrey. Copyright © 1993 by Patricia Buckley Ebrey.

234 "North and South Korean Declaration Text: June 2000." Reprinted by permission of the Embassy of Korea, Washington D.C.

235 From "Declaration of Independence," by Ho Chi Minh, Sept. 2, 1945, (www.vietnamembassy-usa.org/learn/gov-declaration.php3).

240 Extracts from writings and words of Mahatma Gandhi, compiled in *The Essential Gandhi: An Anthology*, ed. Louis Fischer (1962). Reprinted by permission of the Navajivan Trust.

241 "Speech to Pakistan's Legislature," by Mohammed Ali Jinnah, from *Sources of Indian Tradition: Volume Two: Modern India and Pakistan*, ed. Stephen Hay (New York: Columbia University Press, 1988), 385-87.

244 Reprinted by permission of University of California Press from *Punjabi Century 1857–1947*, by Prakash Tandon. Copyright © 1968 Prakash Tandon.

246 Reprinted by permission from *Behind Mud Walls, 1930–1960*, by Charlotte